GREEK AND
ROMAN EDUCATION

Modern Western education finds its origins in the practices, systems, and schools of the ancient Greeks and Romans. It is in the field of education, in fact, that classical antiquity has exerted one of its clearest influences on the modern world. Yet the story of Greek and Roman education, extending from the eighth century BC into the Middle Ages, is familiar in its details only to relatively few specialists.

Containing nearly three hundred translated texts and documents, *Greek and Roman Education: A Sourcebook* is the first book to provide readers with a large, diverse, and representative sample of the primary evidence for ancient Greek and Roman education. A special feature of this source-book is the inclusion of not only the fundamental texts for the study of the subject, but also unfamiliar sources that are of great interest but not easily accessible, including inscriptions on stone and Greek papyri from Egypt. Introductions to each chapter and to each selection provide the guidance which readers need to set the historical periods, themes, and topics into meaningful contexts. Fully illustrated and including extensive suggestions for further reading, together with an index of passages explored, students will have no further need for any other sourcebook on Greek and Roman education.

Mark Joyal is Professor and Head of the Department of Classics at the University of Manitoba. **Iain McDougall** was Professor of Classics and Chair of Department at the University of Winnipeg. **J.C. Yardley**, formerly Head of Classics at the Universities of Calgary and Ottawa, is now Emeritus Professor at the University of Ottawa.

GREEK AND ROMAN EDUCATION

A Sourcebook

Mark Joyal, Iain McDougall,
J.C. Yardley

Routledge
Taylor & Francis Group

LONDON AND NEW YORK

First published 2009
by Routledge
2 Park Square, Milton Park, Abingdon, Oxon OX14 4RN

Simultaneously published in the USA and Canada
by Routledge
270 Madison Ave, New York, NY 10016

Routledge is an imprint of the Taylor & Francis Group, an informa business

Typeset in Times New Roman by
Book Now Ltd, London
Printed and bound in Great Britain by
CPI Antony Rowe, Chippenham, Wiltshire

British Library Cataloguing in Publication Data
A catalogue record for this book is available from the British Library

Library of Congress Cataloging in Publication Data
Joyal, Mark.
Greek and Roman education: a sourcebook/Mark Joyal, Iain McDougall,
J.C. Yardley.
p. cm.
Includes bibliographical references and index.
1. Education, Greek. 2. Education–Rome. I. McDougall, Iain. II. Yardley,
J.C., 1942– III. Title.

LA71.J69 2008
370.938–dc22   2008010910

ISBN10: 0–415–33806–9 (hbk)
ISBN10: 0–415–33807–7 (pbk)

ISBN13: 978–0–415–33806–6 (hbk)
ISBN13: 978–0–415–33807–3 (pbk)

CONTENTS

CONTENTS

ILLUSTRATIONS

PREFACE

Like most areas of classical studies, Greek and Roman education has in recent decades been the object of significant attention in scholarly research and publication. While much of this work has contributed greatly to our understanding of the subject, none of it has had the aim of providing readers with a large and representative sample of the enormous body of relevant primary evidence. It is this basic and longstanding need that the present volume is intended to fill.

Even though this sourcebook contains nearly 300 translated texts and documents, as well as 10 illustrations, its coverage is by no means complete. The chronological scope of this field, extending as it does from the eighth century BC (at least) to the end of antiquity – even to the early Middle Ages – precludes such a treatment. In some cases our decision about what to include and what could be omitted was based on practical considerations. For instance, it was impossible to present in their entirety the two long passages from the *Republic* on the educational schemes in Plato's ideal state (selections 5.8 and 5.9) without sacrificing many shorter but important and less-familiar items; and although we have severely limited what we printed from these two passages, we have identified the full contexts for our readers in the knowledge that translations of the *Republic* are easily accessible. Notwithstanding decisions such as these, we are confident that this book contains most of the central texts, and much else besides, for the serious study of Greek and Roman education. Furthermore, its organization, including the introductions to each chapter and to each selection or set of selections, as well as the suggestions for further reading, should enable the reader to gain a deep understanding of this unusually fascinating and influential element of ancient life and society. Although scholars in many disciplines will find a great deal in this book to interest them, we have tried to keep the needs of students and non-specialist readers clearly in view.

The three contributors to this book were each responsible for different parts of the overall project. McDougall translated approximately two-thirds of the Greek texts, including all the papyri and most of the inscriptions, and Yardley translated all but a handful of the Latin texts. Joyal translated the remaining texts, organized the material, and wrote the general introduction, the chapter introductions, the introductions to each of the selections, the footnotes, and the indexes. At several stages all three of us took the opportunity to comment on each other's work.

Over the time in which this book has gradually reached completion we have received help from several friends and colleagues. Many years ago Alan Booth compiled an initial list of passages which formed the basis for the much larger collection that has since developed. Mark Golden read an advanced version of the book as it was nearing completion and offered many suggestions for improvement which we have gratefully adopted. Annette Tefeteller provided bibliographical help and other advice on Chapter 1. At Routledge, Richard Stoneman, Amy Laurens and Lalle Pursglove showed exemplary patience and support even as we failed to meet one deadline after another. At an early stage the anonymous readers for the press also provided sensible criticism and guidance. Chris Kelk, a friend of the three authors, generously took time out from his acting career to proofread the final version. The University of Manitoba provided the resources necessary for the purchase of the images and permissions listed in the Acknowledgements.

ACKNOWLEDGEMENTS

Figures 3.1a and b: Bildarchiv Preussischer Kulturbesitz/Art Resource, NY
Figure 3.2a: Photo © The Trustees of the British Museum
Figure 3.2b: Réunion des Musées Nationaux/Art Resource, NY
Figure 6.1: The Center for the Tebtunis Papyri, The Bancroft Library, University of California, Berkeley
Figure 6.2: Deutsches Archäologisches Institut, Berlin, from P. Schazmann, "Das Gymnasium," *AvP* VI (Berlin 1923) pl. 1–2
Figure 8.1: Erich Lessing/Art Resource, NY
Figure 8.2: © British Library Board. All Rights Reserved (Add. 34186)
Figure 8.3: Soprintendenza per i Beni Archeologici delle province di Napoli e Caserta
Figure 8.4: The Mistress and Fellows, Girton College, Cambridge
Translations in selections 10.15 and 10.17: Pharr, Clyde; *The Theodosian Code and Novels and the Sermondian Constitutions.* © 1952 in the name of the author, 1980 renewed in name of Roy Pharr, executor. Reprinted by permission of Princeton University Press.
Translation in 10.7c: J. Richards, *Consul of God: The Life and Times of Gregory the Great*, London: Routledge and Kegan Paul 1980, 28–29.

ABBREVIATIONS

CIL	*Corpus Inscriptionum Latinarum*
FIRA	*Fontes Iuris Romani Antejustiniani*
IG	*Inscriptiones Graecae*
LIMC	*Lexicon Iconographicum Mythologiae Classicae*
PBour	*Les Papyrus Bouriant*
PGiss	*Griechische Papyri im Museum des oberhessischen Geschichtsvereins zu Giessen*
POxy	*Oxyrhynchus Papyri*
PSI	*Papiri greci e latini* (Pubblicazioni della Società Italiana per la ricerca dei Papiri greci e latini in Egitto)
PSorb	*Papyrus de la Sorbonne*
SB	*Sammelbuch griechischer Urkunden aus Ägypten*
SEC	*Supplemento epigraphico cirenaico*
SEG	*Supplementum Epigraphicum Graecum*
SIG	*Sylloge Inscriptionum Graecarum*
SLG	*Supplementum Lyricis Graecis*

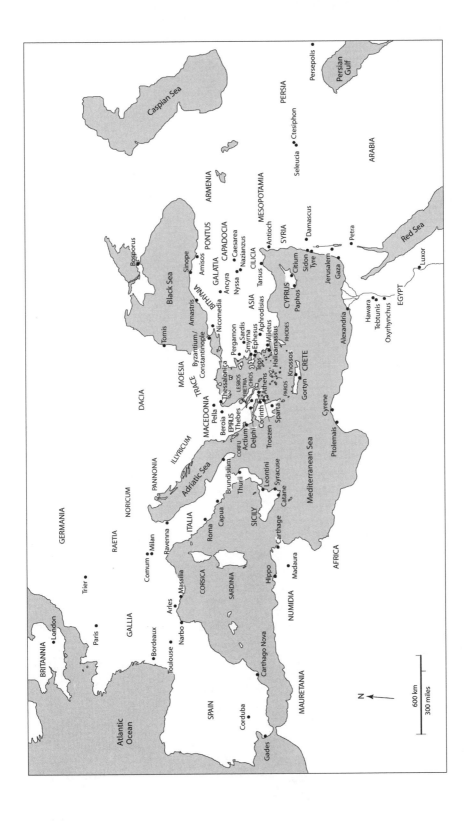

INTRODUCTION

The purpose of this book is to provide readers with a wide but coherent range of important textual and material evidence for ancient education. All texts are translated from their original Greek or Latin. Each item is accompanied by an introduction which is intended to place the evidence within its broader historical, social and intellectual contexts. In almost every instance, suggestions for further reading are given for those who want to investigate the evidence in greater detail or to dig deeper into a topic or problem.

We envisage a diverse readership: not only university students who are making a specialist study of ancient education, but also students and scholars of the Greeks and Romans who need easy access to, and guidance through, a substantial body of material on ancient educational practice and theory; educational, philosophical and cultural historians; and interested readers in general who want to learn more about an unusually important and influential side of ancient Greek and Roman life. It is very difficult to satisfy all the needs of such an audience, but it will be helpful to many readers if we explain briefly the nature of the sources we have drawn upon and offer some practical advice to increase the book's usefulness.

Literary sources

The translated sources in this book are extracted from works of Greek and Latin literature which cover roughly two thousand years, from the eighth century BC to the twelfth century AD. Some of these works are very famous, while others are known and read by only a few people.

Poetry

The earliest Greek literature is poetry. For our study of early educational practices and early beliefs about education, we rely on the epic poetry of Homer, the didactic (instructional) poetry of Hesiod, the elegiac poetry of Theognis and Tyrtaeus, and the lyric poetry of Pindar and Sappho (e.g. **1.1**, **3–8**). In view of the imaginative and allusive nature of poetry, the use of these sources requires careful interpretation, especially when we are dealing with mythological subject-matter (e.g. **1.10–11**). Latin poetry also provides evidence for practices in the Roman world, though not to the same extent that Greek poetry does; and it is subject to similar interpretive limitations as Greek poetry (e.g. **8.25**).

Comic drama

From the fifth and fourth centuries BC we can draw evidence from Athenian comedy, especially (but not only) from the works of the playwright Aristophanes (e.g. **3.11, 5.17**). Comic drama in this period tends to be highly topical, dealing with current themes and events that were immediately recognizable to the play's original audience. Relevant passages therefore have the potential to shed light on education as it was practised in contemporary Athens. Readers must keep in mind, however, that Athenian comedy frequently indulges in fantasy and that it aims above all to be funny. Realistic depiction is not necessarily the playwright's primary aim.

Forensic, political and diplomatic speeches

Many references to teachers, students, schools, curriculum and the teaching profession are to be found in speeches made by Greeks and Romans such as Isocrates, Demosthenes, Aeschines and Cicero (e.g. **3.24**). These speeches can be a helpful source of information, but it is important to remember that, in order to win favour, speech-writers frequently frame their arguments to conform to their audience's opinions and prejudices. They are also prone to exaggerate their own virtues or those of the person they are extolling, and to magnify their opponents' faults. These are habits which can easily lead to the misrepresentation of facts.

Historiography

Historical writing – understood as the attempt to explain events rationally through research and inquiry – began with the work of some fifth-century Greeks, most famously Herodotus and Thucydides, and continued to the end of antiquity and beyond. Greeks and Romans had a tremendous curiosity about their pasts, and ancient historical writings in both Greek and Latin survive in abundance. The information which ancient historians provide about education is often given incidentally (e.g. **3.23**); in these cases there does not usually seem to be cause to doubt the truth of a statement. On other occasions, an author's desire to make a special point or to win his audience over to a certain belief may influence the way that he presents his readers with details about educational practices (e.g. **7.1b**).

Philosophical literature

Philosophers tend to formulate their ideas at a high level of generality, and the views which such figures as Plato, Aristotle, Seneca and Musonius Rufus expressed about education are sometimes heavily theoretical. Plato's dramatic representations of Socrates and the sophists pose special problems of interpretation, since these are undoubtedly imaginative recreations. Yet there are good reasons for us to pay close attention to what ancient philosophers had to say about education. For one thing, their theories were usually devised on the basis of contemporary practices and were not simply divorced from reality (e.g. **5.8**). Moreover, the role which ancient philosophers have played in the history of education is an influential one (e.g. **10.27**). Finally, their discussions are intrinsically interesting and worthy of study.

Biographical works

The many biographies and autobiographies that survive from Greek and Roman antiquity (sometimes as a section within an author's larger work) reflect a keen interest in human character. Since a person's childhood was seen as influential on the kind of adult that person would become, his or her upbringing and education frequently play an important role in ancient biographies (e.g. **10.10**). Many biographical accounts of teachers also survive (e.g. **10.20**).

Essays and technical treatises

A disparate group of works is captured under this category. These works include, for instance, "display speeches" and "declamations" by teachers and students of rhetoric (e.g. **4.9**, **9.12**), as well as instructional works that explain good rhetorical practice (e.g. **9.8b**); treatises that relate to elements within the educational system (e.g. **10.2**); works which set out a state's constitution (**3.25**); political tracts (**3.16a**); and polemical works (e.g. **5.3**).

Legal texts

Two collections of laws that are relevant to our study were published in late antiquity, the Theodosian Code in AD 438 and the Code of Justinian in AD 534. The first of these two, in particular, contains the record of many legal provisions and regulations for students, teachers and schools; both collections inform us about the state's role in the education of its citizens (e.g. **10.15, 26b**).

Christian literature

This general heading comprises a large variety of works whose dates range from the second century AD to the Middle Ages. Many of them were composed by the "Church Fathers," such as St. Augustine and St. Basil. These writings include, for example, theological treatises, essays containing instruction and advice, sermons, and apologetic works (e.g. **10.4, 7**).

Documentary sources

Unlike the evidence from literary works, "documentary" evidence derives from a variety of "non-literary" sources which are not distinguished by their artistic qualities. They are most easily discussed according to the writing-material on which they are found.

Papyri

Papyrus is a reed plant which was harvested in ancient Egypt, manufactured into sheets, and then sold abroad as a writing material. It was, in fact, the ancient counterpart of paper. Most of the papyri that have survived from the ancient world were discovered in Egypt, where the dry sands encouraged their preservation. A large proportion of these papyri contain subject-matter that was intended only for the eyes of the writer and his or her recipient. Hence they can provide unique insight into the often unguarded thoughts and feelings of average Greeks and Romans living in Egypt in the Hellenistic and Roman periods.

Two kinds of papyrus text are of special importance for the study of ancient education: first, students' schoolbooks and teachers' notebooks, both reflecting the specific content of the education that students were receiving (e.g. **6.1**); and secondly, letters from student to parent or vice versa (e.g. **9.17**). Most papyrus documents have not survived without damage; it is usually the case that letters, words, or whole sections of a document have been lost as a result of the harm that it has suffered from the passage of time. These gaps in a papyrus document are indicated in our translations by a sequence of dots.

Inscriptions

Greeks and Romans regularly made permanent records of the official decisions taken by their cities and states by inscribing them on stone. Important people often did the same when they wanted their good works to be remembered. Thousands of Greek and Latin inscriptions have survived from the ancient world. The ones that concern us most are decrees which honour individual people for the special service they have given to students, teachers, schools and other educational institutions; those which recognize students' participation in official forms of education or training; and those which a citizen, king or emperor has set up to record his benefaction to a state's educational system (e.g. **6.8**, **8.17b**). From later antiquity in particular there are many tombstones that record and comment on a person's status as a teacher or pedagogue (e.g. **8.10**, **28**). Like papyri, inscriptions on stone have frequently suffered physical damage, with the result that in many cases it is impossible to read the entire document. Again, a sequence of dots indicates a gap in the text of an inscription.

Writing on other materials

The Linear B clay tablets from the Bronze Age, mentioned in the introduction to Chapter 1, are the earliest Greek inscriptional evidence. Some school exercises are preserved on ostraka (pieces of broken pottery, e.g. **9.8c**), others on wood (e.g. **8.29**), and still others on wax tablets (e.g. **8.6**).

Artistic and architectural evidence

Under this category of evidence are included painting (especially on pottery), sculpture, and architecture. School scenes are a familiar theme on Greek painted pottery of the sixth and fifth centuries BC (e.g. **3.13**); so are scenes in which people (especially women) hold book-rolls (e.g. **3.21**), as well as scenes involving mythological and legendary figures who are associated with education or initiation (e.g. Chiron, Phoenix and Linus: **1.10**, **13**). In small-scale sculpture, teachers are frequently depicted with one student or more (e.g. **8.2**), as are sophists (rhetorical teachers) on a larger scale, often holding a papyrus book-roll. Archaeological excavations have unearthed the remains of many gymnasia throughout the Greek and Roman worlds (e.g. **6.21**); these supplement what we know from papyrological and inscriptional records and, to a smaller degree, from literary evidence.

Advice on the use of this book

The material in this book is presented in a broadly chronological framework. Those who use it to investigate special topics in ancient education (e.g. students who are writing essays on pedagogues, women, slaves, discipline, salaries, and so on) will find that these topics are not confined to single chapters, but rather that relevant evidence is scattered throughout several historical periods. In these cases, quick progress in locating the evidence can be made by consulting the general index at the back of the book.

We have not provided a general introductory sketch to outline the development of ancient education over the long stretch of time covered by this book. Such a narrative is unnecessary in view of the general introductions that begin each chapter, but readers who want basic context and orientation will find guidance under the heading *General background* which appears at the end of each chapter-introduction.

Most of the introductions to individual selections contain advice for further reading in the extensive scholarly literature on ancient education; with only a few exceptions, references are restricted to works in English. The books and articles which are cited there usually contain their own bibliographies that will lead readers still further afield.

Some of these introductions supply brief but essential information about the authors of the translated passages. Users of this book should be aware that in our recommendations for further reading we have not cited articles that appear in standard reference works, where more detailed biographical or other basic information can be easily found. We have instead taken it for granted that readers will consult these works as they see fit. They include the following:

- Hubert Cancik and Helmuth Schneider (eds), *Brill's New Pauly: Encyclopaedia of the Ancient World*, in 20 volumes (Brill 2002–); also available on-line. Articles have been translated from German. This project is nearly exhaustive in its coverage.
- Simon Hornblower and Anthony Spawforth (eds), *The Oxford Classical Dictionary*, third edition (Oxford University Press 1996). A standard, authoritative work of reference; many readers will find it a more useful starting-point than the *New Pauly*.
- Lin Foxhall, David Mattingly, Graham Shipley and John Vanderspoel (eds), *The Cambridge Dictionary of Classical Civilization* (Cambridge University Press 2006). Articles are reliable and often cover topics not treated in *The Oxford Classical Dictionary*, but they are usually shorter and less detailed.
- Simon Hornblower and Anthony Spawforth (eds), *The Oxford Companion to Classical Civilization* (Oxford University Press 1998). Less comprehensive than any of the foregoing, but contains many good articles, and is illustrated.
- Simon Hornblower and Anthony Spawforth (eds), *Who's Who in the Classical World* (Oxford University Press 2000), and John Hazel, *Who's Who in the Greek World* and *Who's Who in the Roman World* (Routledge 2000 and 2002). Convenient and concise.

1

EARLY GREECE TO
c. 500 BC

The earliest written evidence for the Greek language dates to *c*. 1450–1200, a time frequently called the Mycenaean Period after the most famous Bronze Age site on the Greek mainland. The writing appears usually on clay tablets formed in the shape of either palm-leaves or pages; these tablets were preserved only because they were baked hard from fires that destroyed the buildings on the mainland and the islands where the tablets were stored, in centres such as Pylos, Mycenae, Thebes and Knossos. This writing was not expressed in the Greek alphabet familiar to us today, which did not come into use until perhaps three or four hundred years after the end of the Bronze Age. Instead it was transmitted in a "pictographic" script (i.e. images of familiar things representing complete syllables and their sounds) which scholars call Linear B. The thousands of Linear B tablets and fragments that have come to light do not, however, provide direct evidence for education in Bronze Age Greece. They are instead mainly inventories and official records from Mycenaean palaces, and inform us about palace administration.

There is little evidence that in this period literacy extended beyond its use in the Mycenaean palaces. Since the script of Linear B contains over ninety symbols, it must have been difficult to master and probably required special training (some tablets within a single collection have even been identified as students' writing exercises; Chadwick 1968: 17–21). We do not know, however, whether a class of Mycenaean "scribes" existed: no reference to that profession has been identified in the tablets, nor do the authors make any mention of themselves (Palaima 2003: 173–77).

The period that lasted roughly 300 years after the Bronze Age is frequently referred to as the Greek "Dark Age," largely because of its economic and cultural degeneration. This degeneration included, apparently, the complete collapse of literacy. Most education in this period, indeed until about 500 BC, must have involved the transmission of skills in farming or in other trades (**1.1**). Tradesmen no doubt learned their skills through an apprenticeship, probably with their fathers, as perhaps professional singers like Phemius and Demodocus in the *Odyssey* did too (though

1

in *Odyssey* 22.347 Phemius claims to be "self-taught," *autodidaktos*). Such a system is reflected in the tradition about Solon's law on the teaching of trades, which, if historical, would date to the early sixth century BC (**1.2**). Another element of "popular" education in early Greece, though in this case containing a heavily ethical ingredient, is reflected in "wisdom literature," which took the form of instructional (or "didactic") poetry (**1.3**).

For the period *c.* 800–500 we are able to form a picture of "élite" education, mainly from the poets Homer, Theognis and Pindar (**1.4–7**). This education was really a moral training that a young person received from his association with an older role-model. Something similar may possibly be said about the relationships with young females that the poet Sappho describes, but the evidence for her educational influence is both late and uncertain (**1.8**).

The centaur Chiron plays an intriguing role in the upbringing of numerous mythological figures, most prominently Achilles and Asclepius (**1.10–11**). This relationship defies secure interpretation; it may be that Chiron's role is to be linked with initiation rites, such as we find on Crete (**1.12**). Initiation rites also played a role in the upbringing of girls, especially through their performances in choruses (Ingalls 2000; Skinner 2005: 71–78).

Some time between about 900 and 800 BC, under circumstances that are unclear, the Greeks adopted and adapted the Phoenician writing system for their own use. The Greeks themselves preserved fairly specific memories about the origin of their alphabet, though they ascribed it to their mythical past (**1.14**). Evidence for the earliest Greek schools relates to the end of the period surveyed in this chapter (**1.15**).

General background: Pomeroy *et al.* 1999: 1–130; Sansone 2004: 1–47; Morris and Powell 2006: 60–92, 148–70. *Linear B and the Bronze Age*: Chadwick 1967: 126–31; Ventris and Chadwick 1973: 109–17; Chadwick 1976: 15–33; Castleden 2005: 85–91. *Early Greece*: Marrou 1956: xi–xviii, 3–13; Bowen 1972: 43–50, 57–62; Barrow 1976: 14–22; Griffith 2001; van Wees 1997.

1.1. Professional craftsmen

Homer, *Odyssey* 17.381–86

Homer identifies a special class of workers, called *demioergoi* (lit. "workers for the people"; cf. *Odyssey* 19.134–35), who are distinguished by the fact that they hire their services to the public. Their areas of expertise are among the most prized in the society that Homer depicts. The appearance of these specialists shows that a system of training in crafts that were in heavy demand existed in Homer's time and earlier. The speaker in this extract is Eumaeus, Odysseus' swineherd; Antinous is one of the suitors of Odysseus' wife Penelope. Further reading: Finley 1978: 36–37, 55–57; Burkert 1992: 14–25; Griffith 2001: 29–33.

> Antinous, a nobleman you are, but the words you speak are a disgrace. For who summons strangers from foreign lands and brings them here on his own unless they are those who work for the people (*demioergoi*) – a seer, or a healer of diseases, or a carpenter, or even an inspired singer, who delights others with his songs? These are men who are invited over the vast expanse of the earth.

1.2. Solon's law on teaching trades

Plutarch, *Life of Solon* 22.1

Athenians of the fifth and fourth centuries often attributed to Solon (*c.* 630–560 BC) certain laws which were established only much later. The law which required a father to teach his son a trade, however, is coherent with the general nature of the other laws that we know Solon laid down, since those too seem to have focused on the family. Further reading: Ehrenberg 1973: 71–75; MacDowell 1978: 43; Osborne 1996: 220–21.

> Solon noted that the city was becoming full of people continuously streaming into Attica from all directions in order to find security against the dangers they faced, that most of the land was mediocre and unproductive, and that those who came by sea to trade were not in the habit of bringing anything into the Athenian market for those who had nothing to offer them in return. He therefore focused the attention of his fellow-citizens on the skills required in craftsmanship and drew up a law whereby no son was under obligation to support his father if he had failed to teach him a trade.

1.3. Traditional wisdom

Hesiod, *Works and Days* 286–319

In the *Works and Days* (composed *c.* 725–700 BC), Hesiod assumes the role of moral advisor, dispensing wisdom in large quantities to his brother Perses. Partly for this reason, the poem is commonly classified as "wisdom literature," a very old genre with near-eastern, non-Greek relatives, and concerned especially with the transmission of traditional knowledge. Further reading: Beck 1964: 66–69; Walcot 1966: 80–103; West 1978: 3–40, 1999: 76–78, 306–33; Heath 1985: 253–63.

> With good purpose shall I speak to you, most foolish Perses. You can easily choose Inferiority in abundance; the path is smooth, and it lives

3

very near. But the immortal gods set sweat in front of Superiority, and the road to it is long and straight and rough at first. When one reaches the summit, then it is easy, despite its former difficulty.

By far the best man is he who perceives everything on his own, contemplating what will be better later and in the end. He too is a noble person who follows good advice. But he who neither perceives on his own nor takes to heart what he hears from another, that man is useless. But you, Perses, always bear in mind my instruction, and work, you who are sprung from Zeus, so that hunger may hate you and revered Demeter of the fair crown favour you and fill your granary with food. For hunger always accompanies a lazy man. Gods and men are hostile to that man who lives an idle life, with a temper like blunt-tailed drones who in their laziness wear down and eat away the toil of the bees.

May your tasks be welcome to you, to order them in due measure, so that your granaries may be full of food in its season. As a result of work men are rich in flocks and wealthy, and he who works is far dearer to the gods. Work is no reproach, but laziness is a reproach. If you work, a lazy man will at once envy you as you gain wealth. Superiority and honour accompany wealth. But whatever state your fortune is in, working is better, if you turn your dim-witted heart from other people's possessions towards work and take thought for your livelihood as I tell you to do. Modesty is not good at providing for a needy man – modesty, which is a great harm and a great help for men. Modesty accompanies poverty, boldness accompanies prosperity.

1.4. Phoenix and Achilles

(a) Homer, *Iliad* 9.485–95, (b) Homer, *Iliad* 9.438–45

The relationship between Phoenix, the speaker in these two passages, and Achilles, the son of Peleus and central character in the *Iliad*, resembles that between master and apprentice: the younger member learns – by prolonged association, observation and practice – the skills that enable him to become successful and to gain honour among his peers. The result of this association, in the present case at least (**b**), is intellectual and physical excellence, i.e. skill in counsel and war. The role which Phoenix plays is like that of the pedagogue (*paidagogos*), who was to become a central figure in the upbringing of both Greek and Roman children (e.g. **3.3–5**). The *Iliad* was probably composed some time in the second half of the eighth century BC. Further reading: Jaeger 1947: 26–29; Beck 1964: 60–62; Marrou 1956: 7–8; Held 1987: 248–53.

a

I made you the man you are today, godlike Achilles, and loved you from the bottom of my heart. You refused to go to a feast in the company of any other man or to take your meals in the hall until I had given you a seat upon my knees and given you your fill of the food, cutting the first slice for you and offering the wine. Frequently you soaked the tunic on my breast as you sprayed wine from your mouth in your annoying childishness. Thus countless are the sufferings and toils I have endured on your behalf, as I bore in mind that it was not the will of the gods that I should have a child of my own. Instead, godlike Achilles, I made you my son so that one day you might protect me from the disgrace of ruin.

b

Old Peleus, that driver of horses, sent me to you on the day when, as a young child, you were dispatched from Phthia to join Agamemnon. As yet you knew nothing of war, the great leveller, or of the assemblies where men win great distinction. It was on this account that he sent me to teach you all these things, to become skilled at making speeches in public and performing deeds of war. Therefore, dear child, I would not wish to be left behind without you.

1.5. Learning through association

Theognis 27–36

In this extract Theognis offers advice to his friend Cyrnus which he himself learned when he was a child (*pais*). It is therefore likely that Cyrnus too is a boy or a young man. The instruction which Theognis presents here is heavily ethical and reminiscent of the content and tone of passages in Hesiod's *Works and Days* (**1.3**); and we can imagine that the broad topics which it involves are the kind that Phoenix would have concerned himself with in his teaching of Achilles (**1.4**). Theognis' dates are difficult to fix; suggestions for his birth have ranged from about the middle of the seventh century to the late sixth century BC. Further reading: Jaeger 1947: 194–204; Adkins 1960: 75–79; Thomas 1995: 117–23; Konstan 1997: 49–52; Raaflaub 2000: 38–39.

It is due to my concern for you, Cyrnus, that I shall lay before you the lessons I learned from good men when I was still a child. Be wise and do not try to win honour, virtue or wealth for actions which are shameful or do wrong to others. Fix this advice in your mind: do not associate with evil men, but be the constant attendant of those who are virtuous. Be with them when you drink and take your meals. Take your seat in their company and win their approval, since they have

5

great influence. It will be from good men that you will learn good lessons. If you keep company with evil men, you will destroy the intelligence you currently possess.

1.6. Inherited wisdom

Theognis 429–38

Theognis says nothing in **1.5** about formal schooling or about the systematic learning of practical, useful subject matter. That is because he does not believe a person can be taught to have good sense or to be good. Instead, goodness must be something that a person is born with. Since Theognis uses the adjective *kakos* ("bad") and its antonyms *esthlos* ("noble") and *agathos* ("good") as class labels (likewise *kakotés*, "wickedness"), he is restricting the possibility of improvement through learning to members of a single class whose natures he already approves of. Further reading: Jaeger 1947: 194–204; Adkins 1960: 75–79; Lloyd-Jones 1971: 46–48; Mitchell 1997.

> It is easier to beget and raise a person than it is to implant good sense in him. No one yet has devised a way to make the fool wise or to make him noble (*esthlos*) if he is bad (*kakos*). If god had given the followers of Asclepius [i.e. physicians] the ability to heal wickedness (*kakotés*) and men's deluded minds, they would earn great fees in abundance; and if sense could be created and implanted in a man, no son of a good (*agathos*) father would ever become wicked (*kakos*), because he would rely on good advice. But never will a person make the bad man (*kakos*) good by teaching him.

1.7. Pindar's criticisms of education

(a) *Olympian Ode* 2.86–88, (b) *Nemean Ode* 3.40–42,
(c) *Olympian Ode* 9.100–104

In **a**, the Boeotian poet Pindar (518–*c.* 440) takes the assumptions about learning that we find in Theognis one step further: he disparages those who have had to learn what they know and extols as wise those who know things "by nature." In Pindar's view, those who know "by nature" are those who have been born into the right families – the aristocrats and other nobility to whom he addresses his poems. Further reading: Jaeger 1947: 3.113–14; Guthrie 1969: 250–53.

a

Wise (*sophos*) is the man who knows many things by nature; but boisterous windbags who learn are like crows that shriek aimlessly against the divine bird of Zeus.

6

b

One who has glory that he is born with is far the mightier, but a man who has learning is shadowy, always changing his plans; he never embarks with a precise step, but dabbles in countless feats with an imperfect mind.

c

Everything that comes by nature is best. Many men are eager to win glory with skills (*aretai*) that are taught. But without god's help, each deed is no worse when it remains quiet; for some paths are longer than others, and one training will not develop us all.

1.8. Sappho

(a) Maximus of Tyre, *Oration* 18.9, (b) S 261A.7–11 *SLG*

Sappho lived on the island of Lesbos probably in the last decades of the seventh century BC and the early years of the sixth. The aspect of her life which has provoked the greatest controversy is her relationship with the females whom she mentions in her poetry. The well-known image of Sappho as a teacher of young women with whom she may have had erotic attachments depends mainly on late evidence of the kind presented below. Maximus (**a**) lived in the second century AD; that is also the likely date of the papyrus fragment (**b**). For Socrates' relationships with young men (mentioned in **a**), see **4.13–16**. Further reading: Marrou 1956: 33–35; Dover 1978: 173–79; Parker 1993; Lardinois 1994; Skinner 2005: 74–77.

a

What else could the love (*eros*) of the Lesbian woman [Sappho] be but Socrates' art of love. For they seem to me to have practised love in their own way, she the love of women, he the love of men. They said they loved many and were captivated by all things beautiful. What Alcibiades, Charmides and Phaedrus were to him, Gyrinna, Atthis and Anactoria were to her; and what the rival craftsmen Prodicus, Gorgias, Thrasymachus and Protagoras were to Socrates, Gorgo and Andromeda were to Sappho. Sometimes she criticizes them, sometimes she examines them and uses irony, just as Socrates does.

b

She [Sappho], in peace, teaching not only the best girls from among her compatriots but also those from Ionia . . .

7

1.9. Criticisms from early philosophers

(a) Xenophanes frs. 10, 11, (b) Heraclitus frs. 42, 40

Theognis and Pindar were not the only Greeks in this period to criticize learning (**1.6–7**). Xenophanes (*c.* 570–480) focused some of his attacks upon the anthropomorphism of Greek religion, which assigned human qualities to Zeus and the other gods (cf. frs. 14–16). It was on this ground that he criticized Homer, yet he could not deny that Homer was basic to Greek learning. The fact that Xenophanes attacks conventional education and its sources is characteristic of many Greek philosophers in all periods of antiquity. Heraclitus (born *c.* 540) provides other examples of this criticism. Further reading: Beck 1964: 69–70; Raaflaub 2000: 23–27, 48–50.

a

Homer and Hesiod have attributed to the gods all the things that are a source of criticism and reproach among human beings: theft, adultery, and mutual deception.

Since all from the beginning have learned from Homer.

b

Heraclitus said that Homer deserved to be banished from the contests and whipped, and Archilochus deserved to be too.

Learning many things (*polumathie*) does not teach sense, for if it did it would have taught Hesiod and Pythagoras,[1] and likewise Xenophanes and Hecataeus.[2]

1.10. Chiron and Achilles

(a) Homer, *Iliad* 11.828–32, (b) Homer, *Iliad* 16.141–44

In the relatively few references to educational relationships and practices that we find in early Greek sources, the centaur Chiron often plays a prominent role. This is a remarkable fact, since Chiron was not a man but a centaur (part-horse, part-man), and since these mythical beasts were characterized in the stories about them especially by their irrational behaviour;

---

1 Scientific and religious thinker, born on the island of Samos in the sixth century BC.
2 A prose-writer from Miletus, born around 550 BC.

numerous tales emphasize their sexual impulses, violent inclinations, and weakness for alcohol. Chiron, however, is the exception to this pattern. By Homer's time he was believed to have been Achilles' teacher; and he is depicted on many vases of the seventh, sixth and fifth centuries either as receiving Achilles from Achilles' father Peleus or as being in the act of teaching him (Beck 1975: 9–12, and figs 1–20). Elsewhere in the *Iliad* it is the aged Phoenix who is said to have been Achilles' teacher (**1.4**). The skill with which Chiron is most closely connected is medicine, as in **a**. Many legendary heroes besides Achilles are also reported to have received military training from him; see Xenophon, *On Hunting* 1.1–3 and 17; also Pindar, *Nemean Ode* 3.43–63. Chiron's knowledge of, and ability to teach, both healing and killing may reflect his essential nature as part-human, part-animal. Further reading: Marrou 1956: 7–8; Beck 1964: 49–51, 73–75; Kirk 1970: 152–62; Sergent 1986: 252–54; Griffith 2001: 34–35; *LIMC* III.1, 241–44.

a

[The speaker is Eurypylus, a Greek warrior wounded by the Trojan prince, Paris.] But save me and take me to my black ship. There cut the arrow from my thigh, wash the dark blood away from it with warm water, and sprinkle on it the excellent, soothing herbs which they say you learned from Achilles, who was taught by Chiron, the most civilized of the centaurs.

b

No other Achaean could brandish this spear; only Achilles knew how to brandish it, the Pelian ash from Pelion's crest, which Chiron gave to his beloved father [Peleus] to be death for heroes.

1.11. Chiron and Asclepius

(a) Homer, *Iliad* 4.192–97, 210–19, (b) Pindar, *Pythian Ode* 3.1–7, 45–46

Asclepius was the Greek god of medicine and the son of Apollo. As we saw in **1.10a**, Homer knew a tradition according to which Chiron was responsible for at least some of Achilles' knowledge of healing-herbs; here he credits Chiron with Asclepius' similar knowledge (**a**). Writing some time between 476 and 467, Pindar presents a more elaborate story in which Chiron's involvement in Asclepius' upbringing and training begins from his birth (**b**). Further reading: Jaeger 1947: 218–19; Beck 1964: 50; Robbins 1993: 12–20; *LIMC* III.1, 246.

a

Agamemnon then addressed Talthybius, the godlike herald: "Talthybius, with all the speed you can muster, summon here Machaon, the son of Asclepius with his matchless skill as a doctor, so that he may examine warlike Menelaus. Someone from the ranks of the Trojans or Lycians . . . hit him with an arrow. . . ." . . . When they reached the spot where golden-haired Menelaus had been wounded . . ., the man of godlike stature Machaon stood in their midst and from the close-fitting belt he pulled the arrow whose sharp barbs were broken back as it was being pulled out. He unfastened the gleaming belt, the loin-cloth beneath, and the metal plate at his waist, the work of bronze-smiths. But when he saw the wound where the sharp arrow had struck him, he sucked out the blood and, drawing on his expert knowledge, sprinkled over it the soothing herbs which Chiron, with kindly intent, had presented to his father at some point in the past.

b

I would want the departed Chiron, son of Philyra, to be alive, wide-ruling offspring of Uranus' son Cronus, and to be ruling in Pelion's glens, a wild beast with a mind friendly to men, just as he was when he once raised Asclepius, the gentle craftsman who strengthens limbs by bringing relief from pain, hero and defender against all kinds of diseases. . . . Apollo took Asclepius and gave him to the Magnesian centaur to teach him how to heal diseases painful to men.

1.12. A Cretan rite of initiation

Strabo, *Geography* 10.4.16, 21

Chiron's prominent place in the education of legendary Greek heroes has been explained as reflecting a dimly remembered initiation ritual that signi-fied passage into manhood: the youth leaves his family and familiar surroundings to live with an adult male; after a certain period he returns, now a member of adult society. Whatever may be the truth in this sugges-tion, there is no doubt that the passage from one stage of life into another played an important role in the education and training of Greek youths.

The following passage is a remarkable account by the fourth-century historian Ephorus, recorded by Strabo (first century BC), of an initiation ritual in Crete. The first part of this extract sets out the general structure of Cretan society and the life that free males live (compare Xenophon's description of the Spartan system of education and training, **2.2**). Several chapters then follow (not included here) in which Ephorus considers

10

whether the customs he has just explained have their origins in Sparta or in Crete. The second part of the extract is Ephorus' description of the initiation ritual itself. The rite described here has recently been traced back to the Bronze Age through the evidence of Minoan art (Koehl 1986, 1997). Further reading: Dover 1978: 189–90, 1988: 117, 122–23, 124–26; Bremmer 1980: 283–87; Sergent 1986: 7–39; Percy 1996: 61, 64–67; Calame 1999: 280–88; Griffith 2001: 74–80; Graf 2003: 9–20; Skinner 2005: 62–71.

(16) They order the boys to join the "herds" (*agelai*[3]), as they call them, and the grown men to eat in the common messes, which they call "men's quarters," so that, being fed at public expense, the less well-off will have an equal share of the provisions. In order that courage rather than cowardice prevails from childhood, they raise them together in armour and hard work, with the result that they have no concern about heat, cold, a steep, rough road, and blows in gymnasia and on the battle-line. They train them in archery and in dancing with armour, which the Couretes[4] first showed them, as later Pyrrhichus did too, who invented the "Pyrrhic dance," as he called it; and so even their entertainment is not without its usefulness for war. . . . They also wear warlike clothing and shoes, and their weapons are their most valuable gifts. . . .

(21) Their custom concerning love affairs is peculiar, for they win over the ones they love (*eromenoi*) not by persuasion but by abduction. Three or four days beforehand, the lover (*erastés*) gives advance notice to the boy's friends that he is going to carry out the abduction. It is absolutely shameful for them to conceal the boy or not to let him go on the appointed road; it is as though they were admitting that the boy was unworthy of gaining a lover like this. If, when they meet, the abductor is equal or superior to the boy in rank and in other respects, the friends pursue him and grab him half-heartedly, satisfying tradition, but then they hand him over cheerfully to be led away; but if the abductor is unworthy, they take the boy away from him. The pursuit is not ended until the boy is led into the men's quarters in the abductor's house. The Cretans consider desirable not the boy who has exceptional beauty but the one who excels in manliness and good behaviour. After giving the boy a gift, the lover takes him away to any place in the countryside he wishes; those who were present at the abduction follow them.

After eating and hunting together for two months (it is not permitted to keep the boy any longer than this), they return to the city.

---

3 The term that Plutarch uses to describe the organization of Spartan youths into "companies" in **2.6** (16.5) and **2.9**.
4 A mythical band of youthful warriors.

The boy is let go, having received gifts of a military outfit, an ox, and a drinking cup (these are the gifts prescribed by law), as well as many other expensive gifts, so that the friends make contributions because of the great cost. The boy sacrifices the ox to Zeus and provides a feast for those who returned with him; then he makes known whether or not he is satisfied with the time he has spent with his lover, for the law provides that, if any violence was used on him in the abduction, he can on that occasion get revenge and be rid of his lover. For good-looking boys who have distinguished ancestors it is a disgrace not to have lovers, since people think this has happened to them because of their character. Those who have been abducted are called "standers-beside" (*parastathentes*). They are honoured, for in both the dances and the foot-races they hold the most prestigious positions, and they are allowed to dress differently from the others in clothing given to them by their lovers. They wear distinctive clothing not only at that time but also when they are grown men; from this clothing each one can be recognized as having been "glorious," for the beloved one (*eromenos*) is called "glorious" (*kleinos*) and the lover (*erastés*) is called "friend" (*philetor*). These are the customs concerning love affairs.

1.13. Heracles and Linus

Diodorus of Sicily, *Library of History* 3.67.2

The following story is drawn from Greek mythology, but it reflects assumptions about the use of physical punishment in real educational environments. Although Diodorus lived in the first century BC, the story of Heracles' retaliation over his teacher's punishment dates to no later than about 500 BC, since it begins to appear on painted pottery at about that time (Beck 1975: 13 and pls. 5–6).

> Linus was admired for his poetry and singing and had many pupils, but three very illustrious ones, Heracles, Thanyras and Orpheus. When Heracles was learning to play the lyre but was unable to understand what he was being taught – for he was dim-witted – Linus punished him with blows. Heracles became very angry and killed his teacher by striking him with the lyre.

1.14. The introduction of the alphabet into Greece

Herodotus, *Histories* 5.58–59

The Greeks preserved a tradition, first mentioned by Herodotus, that they had adopted and developed their alphabet from the Phoenicians. Though essentially correct, Herodotus' account also contains a significant error. Whereas the mythical Cadmus, who is credited with introducing the alphabet into Greece, was a Phoenician, in Greek legend he is also the founder of the city of Thebes. Since there is a gap of as much as 800 years between the founding of Thebes around 1600 BC and the introduction of the alphabet into Greece, probably between around 900 and 800 BC, Cadmus could not have been responsible in any sense for the Greeks' adoption of the alphabet – if in fact this character from mythology even existed. Further reading: Jeffery 1961: 1–21, 1982: 819–33; Coldstream 1977: 295–302; Powell 1991: 5–20; West 1999: 24–27; Burkert 1992: 25–33; Snodgrass 1980: 78–84; Thomas 1992: 52–73.

(58) The Phoenicians who came with Cadmus . . . settled this land and introduced many skills to the Greeks, above all letters, which the Greeks, I believe, did not previously have. At first these were the letters which all the Phoenicians use, but over time, as they changed their language, they also changed the flow of the letters. The Greeks who lived around them in these parts at that time were mainly Ionians. They learned the letters from the Phoenicians, and after changing the shapes of a few of them they put them to use. Since the Phoenicians had introduced these letters into Greece, it was only right that the Greeks called them "Phoinikeïa." . . . (59) I myself saw Cadmean letters engraved on tripods in the temple of Apollo Ismenias in Boeotian Thebes, similar in most respects to the Ionian letters.

1.15. An early Greek school

Herodotus, *Histories* 6.27.1–2

The events in this extract occurred on the island of Chios in 496 BC. The children who died in the incident are described as *paides* and as engaged in the learning of letters (*grammata*, i.e. reading and writing); they are therefore in the early years of their education. This is our earliest reference to the delivery of formal education in a Greek "school."[5] Even though that term does not occur in this passage, it is hard to imagine how one hundred and twenty children could be accommodated unless it was in a building dedicated to the purpose. The large number of students who are said to have been learning to read and write is striking. Further reading: Beck 1964: 88–91; Harris 1989: 58–59.

---

5 Solon's school laws, if genuine, would belong to an earlier period, but they are probably a later invention; see **3.3**.

There is normally some advance warning whenever great misfortune is going to fall on a city or nation. In the case of the people of Chios there were substantial signs before the event just related. In the first place, when they sent a choir of young men to Delphi, only two returned home; the others, all ninety-eight of them, were stricken with plague and died. Then again, in the city at the very same time and shortly before the sea-battle, a roof collapsed on children (*paides*) who were learning their letters (*grammata*). Of the hundred and twenty children only one survived.

2

SPARTA

Direct evidence for educational practices in Sparta comes primarily from two sources, Xenophon (late fifth century and first half of the fourth century BC) and Plutarch (AD 46–c. 120), who made extensive use of Xenophon's writings on Sparta. Plato, a contemporary of Xenophon, also provides information about Sparta, as do some other writers, in particular Aristotle and the second-century AD writer Pausanias. Inscriptional evidence, however, is not nearly as abundant or helpful for the study of Sparta in the fifth and fourth centuries BC as it is for Athens and many other cities; and since written works from Spartan authors after the late seventh century BC are almost non-existent, we are forced to rely upon the perspectives of non-Spartans for our understanding of Spartan education.

The Spartan educational system was tightly woven into the fabric of Spartan society. The ancient Spartans (Lacedaimonians) themselves attributed the structure and character of their institutions, including the educational system frequently referred to as the *agogé*, to the work of a lawmaker named Lycurgus whose date, and even existence, are uncertain (**2.2, 6**). Like the legendary Lycurgus, Spartan society is something of a mystery, but it is clear that it was organized so that personal interests and comfort were subordinated to the state's security. To this day, this remains Sparta's most notorious characteristic (e,g, **2.4–5, 10**). The kind of person that the Spartan system aimed to produce may be seen from lines of the late seventh-century BC Spartan poet Tyrtaeus (fr. 12.10–28 West):

A man does not prove himself courageous in war unless he can bear to see bloody slaughter and can aim at the enemy as he stands near him. Among mankind this excellence, this prize, is the best and finest thing for a young man to win. The city and all the people share in this noble thing, whenever a man, feet planted firmly, stands relentlessly in the front ranks and pays no thought at all to shameless flight as he shows a steadfast heart and soul. He stands beside the man who is near him and encourages him with his words. This man proves himself courageous in war. All at once he routs the rugged battalions of the

15

enemy and eagerly holds back the wave of battle. The man who falls in the front ranks and loses his life, giving honour to his city, his people, and his father, who has suffered many wounds in his chest from a spear that came through the centre of his shield and through his breastplate, this man do young and old alike lament, and in painful longing the whole city mourns for him.

Over seven hundred years later, Plutarch neatly linked the nature and duration of Spartan upbringing with the military character of Spartan society (*Life of Lycurgus* 24):

> Their education continued until they were fully grown men, and nobody was allowed to live his life according to his own wishes. Instead their life in their city resembled that of a military camp, in that they had a set pattern of life and spent their time in the service of the state, believing that their country, not themselves, had complete ownership of their persons. If no other duty had been assigned to them, they constantly kept watch over their boys and provided them with instruction in matters of practical benefit; either that, or they would themselves receive such lessons from their elders.

It can hardly be assumed, however, that Spartan society, or by implication its educational system, remained static throughout the city's history. In fact, one of the difficulties in studying Spartan education is the probability that some of the features presented as part of its early core are really later additions or distortions of early elements (e.g. **2.6, 10**).

To the modern mind the Spartan educational system, though certainly systematic, may not seem to involve education as much as an initiation into society (e.g. **2.8–9**). There is much truth to this view, and initiatory features can be seen in the systems of other Greek states too. For instance, some of the features of the Spartan system described in selections below are worth comparing with the rites described in **1.12** and with the *ephebeia* in **3.25–26**.

General background: Ehrenberg 1973: 28–49; Pomeroy *et al.* 1999: 131–58; Morris and Powell 2006: 193–204. *Agogé*: Marrou 1956: 14–25; Rawson 1969: 12–115; Bowen 1972: 50–57; Barrow 1976: 23–30; Cartledge and Spawforth 1989: 176–83; Kennell 1995: 5–27; Hodkinson 1997; Cartledge 2001: 79–90; Powell 2001: 218–70, esp. 231–36; Ducat 2006: ix–xvii.

2.1. The state as *paidagogos*

Plutarch, *Life of Lycurgus* 30.4–6

The following passage expresses the view that a Spartan's education was a life-long process tightly connected with his or her membership in Spartan society. To the characterization of Sparta as a *paidagogos*, compare Pericles' statement that Athens is the "schooling (*paideusis*) of Greece" (**3.1b**). Further reading: Powell 2001: 218–70.

> The Spartans instilled in the rest of Greece not only obedience but a desire to place themselves under their authority and to receive orders from them. When they sent requests to Sparta, they would ask them for a single Spartan commander, not ships, hoplites or money. When they received their commander, they would treat him with respect and awe. . . . In each place these men were called regulators (*harmostai*) and chasteners (*sophronistai*) of the people and magistrates, since people were inclined to look upon the city of Sparta as a whole as the teacher or *paidagogos* of a well-balanced way of life and a well-regulated constitution. It was of this characteristic of Sparta that Stratonicus[1] appears to have been making fun, when he humorously framed a law requiring that the people of Athens conduct mysteries and sacred processions, and that the people of Elis organize athletic festivals, on the grounds that these were the things that they did best; in the case of the Spartans, however, they were to be flayed alive if these other peoples misbehaved. Stratonicus was only speaking in jest. However, when Antisthenes, the Socratic, saw the Thebans putting on airs after the Battle at Leuctra,[2] he declared that they were behaving just like little boys who prance about because they have given their *paidagogos* a beating.

2.2. The character of Spartan education

Xenophon, *Constitution of the Lacedaimonians* 2.1–4.6

The following extract is of fundamental importance for our knowledge of the Spartan educational experience; it is also our earliest source on the topic (early fourth century BC). Certain famous features of the Spartan system emerge in this account. As we shall see, these are treated in greater detail by Plutarch, who provides our most expansive account of Spartan education and upbringing. These features include:

i   the promotion of toughness in Spartan youths through the provision of minimal clothing;

1 Athenian lyre-player, *c.* 410–360 BC, known for his wit.
2 371 BC, between the Spartans and the Thebans. The defeat of the Spartans ended their domination on the battlefield which had endured for two centuries. Leuctra is in Boeotia.

ii the teaching of self-sufficiency, illustrated here by the encouragement youths receive to steal food in order to supplement their rudimentary diet;

iii the prominence of the *paidonomos* and the role that he and his assistants play in administering strict discipline;

iv membership in a common mess (*phidition, sussition*);

v   the division of Spartan youths into age-groups;

vi the acceptance of pederasty as serving an educational purpose.

Some of these features find parallels in the practices of other Greek states in the Archaic and Classical Periods, in particular iv–vi; cf. **1.12**, **3.25–26**, **6.20**, **24**. Xenophon presents the Spartan educational system as an integrated aspect or expression of Spartan society rather than as a distinct institution. Further reading: Murray 1980: 153–72; Proietti 1987: 44–79; Kennell 1995: 116–36; Powell 2001: 231–36; Griffith 2001: 36–66; Cartledge 2004: 60–65; Ducat 2006: 1–22, 69–117.

(2.1) Having explained the issues relating to birth, I also wish to clarify the difference between the Spartan educational system and that of other Greek states.

In the rest of the Greek world, those who claim to provide their sons with the best education place their children in the care of a *paidagogos* as soon as they can understand what is said to them, and they send them to school to learn letters, music and the activities of the *palaistra* (wrestling school). In addition, their children's feet are allowed to remain soft through the use of sandals, and the strength of their bodies is undermined by the use of different forms of cloak. Furthermore, the capacity of the stomach is traditionally used to measure the amount of food to be eaten.

(2.2) By contrast, instead of having each man privately assign slaves to serve as *paidagogoi*, Lycurgus placed boys under the authority of a man appointed from the ranks of those who are eligible to hold the highest magistracies. This person is called the *paidonomos*, and Lycurgus gave him the authority to gather the boys together, to keep a watchful eye on them, and to punish anyone who was inclined to laziness. A number of young men who carried whips were also assigned to him to inflict punishment whenever necessary. As a result, there exists in Sparta a combination of respect and obedience at a very high level. (2.3) Instead of letting the feet become soft through the use of sandals, he decreed that children should toughen their feet by going barefoot, in the belief that, if this became their normal practice, it would be much easier for them to climb uphill and safer for them to descend steep gradients, and that a boy without shoes whose feet were trained would leap, jump up and run more swiftly than one wearing sandals. (2.4) Instead of weakening them by the use of different cloaks, he legislated that they should become accustomed to using a single cloak throughout the year, in the belief that under these circumstances they would be better prepared to cope with both heat and cold. (2.5) He ordained that each *eiren*[3] should contribute to the common mess just the exact amount of food to ensure that they would never be weighed down by being full and that they would become experienced at living with want. For he believed that those who were provided with this training would have a greater ability, should the need arise, to continue at their labours on an empty stomach and, if instructed to do so, to persevere for a longer period on the same diet; that they would have less need for sophisticated meals and be less concerned about any food they were called upon to eat; and that they would have a healthier life. He also believed that a diet which produced a slim body also resulted in greater height than one which thickened the girth.

(2.6) However, to prevent them from suffering too severely from hunger, and without allowing them to take what they needed effortlessly, he did permit them to provide a remedy for their hunger by stealing. (2.7) Everyone is well aware, I think, that it was not because there was a lack of resources to give them food that he allowed them to use their wits to provide it for themselves. It is quite clear that someone who intends to steal must go without sleep at night, must use deception and lie in wait for his opportunity during the day, and must have his lookouts ready posted if he is going to succeed in stealing something. Therefore, it is plain that he provided this form of education in all these matters because he wished to make the boys more resourceful in providing themselves with the necessities of life and to improve their skills in war. (2.8) The question might be asked why, if he considered theft to be a positive characteristic, he imposed a severe flogging on anyone who was caught. My answer is that in all the other forms of instruction men punish those who are deficient in carrying out their instructions. Thus the Spartans too punish those caught because they have been deficient in their thieving. (2.9) While Lycurgus established that it was an honourable practice to steal as many cheeses as possible from Artemis Orthia,[4] he assigned others to flog the thieves, because he wished to demonstrate thereby that it is possible to achieve the joy of a lasting distinguished reputation by

---

3 *Eiren*, pl. *eirenes*: thirty-year olds, the oldest in the Spartan age-classes.
4 The most important cult of Artemis in Sparta, closely associated with the *agogé* because of the role its altar played in the cheese-stealing ritual alluded to here, and in the whipping contest (**2.10**); see Kennell 1995: 126–29; Ducat 2006: 249–60.

enduring a brief moment of pain. This practice also reveals that in cases where speed is essential there is minimal benefit in store for the lazy, but rather the maximum amount of trouble.

(2.10) In order to ensure that the boys should never be without someone to take charge of them during the absence of the *paido-nomos*, Lycurgus required any citizen who happened to be present at any given moment to assume authority, to give the boys whatever instructions he thought fit, and to punish any misdeed. By so doing, he engendered a more respectful attitude in the boys, since neither boys nor men show as much respect for anything as they do for those in charge. (2.11) And to ensure that the boys should never be without someone to take charge of them even on occasions when a grown man was not present, he ordained that the *eiren* with the keenest mind should take charge of each unit (*ilé*). As a result, in Sparta there is always someone in charge of them.

(2.12) I think that I must also say a word about sexual relations with boys, since that too is relevant to education. In other Greek states, it is the tradition either for man and boy to be bound together in an association with each other, as among the Boeotians, or for men to enjoy the bloom of youth in return for favours, as in Elis. There are also some states which completely ban lovers from engaging in conversation with boys. (2.13) Lycurgus adopted a policy which was at variance with all these traditions. When he saw that a man of upright character admired the inner being of a boy and was attempting to establish a friendship with him which was beyond reproach and to spend time with him, he approved of the relationship and considered this to be an excellent form of education. On the other hand, if a man was clearly lusting after a boy's body, he saw this as an utterly shameful practice and brought it about that in Sparta, in terms of sexual matters, lovers keep their hands away from their beloved just as much as fathers do from their sons or brothers from their brothers. (2.14) I am not surprised, however, that some people refuse to accept that this is the case, since the laws in many cities are not framed to oppose the desire for sexual relations with boys. . . .

(3.1) At the point when boys proceed from childhood to puberty, in the rest of Greece they are released from their *paidagogoi* and their schoolmasters; they are no longer subject to anyone's control and are allowed complete personal freedom. Here, too, Lycurgus came to a decision which was at variance with this practice. (3.2) On the basis of his observation that boys of this age develop a large measure of high spirits, that their insolent behaviour, in particular, predominates and that they are beset by the most powerful desires to pursue pleasure, at this stage of their development he forced them to undergo a great deal of hard labour and cleverly contrived that the time they had for leisure was minimal. (3.3) Also, by penalizing anyone who shirked these tasks with exclusion from all future privileges in civic life, he ensured that not just public officials but also each boy's relatives focused their attention on preventing them from completely destroying their reputation in the city by flinching from their responsibilities. (3.4) In addition, because Lycurgus wanted respect to be instilled in them as a dominant characteristic, he decreed that they should keep their hands under their cloaks even on the streets, that they should maintain silence as they walked, and that they should not look about them in any direction, but keep their eyes fixed on the ground before their feet. As a result of this requirement it became clear that the male sex had greater powers of self-control than was the case with the natural disposition of the female sex. (3.5) At all events, you would be more likely to hear a statue of stone use its voice than these youths, you would be more likely to cause a bronze image to divert its gaze than you would theirs, and you would be inclined to think them more bashful even than a young maiden in her bridal chamber. Whenever they entered the common mess (*phidition*), you must be satisfied if you even hear them answer a question. Such was the careful attention Lycurgus devoted to boys in their adolescence (*paidiskoi*).

(4.1) By far his most serious attention was focused on boys when they reached the prime of their youthful years (*hebontes*).[5] It was his belief that, if they developed as they ought to, they had the strongest capacity to benefit the state. (4.2) Noting that the choral singing which was most worth listening to and the athletic competitions which were most worth watching were those in which the will to win was particularly strong, he came to the conclusion that youths in their prime (*hebontes*) also could reach the highest level of bravery if he could match them against each other in a fierce struggle to display their valour. Let me explain, therefore, how he brought about these matches. (4.3) The ephors[6] select three men from those in the prime of life. These officials are called the *hippagretai*, and each of them draws up a list of a hundred men, providing a clear explanation why particular individuals were given preference and others rejected. (4.4) Consequently, those who fail to achieve the honour of selection are in a state of war with both those who rejected them and those who are picked instead of themselves, and they maintain a keen watch on each

---

5 Probably the period from the ages 20 to 30; see Kennell 1995: 117–18; Ducat 2006: 99–112.
6 Five Spartan magistrates elected annually; they held wide powers in both domestic and foreign affairs.

other to see if anyone violates what is considered to be honourable practice by taking things too easily. (4.5) This form of competitive rivalry is particularly dear to the gods and meets the highest standard of civic conduct. As it occurs, there is a clear demonstration of how the courageous man must act; each of the two groups strives separately to achieve permanent superiority and, should the need arise, at the individual level, to defend the interests of the state with all their might. (4.6) They are also forced to pay serious attention to their physical fitness, since their rivalry leads them to engage in fisticuffs with each other whenever they meet, although any man present has the authority to intervene to break up the fight. If anyone refuses to obey this intervention, he is brought before the ephors by the *paidonomos* and punished severely in order to bring him to the point where he never allows his anger to prevail over obedience to the laws.

2.3. Spartan women

Xenophon, *Constitution of the Lacedaimonians* 1.3–4

Spartan society seems to have made greater provision for the education of females than other Greek states did, though their educational program was not fully parallel with the one that Spartan males underwent. Further reading: Scanlon 1988; Pomeroy 2002: 3–32, 2004: 203–5; Cartledge 2004: 212–16; Ducat 2006: 223–47.

(3) Among other peoples, girls who are destined to bear children and who are brought up in what appears to be the acceptable way receive a diet of the simplest food possible and a minimum of dishes requiring careful preparation. Indeed, they see to it that the girls either abstain from wine altogether or drink it well diluted with water. Other Greeks see fit to have their girls take no exercise at all and sit working at their wool, just like the majority of those involved in handicrafts. How on earth can a girl who is brought up in that way be expected to bear a magnificent child? (4) By contrast, Lycurgus believed that even slave women were capable of producing clothing, but that the principal responsibility of a freeborn woman was the production of children. Thus, he first laid down that physical exercise be a requirement for females just as much as males, and then established competitions in running and strength for women just as he had for men. He did so in the conviction that children are born healthier when both their parents are strong.

2.4. Pericles compares Spartan and Athenian education

Thucydides, *The Peloponnesian War* 2.39.1

This extract is drawn from the funeral speech which – according to Thucydides – Pericles delivered as a tribute to the Athenian soldiers who had died in the first year of the Peloponnesian War (431 BC). The speech is perhaps the most famous encomium of ancient Athens and of the Athenian character. Here Pericles summarizes the essential differences which he sees between the Spartan and Athenian systems of education. Further reading: Rawson 1969: 20–24; Ducat 2006: 38–40.

> The city we show the world is open to everyone, and we never use expulsions of foreigners to keep anyone from learning or observing, even though an enemy might gain an advantage if he saw what was not hidden. We rely on our innate courage, not on plans and deceit. In regard to our educational systems, they [the Spartans] pursue manhood through oppressive training from the very start of their youth, whereas we have a relaxed style of life yet are just as ready to confront the dangers that we are equal to.

2.5. Pros and cons of the Spartan system

Aristotle, *Politics* 8.1337a21–32, 1338b9–17, 24–38

Aristotle praises the Spartans for the fact that their system is publicly administered, a clear indication to him that the state takes seriously the care of its children; but he also condemns the Spartans for the brutality in their upbringing, observing that physical force is not the way to instil courage in children. Further reading: Rawson 1969: 79–80; Lord 1982: 48–51; Curren 2000: 12–15; Ducat 2006: 61–64.

> (1337a) Since the goal of the state as a whole is a single one, it is apparent that the educational system must be one and the same for everyone, and that the administration of this system must be public and not private, as it is now: each person takes care of his own children, teaching them privately any subject he personally decides on. Things that are of public concern require a training that is public too. Furthermore, no citizen should think that he belongs to himself; rather, all citizens belong to the state, for each person is a part of the state, and by nature the administration of each part looks towards

the care of the whole. The Lacedaimonians can be praised on this account, since they take the greatest pains over their children, and they do so as a community. . . .

(1338b) At the present time some of the states that have the highest reputation for the care they devote to their children produce in them an athletic condition, ruining their appearances and the growth of their bodies. The Lacedaimonians did not make this mistake, but they brutalize their children through excessively hard work, believing that this is the best way to produce courage. Yet people have often pointed out that the care of children should not be carried out with its sole or special focus on courage; and even if the focus is on courage, they are failing in their search for it. . . .

Moreover, we know that the Lacedaimonians themselves were ahead of everyone else so long as they alone applied themselves to demanding exercises, but now they fall short of the rest in both athletic competitions and the contests of war. They used to be set apart not because their young people exercised in the way I have mentioned but because they alone trained while their competition did not train at all. Therefore beauty, not brutality, must take first place, for it is the good man, not the wolf or any of the other wild animals, who could take part in a dangerous, noble competition. The truth is that those people who are too lenient with their children and give them no guidance in what their education really calls for make them mechanical; they make them useful for one political task only, and, as the argument goes, in an inferior degree to others. We must judge the Lacedaimonians not from their former achievements but from their current ones; for they now have competitors in education, whereas before they did not.

2.6. Plutarch on Spartan education

Plutarch, *Life of Lycurgus* 16.3–6, 17.1–4, 18.1

Writing almost 500 years after Xenophon, Plutarch used his *Constitution of the Lacedaimonians* as an important source in composing his own biography of the Spartan lawgiver Lycurgus (e.g. **2.2**). He also supplemented this work with information that he drew from other writers, especially Aristotle. The fact that Plutarch's accounts are much fuller and more precise than Xenophon's produces the impression that he is the better and more useful source, but there is good reason to believe that the system which he describes reflects Spartan education as it existed in the Hellenistic Period and the Roman Empire, after extensive modifications had been made to it, and not as it was in the time of Xenophon or before. Further reading: Kennell 1995: 23–25, 32–35; Ducat 2006: 23–29.

(16.3) Babies were brought up, not tightly wrapped in blankets, but with their limbs and physiques left free to develop, and they were also trained to show no peevishness or fussiness over their diet, to have no fear of the dark or apprehension at being left alone, and to avoid the crankiness and squalling typical of the ill-bred. It was because of these results that several people from elsewhere would purchase Spartan nurses, and it is recorded that Amycla, who nursed the Athenian Alcibiades, was a Spartan.

(16.4) However, as Plato tells us,[7] Pericles appointed Zopyrus to be Alcibiades' *paidagogos*, a man who had nothing to distinguish him from all other slaves. Lycurgus, by contrast, did not subject the sons of Spartan citizens to the supervision of a *paidagogos*, no matter whether purchased or hired. Nor did he permit any Spartan to bring up and educate his son as he chose. Instead, he took over all boys as soon as they reached their seventh birthday and assigned them to companies, in this way ensuring that they would eat together and develop together and become used to sharing their hours of recreation and study with each other. (16.5) He appointed as leader of each company (*agelé*[8]) the boy who displayed outstanding judgment and spirit; the other members of the company would keep their eyes fixed on him, obey his commands, and submit themselves to his discipline, with the result that their training was an exercise in absolute obedience. Older men would observe the boys while they were at play and would constantly try to provoke situations which led them to fight and to show their will to win, maintaining a careful scrutiny to determine each boy's natural disposition to display boldness and a refusal to back down in the confrontations which occurred.

(16.6) While they learned letters for practical application, all the rest of their education was focused on absolute obedience to authority, perseverance in the face of hardship, and victory in battle. For this reason, as they grew older, their training was intensified, their heads were shaved to the skin, and they were forced to become used to walking barefoot and, for the most part, to wearing no clothes when they were at play. Once they reached the age of twelve, they were

---

7 In *Alcibiades* I 122a8–b2.
8 Lit. "herd" (pl. *agelai*), translated as "company" elsewhere in this passage (cf. **2.9**). Ephorus uses *agelé* with a similar reference in his description of the Cretan initiation rite (**1.12**).

denied the use of a tunic and were assigned a single cloak a year. The skin on their bodies was rough and dry, and they had no experience of baths and ointments, except on the few days each year when they were allowed to share in such indulgences. . . .

(17.1) Once boys had reached this age, close associations were established with lovers drawn from those young men who were of good repute. A careful watch was also maintained by the older men, who paid more frequent visits to the places where they exercised and were present when they engaged in fighting and teasing each other. The supervision was rigorous, in the belief that they all were, in a way, the fathers and *paidagogoi* of all of them, with a responsibility to regulate their conduct. As a result, there was no time when or place where a boy who went astray was without someone to reprimand or punish him. (17.2) On top of all that, it was from amongst the men of high character and nobility that they appointed a *paidonomos*, and the elders personally picked without exception the youth with the greatest self-discipline and most warlike spirit to take charge of the companies of those known as the *eirenes*, which is the name given to those who have completed their second year beyond boyhood (the senior boys are called the *melleirenes*[9]).

This *eiren*, then, who would be twenty years of age, is the one who holds command in battle over his subordinates and domestically uses them as servants at dinner. (17.3) In response to his instructions the sturdy fetch wood and those of lesser physique bring vegetables. What they fetch is stolen, some of them trespassing into people's gardens, others slipping into the common messes of the men with great caution and guile. If anyone is caught, he is whipped on the principle that his thieving has been devoid of skill and care. They also steal whatever food they can, as they learn to make clever raids on those who are asleep or maintain a careless watch over their property. (17.4) Anyone who is caught is not only punished with a flogging, but must also go hungry, since they receive a meagre amount of food for their meals in order to force them to use their own initiative to fend off hunger by daring acts of guile. . . .

(18.1) A story is told which illustrates the care which the boys apply to their stealing. One of them, who had just stolen a fox-cub and had wrapped it up in the folds of his cloak, stubbornly allowed his abdomen to be torn apart by the animal's teeth and claws until he died, in order to escape detection. This tale is quite credible on the evidence of the young men (*epheboi*) today, many of whom I have witnessed dying from being whipped at the altar of Artemis Orthia.

---

9 These were probably nineteen-year-olds; see Kennell 1995: 35–37; Ducat 2006: 72–77.

2.7. Spartan literacy

(a) Isocrates, *Panathenaecus* 209, (b) Plutarch, *Spartan Sayings* 237a

In selection **a**, Isocrates speaks in categorical terms about Spartan illiteracy and aversion to literature and literary education. He does so for rhetorical effect, but the basic sincerity of his words is not to be doubted. Selection **b** is Plutarch's expansion of comments in his *Life of Lycurgus* (**2.6** [16.6]). The low value which the Spartans apparently placed on literary education should not be taken as a lack of interest in poetry or song (see Plutarch, *Life of Lycurgus* 21.1–3). The most famous Spartan poets were Tyrtaeus (see chapter introduction) and Alcman, who belong to the second half of the seventh century BC. Further reading: Cartledge 1978, 2001: 39–54; Boring 1979; Harris 1989: 112–14; Ducat 2006: 119–24.

a

Whereas it is clear that the barbarians have been students and teachers of many discoveries, the Spartans have fallen so far short of our common education (*paideia*) and pursuit of wisdom (*philosophia*) that they do not even learn letters (*grammata*), a subject which has so much power that those who understand them and use them become knowledgeable not only in what their own generation has accomplished but also in the accomplishments of all who have gone before them.

b

The Spartans would learn letters for practical application. However, they excluded from their society all other forms of education, written material just as much as individual practitioners. Their educational system was focused on absolute obedience to authority, perseverance in the face of hardship, and accepting the alternatives of victory or death in battle.

2.8. The common mess

Plutarch, *Life of Lycurgus* 12.4–6

As he does elsewhere, Plutarch here expands on a subject that Xenophon had treated briefly (**2.2** [3.5]). This time the topic is the common mess (*phidition, sussition*), which was an important ingredient in the acculturation of Spartan youths into adult society. Further reading: Kennell 1995: 130–31; Hodkinson 1997: 90–91; Powell 2001: 228–31; Cartledge 2004: 70–72; Ducat 2006: 81–86, 93–94.

(4) Boys also would regularly attend the common messes, rather as if they were being taken to schools in which they would learn self-control. There they would listen to discussions about public affairs and observe those who served as their models instructing them in the qualities of the freeborn. They personally became accustomed to have fun, to make jokes without being coarse, and not to show resentment when they were made the butt of jokes. In fact, this capacity to put up with a joke appeared to be a particularly Spartan characteristic. If, however, someone found he could not do so, he had the right to appeal to the person poking fun at him to stop, (5) and stop he did. When each member entered the mess, the eldest pointed to the doors and said to him: "Nothing said here passes outside through these doors." It is said that the membership of anyone applying to join the mess was approved by the following process. Each member of the mess would pick up a piece of soft bread and, as an attendant carried around a bowl on his head, deposit it in the bowl like a ballot without saying a word: someone voting for admission would deposit the piece of bread without doing anything to it, while someone voting for exclusion would do so after squeezing it tightly in his hand; (6) a piece of bread which had been so squeezed was the equivalent of a negative vote. If a single ballot of this kind was found in the bowl, the applicant for admission was rejected on the grounds that it was their wish that their association with each other should give pleasure to all members. They say that a candidate who has been rejected in this manner has been "kaddized," because the bowl in which the pieces of bread are placed is known as a *kaddichos*.

2.9. Homosexual ties

Plutarch, *Spartan Sayings* 237b–c

Xenophon deals with the topic of pederasty in relationships between younger and older Spartan males (**2.2** [2.12–14]). He firmly rejects the possibility that these relationships possess a sexual dimension. In this extract Plutarch repeats this view. It seems naive, however, to believe either Xenophon or Plutarch in this matter. Further reading: Dover 1978: 185–96; Cartledge 1981, 2001: 91–105; Powell 2001: 228–30; Skinner 2005: 62–71; Ducat 2006: 164–69, 196–201.

(b) The practice was for the young men to sleep together, according to their unit (*ilé*) and company (*agelé*), on mattresses which they personally stitched together after breaking off the tops of reeds growing beside the Eurotas. This they did with their bare hands without the use of any knife. During winter they would place underneath and blend into their mattresses plants known as Lycophon, whose tissues appeared to possess a capacity to contribute warmth. Although they were permitted to form an affectionate bond with boys of good character, (c) to have sexual contact was considered a disgrace on the grounds that such love was focused on the body and not the soul. Anyone accused of this form of disgraceful sexual intimacy lost his civic rights for the rest of his life.

2.10. The whipping contest

(a) Plutarch, *Spartan Sayings* 239c–d, (b) Pausanias, *Description of Greece* 3.16.10–11

One of the most bizarre elements to be reported about the upbringing of Spartan youths is the event called the "whipping contest." Detailed evidence for this contest is late, but the earliest hints of it are in Xenophon (**2.2** [2.7–9]) and Plato (*Laws* 633b). The extracts translated below date to the beginning and middle of the second century AD respectively. The exhibition which Plutarch and Pausanias saw with their own eyes was a later development, not part of the Spartan upbringing which Xenophon and his contemporaries knew. Further reading: Burkert 1985: 262–63; Kennell 1995: 70–83, 149–61 (texts and translations relating to the whipping contest); Ducat 2006: 191–94, 249–60.

a

(c) In Spartan society boys are thrashed with whips all day long at the altar of Artemis Orthia, frequently to the point of death. They bear this unflinchingly and proudly maintain a cheerful spirit (d) as they compete with each other to secure the victory of being the one who can endure receiving a more protracted and severe beating than the rest. The winner is held in particularly high esteem. The competition, which takes place annually, is called the "Whipping."

b

(10) At this the Spartans received an oracle that they should make the altar run with human blood, and they would offer as sacrifice an individual chosen by lot. As a reform of this practice, Lycurgus instituted the whipping of young men (*epheboi*), and that is the method used to cover the altar with human blood. The priestess takes up a position beside them holding the wooden statue of the goddess. Although under other circumstances the small size of the statue makes it light, (11) if those administering the whipping ever use the lash with

restraint due to the beauty or rank of one of the youths (*epheboi*), at that moment the statuette immediately becomes heavy in the woman's hands and is no longer easy to hold. She holds the scourgers responsible and claims that the weight she is carrying is their fault. In this way, ever since the time of the sacrifices in Tauric territory, the image has been continuously appeased with human blood.

3

ATHENS IN THE FIFTH AND
FOURTH CENTURIES BC

We know far more about life and society in Athens during the fifth and fourth centuries BC than we do about any other Greek state during the same period. This was the time when educational practices in Athens assumed a recognizable form. As it is presented in numerous sources (**3.13–15**), the pattern that prevailed in this period consisted essentially of three elements: physical training (*gymnastiké*), which included wrestling, running, javelin-throwing and other competitive activities; music (*mousiké*), which included the memorization of poetry, instruction in the playing of the lyre (a stringed instrument), singing, and dancing; and letters (*grammata*), which involved reading, writing and the study of literature. The evidence of **3.11** suggests that letters may not have held a central place in the curriculum in the first half of the fifth century. If this inference is correct – though our sources may reflect a social bias in this matter (**3.16**) – the situation was to change rapidly (**3.17–19**).

In other ways, however, we find a great deal of educational continuity with the past. Seen as the production of good citizens – more generally as their "cultivation" and "improvement" – education was considered to be something that took place not simply in schoolrooms. Many sources show clearly that Athenians took a broad view in defining education (**3.1**), as their predecessors in the rest of Greece had done as well. Given this outlook, it is not surprising that the formalized practice of pederasty, which is prominent either explicitly or implicitly in earlier evidence for educational relationships, retains a place in Athenian society (**3.2–3**). As before, Athenians looked to poets as a source of wisdom; these poets naturally included Homer, but now tragic poets were included too (**3.8–9**). There was no public provision for the education of children and youths (**3.22**), though this was to change in Athens with the introduction around 335 of the two-year mandatory military service called the *ephebeia* (**3.25–26**).

The fifth century witnessed the emergence of schools in Athens and elsewhere (cf. **1.15**). The earliest formal schooling of Athenian children for which we have evidence occurred not in Athens but in Troizen (**3.10**), and by the late fifth century schools must have been widespread, even in small communities (**3.23**). The status of teachers, however, was poor (**3.24**).

In 508 BC Athens underwent a remarkable development in its political life with the adoption of a system of direct democracy. Now Athenian citizens (males eighteen years of age and older) were eligible to attend, speak at, and vote in the Popular Assembly (*ekklesia*), where most of the city's important business was conducted. Those thirty and older could serve on the Council of Five Hundred (*boulé*) and hold one of the numerous annual magistracies (service in which was determined by lot, not election). This new political structure prepared the ground for an intellectual upheaval in the fifth and fourth centuries which has had a profound and permanent influence on Western thought and education. The middle of the fifth century saw the advent of the "sophists" as an important professional class of teachers offering a kind of "higher" education which focused especially on the use of language. The second half of the fifth century was also the time when Socrates was testing many of the well-entrenched beliefs of his fellow Athenians, as well as the claims of the sophists. The sophists and Socrates are given a chapter to themselves (Chapter 4). Three figures who belong to the fourth century BC – Isocrates, Plato and Aristotle – are important enough because of their contributions to the practice and theory of education that they too must be given a separate treatment (Chapter 5). Yet all of these people and their activities can be understood only within the context provided by the evidence of this chapter.

General background: Ehrenberg 1973: 192–258; JACT 1984: 196–243; Pomeroy *et al.* 1999: 246–86; Sansone 2004: 94–105; Morris and Powell 2006: 204–20, 268–87.

3.1. Civic education

(a) Simonides, fr. 90 West, (b) Thucydides, *The Peloponnesian War* 2.41.1, (c) Plato, *Apology* 24c10–25b8, (d) Plato, *Protagoras* 320a4–7

Selection **a** is the translation of a three-word fragment from a poem written late in the sixth century or early in the fifth century BC by the poet Simonides (from the Aegean island of Ceos). It expresses what must have been viewed as a general truth about the Greek city-state (*polis*) for a free person who was engaged in its day-to-day life. The second extract is drawn from Pericles' celebrated funeral speech (see also **2.4**); it occurs roughly halfway through the speech and summarizes the lavish praise of Athens that has preceded. Extract **c** is from the speech Plato presents Socrates as delivering on the day of his trial in 399. Here Socrates demonstrates to his accuser

Meletus that it is absurd to claim that Socrates alone corrupts the young men of Athens while everyone else improves them. Although Meletus' position is presented in an extreme form, it reflects assumptions that democratic Athens made about the education of its young (cf. Plato, *Protagoras* 320c8–328d2). The final extract, also from one of Plato's works, provides a specific example of an association between a younger Athenian male (Clinias) and an older one (Ariphron) which is outside any formal educational arrangement. Further reading: de Strycker and Slings 1994: 107–13; Ober 2001; Too 2001; Brickhouse and Smith 2004: 105–20.

a

The city (*polis*) teaches a man.

b

In a word, I say that the whole city (*polis*) is the schooling (*paideusis*) of Greece.

c

(24c) SOCRATES: Come here, Meletus, and tell me: (d) your greatest concern is how the young will be as good as possible, isn't it?

MELETUS: It certainly is.

SOCRATES: Come on, tell these men [i.e. the jury]: who improves them? ... You say you've discovered the one who corrupts them – me – and you bring me before these jurors here and accuse me. Come then, tell the jurors who improves them; reveal his identity. Do you see, Meletus, that you're silent and don't know what to say? Don't you think it's shameful, and adequate evidence of precisely what I'm saying, that you've had no concern about this? Tell us, my good man, who improves them? – The laws.

(e) SOCRATES: But that's not what I'm asking, my good friend. What *man* is it who knows this very thing in the first place, namely the laws? – These men here, Socrates, the jurors.

SOCRATES: What do you say, Meletus? Can these men teach the young and improve them? – Of course.

SOCRATES: All of them, or some of them but not others? – All of them.

SOCRATES: I'm delighted to hear that – you're talking about an unlimited number of benefactors. And do these spectators here improve them, (25a) or not? – They do too.

SOCRATES: What about the members of the Council (*boulé*). – So do they.

SOCRATES: But surely, Meletus, the men who attend the Assembly (*ekklesia*) don't corrupt the young. Do all of them improve the young too? – They do too.

SOCRATES: So all the Athenians except me, it seems, turn them into fine upstanding citizens, whereas I alone corrupt them. Is that what you mean? – That's exactly what I mean.

SOCRATES: That's a very difficult spot you think I'm in. Answer another question: do you think that the situation with horses is this, (b) that the people who improve them include everyone except the one person who makes them worse? Or is it precisely the opposite of this: the one who can improve them is a single person, or very few people – those who are skilled in horses – whereas the majority of people make them worse if they are around them and use them. Isn't that the way it is with horses and all other animals, Meletus? . . . Our young people would be very fortunate if only one person corrupts them while everyone else improves them.

d

Clinias, the younger brother of Alcibiades over here, is under the guardianship of the famous Pericles. He was afraid, no doubt, that Alcibiades might corrupt Clinias, so he dragged him away from Alcibiades, put him in Ariphron's house, and tried to have him educated there. Before six months were up, Ariphron gave Clinias back because he didn't know what to do with him.

3.2. Educational pederasty

Plato, *Symposium* 184b6–185b5

Pederasty (*paiderastia*, literally "love of boys") sometimes played a central role in the upbringing of Greek males (**1.12**, **2.2**, **6**, **9**). As the following extract makes clear, the customs associated with these educational pederastic relationships persisted in Athenian society in the fifth and fourth centuries BC. Here Pausanias – lover of the tragic playwright Agathon, at whose house the symposium (dinner party) depicted by Plato is being held – explains the custom (*nomos*) that regulates serious relationships between (mainly upper-class) males in Athens. Further reading: Marrou 1956: 26–35; Dover 1978: 89–91, 201–3; Cohen 1987; Robb 1994: 197–207; Hindley 2004.

(184b) We have a custom (*nomos*) whereby, in the same way that lovers may willingly undergo any form of slavery to the boys they love without their conduct being seen as fawning or disgraceful, (c) there is just one other form of voluntary slavery which is not seen as shameful, namely the slavery involved in the pursuit of goodness (*areté*). For it is our established practice not to see either flattery or scandal in the voluntary slavery which occurs when someone of his own free will pays court to another man in the belief that through him he will become a better person in terms of either some aspect of wisdom or any other form of goodness. If we are to conclude that it is a fine thing for a lover to be gratified[1] by the boy he loves, we must compare these two customs, the one dealing with pederasty and that dealing with the pursuit of wisdom and all other forms of goodness.

(d) Whenever a lover (*erastés*) and his beloved come together, each has his own code of conduct: that the lover would be justified in performing any service for his beloved in return for favours granted, while his beloved would be justified in performing any service to the man who is making him wise and good; that the former has the capacity to contribute to his beloved's intelligence as well as his good-ness, (e) while the latter is eager to be taught and to become wise as well. Only then, and in no other circumstances but this, when these two codes of conduct coincide, is it a fine thing for a boy to confer his favours on the man who loves him. In this context there is nothing shameful about being deceived in one's expectations, whereas in all other contexts there is shame no matter whether expectations are met or not.

(185a) For example, if a boy were to confer his favours on a lover for the sake of wealth, in the belief that his lover was a wealthy man, and if his expectations were not met and he received no money, when the truth was revealed that his lover was poor, his conduct would be scandalous nonetheless. This is because such a boy is seen to have revealed the personal characteristic that he would perform any service for any man for the sake of money, and there is no honour in that. By the same line of reasoning, if he were to confer his favours on a man he believed to be good, on the assumption that he would become a better person through his friendship with his lover, and if his expectations were not met when his lover was revealed to be base and devoid of goodness, there would be honour in the deception regardless. (b) For he, by contrast, is deemed to have revealed this about himself, that he would be eager to do anything for anybody for the sake of goodness and in order to become a better person. Conduct stemming from this motivation is the most honourable of all.

---

1 In this passage, "be gratified," "confer favour," and "perform a service" all allude to sexual contact of one form or another.

3.3. Solon's school laws

Aeschines, *Against Timarchus* 9–12

Aeschines' speech *Against Timarchus* was delivered in Athens in 346 BC. The Athenians believed that the regulations explained below had been introduced by the lawgiver Solon, who brought wide-ranging constitutional reforms to Athens in 594 or 590 BC. But despite the interval of 250 years, this speech is the earliest evidence that we have for Solon's educational laws, and many scholars do not believe that Solon was actually responsible for them (for instance, the requirement for a *choregos* to be over forty years old [11] is a fourth-century innovation: Golden 1990: 65–67). By associating Solon with these laws, Aeschines sought to increase their authority in the eyes of his jurors. Whatever their origin, it is apparent that the laws dealt mainly with morality rather than with the practical delivery of education. The main purpose underlying the prescriptions set out here is to prevent unsanctioned sexual relations between younger and older males. For other elements of Solon's school laws, see **1.2**. Further reading: Marrou 1956: 42–43, 382; Beck 1964: 92–94; Ehrenberg 1973: 71–76; Dover 1978: 19–23; MacDowell 1978: 43; Percy 1996: 176–79; Skinner 2005: 112–13.

(9) First of all, let us take a look at the legislation about the teachers (*didaskaloi*) into whose care we have no option but to place our own children. Although their very livelihood depends on their ability to control themselves, and although a life of poverty faces those whose behaviour is the opposite, nonetheless the lawgiver [i.e. Solon] clearly showed little confidence in them. For he explicitly designates first the hour at which the freeborn boy should go to the school (*didaskaleion*), then the number of boys who should enter the school with him, and the hour for departure. (10) He prohibits teachers from opening their schools and the physical trainers (*paidotribai*) from opening their wrestling schools (*palaistrai*) before the sun has risen, and he specifies that they must close them before sunset. The reason is that he views with the greatest suspicion the prospect of a boy being alone with his teacher in the dark. He further stipulates which young lads are to attend school, what age they should be, and which magistrate shall have the responsibility for supervising them. He makes provision for the supervision of *paidagogoi*, and for the attention to be paid to the Muses in the school and to Hermes in the *palaistra*. Finally he specifies the company the boys are to keep when they go to school and the manner in which the cyclic dances are to be conducted. (11) For he

lays down that the *choregos*[2] who intends to incur expenditure on your behalf may only do so if he is over forty years of age. The purpose is to ensure that the *choregos* has reached the years of greater self-control before he is involved with your children. These laws will be read out to you so that you may see that the lawgiver believed that a boy who has been well brought up will be a useful citizen to the state when he becomes a man and, conversely, that once the education of a man's natural character has started with exposure to bad influences, that man will turn out to be a citizen just like Timarchus here because of his deficient upbringing. Read them these laws:

(12) "Teachers of boys must not open their *didaskaleia* before sunrise and must close them before sunset. It is forbidden that, once the boys are in school, anyone older than the boys should enter with the exception of the teacher's son, his brother, or his son-in-law. If anyone does enter the school in contravention of these regulations, the penalty will be death. The *gymnasiarchoi*[3] must not under any circumstances allow a man who has reached maturity to come down to celebrate the rites of Hermes with boys. Should he permit it and not debar such a person from the gymnasium, he shall be liable under the law governing the seduction of freeborn boys. The *choregoi* appointed by the people must be over forty years of age."

3.4. Themistocles and the *paidagogos*

Herodotus, *Histories* 8.75.1

According to **3.3** (10), Solon regulated the activities of pedagogues (*paidagogoi*), i.e. attendants (usually slaves) who accompanied children from place to place during the course of a day, safeguarded them, and sometimes provided instruction. The first certain reference to the position of *paidagogos* is, however, the following passage from Herodotus, who is describing an event shortly before the Battle of Salamis in 480 BC. Themistocles was an important Athenian politician and general at the time of the Persian Wars. Further reading: Marrou 1956: 143–44; Young 1987.

---

2 Literally "chorus leader," one of the annual "liturgies" in Athens, i.e. public services which a private citizen was expected to perform at his own expense. The *choregos* paid the cost of a chorus for its performance at a festival.

3 *Gymnasiarchos* = "superintendent of the gymnasium" (another liturgy). He paid for the maintenance of one of the city's gymnasia, including especially the provision of olive oil.

At the moment when the Peloponnesians were outvoting him, Themistocles secretly left the assembly; he then sent a man by ship to the Persian fleet after he had told him what to say. His name was Sicinnus; he was Themistocles' servant and his sons' *paidagogos*.

3.5. The pedagogue in a wealthy family

Plato, *Lysis* 208c1–d2, 223a1–5

Plato's dialogue *Lysis*, written probably around 390 BC, is the representation of a fictional encounter between Socrates and the young Lysis, whom he meets in a wrestling school (*palaistra*). The dialogue as a whole provides valuable evidence for the role of pedagogues and the life of privileged boys in Athens in the late fifth century BC. Further reading: Beck 1964: 105–9.

(208c) "Tell me this," I [Socrates] asked. "Do your parents allow you control over your own activities?" "Of course they don't," replied Lysis.

"Who does exercise that control?" I asked. "This man here, my *paidagogos*."

"Not a slave, surely?" "Of course he's a slave," he said.

"How odd!" said I. "A free man under the control of a slave! What does this *paidagogos* do to exercise that control?" "He takes me to school, I suppose," he replied.

"I presume that the teachers at school do not exert authority over you as well," I said. "Of course they do," he replied.

(d) "Then your father has deliberately appointed a large number of people to control you and dictate to you.". . . .

[Later, the pedagogues of Lysis and his friend Menexenus arrive.] (223a) I had it in mind to start something with another of the older men there. But then, just as though they were divine beings, the *paidagogoi* of Menexenus and Lysis arrived together with the boys' brothers. They called for them and told them to come home, since by now it was late. At first we tried to drive them off, but they paid no attention; instead they got annoyed and went on calling in their foreign accents.

3.6. What should an Athenian girl learn?

Xenophon, *The Estate Manager* 7.3–6

Xenophon's *Estate Manager* deals broadly with the subject of household management. In this extract Xenophon reports a fictional encounter between Socrates, the main character in the work, and Ischomachus, a farmer. Ischomachus' words are usually considered to be important evidence for the upbringing and married life of freeborn Athenian women. Further reading: Lacey 1968: 163; Pomeroy 1975: 71–74; Powell 2001: 252–56.

(3) "So, Socrates," he said, "to answer the question you put to me, I do not at all spend my time indoors. After all, my wife is perfectly capable of running the house on her own."

(4) "Well, Ischomachus," I said, " . . . did you personally give your wife her training so that she has turned out as she should be? Or did she have knowledge of her responsibilities when you received her from her father and mother?"

(5) "Look here, Socrates," he replied, "she hadn't reached her fifteenth birthday when she came to me. She had lived her entire life until that time under scrupulous supervision so that she should see, hear and say as little as possible. What knowledge could she have had when I took her over? (6) Don't you think it satisfactory that her only piece of knowledge when she arrived was how to take wool and produce a garment, and that the only thing she had seen was how the spinning assignments were handed out to the slave girls? After all, she had received a meticulous training in matters of diet and, in my opinion, this type of education is of fundamental importance for both men and women."

3.7. Aspasia

Plato, *Menexenus* 235e–236c, 249d

In contrast to Ischomachus' wife (**3.6**), Aspasia – companion of Pericles and mother of one of his children – was not an Athenian citizen and therefore not as restricted in the kinds of activities in which she could participate. Even if allowance is made for this fact, however, the remarkable claim that Aspasia taught Socrates rhetoric is difficult to take seriously, since it is very hard to believe that Socrates ever took lessons in rhetoric, that Aspasia taught the subject, or that the aristocratic Pericles, Athens' foremost orator during his adult life, learned his craft from her. Further reading: Pomeroy 1975: 89–91.

(235e) SOCRATES: Menexenus, it is not surprising that I should be able to deliver that speech. After all, the woman who was my teacher was no mean exponent of the art of rhetoric and produced many other excellent orators, amongst whom was Pericles. . . .

MENEXENUS: Who was she? Or should I assume that you mean Aspasia?

SOCRATES: That is whom I mean, though I might also mention Connus. (236a) Those two were my teachers, he in music and she in rhetoric. So there is nothing very remarkable that a man who had received such an education should be capable of making the speech. Even a man with an inferior education, who had been taught music by Lamprus and rhetoric by Antiphon of Rhamnus, could gain credit for himself by eulogizing the Athenian people before an Athenian audience.

MENEXENUS: Suppose you had to speak. What would you have to say?

SOCRATES: Perhaps nothing original. (b) But just yesterday I listened to Aspasia delivering a funeral oration on that very topic. She had heard the story that you told me, that the Athenians were going to pick someone to make the speech. She went through with me what she had to say, some of it off the cuff, the rest worked out carefully earlier when, I believe, she composed the funeral speech which Pericles delivered. She pieced together various passages from that.

MENEXENUS: Can you actually remember what Aspasia said?

SOCRATES: Yes, if I am not very much mistaken. You see, I learned it by heart from her (c) and I came within an inch of being beaten when my memory failed.

MENEXENUS: Then, why don't you recite it to me?

SOCRATES: So that I don't incur the wrath of my teacher for publishing her speech. . . . .

(249d) That, Menexenus, is the speech made by Aspasia from Miletus.

MENEXENUS: Good Lord, Socrates! If Aspasia can compose a speech like that despite the fact that she is a woman, the Aspasia you describe is fortunate indeed.

3.8. The poet as teacher

(a) Aristophanes, *Frogs* 1030–36, (b) Aristophanes, *Frogs* 1500–503

Like Greeks of the Archaic Period (*c.* 800–500 BC), Athenians in the fifth and fourth centuries looked to poets, including writers of tragedy, for instruction. This reliance explains the plot of Aristophanes' comedy *Frogs*: the god Dionysus descends to the Underworld to fetch either Aeschylus or Euripides (both deceased at the time of the play's production in 405) to become the poet of Athens; Aeschylus (the speaker in **a**) wins a competition with Euripides, and in **b** the god Pluto explains what is now expected of him. The public, popular nature of Greek tragedy – plays were performed in the outdoor Theatre of Dionysus, which seated well over 10,000 people – enhanced the status of the tragedian as educator. Further reading: Redfield

1990; de Strycker and Slings 1994: 280–81; Thomas 1995: 117–23; Ford 1999; Raaflaub 2000: 27.

a

Just consider the beneficial effects originally conferred by poets of nobility. Orpheus introduced us to the rites of the Mysteries and taught us to avoid murder; Musaeus taught us about oracles and how to cure diseases; Hesiod provided us with instruction on working the land, on the seasons for crops, and on ploughing. And what was the basis for the honour and fame held by the divine Homer if it was not the valuable lessons he taught us in courage, drawing up lines of battle, and arming men for war?

b

Go on, Aeschylus, farewell. Good luck on your journey. Bring salvation to our city with the soundness of your judgement and educate those who are devoid of intelligence. No small number there!

3.9. The educational role of Homer's poems

Xenophon, *Dinner Party* 3.5, 4.6–7

Of all poets, Homer held the most important place in the education of Greeks both young and old. There is no need to doubt Niceratus' claim below that he could recite all of Homer's two poems (about 30,000 lines), since such feats of memory are well attested in the ancient world. Further reading: Beck 1964: 117–22; Raaflaub 2000: 27–34.

(3.5) "Well then," said Socrates, "once each of you has specified what he possesses to the benefit of others, I will happily reveal the craft I have by which I produce this effect. But what about you, Niceratus? What sort of knowledge produces your feelings of pride?"

"My father focused his care on ensuring that I would turn out to be a good man," he replied, "and forced me to learn every line of poetry Homer wrote. Even now I could recite the whole of the *Iliad* and the *Odyssey* by heart." . . .

(4.6) At this point Niceratus said: "Why don't you let me tell you the areas in which you will be improved if you associate with me? You are aware, of course, that Homer, that paragon of wisdom, has included in his poetry just about every dimension of the human condition.

41

Therefore, if any of you wishes to develop skills in managing a household, or in making speeches in public, or in generalship, or to become like Achilles, Ajax, Nestor or Odysseus, he should, I suggest, pay court to me. All these matters fall within the scope of my knowledge."

"Really?" said Antisthenes. "Do you also know how to exercise royal power just because you are aware that Homer praised Agamemnon as 'a good king and mighty spearman'?"[4]

"By Heavens, of course!" he replied. "And I also know that, when driving a chariot, a man must bring it close to the turning-post when making a turn and that 'he should lean a little bit to the left in the chariot and should, with shouts of encouragement, apply the goad to the horse on the right and slacken the reins in his hand to give it its head.'[5] (4.7) There is another piece of knowledge I have in addition to that, one which you can put to the test right this minute. Somewhere Homer states that 'besides, an onion serves as relish for a drink.'[6] So, if someone brings us an onion, you will receive this immediate benefit, at least, since your drinks will give you greater pleasure."

3.10. Early Athenian schooling

Plutarch, *Life of Themistocles* 10.2–3

The following event is supposed to have taken place in 490 BC, when Athens was under dire threat from the Persian invasion. If Plutarch's account is genuine, it is evidence for the earliest formal education of Athenian children that we know of and suggests that this was not an unusual thing at the time. Even if the story is true, however, it cannot be taken as proof for the existence of universal or compulsory education. Troizen was about thirty miles southeast of Argos. Further reading: Marrou 1956: 43; Jameson 1960: 210–11; Beck 1964: 84.

When Themistocles' decree had been ratified, the majority of Athenians brought their wives and families to Troizen for safe-keeping. The people of Troizen gave them a very warm welcome and indeed decreed that they should be supported at public expense, allocating a daily allowance of two obols to each family. The decree also made provision to permit the boys to pick fruit anywhere and, in addition, to pay fees for teachers for them. It was Nicagoras who drew up the bill.

---

4 Homer, *Iliad* 3.179.
5 Homer, *Iliad* 23.335–37.
6 Homer, *Iliad* 11.630.

3.11. The "old system of education"

Aristophanes, *Clouds* 961–1023

Aristophanes' comedy *Clouds* (produced in 423 BC, revised between 420 and 417) presents a stage character named Socrates – a caricature of the philosopher born in 469 and executed in 399 – who operates a school where students are taught (among much else) the ethically dubious skill of making weak arguments appear more powerful and persuasive and strong arguments appear unconvincing (see also **4.18**). The play includes a contest in which two personified characters – the "Stronger Argument" and the "Weaker Argument" – compete over the right to train the young man Pheidippides, son of the farmer Strepsiades, who is the play's main character. The Stronger Argument's description of the "old system of education" (*archaia paideia*) is intended to reflect the curriculum and character of education in the first half of the fifth century. There is a strong military element and purpose in the "old system" as it is represented here; note that reading and writing are not mentioned. Further reading: Marrou 1956: 36–45; Beck 1964: 80–85, 127–29; Dover 1968: lviii–lxiv, 1972: 109–16; Ostwald 1986: 229–38; Morgan 1998: 10–13, 1999: 47–53; Pritchard 2003: 302–11.

Stronger Argument: I'll describe to you, then, the old system of education which prevailed when I was in vogue because I used just arguments, and when self-control was the order of the day. First of all, there was no obligation to listen to a child's inarticulate grunts. Second, children from the various quarters of the city had to march through the streets to the *kitharistés'* school in an orderly manner, and they had to do so in groups without wrapping themselves in layers of clothing, even if the snow was falling thick as meal. Again they were taught to learn a song by heart without squeezing their thighs together, something like "Pallas the Terrible Sacker of Cities" or "A Far-reaching Cry,"[7] and they had to maintain the key in which it had been passed down by their fathers. If any of them played the fool or indulged in some form of modulation, like the intricate flourishes made fashionable by Phrynis[8] and used by the modern generation, he was crushed under a shower of blows for doing away with the Muses. At the school of the *paidotribés*, when the boys were sitting down, they had to place their thigh in front of them in order to avoid displaying anything which might cause anguished excitement for those outside.

---

7 These two songs and their authors are unknown. The Weaker Argument's reference to them shows that they belonged to an earlier generation and at the time of the play were considered old-fashioned.

8 A poet who was active around the middle of the fifth century.

Then, when they got up again, they had to rake over the sand, taking care that they didn't leave behind an impression of their youthful splendour for their lovers. No boy would have anointed himself with oil below his navel. As a result, the dew and down blossomed on their genitals just as it does on peaches. Nor would he have gone up to his lover assuming a soft and sexy voice and making a whore of himself with his eyes. At dinner sons could not have picked up even the top of a radish or grabbed dill or celery before their elders. A diet of dainty foods, giggling, and cross-footed postures were out.

Weaker Argument: That's out-of-date nonsense, like the festival of Zeus Polieus. It smacks of cicadas, Cecides, and the Bouphonia.[9]

Stronger Argument: But that's the approach my form of education adopted to bring up the men who fought at Marathon.[10] You, by contrast, teach the youths of the modern generation to wrap themselves in heavy clothes, so that I'm ready to choke when they have to dance at the Panathenaea.[11] They hold their shield in front of their cock and show no respect for Athena. Therefore, young man, have confidence and let your choice fall on me, the Stronger Argument. You will learn to hate the *agora* (marketplace), to stay away from bath-houses, to be embarrassed at what is shameful, and to flare up if someone makes fun of you. You will learn to get up from your seat for your elders when they arrive, not to behave badly towards your parents, nor to commit any other shameful act. . . . You will be taught not to fly off to a dancing-girl's house, so that you won't make a shipwreck of your good reputation, gaping in amazement at what you find there and struck by some tart's apple. Finally, you will learn to avoid contradicting your father or calling him Iapetus,[12] thus reproaching that time of his life when he brought you up as the darling of his nest.

Weaker Argument: Bloody Hell! If you follow his advice, young man, you will have to back down before Hippocrates' kids[13] and people will call you "mummy's little darling."

Stronger Argument: But you will spend your time in the gymnasium, radiant and blooming with a healthy glow, instead of indulging in subtle chatter in the *agora* like people today, or being hauled off to

9 The custom of wearing a brooch in the shape of a cicada was considered unfashionable. The identity of Cecides is uncertain; he was apparently a poet. The Bouphonia was part of the festival of Zeus Polieus.
10 "The men who fought at Marathon" (*Marathonomachoi*) was a proverbial designation to evoke the courage and toughness shown by the soldiers of an earlier generation who saved Athens from the Persians; see Loraux 1986: 155–71.
11 An annual festival in Athens dedicated to Athena, the patron goddess of the city.
12 A Titan, brother of the early god Cronus, and therefore considered a "has-been."
13 Hippocrates is probably the Athenian general killed in 424; his sons are elsewhere ridiculed as dim-witted.

court to deal with a case that requires petty quibbles and brass-necked knavery. In place of all that, you will go down to the Academy and will run off beneath the sacred olives with a chaste friend of your own age, wearing crowns of white reeds. . . . If you follow my suggestion and concentrate on these activities, you will always have a chest sleek with muscle, a bright healthy complexion, broad shoulders, a tiny tongue, a huge rump, and a tiny cock. However, if you follow the modern way, first you will have a pale complexion, narrow shoulders, a thin chest, a huge tongue, a tiny rump, a huge cock, and a lengthy decree. He will convince you to view everything foul as fair, and everything fair as foul. To cap it all, he'll give you a good dose of the sort of buggery Antimachus[14] loves.

3.12. Discipline

(a) Plato, *Protagoras* 325c5–d7, (b) Xenophon, *Anabasis* 2.6.12

According to the Stronger Argument (**3.11**), students in the old days were kept in line through physical force. Corporal punishment and threats were not, however, characteristic of education only in the early fifth century; they were used by teachers throughout the fifth and fourth centuries (and later) as well. Protagoras is the speaker in **a**, a passage drawn from Plato's dialogue of that name (see **4.3** for general brackground). In **b**, Xenophon is describing the personality of the general Clearchus. Further reading: Beck 1964: 100–105; Booth 1973.

a

(325c) Starting from when their children are very small, they instruct and chastise them as long as they live. As soon as a child understands what is said to him, his nurse, his mother, his *paidagogos* (d) and his father in person devote all their energies to ensure that he is as good as can be. Whatever he says or does, they give him the benefit of their instruction and show that one thing is right and another wrong; one thing the mark of a man of nobility, another of a base man; this the mark of piety, that of impiety; he should do this, not do that. If he is obedient and willingly so, all is well. If not, they straighten him out with threats and blows, like a piece of wood which is warped and crooked.

---

14 Unknown, but attacked elsewhere by Aristophanes.

b

For there was nothing pleasant about Clearchus' manner, only a constant harshness and severity. Thus his soldiers' relationship with him was identical to that of boys towards their schoolmaster.

3.13. The curriculum on a drinking cup

This famous cup was painted in Athens by Douris around 485 BC. It depicts educational scenes involving reading and writing (*grammata*), lyre-playing and flute-playing. On the right-hand side of each photograph, a *paidagogos* sits holding a staff; his presence in these scenes is evidence that we are looking at public education outside the home rather than private education inside it (cf. **3.3**). That the students in the paintings are learning to play musical instruments is of course no surprise, nor is it unexpected that poetry is being taught as well (in Figure 3.1a the teacher holds an open scroll[15]). This cup, however, provides solid evidence that the educational scheme described as the "old system of education" (*archaia paideia*) by the "Stronger Argument" in **3.11** is probably a distortion, since that description excludes any mention of training in writing, which is depicted on this cup. The cup has also been taken as evidence both for the concurrent learning of subjects (Beck 1964: 80–83; Marrou 1956: 148, 374–76; Pritchard 2003: 306–8) and for the learning of subjects in sequence (*grammata* first, *mousiké* later: Booth 1985). Further reading: Bundrick 2005: 61–63.

3.14. A standard curriculum

(a) Plato, *Charmides* 159c3–12, (b) [Plato], *Alcibiades* I 106e4–9, (c) [Plato], *Theages* 122e8–11

Physical training, together with *grammata* and *mousiké* (**3.13**), came to be seen as comprising a standard curriculum of basic subjects (cf. **3.15**, **4.4**, **4.19**, **5.6** [267]). Further reading: Marrou 1956: 40–43; Beck 1964: 80–85, 111–41; Pritchard 2003.

a

SOCRATES: Is it best to write the same letters quickly or in a relaxed way when you are at the writing-teacher's (*grammatistés*)?
CHARMIDES: Quickly.
SOCRATES: What about reading – quickly or slowly?

---

15 The words on the scroll are the opening lines of a lost poem by Stesichorus: "O Muse, I begin to sing of broad Scamander."

Figure 3.1 (a and b) School scenes. Douris' Cup, Berlin, Staatliche Museen F2285

CHARMIDES: Quickly.

SOCRATES: And, of course, to play the lyre quickly and to wrestle aggressively is better than to do them in a relaxed way and slowly?

CHARMIDES: Yes.

SOCRATES: What about boxing and the *pankration?*[16] Isn't it the same with them?

CHARMIDES: Yes.

16 *Pankration* = "all-in wrestling," literally "total mastery"; see Golden 2004: 127–28.

b

[Socrates is the speaker, addressing Alcibiades, who is nearly twenty.] Now, I know pretty well what you've learned; but tell me if there's something I've missed. As far as I recall, you've learned letters, lyre-playing, and wrestling – you refused, of course, to learn the *aulos*.[17] These are the things you know, unless, I suppose, you've been learning something without my knowing it.

c

[Socrates is the speaker, addressing the young Theages and his father Demodocus.] Didn't your father have you taught and educated in the same subjects that the others – the sons of good and noble fathers[18] – have been educated in, I mean letters, playing the lyre, wrestling, and competition in general?

3.15. A traditional education in Athens

Plato, *Protagoras* 325d7–326e5

Like other professional teachers ("sophists": Chapter 4) in the second half of the fifth century, Protagoras claimed to be able to teach *areté* ("goodness," "excellence," "virtue") for a fee (**4.7, 12, 5.4**). This claim, however, treated *areté* as a commodity and flew in the face of traditional Greek assumptions about the nature of goodness (**1.6–7, 3.2**). Protagoras' tactic here is to demonstrate that his claim is not an extravagant one, since the goal of Athenian education is moral and intellectual. Further reading: Marrou 1956: 39–40, 47–48, 57–58; Guthrie 1969: 250–60; Kerferd 1981: 131–38; de Romilly 1992: 44–52; Benson 1997: 327–32; Curren 2000: 43–48.

> (325d) Then parents send their children to teachers and instruct them to pay closer attention to their children's good behaviour than to letters and the lyre. (e) These are the things on which their teachers concentrate. When they have learned their letters (*grammata*) and are at the stage of understanding the written word as they earlier did the spoken, the teachers set on the benches before them the works of good

---

17 A reed instrument, something like the oboe. For Alcibiades' refusal to learn the *aulos*, see Plutarch, *Life of Alcibiades* 2.5–6.

18 "Good and noble" translates the stock phrase *kaloi te kagathoi*; in **3.13b** it is translated "outstanding members of society." For the implications of this Greek phrase, see Dover 1974: 41–45; Marrou 1956: 43–45.

poets which they have them read aloud. (326a) They compel their pupils to learn by heart many passages which contain words of warning, and which describe in great detail and praise fulsomely virtuous men of the past. Their objective is that the child may emulate and imitate them and make it his goal to become like them. The *kitharistai* (lyre-players) in their turn focus on self-control by other means and attempt to ensure that the young do no wrong. Furthermore, once the children have learned to play the lyre, they go on to teach them the works of other distinguished poets, who composed in lyric meters. Setting these poems to music for the lyre, (b) the teacher ensures that the children's inner soul becomes familiar with their rhythms and harmony. The purpose is to make the pupils more civilized by developing a sound inner rhythm and harmony, thus producing citizens useful in both word and deed. For every man requires a sound rhythm and harmony in his life. In addition to these teachers, parents also send their children to a *paidotribés* for physical conditioning so that they may thus have a body capable of serving their superior intelligence (c) and no cause for cowardice either in war or other activities on grounds of physical deficiency.

That is the typical pattern of education chosen by those with the greatest means, that is, the wealthiest. Their children start going to school earliest in their lives and stay there longest. When they do leave school, the city in its turn makes them learn the laws and live their lives according to the pattern there laid down. The objective is to prevent them acting on their own without guidance. (d) You are aware how the *grammatistai* trace lines with their stylus for those whose writing skills are as yet undeveloped; they pass out the writing-tablets and have their pupils form their letters according to the outline they have traced for them.[19] Similarly, the city traces out laws, which have been devised by excellent law-givers from the past, to serve as guidelines for behaviour, and it compels men to rule and be ruled in keeping with their requirements. Whoever deviates from the laws is punished. This punishment is called correction, (e) both in your state and everywhere else, because the punishment corrects. Thus, Socrates, considerable attention is devoted to goodness (*areté*) both privately and by the state. Are you then surprised or puzzled that it should be teachable?

---

19 For the practice of drawing parallel lines to provide guidance for the student, see Muir 1984. It is illustrated by **8.4** and by Cribiore 1996: pls. 51 and 61 (both from the third century AD).

3.16. Athletics and music

(a) [Xenophon], *Constitution of the Athenians* 1.13, (b) Aristophanes, *Wasps* 954–61, (c) Aristophanes, *Frogs* 727–29

Some passages suggest that in the fifth century, music and physical training were associated especially with the education of well-born children (cf. **3.11**). The *Constitution of the Athenians* (**a**) was probably written between about 425 and 415 BC. The "young men" referred to in this extract are identified in the sentences that follow it as belonging to the wealthy classes. Confirmation of the role played by music in élite education is provided by the argument (**b**) that an inability to play the lyre is evidence of a lack of breeding (cf. *Wasps* 986–89). In *Wasps* the character Bdelycleon ("Cleon-hater") tries to satisfy the obsession with jury-duty from which his father Philocleon ("Cleon-lover") suffers by staging a mock trial in his father's home. The defendant is a dog accused of stealing cheese. *Frogs* (**c**) was produced in 405. Further reading: Morgan 1998: 9–14; Pritchard 2003: 318–31.

a

In Athens the masses have put a stop to the young men exercising in the gymnasium and practising music; they think that these pursuits aren't good, since they realize that they are incapable of practising them.

b

BDELYCLEON: No, he's the best of dogs alive today, capable of watching over a large flock.
PHILOCLEON: What good is that, if he gulps down the cheese?
BDELYCLEON: What good? It's you he fights for, and he guards your door; all-round he's an outstanding dog. Forgive him if he made off with the cheese, since he doesn't know how to play the lyre.
PHILOCLEON: I'd prefer he didn't know how to write either; then the scoundrel wouldn't have submitted his account to us.

c

Those of our citizens who we know are true-born and well-behaved men, just and outstanding members of society, and who were raised in wrestling schools and learned dancing and music, we treat them with contempt. . . .

3.17. Education for public life

Aristophanes, *Knights* 182–93

Like the sausage-seller in this selection, boys often did not progress far beyond the rudiments of reading and writing, especially if their livelihoods did not depend on those skills (contrast **3.15** [326c]). Illiteracy, or at any rate poor skills in reading and writing, are seen here as the mark of a new, demagogic kind of politician, exemplified in this play by the Athenian Cleon, who is the main target of Aristophanes' attacks. *Knights* was produced in 424. Further reading: Beck 1964: 80–85; Dover 1972: 95–100; Harris 1989: 101, 109–10; Pritchard 2003: 309–11.

SAUSAGE-SELLER: I don't think that I deserve great power.

DEMOSTHENES: Bloody Hell! Why do you say that you don't deserve it? I do believe that you've a guilty secret about some fine quality you're hiding. You don't come from a gentlemanly background, do you?

SAUSAGE-SELLER: Heavens, no! The lineage is strictly dishonest.

DEMOSTHENES: You're lucky about your station in life. You've got an excellent grounding for politics.

SAUSAGE-SELLER: Look here, chum! I've no learning. I just know my letters, though even there my knowledge isn't very good.

DEMOSTHENES: Just about the only strike against you is that you've got even that knowledge, however deficient. Popular leadership is no longer for the educated man or the man of virtuous character. It's the uneducated rogue who fits the bill.

3.18. Literacy as the goal of Athenian schooling

Xenophon, *Education of Cyrus* 1.2.6

To Xenophon, the one element that comes to mind in describing the purpose of Athenian schooling is the learning of letters (contrast **3.11, 16**). The following passage may also be taken as evidence that the school, not the home, was at this time generally seen as the place where reading and writing were learned. Further reading: Rawson 1969: 50–54; Harris 1989: 65–115.

The boys go to school and spend their time learning about justice. That is the purpose for which the Persians say they attend school, just as we say that our boys go to learn letters (*grammata*).

3.19. Some literary basics

Plato, *Statesman* 277e2–278c1

The system described below for teaching students how to form letters, sylla-bles and words remained in use until the end of antiquity; see **6.1**, **8.4–5**, **10.1**. Selection **3.15** supplements what is said here. Further reading: Beck 1964: 114–17.

> (277e) VISITOR: I suppose we know that when children are just becoming skilled in letters . . .
> YOUNG SOCRATES: Know what?
> VISITOR: That they are good enough at distinguishing each of the letters in the shortest and easiest syllables, and that they can demon-strate what is true in regard to them.
> (278a) YOUNG SOCRATES: Of course.
> VISITOR: But in regard to these same letters in other syllables, they make mistakes again, and their thoughts and words are false.
> YOUNG SOCRATES: Certainly.
> VISITOR: Then isn't this the easiest and best way to lead them on to the things that they don't yet know?
> YOUNG SOCRATES: How do you mean?
> VISITOR: To lead them back first to those instances in which they were forming correct beliefs on these same matters and, after we've brought them back, to set these beside the things that they don't yet know. (b) As we're comparing them, we should demonstrate that in both sets of combinations there are the same points of contact and basic features, until the ones that they are right about are set beside all the ones that they don't know and are shown to them. After they've been shown, and in this way become models, they will see to it that each of all the letters in all the syllables is called different, since it is different from the others, and the same, (c) since it is always the same as itself in the same respects.

3.20. The school of hard knocks

Aristophanes, *Knights* 1228–52

In this extract a contrast of a familiar (and universal) kind is drawn between formal education and the very practical (and brutal) education which the sausage-seller in Aristophanes' play received in his youth. It is a far cry from the "civic education" envisaged by Simonides, Pericles and Socrates in **3.1a–c**. Further reading: Ostwald 1986: 199–229; Morgan 1999: 49.

SAUSAGE-SELLER: Quickly now. Put it[20] down, you rogue.

CLEON: I won't. I've got an oracle from Delphi which describes the only man destined to defeat me.

SAUSAGE-SELLER: Yes. It gives my name, and very clearly too.

CLEON: It's proof I want. I'd like to put a question or two to you to see if you match the description in the god's oracle. The first question I'll ask you is this. Which teacher's school did you attend when you were a boy?

SAUSAGE-SELLER: It was in the scorching-chamber of the slaughter-house that a set of knuckles taught me to behave.

CLEON: What did you say? This oracle's really affecting my mind. Let's leave that. Describe the style of wrestling you learned in the school of the *paidotribés*.

SAUSAGE-SELLER: When I stole, I learned to look a man right in the eye and to swear by all that's holy that I hadn't taken a thing.

CLEON: Oh Phoebus, Lycian[21] Apollo! What are you trying to do to me? What trade did you take up when you became an adult?

SAUSAGE-SELLER: I sold sausages. And got screwed a bit as well.

CLEON: Oh, dear me! I'm a luckless wretch indeed. I've had it now. 'Tis a slender hope on which I'm borne.

3.21. Women with scrolls

From the middle of the fifth century BC it became common to find depictions on Athenian vases of women reading from scrolls. The following examples date to *c.* 450–440 and 440–430 respectively. The natural inference to draw from these depictions is that some Athenian women received enough education to enable them to read. While this inference may be correct, an alternative interpretation has been proposed: the depiction is symbolic of the social and political weakness of women, with whom a static, passive form of communication is associated, in contrast with the use that men made of the more dynamic spoken word in political assemblies and law courts (Glazebrook 2005). Adult Athenian males are not similarly depicted with scrolls. Further reading: Beck 1964: 85–88, 1975: 55–58 and pls. 69–75.

3.22. A parent's obligation

Plato, *Crito* 50d–e

Plato's dialogue *Crito* is set in the Athenian prison-house where Socrates was held in the period between his trial and the day of his execution in

---

20 "It" is the crown worn by a speaker in the Assembly (*ekklesia*) in Athens.

21 I.e. from Lycia, a city in Asia Minor with which Apollo is often associated.

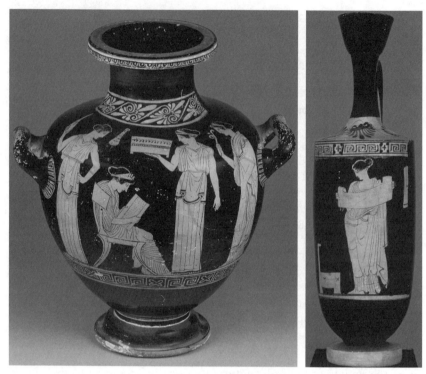

Figure 3.2 a) Woman reading a scroll: Red-figure hydria, British Museum E190.
b) Muse reading a scroll: Red-figure lekythos, Louvre CA 2220

399 BC. Socrates' friend Crito tries to persuade him to escape from prison and live out his days in another city. Socrates rejects this proposal; to support his position he cites the argument that the Laws of Athens (the personified speakers in this extract) would make to him. This passage seems to suggest that parents were legally obliged to provide for their sons' education (compare Solon's laws, **1.2**). However, the Greek word *nomos* (plural *nomoi*), which is translated below by "law," also means "custom," and it is the force of custom which Socrates must be invoking here. Further reading: Marrou 1956: 382; Harris 1989: 99; Beck 1964: 92–94; Ober 2001.

(d) "So tell us, do you have any complaint to make about us, who are the laws governing marriage?" "No, I have none," I would reply. "Well then, about the laws regulating a son's upbringing and education, which you too received? The laws entrusted with that function instructed your father to give you an education in the arts (*mousiké*) and physical exercise (*gymnastiké*). Was there anything wrong with our requirement?" (e) "No, nothing wrong at all," I would reply.

3.23. A late fifth-century school in Boeotia

Thucydides, *The Peloponnesian War* 7.29.4–5

Thucydides describes an incident which occurred in the summer of 413 BC. Mycalessus (near Thebes) was not a large town, as Thucydides himself observes, but it possessed more than one school. On the basis of this passage it seems reasonable to infer that by this time schools were a feature in most Greek *poleis*. Further reading: Beck 1964: 88–91; Harris 1989: 101.

(4) Rushing into Mycalessus the Thracians sacked the houses and temples and put the population to the sword. . . . Just like those barbarians with the greatest thirst for blood, the Thracians are at their worst when they are carried away by their own audacity. (5) The confusion they caused was widespread and death was present in every form. In particular, they attacked a school (*didaskaleion*), the largest in the town, just after the children had arrived, and slaughtered them all. The disaster which befell this entire community has no parallel.

3.24. Aeschines and his father

Demosthenes, *On the Crown* 129, 257–58

The speech *On the Crown* was delivered in 330 BC and contains intense criticism of Aeschines, Demosthenes' political opponent (and author of the speech *Against Timarchus*, **3.3**). Demosthenes' vilification of Aeschines displays a considerable amount of caricature and exaggeration; it is therefore difficult to assess the truth of all his comments. For instance, whereas Aeschines' father is described as a teacher's assistant in 129, in 258 he is presented as a teacher. But the claim that Aeschines' father was both a slave and the assistant to a teacher serves a purpose: Demosthenes expects to evoke the jurors' contempt towards Aeschines, since, as we see elsewhere, the teaching profession at this time was not highly esteemed. Further reading: Dover 1974: 30–33; Booth 1981; Harris 1989: 98, 135–36.

(129) Shall I describe how your father, Tromes, was the slave of Elpias who teaches letters near the Theseum[22] and used to wear a set of stout shackles and a wooden collar? . . .

(257) When I was a boy, Aeschines, it was my privilege to attend the proper schools and to have everything a boy should to prevent him doing anything shameful from sheer need. . . . (258) You, by contrast, who are an arrogant man and spit on the rest of the world, must reflect

22 The temple of Theseus, situated in the centre of Athens.

55

on the nature of the fortune which you have enjoyed in comparison with mine. Because of that fortune, when you were a boy, you were brought up amid great poverty and attended your father in the *didaskaleion*, grinding the ink, wiping down the benches and sweeping out the room for the *paidagogoi*. Your position was that of a menial, not a freeborn boy.

3.25. The Athenian *ephebeia*

[Aristotle], *The Athenian Constitution* 42

The author of this work[23] describes a system of two-year mandatory military service in Athens for males who had reached the age of eighteen. The system was introduced in 335 or 334 BC and represents the first state education or training to be established in Athens. By the end of the fourth century BC, service was reduced to one year and was probably voluntary. This institution was named the *ephebeia*, since the young men who underwent its training belonged to the age-designation *ephebos* (18–19 years). The *ephebeia* existed also in other Greek states, though in different forms (Chapter 6). Although it is only in the second half of the fourth century that the institution of the *ephebeia* was established in Athens, its purpose as a rite of passage, and some of its specific elements, are much older than this and can be paralleled in many other Greek and non-Greek societies.[24] Further reading: Forbes 1929: 100–178; Marrou 1956: 105–12; Pleket 1969: 286–98; Reinmuth 1971: 123–38; Siewert 1977; Vidal-Naquet 1986; Rhodes 1992: 493–510; Ober 2001: 202–5; Polinskaya 2003; Kennell 2006: vii–xv.

> Those who have Athenian parentage on both sides are entitled to hold citizenship and are registered in their demes when they reach the age of eighteen. When the registration takes place, the members of their deme swear an oath and decide by ballot, first whether the candidates appear to have reached the age prescribed by law . . . , and second, whether they are of free and legitimate birth. If the demesmen vote that a man is not of free birth, the matter is referred to the jury-court, and the members of the deme select five of their number to present their case. If it is decided that the accused's registration is illegal, the city sells him as a slave; if, however, he wins his case, his deme has no option but to proceed with his registration. Afterwards the Council (*boulé*) reviews those who have been registered and, if it decides that

23 Not Aristotle, but more likely one of his students. The *Athenian Constitution* was written around 330 BC.
24 E.g. the Roman *Collegia Iuvenum*; see Marrou 1956: 299–301; Pleket 1969.

anyone under the age of eighteen has been enrolled, it fines the members of the deme responsible. Once the *epheboi* have passed this review, their fathers gather together by tribe and under oath select three members of their tribe over the age of forty whom they believe to be the best and most suitable men to supervise the *epheboi*. Of this group one from each tribe is elected by the people as *sophronistés*,[25] and one man is elected from the entire body of Athenian citizens as *kosmetés*[26] to take charge of everyone. When these men have gathered the *epheboi* into a group, they first make the rounds of the temples, then they march off to Piraeus, where some of the *epheboi* serve as the garrison of Munichia, others of Akte.[27] The people also elects two *paidotribai* and other teachers whose responsibility it is to instruct the *epheboi* in the use of hoplite arms, the bow, the javelin and the sling. The *sophronistai* are allotted one drachma each for maintenance, while the *epheboi* are allotted four obols each.[28] Since the latter live in messes according to tribe, each *sophronistés* receives the money allotted to the members of his tribe and purchases the provisions as a common stock to be shared by all, and takes care of all other matters. . . . In the second year an assembly is held in the theatre and the *epheboi* give the people an exhibition of their battle-formations, after which they receive a shield and a spear from the city. Then they make patrols through the countryside and put in their time garrisoning the forts, serving thus for two years. Their dress is the short military mantle and they pay no taxes. They do not appear in courts of law either as plaintiffs or defendants, so that they have no excuse for absenting themselves from their duty. An exception is made in cases involving an inheritance, the marriage of an heiress, and hereditary priesthoods. Once their two years have elapsed, they duly join the rest of the citizen-body.

25 So called because his responsibility was to keep the young men *sophronés*, "well-behaved," by punishing those who fell out of line. He probably served for one year only, possibly with responsibility for the discipline of first-year *epheboi*. For the requirement that the *sophronistés* be forty years of age, compare the same requirement for the *choregos* stipulated in Solon's laws (**3.3**; so also *The Athenian Constitution* 56.3), and for the *paidonomos* in **6.8**. The position of *sophronistés* is associated especially with Sparta (**2.1**).

26 Literally "one who keeps order (*kosmos*)." Like the *sophronistés*, his service probably lasted for a year, and he too probably had to be forty years of age.

27 Munichia is the hill on the eastern side of Piraeus; Akte is the peninsula south of the main harbour.

28 One drachma was a common daily wage for a skilled worker in Athens around 400 BC. Six obols = one drachma.

3.26. Honours granted to the *epheboi* of the tribe Cecropis

IG II² 1156, lines 36–44 (= *SIG* 957)

One reason why scholars have fixed the introduction of the Athenian *ephebeia* to 335 or 334 BC (**3.25**) is the appearance from that time forward of inscriptions that relate to the activities of this institution. The following inscription, which dates to 334, records the honours given by decree to *epheboi* from the Athenian tribe Cecropis in recognition of their performance of duties. These *epheboi* did garrison duty in Eleusis (16 km west of Athens), even though only Munichia and Akte are mentioned in **3.25** as sites for this service. The first 25 lines of this inscription, which are in a fragmentary state, contain the names of about 45 *epheboi* from the demes of Cecropis. The inscription contains three similar motions, only the second of which is presented here; the final part of the inscription has also been omitted. Further reading: Reinmuth 1971: 5–10.

Hegemachus son of Chairemon from the deme of Perithoidai presented the following motion: that, since the *epheboi* of the tribe Cecropis stationed at Eleusis are maintaining a high standard and are showing commitment in carrying out the duties imposed upon them by the Council (*boulé*) and People (*demos*), and conducted themselves in accordance with the principles of good discipline, they receive public commendation, and each one of them be awarded a crown of fresh leaves in recognition of their orderly conduct and discipline; that their *sophronistés*, Adeistos son of Antimachus from the *deme* of Athmonia, is to receive public commendation and be awarded a crown of fresh leaves whenever he has undergone scrutiny for his term of office; that this decree be inscribed on a votive tablet to be erected by the *epheboi* of the tribe Cecropis during the archonship of Ctesicles.

4

THE SOPHISTS, SOCRATES, AND THE FIFTH-CENTURY ENLIGHTENMENT

Children in the fifth century who were able to continue their formal education to completion normally stopped at about the age of fourteen or fifteen. This traditional education in letters, music and physical training did not in itself, however, provide people with all the knowledge and skills that they needed to be successful in life. In particular, many people who were otherwise prosperous were at a disadvantage if they did not belong to traditional, well-connected families, especially aristocratic ones, and did not therefore possess some of the advantages that inherited status conferred. It was in this environment that professional educators called "sophists" made their appearance around the middle of the fifth century. Most of them were non-Athenian Greeks. Although they taught a wide range of subjects (**4.5–8**), all of them offered people the opportunity to learn the "art of persuasion" – rhetoric – provided that these people were willing and able to pay the fees they charged (**4.9–10**). By adopting the name "sophist," whose meaning is literally "practitioner in *or* purveyor of wisdom," they were appropriating for themselves the status of traditional educator, since in its earliest use this term had been applied above all to poets, who were seen as the transmitters of received wisdom in Greek society (**4.3, 6**).

In important respects the educational movement which the sophists initiated was a democratic one: their teaching was available to anyone who could pay (**4.12**), regardless of inherited social class, and it is no coincidence that they came to be connected most closely with Athens. In 461 BC, Athens instituted reforms to its democratic system which in principle removed from the aristocratic classes many of the privileges that they had traditionally possessed and passed them to the general body of Athenian citizens. A driving force behind these democratic reforms was Pericles, himself an aristocrat from an old and prominent family who seems to have played a significant role in the arrival and cultivation of the sophists, as well as other intellectuals and artists. Subsequent reforms in the fifth century included the introduction of pay for jury service, for membership on the Council of 500 (the *boulé*), and for the most influential magisterial positions.

In democratic Athens the ability to influence others through persuasive speech was of paramount importance. The city therefore provided a ready market for the kinds of practical skills that the sophists undertook to teach; and although their lessons were restricted to those who could afford them, their clientele extended beyond the children of the old aristocratic families. It is fair to say that the sophists not only profited from the existence of Athenian democracy but also (despite severe criticism from some quarters: **4.11**) helped to further its cause. Indeed, it is difficult to imagine how the sophists could have flourished in any setting but a democratic one.

The importance of the sophists, however, lies especially in the fact that they were humanists: their thought was focused upon the human being and the human condition, they asked fundamental questions about human nature, and they sought answers to these questions from the perspective of human individuals and their innate limitations (**4.1**). Their radical thinking, tied closely to the political life of the city, helped to free Greek education from the well-worn path that it had taken for centuries with only modest changes.

Socrates' activity is best understood, both chronologically and intellectually, within the context of this movement (**4.13–21**). Despite the fact that he seems to have acknowledged the importance of irrational forces in his associations with other people (**4.15–16**), his most prominent intellectual characteristic was his relentless dedication to reason and his resistance to society's traditional, often untested, assumptions. It is, however, a gross error to confuse him with the sophists (e.g. **4.18**), as some of the evidence presented below will show.

General background: Pfeiffer 1968: 16–56; Guthrie 1969; Ehrenberg 1973: 333–83; Kerferd 1981, 1997; de Romilly 1992: 1–29; Benson 1997. *Translated sources*: Dillon and Gergel 2003.

4.1. The sophists and the human-centred world

(a) Antiphon, *On Truth* fr. 44(b) II–III, (b) Protagoras, *On Truth* fr. 1

Theognis, Pindar and others believed that a person's heredity and innate character (*phusis*) determined his chances for success in the world (**1.6–7**). They assumed, however, that only those who belonged to the social élite possessed the right kind of *phusis*. Writing around 425 BC, the sophist Antiphon (**a**) expressed a different view: *phusis* is not "heredity" but rather "human nature," a quality which all people share by virtue of their membership in the human race. By implication, the factor which differentiates Greeks from non-Greeks (i.e. barbarians) is not *phusis* but *nomos*, i.e. "custom" or "convention." A further implication of Antiphon's position must follow: with the right upbringing, including exposure to certain cultural norms, a barbarian could acquire the characteristics associated with a Greek (language, religious observances, political organization, etc.). Differences between people, not only Greeks and barbarians but also the well-born and the low-born, could be minimized if not eliminated through education and acculturation.

Since the sophists accepted students on the basis not of their social standing but of their ability to pay fees (which were sometimes very high: **4.12**), they naturally adhered to the belief that differences among members of their potential clientele also existed generally because of *nomos*, not *phusis*. Hence a person of intelligence and talent would not be prevented from achieving worldly success simply because he did not come from old money; provided he (or his parents) could pay, he would learn from the sophists the skills and techniques that he needed. Furthermore, if important differences between cultures and between individual people depend upon *nomos*, which is changeable from culture to culture, rather than on unchanging *phusis*, the beliefs that the individual person holds, fallible though they may be, will count for a great deal, whereas absolute truths will be difficult if not impossible to establish. Protagoras' famous words (**b**) express the human-centred and relativistic view that the only criterion of what is true and real is the judgement of the individual person rather than an ideal, impersonal standard. This view of the world lies at the heart of the conflict between Socrates and the sophists, as well as between Plato and his philosophical rivals in the fourth century. Further reading: Kerferd 1981: 49–51, 83–130, 1997: 249–51, 260–62; Ostwald 1986: 250–73; Long 2005.

a

... [the customs of those near us] we know and respect, but the customs of those who live far away we neither know nor respect. In this we have become barbarians in the eyes of one another. And yet by nature we are all naturally disposed in the same way to be either barbarians or Greeks. It is possible to examine ... the things necessary by nature for all people ... none of us has been marked off as either barbarian or Greek. For we all breathe into the air through the mouth and nostrils; we laugh when we are pleased and cry when we are pained; with our sense of hearing we receive sounds; with our sense of sight we see with the ray of light; we work with our hands; we walk with our feet. ...

b

A person is the measure of all things, of the things that are, that they are, of the things that are not, that they are not.

4.2. An educational simile

Antiphon, *On Concord* fr. 60

The comparison of education with farming – the most common simile in ancient education (e.g. **5.21**, **8.18**) – involves analogy with a rational occupation, agriculture, which was considered to require skill and knowledge. Use of the simile here reflects the theoretical analysis of education which began in the fifth century BC. Further reading: Jaeger 1947: 312–14; Guthrie 1969: 168; Morgan 1998: 240–70; Pendrick 2002: 409–12.

> The most important thing of all, I think, is education (*paideusis*). For whenever someone begins any matter whatsoever in the right way, its completion is likely to turn out right as well. Whatever kind of seed a person plants in the ground is just the kind of crop one ought to expect; and whenever the education that one plants in a young body is good, the final product lives and flourishes throughout its whole life, and neither rain nor drought destroys it.

4.3. The sophists in their historical context

Plato, *Protagoras* 316d3–e5

Plato's dialogue *Protagoras* is set in the house of the wealthy Athenian Callias, perhaps in the late 420s BC. It depicts a meeting between Socrates and Protagoras, the most famous and important of the fifth-century sophists; also in attendance are other prominent sophists, including Prodicus (from the island of Ceos) and Hippias (from the city of Elis in the northwestern Peloponnese). In the following passage Protagoras places his profession in its historical context by comparing it and linking it to the activities of earlier "wise men," in particular poets and seers. For the importance of poets, especially Homer, in traditional education, see **1.9**, **3.8–9**. Further reading: Morrison 1949; Guthrie 1969: 27–34; Kerferd 1981: 15–44; Ostwald 1986: 238–50.

> (316d) I claim that the sophist's skill is an old one, but that those men of an earlier time who practised it created a pretext and covered it up because they feared that it was resented. Some presented it as poetry, for instance Homer, Hesiod and Simonides; others – Orpheus, Musaeus and their followers – as sacred rites and prophecy. I have noticed that some others have presented it as physical education (*gymnastiké*) too, such as Iccus of Tarentum and, still to this day, Herodicus of Selymbria, originally from Megara and a sophist second to none. (e) Your man Agathocles, who was a great sophist, made music his pretext, as did Pythoclides from Ceos and many others. All

these men, as I was saying, used these skills as screens because they were afraid of resentment.

4.4. The sophists and "liberal education"

Plato, *Protagoras* 312a7–b6

At the beginning of the *Protagoras*, Socrates discusses with the young Hippocrates whether Hippocrates should go to Protagoras for the next stage in his education. Hippocrates has completed the regular curriculum (*grammata, mousiké, gymnastiké*: **3.14–15**), which is said to be suited to a "freeborn layman" and therefore comprises a "liberal education" (see also **5.24**). As such, this kind of education is thought to be like that which Protagoras offers to his students. Further reading: Marrou 1956: 46–60; Guthrie 1969: 35–40, 44–48, 50–51; Kerferd 1981: 15–23.

(a) "But, Hippocrates, perhaps you imagine that the education you will receive from Protagoras will not be like that [i.e. like that of professionals], (b) but rather of the sort you received from the *grammatistés, kitharistés* and *paidotribés*. You didn't learn any of these skills so that you might become an expert practitioner, but only to gain the kind of education that befits a freeborn layman."

"Well," he said, "in my opinion, that's rather more like the education one would receive from Protagoras."

4.5. What do the sophists teach?

Plato, *Protagoras* 318a6–319a7

The claim by Protagoras in this extract that he can improve his students and make them better citizens reflects a traditional Greek expectation about the teacher's role. The fact that Socrates gives the name "political skill" to the characteristic quality of the good citizen is less surprising when we realize that "citizen" in Greek is *polités*, and "political skill" is *politiké*. Protagoras' reference in this passage to sophists who teach "arithmetic, astronomy, geometry and music" (he is thinking of Hippias) has special importance for the history of Western education, since it is the first instance in which the subjects of the medieval *quadrivium* are grouped together (see **10.27**). Further reading: Dillon and Gergel 2003: 1–42 (translated sources for Protagoras); Guthrie 1969: 14–26, 44–48; Kerferd 1981: 1–3, 37–39; Scolnicov 1988: 21–29; de Romilly 1992: 196–203; Ford 2001.

(318a) Protagoras said in reply, "Young man, if you associate with me as your teacher, it will be your good fortune to return home a better man on the day you join me. . . . Each day thereafter will see consistent improvement." . . .

[Socrates presses Protagoras to be more precise.] (d) "If Hippocrates here comes to study with Protagoras and departs a better man the very day he begins his association, and if there is further improvement on each subsequent day, where will that improvement be found, Protagoras?. . . ."

When he had heard what I had to say, Protagoras replied, "Your question is a good one, Socrates. . . . If Hippocrates comes to me, his experience will be different from what it would have been had he gone to study with any other sophist. The others damage the young by forcing them back against their will to the technical subjects from which they have fled. (e) For these sophists teach them arithmetic, astronomy, geometry and music." At this point he glanced at Hippias. "If, however, Hippocrates comes to me, he won't learn anything other than what he has come to learn. The purpose of my instruction is to teach sound judgement, first in his handling of private affairs, so that he can manage his household in the best way possible, then in handling affairs of the state, (319a) so that in the public domain he may reach the highest level of competence in his action and speech."

"Am I following your line of argument correctly?" I asked. "I believe that you are talking about political skill, and that you are guaranteeing to make men good citizens."

4.6. The sophists and poetry

Plato, *Protagoras* 338e6–339a6

By taking it upon themselves to teach the analysis of poetry ("literary criticism"), the sophists were incorporating an activity into their curriculum which held a traditional place (and would continue to do so); see **1.9**, **3.8–9**, **4.3**. Further reading: Kerferd 1950, 1981: 24; Jaeger 1947: 1, 295–97; Ford 2001: 103–7.

(338e) Protagoras began to ask his questions in roughly the following manner. "I believe, Socrates, that it is critical for a man's education to have him become an expert about poetry. (339a) That entails the ability to understand which passages of a given poet are properly composed and which are not, to know how to distinguish between them, and to give an explanation, when asked. My question now will be about the issue which you and I have made the subject of our discussion, that is, goodness (*areté*). I have, however, transferred the context to the realm of poetry, and that will be the only difference."

4.7. Gorgias on the teachability of goodness (*areté*)

Plato, *Meno* 95b1–d1

Can goodness (*areté*) be taught, or is it transmitted by innate character (*phusis*)? If it can be taught, who teaches it? These questions represent one of the great intellectual controversies of the fifth century, with wide social ramifications, and they continued to be debated long after (see also **3.15**; Kidd 1988: 100). As he does in the *Protagoras*, so here Plato considers these problems. Gorgias (from the Greek city of Leontini in Sicily) is viewed as different from other sophists because of his reluctance to claim that he teaches *areté*; his aim is the more practical one of turning men into clever speakers, that is, of making them skilful in *rhetoriké*. Further reading: Dillon and Gergel 2003: 43–97 (translated sources for Gorgias); Harrison 1964; Guthrie 1969: 271–73; Kerferd 1981: 44–45, 131–38, 1997: 253–56; de Romilly 1992: 44–47, 203–7.

> (95b) SOCRATES: Well then, tell me. Are these people[1] willing to offer themselves as teachers of the young? Are they prepared to agree that they are teachers and that goodness (*areté*) can be taught?
>
> MENO: Oh, not at all, Socrates. One minute you might hear them say that it can, the next that it can't.
>
> SOCRATES: Then are we to describe them as teachers of this thing, when they can't even agree on that point?
>
> MENO: No, Socrates, I don't think so.
>
> SOCRATES: Well, let's turn to the sophists. They are the only men who make that claim. Do you believe that they are teachers of goodness?
>
> (c) MENO: Oh, Socrates, that's why I really admire Gorgias. You'd never hear him making that promise. He laughs at the others when he hears them doing so. He sees it as his function to make men clever speakers.
>
> SOCRATES: So, you yourself do not believe that the sophists are teachers?
>
> MENO: I can't say, Socrates. My reaction is just like that of the majority of people. One moment I think that they are, the next that they are not.
>
> SOCRATES: Do you think that you and your fellow-politicians are the only people who can't make up their minds on its teachability? (d) Why, the poet Theognis says the very same thing.[2]

---

1 The *kaloi kagathoi*, literally "good and noble men," i.e. "outstanding members of society," referred to just before this extract. For this phrase, see Ch. 3 n. 18.
2 Socrates now quotes Theognis 33–36 (**1.5**) and 435, 434 and 436–38 (**1.6**) to demonstrate ancient disagreement and confusion over the teachability of *areté*.

4.8. Hippias the polymath

Plato, *Hippias Major* 285b7–d4

Of all the sophists, Hippias was reputed to possess knowledge over the widest range of subjects. The following passage provides a partial indication of the breadth of the expertise to which he laid claim. Sparta was much nearer Hippias' home of Elis than Athens was, so his visits there are understandable. His interest in human and divine family relationships and in the past in general likely reflects the feats of memory for which he was famous (see Xenophon, *Dinner Party* 4.62; Plato, *Hippias Minor* 368d2–7). Further reading: Dillon and Gergel 2003: 118–32 (translated sources for Hippias); Guthrie 1969: 280–85; Kerferd 1981: 46–49, 1997: 258–60.

> (285b) SOCRATES: What then, Hippias, are the subjects which the Spartans love to hear you discuss ... ? Or is it obvious that it is those subjects on which you are an expert, (c) astronomy and the phenomena of the heavens?
>
> HIPPIAS: Not at all. They refuse even to tolerate those topics.
>
> SOCRATES: But do they enjoy hearing you discuss geometry?
>
> HIPPIAS: Absolutely not. For many of them, so to speak, do not even know how to count.
>
> SOCRATES: Then they are far from ready to put up with you giving a talk about making calculations.
>
> HIPPIAS: By God, miles from it!
>
> SOCRATES: Well then, those topics on which you have the knowledge to make more accurate pronouncements than any other man, (d) the function of letters, syllables, rhythm and harmony?
>
> HIPPIAS: What sort of harmonies and letters could you be referring to?
>
> SOCRATES: Well, what are the subjects they are happy to listen to and of which they approve? . . . .
>
> HIPPIAS: The family relationships of heroes and men, Socrates, the settlement of cities founded in the distant past, and, to put it in a nutshell, the entire field of ancient history.

4.9. Sophists in action (I): rhetorical display (*epideixis*)

(a) Gorgias, *Encomium of Helen* 6–9, 15,
(b) Xenophon, *Memoirs of Socrates* 2.1.21–23, 27–28

Different sophists taught different subjects and skills, and specialization enabled one sophist to differentiate himself from the others in selling his talents on the open market. In one way or another, however, all sophists taught *rhetoriké*, "the art of speaking." One of the ways in which they attracted students to themselves was through the public delivery of a "display-speech" (*epideixis*) which demonstrated the level of rhetorical skill to which a prospective student might hope to aspire. These display-speeches frequently took for their themes some mythological topic – not surprisingly, since such themes reflect the subject-matter of so much in a young Greek's education. The following extracts are drawn from two of the very few examples to survive from the fifth century. In **a** an attempt has been made to provide some indication of the artificial verbal effects that Gorgias tried to achieve. Extract **b** is preserved in Xenophon's *Memoirs of Socrates* expressly as the composition of Prodicus. Its moralistic account of Heracles' choice between virtue and vice is strongly reminiscent of the traditional wisdom that Hesiod communicated in his *Works and Days* (**1.3**). Further reading: Pfeiffer 1968: 45–49; Guthrie 1969: 41–44; Kerferd 1981: 45–46, 78–82; Ostwald 1986: 236–50; de Romilly 1992: 57–73; Ford 2001: 94–97; Dillon and Gergel 2003: 76–84 (full translation of the *Encomium of Helen*), 111–16 (full translation of the *Choice of Heracles*).

a

(6) It is either because of the wishes (*boulemata*) of Chance and the plans (*bouleumata*) of the gods and the decrees (*psephismata*) of Necessity that Helen did what she did, or because she was abducted by force, or persuaded by words, or captured by love. If it was because of the first, the accuser deserves to be accused, since it is impossible to hinder the desire (*prothumia*) of a god with human forethought (*promethia*). For it is natural not for the stronger to be hindered by the weaker but for the weaker to be controlled and led by the stronger, and for the stronger to guide and the weaker to follow. A god is a stronger thing than a human being in terms of force and wisdom and other things; so if the responsibility must be attributed (*anatheteon*) to Chance and God, Helen must be absolved (*apoluteon*) of her infamy.

(7) But if she was abducted by force and unlawfully violated and unjustly assaulted, clearly the man who seized her or assaulted her acted unjustly, and the woman who was seized or assaulted suffered misfortune. So the barbarian who undertook a barbaric undertaking in speech and law and deed deserves to receive blame in speech, loss of rights in law, and punishment in deed; and as for the woman who was violated and deprived of her homeland and bereaved of her loved ones, how would it not be reasonable that she be pitied rather than slandered? For he carried out terrible acts, while she endured them; so it is just to pity the one and to hate the other.

(8) But if that which persuaded and deceived her mind was speech, it is not difficult as well to make a defence in the face of this and to

dispel the accusation in the following way. Speech is a great ruler, since it accomplishes deeds most divine with a body most minute and invisible. For it can stop fear and remove pain and instil joy and increase pity. I shall demonstrate that this is so; (9) but I must also demonstrate (*deixai*) it to my listeners by opinion (*doxê*). . . .

(15) That she did not commit a crime but suffered misfortune if she was persuaded by words has been stated; and I shall examine the fourth charge in the fourth part of my speech. If the force that did all these things was love (*erôs*), it will not be difficult for her to escape the blame for the crime that is said to have occurred.

b

[Socrates is the speaker] (21) The wise man Prodicus sets forth the same view about goodness (*aretê*) in that famous composition about Heracles which he puts on display. As far as I remember he tells it like this. When Heracles was setting out from childhood into manhood, at the stage at which young men become independent and show whether they will follow a virtuous or a wicked path in life, he went out to a peaceful place and sat down, wondering which of the two paths he should take. (22) It appeared to him that two tall women were approaching. One of them was attractive and had a noble air about her; her body was clean, her expression modest, her bearing sensible, and her clothing white. The other had been fed in such a way that she was corpulent and soft; she was made up so that, he thought, her colour appeared whiter and redder than it really was, her bearing was more upright than was natural, her expression was brazen, and her clothing revealed as much of her charms as possible. She examined herself constantly, checked to see if anyone else was looking at her, and gazed at her shadow. (23) When they were nearer to Heracles, the one I mentioned first walked in the same way, but the other, wishing to get there first, ran up to Heracles and said: "I see, Heracles, that you don't know which path to take in your life. If you make me your friend, I will take you along the most pleasant and easiest path; there are no pleasures that you won't taste, and you will live your life without knowing any hardships. . . . "

(27) The other woman went up to him and said: "I have come to you, Heracles, because I know your parents and have learned your nature in the course of your education. I therefore expect that if you should take the path that leads to me you would become a noble performer of outstanding deeds, and I would appear yet more honourable and more glorious for my noble acts. I shall not deceive you with promises of pleasure to come, but I shall truthfully explain how the gods have arranged things as they really are. (28) None of the things

that are truly good and attractive do the gods give to people without exertion and practice. If you want the gods to be favourable to you, you must worship the gods; if you want your friends to love you, you must do good by your friends; if it's your desire that some city honour you, you must help that city. . . ."

4.10. Sophists in action (II): argumentation (eristic)

Plato, *Euthydemus* 275d2–277c7

Rhetoric can be a competitive skill if it is directed towards winning arguments. For this reason some sophists taught students to debate and win, regardless of the side they took in a dispute. They used two related techniques, "antilogic," which involved arguing opposing sides of a single proposition, and "eristic," which was devoted to refuting one's opponent regardless of the paradoxical nature of the conclusions that were reached. Good examples of the logical bases and assumptions underlying antilogic can be found in the anonymous treatise called *Double Arguments* (*Dissoi Logoi*), which dates to about 400 BC or shortly after (translation in Dillon and Gergel 2003: 39–42, 266–82, 318–33).

Both antilogic and eristic could be used "to make the strong argument weak and the weak argument strong" (see **3.11**), and in the hands of the unscrupulous this approach to words and their meanings had the potential to descend into mere verbal gymnastics. Plato provides us with an entertaining example of the ludicrous contortions that two sophists, Euthydemus and Dionysodorus, achieve at the expense of an inexperienced young interlocutor. His depiction of these sophists contains plenty of caricature. Further reading: Kerferd 1981: 53–54, 59–67, 1997: 246–48; Rankin 1983: 15–21; de Romilly 1992: 69–92; Scholz 2003.

(275d) Euthydemus began something like this, I believe: "Clinias, which people are the learners, the wise or the ignorant?" Since the question was a big one, the boy blushed and looked at me, not knowing what to do. I realized that he was confused, so I said, "Don't be afraid, Clinias; be a man, and give whichever answer seems right to you. (e) It may be that you will get a great deal of good from it."

At this moment Dionysodorus was leaning a little towards me; he had a big smile on his face and said in my ear: "Look, Socrates, I predict that no matter which answer the boy gives, he will be refuted." Just as he was saying this Clinias answered, so that I didn't even have the opportunity to warn the boy to be careful. (276a) Instead he answered that the wise are the learners.

Euthydemus then said, "Are there some people you call teachers, or not?" – He acknowledged that there were.

"So the teachers are teachers of the learners, just as the lyre-player and the writing-master (*grammatistés*) were, of course, the teachers of you and the other boys, and you were the learners?" – He agreed.

"Now, when you were learning, you didn't yet know the things you were learning, did you?" – "No," he replied.

"So were you wise when you didn't know these things?" – (b) "Of course not," he said.

"If you weren't wise, then, you were ignorant." – "Yes indeed."

"So since you were learning what you didn't know, you were learning when you were ignorant." – The boy nodded his head.

"Then it's the ignorant who learn, Clinias, not the wise, as you think."

After he said this, the two men's followers shouted and laughed, just like a chorus after their leader had given it a signal. (c) Before the boy had fully regained his breath, Dionysodorus took over and said, "When the writing-master dictated to you, which children would learn what was being dictated, the wise or the ignorant?" – "The wise," Clinias said.

"So it's the wise who learn, not the ignorant, and you didn't give Euthydemus a good answer a moment ago?"

(d) At this very moment the two men's admirers let out a huge, boisterous laugh, delighted with their wisdom. The rest of us kept quiet out of astonishment. Noticing that we were astonished, Euthydemus wouldn't let the boy go, so that our admiration of him would be greater still. He continued his questions, and like a skilful dancer he twisted the same question two ways: "Do the learners learn what they know or what they don't know?"

Again Dionysodorus whispered quietly to me: (e) "Here's another one, Socrates, just like the first."

"Good heavens," I said, "I certainly thought the first question was good!"

"All our questions, Socrates," he said, "are inescapable in just that way."

"That's why, I think, your pupils have such a high opinion of you."

Meanwhile Clinias answered Euthydemus that the learners learn what they don't know. Then Euthydemus asked him the same series of questions as before: (277a) "But don't you know letters?" he said. – "Yes," Clinias replied.

"All of them?" – He agreed.

"So whenever someone dictates something, isn't he dictating letters?" – He agreed.

"Then is he dictating things you know, if you really do know them all?" – He agreed to this too.

"So you're not the one who is learning what someone is dictating, but it's the one who doesn't know letters who is learning?" – "No," he said, "I'm the one who is learning."

"So you are learning what you know," he said, (b) "if in fact you know all the letters." – He agreed.

"Then your answer was wrong," he said.

Euthydemus had not yet finished saying this when Dionysodorus took over the argument as though it were a ball and aimed it at the boy again, saying: "Euthydemus is deceiving you, Clinias. Just tell me, isn't learning the acquisition of knowledge of what one is learning?" – Clinias agreed.

"As for knowing, isn't it the possession of knowledge already?" – He agreed.

"Then not knowing is not yet having knowledge?" – (c) He agreed with him.

"So are those who acquire something the ones who possess it already or the ones who don't?" – "The ones who don't."

"Then you're in agreement that the ones who don't know belong to the category of those who don't possess something?" – He nodded.

"Then the learners belong to the category of those who are acquiring something," he said, "not of those who possess it?" – He agreed.

"So those who don't know," he said, "are learning, not those who know."

4.11. A contemporary view of the sophists

Thucydides, *The Peloponnesian War* 3.38.3–7

In the summer of 427 BC the city of Mytilene (on the island of Lesbos) revolted from the Athenian Empire. In order to punish the Mytilenaeans and set an example that would discourage similar behaviour from their other subject allies, the Athenians decided in their Assembly to put to death all adult males in Mytilene and enslave all women and children. They immediately dispatched a ship to carry out their decision; but then they thought that this sentence might be unreasonably harsh, so on the next day they reopened the debate over the fate of Mytilene. In this extract – the only place where Thucydides mentions the sophists – Cleon, a leading Athenian politician at this time (see **3.17**), criticizes his fellow citizens for their lack of resolve and complains that their real desire in reconsidering the previous day's decree is to be seduced by fine speeches, as though the words have no relation to real people and real dangers. Further reading: Guthrie 1969: 84–88; Kerferd 1981: 123–25.

(3) In contests like these our city gives prizes to others but assumes dangers itself. (4) You are to blame: you conduct these contests badly,

since it is your habit to watch speeches and listen to deeds. You consider future actions as feasible on the basis of fine words, yet the events that have already happened you consider on the basis of criticisms that people make in an attractive way; even when you have seen it with your own eyes you fail to take what has been done as more credible than what you have heard. (5) You take first-place for being deceived by the novelty of an argument and for refusing to follow the approved course of action. You are slaves to whatever is eccentric and you despise the conventional. (6) Each person's wish, above all, is to have the ability to speak for himself, but failing that, you compete against those who do speak by appearing not to lag the field in following their insight and to express your approval quickly when someone makes a good point, eager to anticipate a speaker's arguments and slow to predict their consequences. (7) Your search is for almost any world other than the one you live in, but when it comes to matters that are right in front of you, your understanding falls short. To put it simply, you are overcome by the pleasure of listening; you are like people who sit around watching sophists rather than deliberating about the city.

4.12. The sophists and payment for teaching

(a) Plato, *Apology* 20a2–b9, (b) Pl. *Hippias Major* 282b4–e8,
(c) Pl. *Cratylus* 384b1–c2, (d) [Plato], *Axiochus* 366c1–3, (e) [Plato],
Alcibiades I 119a1–6, (f) Diogenes Laertius, *Life of Protagoras* 9.52

Precisely how well the sophists were paid has been a matter of considerable debate, since the collected evidence records wildly differing rates. But like the pay that skilled professionals have received in all ages, the fees that a sophist could command would have depended substantially on his reputation. The following extracts represent a sample of the divergent information about individual sophists' fees. In considering the evidence in these passages it is useful to keep in mind (a) that many skilled workers in Athens around 400 BC were paid 1 drachma per day, though some were no doubt paid more and many were paid less, and (b) that 100 drachmas = 1 mina. Further reading: Forbes 1942: 12–19; Guthrie 1969: 35–40; Vlastos 1975: 155–61; Kerferd 1981: 25–28; Blank 1985; Loomis 1998: 62–75, 232–39; Too 2000: 17–31; Rihll 2003: 184–89.

a

(a) [Socrates is the speaker] Now, I happened to meet a man, Callias the son of Hipponicus, who has spent more money on sophists than everyone else put together. Since he has two sons, I asked him:

"Callias, if your sons were colts or calves, we'd be able to engage and pay for a trainer who could make them distinguished at the excellence appropriate to them, (b) and he would be someone skilled at horses or farming. But as it is, since they are human beings, whom do you plan to engage as a trainer? Who is expert in this kind of human, political excellence? . . . Is there someone," I said, "or isn't there?" "Of course there is," he said. "Who is he," I said, "and where's he from, and how much does he charge for his teaching?" "Evenus," he said, "from Paros – for 5 minas."[3]

b

(b) Socrates: This man Gorgias, the sophist from Leontini, came here from his home on public business as an ambassador, since he was considered the most competent man in Leontini at tending to the interests of his city, and it was the general view that he was the most accomplished speaker in their Assembly. In his private capacity he made displays and associated with the young people here, and in this way earned and received a great deal of money from our city. (c) Then again, our friend Prodicus often went to other places on public business. The last time he came here from Ceos for this purpose, just recently, and spoke in the Council, he gained a great reputation, and he made private displays, associated with young people, and received an extraordinary sum of money. But none of those men of old ever thought that he should exact money as payment for his wisdom (*sophia*) or should make displays among people from all sorts of places. (d) They were so simple-minded and had failed to realize how valuable money is. But Gorgias and Prodicus have each earned more money from their wisdom than any craftsman has from any art you can name. Protagoras did the same even before them.

Hippias: You don't know the beauty of this, Socrates, for if you knew how much money I've made, you'd be astonished. Forget about the other occasions. I went to Sicily once when Protagoras was visiting there. (e) He had a great reputation and was older than I was, but even though I was much younger, I made in a short time much more than 150 minas; and from one very small place, Inycus, I earned more than 100 minas. I returned home with this money and gave it to my father; he and his fellow-citizens were amazed. I'm pretty certain that I've made more money than any other two sophists you'd care to mention.

---

3 For Callias' expenditures on sophists, see also Xenophon, *Dinner Party* 1.5.

c

[Socrates is the speaker] (b) Now, the investigation of words is really no trivial subject. If I had heard Prodicus' 50-drachma lecture (*epideixis*) – which, he claims, can provide the listener with an education on the topic – nothing would stop you from knowing immediately the truth about correctness of names. As it is, however, I haven't heard it; instead I listened to the 1-drachma lecture. (c) So I don't know the truth of the matter on these problems.

d

The things I'm saying are echoes of the wise Prodicus, some purchased for half a drachma, others for 2 drachmas, others for 4 drachmas. He doesn't teach anyone for nothing.

e

Now, of all other Athenians or foreigners, name a slave or free man who is reputed to have become wiser by associating with Pericles, just as I can say that Pythodorus and Callias did by associating with Zeno. Each of them paid Zeno 100 minas and has become wise and famous.

f

Protagoras was the first to charge 100 minas as a fee.

4.13. Socrates on the value of education

Xenophon, *Socrates' Defence* 20–21

Our sources sometimes present Socrates as though he were a consultant on the subject of education (e.g. Plato, *Laches* 178a1–180a5, *Euthydemus* 306d2ff.). Whether or not this depiction is faithful to the historical Socrates, it is consistent with the opinion which he is made to express in the following selection. Here Socrates is dealing with the formal accusation that he corrupts the young; his respondent, Meletus, appears also in **3.1c**.

(20) "By god," Meletus said, "I do know those whom you have convinced to listen to you instead of their parents." "I admit it," Socrates said, "at least as regards education (*paideia*). Parents know it's a special concern of mine. When it comes to health, people listen to doctors rather than to their parents. In the assemblies all Athenians listen, as you know, to the most sensible speakers rather than to their relatives. After all, don't you elect as generals those who you think are the most knowledgeable about warfare, in preference to your fathers,

your brothers, and even yourselves?" "It's to our advantage that way," said Meletus, "and it's our custom." (21) "Then don't you think that this too is remarkable, that the people who are most capable in other activities not only receive fair compensation but are even given special honours, whereas I am being prosecuted by you on a capital charge because some people consider me to be preeminent on the subject of education, which is the greatest human good?"

4.14. The Socratic method

Plato, *Meno* 81e3–85d8

The expression "Socratic method" is generally used today to describe a procedure in which the teacher asks questions rather than telling students what they should know, while the students learn through the answers that they are steered towards. Yet the method which the Platonic Socrates followed implies a good deal more than simple interrogation. Socrates claimed that he himself did not know the answers to the ethical questions that he posed, such as "what is justice?" and "what is goodness?" And since he did not know the answers to questions like these, he could not claim to be a teacher or to have students; instead he referred to his "associates," "people who spend time with me" (**4.15–16**). This outlook further implies that both he and his respondents (his "associates") were engaged in joint investigations, searching together for answers which neither of them knew in advance.

In the following passage, Socrates draws out of his respondent a correct conclusion on a geometrical problem – how to double a square – even though neither of them knows the answer at the outset. The passage raises a number of questions: Could Socrates really lead his respondent to the correct answer if he (Socrates) did not know the answer from the start? What significance is there in the fact that Socrates uses a geometrical problem to illustrate his method? Can the procedure set out here be applied not only to problems that involve number and proportion but also to those that involve ethics and morality? What are the pedagogical implications of linking this procedure to the theory that all learning is "recollection"? Further reading: Sharples 1985: 7–10; Scolnicov 1988: 51–59; Brickhouse and Smith 2000: 53–72.

> (81e) MENO: What do you mean that we don't learn but that what we call learning is recollection? Can you teach me that this is so?
> SOCRATES: A moment ago, Meno, I said that you're a scoundrel, and now you're asking if I can teach you, (82a) even though I say that there is no such thing as teaching, only recollection – no doubt so that I will appear to contradict myself right away.

MENO: Of course not, Socrates. That's not why I said this; it was out of habit. But if you can somehow demonstrate to me that it's as you say, please do.

SOCRATES: It isn't easy, but I'm willing anyway to do my best because you ask me. Call over one of your many retainers over there, whichever you want, (b) so that I can use him to show you.

MENO: Of course. Come over here!

SOCRATES: Is he a Greek, and does he speak Greek?

MENO: Certainly – he's been raised in the house.

SOCRATES: Consider carefully whether it seems to you that he is recalling or is learning from me.

MENO: Yes, I will.

SOCRATES: Tell me, boy, you know that a square is like this? [Socrates sketches square ABCD in the sand: Figure 4.1] – Yes.

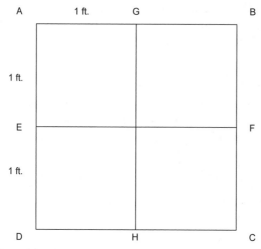

Figure 4.1

(c) SOCRATES: A square has all these four lines equal? – Yes.

SOCRATES: These lines that go through the middle, they're equal too? [EF, GH] – Yes.

SOCRATES: Now, a figure like this could be larger or smaller? – Yes.

SOCRATES: So if this side were two feet long and this side two feet long, how many feet would the whole thing be? Look at it this way: if it were two feet long on this side but only one foot on this side, the area would be two feet once, wouldn't it? – Yes.

(d) SOCRATES: But since it's two feet long on this side too, it comes to twice two feet, doesn't it? – Yes, it does.

SOCRATES: So it's twice two feet? – Yes.

SOCRATES: How much is twice two feet? Work it out and tell me. – Four, Socrates.

SOCRATES: Can there be another figure twice the size of this one, but like it, with all its sides equal, like this one? – Yes.

SOCRATES: How many feet will its area be? – Eight.

SOCRATES: Now, try to tell me how long each of its sides will be. This figure's side is two feet long. (e) What will be the side of the one twice its area? – It'll be twice the length, obviously.

SOCRATES: Do you see, Meno? I'm not teaching him anything; I'm simply asking questions. And now he thinks he knows the length of the side that will produce the eight-feet square. Don't you think so?

MENO: Yes I do.

SOCRATES: Does he know? – Certainly not.

SOCRATES: He thinks it's twice as long, doesn't he? – Yes.

SOCRATES: Observe him recollecting in the right order, as one should recollect. Tell me, do you say that the figure twice the area is made from the line that's twice the length? (83a) Here's what I mean: don't assume a figure that's long on this side and short on that one, but equal on all sides, like this one, but twice the area of this one, eight feet. Just consider whether you still think it will come from the side that's twice the length. – Yes, I think so.

SOCRATES: So this side is twice the length of that one [AB] if we add another here [B] that's the same length? – Yes.

SOCRATES: You think that the eight-feet area will be produced from this line, if there are four lines of this length? – Yes.

(b) SOCRATES: Then let's draw four equal lines on the basis of it. [Figure 4.2: AI, IJ, JK, KA] That would be, in your opinion, the eight-feet area, wouldn't it? – Certainly.

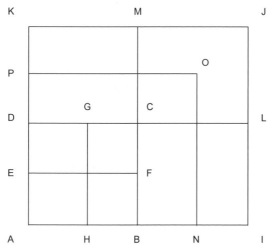

Figure 4.2

SOCRATES: So in it are these four squares, each of them equal to this four-feet square? [Socrates adds the lines CL, CM] – Yes.

SOCRATES: How large is it? Isn't it four times the size? – Of course.

SOCRATES: So four times is the same as twice the size? – Certainly not!

SOCRATES: How many times is it? – Four times.

(c) SOCRATES: So from the side that's twice the length a figure is produced that's not twice the area but four times? – That's true.

SOCRATES: Four times four are sixteen, aren't they? – Yes.

SOCRATES: And from what kind of side does an eight-feet area come? An area four times the size has come from this side, hasn't it? – Yes.

SOCRATES: And the four-feet area here comes from this side that's half the length? – Yes.

SOCRATES: Fine. Isn't the eight-feet area twice the size of this one, but half the size of the other one? – Yes.

SOCRATES: Won't it be made from a side longer than this one but shorter than that one? Don't you think so? – Yes, I think so.

(d) SOCRATES: Good – answer what you think is right. Now tell me: was this line two feet long, and the other one four feet long? – Yes.

SOCRATES: Then the side of the eight-feet figure has to be longer than this two-feet one, but shorter than the four-feet one. – It has to be.

(e) SOCRATES: Now try to say how long you think it is. – Three feet.

SOCRATES: If it's three feet, will it be three feet if we add half of this side? [BN] Here's two, and here's one. And on this side likewise here's two, and here's one. This makes the figure that you mean? [ANOP] – Yes.

SOCRATES: So if it's three feet on this side and three feet on the other, is the whole figure three times three feet? – It seems so.

SOCRATES: But three times three is how many feet? – Nine.

SOCRATES: But the square twice the size had to have how many feet? – Eight.

SOCRATES: Then it isn't from the three-feet side either that the eight-feet figure comes. – Certainly not.

SOCRATES: From what side, then? Try to tell us precisely. If you don't want to count, then just show us the side. – (84a) But Socrates, I just don't know.

SOCRATES: Do you notice again, Meno, where he now is on the path of recollection? At first he didn't know what the side of the eight-feet square was, just as he doesn't yet know the answer even now, but he *thought* he knew it then, and he answered confidently as though he did know, and he didn't think that he was perplexed. But *now* he thinks that he's perplexed; (b) he doesn't know the answer, but neither does he think he knows.

MENO: You're right.

SOCRATES: So is he in a better position now in regard to what he didn't know? – I think so.

SOCRATES: By putting him into perplexity and numbing him as the stingray does, we didn't do him any harm, did we?[4] – No, I don't think so.

SOCRATES: Actually, I think, we've done something useful towards helping him discover the position he's in. For now he would be glad to look for the answer, since he doesn't know it, whereas earlier he thought he could speak easily and effectively, both often and before large crowds, on the subject of the square that's twice the size of another, (c) since he thought the side had to be twice the length. – It looks that way.

SOCRATES: Do you think he would have tried to look for or to learn what he thought he knew (though he didn't know it) before he was thrown into perplexity, when he realized he didn't know and then longed to know? – I don't think he would have, Socrates.

SOCRATES: So it helped him to become numb? – I think so.

SOCRATES: Look at what he will discover as a result of this perplexity simply by searching together with me, even though I'm only asking questions and not teaching him. (d) Watch whether you find me teaching and explaining to him instead of asking for his opinions.

Tell me: do we consider this a four-foot figure? [Figure 4.3: ABCD] Do you understand? – I do.

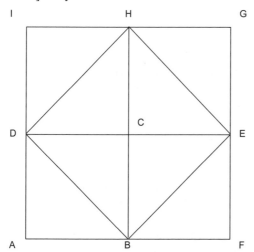

Figure 4.3

4 A little earlier Socrates was compared to a stingray because of his numbing effect on his interlocutors.

SOCRATES: Can we add this figure which is equal to it? [BCEF] – Yes.

SOCRATES: And this third figure too which is equal to each of them? [CEGH] – Yes.

SOCRATES: So can we fill in this space in the corner? [DCHI] – Of course.

SOCRATES: So these must be four equal figures? – Yes.

(e) SOCRATES: Then how many times larger than this one is this whole figure? – Four times.

SOCRATES: But we had to have a figure twice as large – or don't you remember? – I certainly do.

SOCRATES: Does this line, from corner to corner, cut each of these figures in two? – (85a) Yes.

SOCRATES: So these are four equal lines, enclosing this figure? [BEHD] – Yes they are.

SOCRATES: Look it over: how large is this figure? – I don't understand.

SOCRATES: Within these figures, all four of them, each line cuts off half of each, doesn't it? – Yes.

SOCRATES: So how many of this size are in this figure? [BEHD] – Four.

SOCRATES: And how many in this one? [ABCD] – Two.

SOCRATES: And four is how much larger than two? – Twice as large.

SOCRATES: How many feet is this? – Eight.

(b) SOCRATES: On the basis of what line? – This one.

SOCRATES: The one that stretches from corner to corner of the four-foot figure? – Yes.

SOCRATES: Knowledgeable men call this the diagonal; so if its name is diagonal, the figure that is twice as large would be based on the diagonal, according to you. – Exactly, Socrates.

SOCRATES: What do you think, Meno? Is there any opinion this boy gave in his answers which is not his own?

(c) MENO: No, they were his own.

SOCRATES: And yet he didn't know, as we said a little earlier. – That's true.

SOCRATES: And were these opinions in him, or not? – They were.

SOCRATES: So the person who doesn't know – whatever it is that he doesn't know about – are there true opinions in him about the things which he doesn't know? – It appears so.

SOCRATES: And these opinions have been stirred up in him now just like a dream, but if someone asks him these same questions again and again and in many ways, you know that in the end he will have a knowledge about these things which is as accurate as anyone's. – (d) That's likely.

SOCRATES: So he will have knowledge without being taught but only by being questioned, and by finding knowledge in himself? – Yes.

SOCRATES: And to find knowledge in oneself is recollection, isn't it? – Exactly.

4.15. Intellectual obstetrics

Plato, *Theaetetus* 150b9–151c2

The premise which underlies **4.14** – that Socrates does not know the answers to the questions he asks any better than his respondents do, but that he is nevertheless skilled in eliciting correct answers – leads to a celebrated comparison which the Platonic Socrates draws between himself and a midwife: as the midwife is skilled at assisting other women to give birth to the children that they have conceived but is unable to produce children herself, so Socrates is intellectually infertile but is skilled at helping those who are "pregnant" to give birth to their intellectual "offspring." In this passage Socrates also implies that success in his dialectical process may rely on factors that are not fully rational (note his references to the intervention of "god" and of his own "divine sign"). Further reading: Crombie 1964: 15–20, 35–40; Burnyeat 1977; Tomin 1987; Tarrant 1988; Sedley 2004: 28–37.

(150b) This is the most important quality in our [i.e. the midwives'] craft, (c) to be able to test by every means whether the young man's mind is producing an image and a false thing or a genuine and true thing. For this is a characteristic that I share with midwives: I cannot produce wisdom, and the criticism which many people in the past have brought against me is true, that, although I question others, I draw no conclusion on any subject because I possess no wisdom. The reason is this: god compels me to act as midwife but has prevented me from giving birth. Now, I'm not at all wise myself, (d) nor have I made any wise discovery as a product of my own mind. As for those who associate with me, some of them appear at first very unintelligent, but as our association continues, all those whom god allows make astonishing progress. . . . It's clear that they've never learned anything from me, but from themselves they have discovered and produced many fine things. God and I are responsible for this delivery.

(e) Here is the evidence. Many people in the past didn't know this fact and gave themselves credit, while heaping scorn on me; they then left me sooner than they should have, either of their own accord or because they were persuaded by others to do so. After they left me, bad company caused them to miscarry what they still had left and to raise poorly and lose what I helped them bring to birth. They put a higher stock in lies and phantoms than they did in the truth, and in the end they seemed foolish, both to themselves and to others. (151a). . . . Whenever they return, begging to associate with me and stopping at nothing to do it, the divine sign that comes to me prevents me from associating with some of them; but it allows me to associate with others, and these people improve once again.

Now, those who associate with me share the same experience that women have who are giving birth: they feel labour-pains and are filled day and night with a feeling of helplessness, to a much greater degree than pregnant women. My skill can both awaken and put a stop to this labour-pain. (b) These associates of mine have just this experience. However, Theaetetus, there are those who don't seem to me somehow to be pregnant. When I recognize that they have no need of me, I'm very glad to match them up and, God willing, I'm highly competent at guessing from whose association they can get the greatest help. Indeed, I've handed many of them over to Prodicus, and many to other wise and divinely inspired men.

Here's why I've drawn this out at length for you, my fine boy. I suspect that you are pregnant and in labour, as you yourself think. So behave towards me as you would towards a midwife's son who is himself skilled in midwifery: (c) do your best to answer whatever questions I ask you.

4.16. Improvement through *eros*

Aeschines of Sphettus, *Alcibiades* fr. 11

Aeschines, a contemporary of Plato, also wrote dramatic dialogues which featured Socrates in the lead role, though only fragments of them survive today. The speaker in the following passage is Socrates. Like Plato's Socrates (**4.15**, **17**), Aeschines' character disavows knowledge of any skill and attributes the beneficial influence that he has on others to forces less rational than dialectic. In this case, that force is *eros*, "desire," "passion," or "love." Further reading: Field 1967: 146–52; Guthrie 1969: 390–98; Dillon 1994.

Many sick people become healthy, some by human skill, others by a divine gift. Those who become healthy by human skill do so because they are treated by doctors, while those who become healthy by a divine gift do so because a longing leads them to what will help them. They want to throw up just when it will be beneficial for them to do so, and to go hunting when it will be beneficial for them to get some exercise. If I had thought that I could be of help through some kind of skill (*techné*), I would be proving that I am guilty of a great error. But as it is, I thought that in the case of Alcibiades this ability had been granted to me by a divine gift, and that none of this should be cause for surprise. Because of the love (*eros*) which I happened to have for Alcibiades, my experience was no different from that of the women who worship Dionysus. For whenever they become possessed, they draw milk and honey from the same wells that others can't even fetch water from. What's more, although I possess no rational skill which I could teach a man and through which I could help him, nevertheless I thought that by associating with Alcibiades I could improve him through my love (*eros*).

4.17. Socratic ignorance and payment for teaching

Plato, *Apology* 19d8–20a2

Since (as **4.14–16** make clear) Socrates did not lay claim to knowledge or to an ability to teach (and denied that he had any students), it is natural that, unlike the sophists, he did not seek payment from his "associates" for the time that they spent with him. On this basis Plato repeatedly contrasts Socrates with the sophists, sometimes explicitly, as below, but usually implicitly; some other writers draw this contrast as well. For the sophists' fees see **4.12**. Here Socrates presents the unremunerated companionship of a fellow citizen as the alternative to association with a sophist; cf. **3.1c–d**. Further reading: Harrison 1964: 191.

> (19d) None of those claims is true, and if you've heard it said that I set out to teach people and that I exact payment, that isn't true either. (e) And yet I do think that it's a fine thing if someone were able to teach people, as Gorgias of Leontini, Prodicus of Chios, and Hippias of Elis do. Each of them is capable of going to the various cities and of persuading the young men there – who have the opportunity to asso-ciate free of charge with any of their fellow citizens they want – (20a) they all persuade them to abandon their association with those men, to associate with the sophists, to give them money, and to feel grateful on top of it.

4.18. Socrates as head of a school

Aristophanes, *Clouds* 133–84

In his comedy *Clouds*, Aristophanes presents a very different picture of Socrates from the one that we find in Plato, Xenophon, Aeschines and others. *His* Socrates teaches, has pupils, runs a school, charges fees, is willing to steal in order to put food on the table (and encourages his pupils to do the same), is an atheist, and shows a variety of philosophical and scientific interests for which the Socrates who appears in our other sources has little or no time. In this extract the old farmer Strepsiades, father of the dissolute young Pheidippides, knocks on the door of Socrates' school (the *phrontisterion* or "thinkery") and is answered by one of Socrates' students. The butt of Aristophanes' humour in this passage is less Socrates himself than it is all the intellectuals in Athens around this time, especially the sophists and those who speculated on the nature of the physical world. Further reading: Guthrie 1969: 359–407; Dover 1968: xxxii–lvii, 1972: 116–20.

STUDENT: Go to hell! Who knocked on the door?

STREPSIADES: Strepsiades, the son of Pheidon, from Cicynna.

STUDENT: You're a fool; you've kicked the door so unscientifically that you caused an idea that I'd discovered to miscarry.[5]

STREPSIADES: Do forgive me; I live far off in the country. But tell me what miscarried.

STUDENT: It's not lawful to tell about it except to students.

STREPSIADES: Just go ahead and tell me. I've come here to the Thinkery to be a student.

STUDENT: I'll tell you, but you have to treat it as Mysteries.[6] Just now Socrates asked Chairephon how many of its own feet a flea can jump. He asked because a flea had bitten Chairephon's forehead and jumped over onto Socrates' head.

STREPSIADES: How did he measure the distance?

STUDENT: Very cleverly. He melted wax, then he took the flea and dipped its two feet into the wax, and then Persian slippers formed around it as the wax cooled. He slipped them off and measured the distance.

STREPSIADES: King Zeus! What a subtle mind the man has!

STUDENT: Then maybe you'd like to hear about another of Socrates' big ideas?

STREPSIADES: Would I! Please let me in on it.

STUDENT: Chairephon ... was asking him whether he thought gnats sing through their mouth or their arse.

STREPSIADES: Well, what did he say about the gnat?

STUDENT: He claimed the gnat's inside is narrow, and because the passage is thin the wind is forced to travel straight to the arse. And because its anus is a hole attached to a narrow passage, it rings out under the force of the wind.

5 For the metaphor of "intellectual miscarriage," see **4.15**.
6 Religious rites about which the initiates were required to maintain secrecy.

STREPSIADES: So the anus is the gnat's trumpet. The man knows guts like no-one else! Anyone with that knowledge of a gnat's innards could get off easily if he were a defendant!

STUDENT: And just the other day he had a great idea taken from him by a lizard.

STREPSIADES: How? You've got to tell me!

STUDENT: He was looking at the paths and orbits of the moon, and then as he gazed upwards in the dark with his mouth open, a gecko shat on him from the roof.

STREPSIADES: That's a good one! A gecko shat on Socrates!

STUDENT: And yesterday we had nothing to eat in the evening.

STREPSIADES: Alright – so what did he manage to do for food?

STUDENT: He sprinkled fine ash on the table, bent a skewer, then he took a pair of compasses and lifted a cloak from the wrestling school.

STREPSIADES: Thales[7] was a miracle, but he has nothing on this man. Hurry up, open the Thinkery and show me Socrates as fast as you can. I want to be his student. Open the door!

4.19. Criticism of the contemporary curriculum

Plato [?], *Clitophon* 407b1–e3

Although attributed to Plato, the *Clitophon* is usually believed to have been written by someone else, perhaps not long after Plato's death. Much of this short dialogue consists of statements and speeches which the character Clitophon presents as the kind of thing that Socrates was often heard to say. The source of these statements and speeches is probably not the actual utterances of the historical Socrates but rather the ideas he was typically made to express in Socratic literature by Socratic writers. Hence the passage below is probably a fair representation of criticisms which fourth-century readers thought to be typically Socratic. The speaker is Clitophon, who is here assuming the character of Socrates. Further reading: Slings 1999: 1–4, 209–15; Guthrie 1978: 387–89; Rutherford 1995: 96–101; Rowe 2000: 303–7.

(407b) What is your hurry, you people? Don't you know how pointless your actions are? You do your utmost to acquire money, but as for your sons, to whom you are going to leave this money, you don't care whether they will know how to use it for moral purposes; you do not

---

7 One of the "Seven Sages," renowned for his wisdom; he is believed to have predicted a solar eclipse in 585 BC and is often considered to be the first philosopher.

find teachers of morality for them, if it really can be learned, or, if it can be acquired by training and exercise, people who can exercise and train them; nor in fact did you have yourselves taken care of in this way at any earlier time. (c) You see that you and your children have had an adequate education in letters (*grammata*), music (*mousiké*) and physical education (*gymnastiké*), which you believe to be a complete education in goodness (*areté*), and yet you prove to be just as bad in matters of money.

How is it then that you do not despise the current system of education (*paideusis*) and do not look for people to put an end to this lack of harmony? Yet it's because of this tunelessness and neglect, not because of the foot's discord with the lyre, that a brother behaves without measure and harmony towards a brother and cities towards cities; (d) they quarrel and fight, and they commit and suffer the worst acts. You claim that it isn't because of lack of education or ignorance that immoral people are immoral, but that they are like this deliberately; yet still you have the nerve to say that immorality is shameful and hateful to the gods. How, then, could anyone deliberately choose an evil like this? If he is overcome by pleasures, you say. Well, if overcoming them really is deliberate, being overcome by them is not deliberate? Either way the argument proves that acting immorally is not deliberate, (e) and that every man privately, and likewise all cities publicly, must take greater care over this than they do now.

4.20. Socrates and Plato

Diogenes Laertius, *Life of Plato* 3.5–6

Socrates' most famous associate was Plato. The following extract reflects an anecdotal tradition, widely known in antiquity, about the effect which Plato's first meeting with Socrates had on him. It is very doubtful that the details of this story are to be believed; like many anecdotes, this one instead expresses an essential rather than a literal truth. In this case, that essential truth is the decisive impact that Plato's initial encounter with Socrates had in changing the course of Plato's life. Yet the story that Plato wrote tragedies as a young man traces its origin to a relatively early source, Aristotle's student Dicaearchus. Further reading: Riginos 1976: 43–51; Guthrie 1969: 349–55.

(5) [Dicaearchus said that] Plato wrote poems – dithyrambs first of all, and then lyrics and tragedies. . . . But then, when he was about to compete with a tragedy, he listened to Socrates in front of the theatre of Dionysus, and then he burned his poems, saying: "Hephaestus,

come here; Plato now has need of you."[8] (6) It is said that from this time, when he was twenty years old, Plato listened to Socrates continuously.

4.21. Socrates and Aristippus

(a) Plutarch, *On the Education of Children* 4f, (b) Diogenes Laertius, *Life of Aristippus* 2.72

At least one of Socrates' followers departed from Socrates' firmly held principles by charging fees to his students. Although the evidence about Aristippus' fees varies from source to source, there is at any rate ancient consensus that he was a professional teacher. Aristippus (like Plato, apparently) was not with Socrates the day he died,[9] but he was clearly a close follower. Further reading: Guthrie 1969: 490–99; Field 1967: 159–60.

a

Aristippus . . . criticized a father who had no judgement or sense. When someone asked Aristippus how much he demanded as payment for teaching his son, he said, "A thousand drachmas." When the man said, "Good God, what an outrageous demand! I can buy a slave for a thousand!" Aristippus said, "Then you will have two slaves, your son and the one you buy."

b

When someone was criticizing Aristippus for taking money despite the fact that he was Socrates' student, he said, "Of course I do. When people used to send Socrates food and wine, he would take a little and send the rest back. He had the most important people in Athens as his providers, whereas I have Eutychides, whom I've bought with money."

8 An adaptation of Homer, *Iliad* 18.392.
9 See Plato, *Phaedo* 59b5–c6.

5

FOURTH-CENTURY THEORY AND PRACTICE

Isocrates, Plato, and Aristotle

The sophists of the fifth century offered a "higher education" to students who were willing to pay their fees. This education, which usually included the teaching of rhetoric, provided something practical and useful which the traditional curriculum of *mousiké*, *gymnastiké* and *grammata* largely overlooked. These sophists did not, however, establish formal schools in which to carry out their teaching.

The foundation of the first schools of higher education was instead left to three figures of the fourth century, Isocrates, Plato and Aristotle. Isocrates took the lead some time between 395 and 390 by setting up his school near the Lyceum, a gymnasium on the outskirts of Athens. His curriculum lasted as long as four years (Isocrates, *Antidosis* 87) and is said to have cost students 1,000 drachmas ([Plutarch], *Life of Isocrates* 837e). It is unlikely that he ever had more than about six students at one time, but over the course of his career these included some of the most prominent intellectual and political figures in the contemporary Greek world: the historians Theopompus and Ephorus, Nicocles the king of Cyprus, and the Athenian general Timotheus, to name a few. His teaching focused on the spoken and written word and had the practical aim of preparing men to participate in the politics and culture of their city through the exercise of persuasive speech. It is in two works in particular that we learn about Isocrates' educational principles and practices: the short, and possibly unfinished, treatise *Against the Sophists* (**5.1**), and the lengthy *Antidosis* (**5.6, 7**), composed about 40 years later, in 354. Since the *Antidosis* is essentially Isocrates' defence of his life's work, the speech in its entirety is of great importance for understanding both his place in fourth-century education and the character that education was to assume subsequently in the Greek and Roman worlds.

Plato's educational aims were very different from Isocrates', and these differences were the basis of the criticisms that the two directed against each other. Around 385 Plato established a school, the Academy (**5.15–16**), whose activities seem to have been carried out on a much more abstract level than those of Isocrates' school (**5.17–18, 20**; cf. **5.9**). Whereas Isocrates sought to prepare his students for political life as they found it in their contemporary world, Plato's goal was to raise the consciousness of his students beyond the material world, and even to change radically the political reality that they saw around them. In these aspirations education played a central role, and it is no surprise that in those of his works which display the heaviest political focus, the *Republic* and the *Laws*, we find his most explicit reflections on the topic of education (**5.8–14**). Plato was sensitive to the charge that philosophy did not provide a practical education for the real world (**5.19**); he was not, however, merely a theorist, but tried to influence events outside his corner of the world (see Plato, *Letter* 7.328c3–329b7). Some of Plato's most interesting thoughts on education involve his beliefs about the education that women should receive and the role that they should play in the upbringing of children (**5.10, 14**).

In comparing the beliefs, aims and methods of Isocrates and Plato, we can see that a basic source of contention was their difference of opinion over the status of rhetoric. The conflict between them has traditionally been characterized in terms of the age-old battle between rhetoric and philosophy – a contrast between, on the one hand, the practical, attainable goal of acquiring and imparting the means to win debates and adherents to one's expressed opinions, and, on the other, the contemplation of and argument over abstract, eternal truths which may well have little apparent connection to the everyday world around us. From a historical point of view it is convenient to see the conflict in this way, since the contributions of Isocrates and Plato to the western educational tradition reflect this dichotomy. Isocrates' teaching focused on the written word and the acquisition of verbal eloquence, and literature and letters have certainly been central to the western curriculum since antiquity. Plato's emphasis on the inquiry into unchanging realities has never lost its place in the western tradition, not only in the medieval *quadrivium* (**10.27**), but also in the role that mathematical study and philosophy continue to assume. But this dichotomy obscures the fact that other educators were playing prominent roles at the same time, and these people often opposed (and were opposed by) Isocrates, Plato and each other for separate reasons, such as the comparative values of the written and spoken word (**5.1–5**). The dichotomy is also overly simplistic since the terms "philosopher," "philosophy" and "sophist" were used in different senses by different writers. The first two were terms of commendation that one usually reserved for oneself and denied to others, while the third was frequently used as a weapon against one's opponents.

Plato's most talented and famous pupil was Aristotle. His interests ranged far wider than those of either Plato or Isocrates, but he too examined the role of education in the state and the shape that a good system should take. In addition to his comments on the way that children are schooled in other states besides Athens, he confronted such fundamental questions as the role of the law in education (**5.21**), whether a child's education should be provided by the family or the state (**5.22–23**), and the curriculum that ought to be followed (**5.24**). Aristotle established his school, the Lyceum, in Athens in 334 BC and led it until he left the city in 323, the year before he died. Most of his works which survive today, including the *Nicomachean Ethics* and the *Politics*, are products of this period; they are in fact lecture notes from the teaching he undertook in his school.

General background: Jaeger 1944: 46–155; Marrou 1956: 61–91; Wycherly 1961, 1962; Beck 1964: 253–89; Pfeiffer 1968: 57–84; Bowen 1972: 91–129; Muir 2005.

5.1. Isocrates on sophists and rhetoric

Isocrates, *Against the Sophists* 1–13

In *Against the Sophists* Isocrates provides a concise account of his own views on education by criticizing the practices of others. His specific targets are professional teachers of rhetoric; the object of his criticisms includes the exaggerated claims that these teachers make for their subject and their failure even to understand its true nature. The important section translated below raises some of the questions that Plato too would soon be dealing with, in particular the problem of whether rhetoric was – or could reach the level of – a rational skill (*techné*) with its own set of rules (see **5.2**). Further reading: Bowen 1972: 93–94; Lynch 1972: 51–54; Poulakos 1997: 93–104.

(1) If all who undertake to teach were willing to tell the truth and not to promise more than they could fulfil, the general public would not have such a low opinion of them. As it is, those who are bold enough to make extravagant claims so carelessly have made it appear that people who choose to do little have a better plan than people who are engaged in philosophy. Who, in the first place, would not hate and despise people engaged in quarrels who pretend to be seeking the truth but set out to tell lies at the very beginning of their lessons? (2) It is clear to everyone, I think, that it is not in our nature to know the future beforehand; so far are we from this intelligence that Homer . . . has depicted even the gods as sometimes deliberating about this – not because he knew their thoughts but because he wanted to show us that this is one of the things that human beings are incapable of.

(3) These people, then, have become so bold that they try to persuade the young that if they study with them they will know what they have to do and through this knowledge will become prosperous. Once they have set themselves up as teachers and masters of such blessings, they are not ashamed of charging three or four minas for them. (4) If they were selling any other property for a tiny fraction of its value, they would not dispute that they are wrongheaded; yet,

although they place such small value on goodness (*areté*) and prosperity, they claim that they are intelligent teachers of other people. They say that they have no need of money, calling wealth "small silver" and "small gold," yet in striving for a little profit they all but promise to make their students immortal.

(5) But what is most ridiculous of all is that, while they distrust the very people they have to receive their payment from, the ones to whom they intend to impart justice, they deposit the money from their students with people whom they have never taught. In this they take careful thought over their security, but they are doing the opposite of their lessons. (6) For in the case of those who teach some other subject it is appropriate to be exact about debatable points, since there is nothing to prevent those who have become skilled in other matters from being dishonest in dealing with contracts. But it is surely irrational for those who produce virtue and good sense in their students not to trust them above all. To be sure, those who are upstanding and just in their dealings with others will not go wrong in their business with those who have made them the kind of men they are.[1]

(7) Whenever laymen take all these things into account and realize that those who teach wisdom and impart prosperity are themselves in great need and earn little from their students; that they take care over contradictions in words but have no regard over contradictions in actions; furthermore, that they pretend to know about the future (8) but are unable to speak or offer advice about what is called for at the present moment; that those who rely on opinions (*doxai*) are in greater agreement and are more successful than those who claim to have knowledge (*epistemé*) – it is, I think, reasonable for them to despise these people and to believe that occupations such as these are mere chatter and pettiness, and are not cultivation of the soul.

(9) Criticism should be directed not only at the sophists I have just mentioned but also at those who profess to teach the art of making political speeches. These men have no regard for the truth. In their view their craft reposes on the ability to attract the largest number of students by the modest amount of their fees and their vast promises, and on the ability to make a penny or two from these pupils. They themselves are so lacking in common sense ... that although they compose speeches inferior to those which some laymen deliver off the cuff, they nonetheless guarantee to make those who study with them such effective speakers as will not omit any possible argument in the conduct of their affairs. (10) They allow none of the credit for this ability to be attributed to the experience or natural ability of the

---

1 Plato makes the same point in *Gorgias* 519c3–d5 that Isocrates does in this paragraph.

student. On the contrary, they claim to transmit the knowledge of speech-making in exactly the same manner as one would the knowledge of letters. They do so without investigating the intrinsic nature of either of the two branches of learning, in the conviction that because of their extravagant promises they themselves will become objects of admiration, while an education in rhetoric will appear more valuable. They are quite unaware that those who make the arts great are those men who have the ability to convey the capacity of each art, not those who have the nerve to make false pretensions.

(11) For my part, I should have given a small fortune to see philosophy have the influence these men claim it has, since possibly I would not have been left miles behind nor would have benefited so little from it. However, since such is not the case, I would like to put an end to the nonsense they talk; for I observe that abuse falls not only on those who have made this mistaken assumption, but on all the others too who are involved in this aberrant claim.

(12) I am simply astonished whenever I see men judge these people to be suitable teachers for students. They are unaware that they are using an art with a clearly defined set of rules as an analogy for a creative process. Everyone except these sophists knows that the science of letters is fixed and immutable. Consequently, we constantly use the same conjunction of letters to designate the same objects. On the other hand, rhetoric displays quite the opposite characteristic. The words spoken by one speaker cannot be used with similar effect by the speaker who follows him. On the contrary, the speaker who is thought to display the greatest skill is the one who can match his words to his topic and has the ability to discover issues which others have not raised. (13) The most convincing evidence of the distinction between these arts is this: while a speech can only be considered good if it is appropriate to the occasion and reveals a measure of novelty and propriety, in the case of letters there is no need for any of these qualities. It would be a much more just world if those who made use of such analogies paid rather than accepted money, since they are attempting to educate others when their own education calls for a great deal of further care.

5.2. Plato on rhetoric

(a) Plato, *Gorgias* 463a6–b6, (b) *Phaedrus* 270b1–10, (c) *Laws* 937e3–938a4

The following passages span about forty years in Plato's philosophical career. Extract **a** reflects his low view of rhetoric around the time that he opened the Academy, about 385 (**5.15**); **b** was written around 370; **c** is from Plato's last work, the *Laws*, which he left unrevised at his death in 347. In **b** and **c** Plato considers the possibility, at least, that rhetoric may achieve the status of a rational skill (*techné*) rather than a mere "knack" (*tribé*) or "routine" (*empeiria*). Further reading: Jaeger 1944: 182–96.

a

In my opinion, Gorgias, there is a pursuit which is not scientific, but which requires a mind that is intuitive, bold, and naturally skilled in dealing with people. Taken as a whole, I call it flattery. There are, I believe, many parts to this practice, and one of them is pastry-baking. This part appears to be a science, but by my account it is a routine and a knack, not a science. I call rhetoric a part of it, too, and so are adornment and sophistry.

b

SOCRATES: The same method applies to medicine, I suppose, as applies to rhetoric.
PHAEDRUS: What exactly do you mean?
SOCRATES: In both cases you have to determine a nature – of a body in the one case, of a soul in the other – if it is through science, and not merely through a knack and a routine, that you are going to promote health and strength in the body by applying medicines and food, and transmit virtue and whatever conviction you wish by applying words and customary practices to the soul.

c

Although both of these [i.e. justice and advocacy] are noble, they are given a bad name by a kind of corrupt practice which has disguised itself with the respectable name of "science." It claims, first, that a technique for lawsuits exists – namely, itself – both for conducting one's own suits and acting as another's advocate, which is able to win the day regardless of whether in each individual case the people involved acted rightly or wrongly; and it claims that the science itself and the speeches that derive from this science are a gift, provided one pays money in return for it. Now, it is strictly forbidden that this ability [i.e. rhetoric] be allowed to grow in our city, whether it is in fact a science or an unscientific routine and knack.

5.3. Written vs extemporized speeches

Alcidamas, *On those who Compose Written Speeches, or on Sophists* 1–2, 9–10, 15–16

Writing early in the fourth century, the rhetorician and teacher Alcidamas exalted the spoken word over the written. More specifically, he argued for the primacy of extemporized speeches over those which have been worked up in writing. The target of Alcidamas' attacks in these passages is clearly Isocrates, who began his career as a professional speechwriter (*logographos*) but abandoned this occupation in order to open his school and teach his students what he knew. Alcidamas uses the term "sophist" against Isocrates; contrast **5.1** (9, 12). Further reading: Milne 1924: 21–53; Kennedy 1963: 172–73; Pfeiffer 1968: 50–51; Thomas 1992: 123–27; Dillon and Gergel 2003: 283–309.

(1) Some of the so-called sophists have neglected research and education and are no more familiar with speaking ability than laymen are, but are puffed up and proud of themselves because they are trained in writing speeches and display their wisdom through books. They also lay claim to a command over the whole art of rhetoric even though they have acquired only a tiny part of it. For this reason I shall attempt to present a critique of written speeches, (2) not because I consider their ability superior to my own, but because I take greater pride in other accomplishments and think that writing ought to be incidental to a training in speaking. I also believe that those who waste their lives on this very pursuit have fallen far short in rhetoric and philosophy, and I think that it is much more justifiable that they be called poets than sophists. . . .

(9) I believe that in people's lives, speaking is always and in every circumstance a useful thing, whereas the ability to write is seldom appropriate to the occasion. Who does not know that to speak *ex tempore* is a necessary skill for people who are involved in public affairs and in legal trials, and who are creating personal relationships? Frequently and unexpectedly there occur opportune moments in which those who keep silent will seem contemptible, whereas we see those who can speak being honoured by everyone else because they possess a godlike judgement. (10) For whenever we must criticize wrongdoers, console the unfortunate, calm the angry, or do away with accusations that have suddenly been brought against someone, the ability to speak can then assist people in their need; but writing requires leisure and involves periods of time that are too long for the critical moments (*kairoi*)[2] that occur. For these moments demand

2 For *kairos* (pl. *kairoi*), see introduction to **5.7**.

swift assistance for the contests at any given time, but writing completes its speeches in a leisurely and slow manner. What sensible person, then, would admire this ability, which is so deficient at critical moments (*kairoi*)? . . .

(15) It is a strange thing if the person who claims to have something to say about philosophy and who promises to teach others, provided he has a writing-tablet or a book-roll, is able to demonstrate his own wisdom, but if he doesn't have these tools, turns out no better than the uneducated; strange, too, if he is able to produce a speech when given the time but is more tongue-tied than laymen over a subject that is proposed to him on the spur of the moment, and if he advertises manuals for speeches but is shown to have not even the slightest capacity in himself for speaking.

5.4. Counterfeit wisdom

Xenophon, *On Hunting* 13.1–9

In the following extract, Xenophon reproaches the sophists for reasons that Plato also emphasized – for example, their mercenary ways, their disregard for the truth, and their claim to teach goodness (*areté*). This is Xenophon's clearest and most sustained critique of the sophists. Further reading: Gray 1985: 158–63; de Romilly 1992: 27; Waterfield 2004: 83–84.

(1) I am astonished at those who go by the name of sophists, because the majority claim to lead the young on a path towards goodness (*areté*), whereas they lead them in the opposite direction. Nowhere have we seen a man whose goodness resulted from the teachings of the sophists of today, and they have produced no body of literature which encourages men to become good. (2) Instead, a large part of their written work focuses on trivialities which result in the young developing empty pleasures but no goodness. These works are a complete waste of time for those who hope to learn something from them, they keep them away from other works which are useful, and the lessons they teach are evil. (3) Although I reserve my more severe criticism for the sophists' major faults, in the case of their writings I criticize them because, while they have conducted a search for the right words, they have failed to search for intellectual propositions which are correct and which might give younger men an education which leads them towards goodness.

(4) While I am no expert, I do know that the best thing is to be taught what is good by one's natural intuition, and that the second-best thing is to be taught it by those who have a genuine understanding

of something good rather than by those skilled in deception.[3] (5) It may be that I do not express myself in the complicated language of the sophists. Indeed, I am not even attempting to do that, but I am attempting to express ideas which have been properly developed and which well-educated people will need to attain goodness. It is not on words, but on ideas, that an education could be based if they are correct. (6) The sophists of today are not philosophers, and I am not the only one to criticize them for displaying their cleverness with words and not with ideas.

I fully recognize that perhaps a member of their school will claim that something which has been written well and in a logical manner has not in fact been written well and logically. After all, they will find it easy to produce invalid critical comments at a moment's notice. (7) And yet I have written this work as I have in order that it may be correct and produce men who are wise and good, not sophists. It is my wish that my work be useful, rather than seem to be so, in order that it may be beyond refutation for all time. (8) The sophists confer benefit on nobody, because the purpose of their spoken word is deception and their own profit is the objective of what they write. Wisdom never has been, nor is today, a characteristic of any of them, but each is content to be called a sophist, although sensible men use this as a term of abuse. (9) Consequently, my advice is to be on your guard against what the sophists recommend and not to treat the arguments of the philosophers with contempt. The sophists are on the prowl for those who are young and wealthy, whereas the philosophers are the friends of everyone and accessible to all. They do not overvalue or treat with scorn the station men hold in society.

5.5. Aristotle on sophists and rhetoric

Aristotle, *Nicomachean Ethics* 10.1180b32–1181a6, 1181a12–23

Aristotle's criticisms of the sophists resemble those of Isocrates and Plato: they do not know their subject, they are unable to teach, and they make false claims that they can teach political skill.

In all the other sciences the same people – such as doctors and painters – are seen passing on their skills to others and putting these skills to work, but while the sophists profess to teach political skill, none of them practises it; it is done by the politicians, and they would seem to do it by some skill and experience rather than by reason. For we do

---

3 Hesiod makes a very similar remark in **1.3**.

not see them writing or speaking about such subjects (though this would perhaps be a better thing than writing speeches for the law courts or public assemblies), nor again do we see them making politicians of their own sons or of anyone else close to them. . . . The sophists who profess to teach political skill seem to be very far from doing so, since they are completely ignorant of what it is or what it deals with; otherwise they would not equate it with rhetoric, or even lower.

5.6. Isocrates' educational principles

Isocrates, *Antidosis* 261–71, 274–78

Unlike those who wrote handbooks (*technai*) on the subject, Isocrates did not believe that rhetoric could be reduced to precise rules. The method of teaching which he followed was probably that of imitation, whereby students used his own written speeches as examples to be emulated. The following extract from Isocrates' lengthy *Antidosis* was composed in 354, when he was 82; it deals with most of the themes that he had confronted more briefly many years earlier in *Against the Sophists* (**5.1**) and may be treated as complementary to that work. But it is the *Antidosis* that remains the basic source of information for Isocrates' educational principles. His comments early in this extract on "astronomy, geometry and other similar branches of learning" must be a reference to the subjects that students were taught in Plato's school (cf. **5.20**). Moreover, Isocrates' definition of "philosopher" and "philosophy" (270–71) is a direct strike at Plato, who, unlike Isocrates, had as his educational ideal the attainment of secure, unshakable knowledge (*epistemé*) rather than mere opinion or conjecture (*doxa*) (**5.2**). The discussion here about the role in education of subjects such as astronomy and geometry represents one of the earliest statements on the much-debated question of the relationship between the liberal arts on the one hand and philosophy and rhetoric on the other (see further **5.8–9, 9.2–5, 10.3, 7, 27–28**). Further reading: Jaeger 1944: 46–155; Marrou 1956: 87–91; Johnson 1959; Kennedy 1963: 177–79; Too 1995: 179–94; Nightingale 2001: 177–79; Muir 2005.

(261) I believe that those who hold sway in the field of argumentative discourse and those who devote their time to astronomy, geometry and other similar branches of learning do not do any harm to their students, but have some beneficial effect on them. It may be less than they promise, but it is greater than others think. (262) Most people suppose that such studies are but opportunities for useless chatter and nit-picking. They believe that there is nothing there of use for public or private life and that nothing even sticks in the student's mind for any length of time; for these forms of learning do not constitute an

integral part of our normal experiences and needs in life, so they say, but are completely removed from our real necessities. (263) Although I do not hold this view, at the same time, however, neither is my position on the issue so far from it. I believe that those who think that this form of education is of no practical utility for our regular activities are right. Yet, on the other hand, I think that those who hold it in high regard are also speaking the truth. The reason for my having expressed a view which is intrinsically inconsistent is that these branches of learning are by their very nature different from the others we are taught.

(264) The essential nature of the others is such that we receive immediate benefit at the moment when we have acquired the knowledge; in the case of the studies in question, however, no benefit would be conferred on those who have achieved a high degree of proficiency in them, except for those who have chosen to make a living from them. The only benefit comes as students are actually in the process of learning. (265) This is because they spend their time on the precision and elaborate terminology of astronomy and geometry and are forced to focus their minds on topics which are difficult to grasp; they become accustomed to speak about them, to devote their energies to what is said and shown to them, and to keep their attention sharply focused. As a result, because their minds have been exercised and sharpened by these studies, they develop a greater capacity to grasp and learn quickly and without difficulty matters which are of greater importance and deserve more serious attention.

(266) I do not believe that we should use the term "philosophy" to embrace a form of learning which confers no benefit on us in our present circumstances when we are called upon to speak or act. I call this type of study a mental exercise, which prepares the mind for philosophy. It is a form of exercise more appropriate for a grown man, and so above that which children perform at school, although in most respects it is similar. (267) When children devote their efforts to learning letters, music and the rest of their curriculum, there is no improvement as yet in their ability to speak or deliberate on issues. What is improved is their capacity to grasp more important and more serious branches of learning. (268) Consequently, I would advise the young to spend some time on these aspects of education, but not to allow their natural aptitudes to be reduced to skin and bone by these studies, nor to run aground on the arguments of the ancient sophists.[4] One of them claimed that the number of primary elements is infinite,

---

4 Isocrates here applies the term "sophists" to pre-Socratic philosophers.

Empedocles that there are four of them, with love and conflict inter-acting with them, Ion that there are not more than three, Alcmaeon that there are only two, Parmenides and Melissus that there is one, and Gorgias that there is none at all. (269) In my view, such elaborate arguments are just like a juggler's act: they do nobody any good, but attract a large crowd of witless folk. Those who wish to do something of value must remove from the number of their pursuits pointless discussions and activities which contribute nothing to our lives.

(270) On this topic the words I have spoken and the advice I have given must suffice. In the case of wisdom and philosophy it would be inappropriate to discuss these terms, if our lawsuit was over any other issue; the terms have simply no relevance in a court of law. Since, however, this is the very issue on which I have been brought to trial, and since I assert that what some men call philosophy is not really philosophy at all, it is entirely appropriate for me to define and reveal to you what it is, when seen in the right light. (271) My judgement of the matter is really very simple. It is beyond the natural capacity of mankind to acquire a form of knowledge which would enable us to know what to do or say, once it is in our possession. Of the remaining alternatives available to us, I believe that a man is wise if he can, for the most part, hit upon the best course of action by his powers of conjecture. In my opinion philosophers are those who spend their time studying those matters which will enable them to acquire such wisdom in the shortest time possible. . . .

(274) In my opinion, the sort of skill which can produce qualities of goodness (*areté*) and justice in those who are ill-formed by nature has never existed nor does it exist today. I am convinced that those who offer guarantees that they have the ability to do so will collapse from exhaustion and stop talking their nonsense (275) before any such form of education is discovered. Yet I do think that men could improve themselves and be more useful to the community by setting themselves the objective of being able to speak well, by desiring to be able to convince their audience, and, finally, by setting their sights on what is to their own advantage. By advantage I mean not the traditional view of fools, but something which genuinely reflects the meaning of the word. (276) And I trust that I shall soon be able to make you aware of its nature.

First of all, if a man makes a conscious choice to write and deliver speeches which merit praise and honour, he cannot choose as the subject of his discourse issues which are seen as unjust, trivial, or involving a private contract, but rather those which are important, honourable, of benefit to mankind in general and involving public concerns. If he can't find any issues of that nature, he will fulfil none of the things he needs to achieve in order to meet his goal. (277)

Second, from the actions which are relevant to his topic he will select those which are most seemly and advantageous. If a man develops the habit of spending time contemplating and applying his critical standards to such actions, he will have the same capacity in all the other things he does and not just in connection with the discourse in hand. Consequently, those who assume a philosophical approach and concern to achieve distinction when they make a speech will find themselves able to speak and think effectively.

(278) Moreover, if a man wishes to exert powers of persuasion over others, he will not forget about goodness (*areté*). On the contrary, he will purposely focus almost his entire attention upon securing as solid a reputation for fairness as he can among the members of his community. All are aware that words spoken by men of unimpeachable reputation have a more genuine ring of truth than those spoken by men who are the targets of criticism. They know that guarantees based on the manner of a man's life are worth more than those afforded by what he says. As a result, the stronger the desire to persuade one's listeners, the greater the effort one will make to be a man of honour and to enjoy a good reputation in the community.

5.7. A sound mind in a sound body

Isocrates, *Antidosis* 183–85

Isocrates' purpose in comparing physical and intellectual training is to press his point that the aim of the latter – especially rhetorical training – is not "exact knowledge" (*epistemé*) but rather "judgement" or "opinion" (*doxa*). Just as the athlete must be able to respond to the demands of the moment rather than to an abstract ideal, so the speaker must be able to assess his audience and make his words suit their disposition as well as the immediate circumstances (*kairos*, plural *kairoi*; cf. **5.3** [10]).[5] Further reading: Johnson 1959: 26–29; Too 1995: 179–84; Sharples 1985: 10–11.

(183) When *paidotribai* take on students, they instruct those who attend their classes in the positions developed for physical competition, while those involved in philosophy review for their pupils all the forms employed in discourse. (184) Once they have acquainted them with these matters and brought their knowledge of them to a state of

---

5 Cf. Isocrates, *Panathenaecus* 30: "Whom then do I call educated men? First, those who do a good job of handling the circumstances which confront them each and every day, and who exercise a judgement (*doxa*) which exactly matches the circumstances of any given moment (*kairoi*) and which on most occasions demonstrates a capacity to focus on what is beneficial."

perfection, they give them exercises to do and see that they become accustomed to hard work. They force them to link together in practice the various lessons they have learned in order to ensure that they have a firmer command of them and can use their judgement to determine with greater precision what a certain situation requires (*kairoi*). It is impossible to embrace all the various situations within the realm of knowledge, since in all areas of endeavour they simply cannot be known. But those who have the greatest capacity to concentrate their attention on these situations and can for the most part form conclusions about the likely consequences most frequently handle them successfully.

(185) In this manner both sets of teachers provide their attention and training. They can encourage their students' development until they have improved and reached a higher level of intellectual conditioning on the one hand and of physical conditioning on the other. Neither, however, possesses such a form of knowledge that they have the capacity to turn anyone they wish into an athlete or a competent speaker. They may make a contribution, but in general it is those who are provided with a combination of a superior natural aptitude and superior training who achieve these abilities.

5.8. Education in Plato's ideal state (I)

Plato, *Republic* 376d–377e

A substantial part of Plato's *Republic* is occupied with a discussion of the education that the prospective rulers ("guardians") of his ideal state should receive. Plato describes two phases of the curriculum in two separate parts of this work. The first phase, comprising 376d–412b, is the future ruler's early education, and like education in Plato's contemporary Greek world it places a heavy emphasis on Homer's poems. Hence in this part of the *Republic* Plato spends a considerable amount of his time discussing the role of poetry in education. In Plato's curriculum the purpose behind the study of Homer, and of poetry in general, is to present students with models of virtuous behaviour for them to emulate (cf. **3.15** [326a]; also **8.30** [4–9]). Later in the *Republic*, however, Plato will reject any role for Homer in the curriculum on the metaphysical grounds that poetry, as an imitation of our own world, is two removes from reality and is therefore an obstacle to our attaining a clear apprehension of truth. In stressing the importance of the training of both mind and body in the early phase of education, Plato's system reflects standard practice in the contemporary Greek world. The following selection represents only a short part of Plato's explanation of the guardians' primary education; study of the full discussion in *Republic* 376d–412b is therefore strongly recommended. Socrates is the interrogator here and in **5.9**. Further reading: Lodge 1947: 60–87; Marrou 1956: 69–72; Bowen 1972: 104–8; Annas 1981: 79–101; Scolnicov 1988: 112–19; Ferrari 1989: 104–8; Schofield 2000: 214–17.

(376d) "Come then, let us provide the men an education through our discussion, as if we had ample time on our hands and were spinning mythological tales." "Yes, we must."

(e) "What form is this education to take? Or is it difficult to find an improvement on the one which has been devised over the long passage of time, which has gymnastics for the body, and music for the soul?" "That is the case."

"Shall we not, then, start the education in music before that in gymnastics?" "Of course."

"And you include stories under the heading of music, or do you not?" "Yes, I do."

"And stories are divided into two categories, one true and the other false?" "Correct."

(377a) "And education must include both categories, but it must be provided first in those stories which are false?" "I don't understand what you mean," he said.

"Do you not understand," I replied, "that the first thing we do with children is to tell them myths? That, taken as a whole, is the use of falsehood, in spite of the fact that there are aspects which are true. And we employ myths with our children before we do gymnastics." "That is the case."

"That was what I was meaning when I said that we must engage with music before gymnastics." "You were right," he said.

"Are you not aware that the first step is the most important stage in any action, especially with anyone who is young and tender? (b) For that stage is the easiest at which to give each person shape and for him to assume the form one wishes to impress upon him." "Absolutely true."

"Shall we then, without giving it any thought, allow our children to listen to any old myth they come across, fabricated by any old teller of tales, and to absorb into their souls beliefs which are, for the most part, the opposite of those we will think they should hold when they have come to maturity?" "In no way will we allow that."

(c) "Then, it would appear that we must first pay careful attention to those who compose myths and approve any myth they create which is of high quality, while rejecting any which is not. We will convince nurses and mothers to tell their children the myths on the approved list and to use the myths to shape their souls with greater care than they use their hands to shape their bodies. However, we must reject most of those told today." "What sort of myths?" he asked.

"The more important myths," I replied, "will give us a good view of the minor ones, since the major and the minor myths must conform to the same basic form and have the same impact. Or do you not agree?" (d) "Oh, I think so too," he said, "but I have no clear understanding of the more important myths you are referring to."

"The myths told by Hesiod, Homer and the other poets," said I. "These are the men who would tell, and still tell, the false myths they constructed." "What sort of myths do you mean?" he asked. "And what aspect of them are you criticizing?"

"That aspect," I replied, "which must be the first and most emphatic target of our criticism, especially if the falsehood told is unedifying." "What do you mean?"

(e) "Whenever someone's tale gives a poor representation of the essential nature of gods and heroes, just like a painter whose painting utterly fails to capture the image of whatever he wishes to portray."

"Yes, we are right to criticize examples like that," he said. "But what do we mean and which aspects are we talking about?" [Socrates goes on to explain the kinds of myths which children should not be told, quoting many examples from Homer, and he makes the case for the value of education in *mousiké* and physical education.]

5.9. Education in Plato's ideal state (II)

Plato, *Republic* 521c–522c, 525a–d

The second stage of the educational curriculum in Plato's ideal society is purely intellectual and is designed to prepare the guardians for their role as leaders in this state. This preparation is achieved by training the guardians to turn their minds away from the present world – the world of change or "becoming" – towards the world of unchanging reality, the contemplation of which produces real knowledge. The studies which enable the guardians to grasp reality and which they are to follow (to the age of 35) are arithmetic, plane geometry, solid geometry, astronomy and musical theory, leading ultimately to the study of dialectic. They are set out over a long passage (521c–532b) which deserves to be read in its entirety. Plato's views on the kind of education the guardians must receive did not change significantly over the course of his life. At the end of his last work, the *Laws*, he summarizes the curriculum to be undertaken by those responsible for the operation of his hypothetical Cretan state, which he calls Magnesia (*Laws* 989d–992a, not included here); their course of studies is essentially the one that he prescribes in the *Republic*. Further reading: Lodge 1947: 85–113; Marrou 1956: 73–77; Bowen 1972: 104–8; Guthrie 1975: 526ff.; Annas 1981: 272–93; Mueller 1997: 271–89.

(521c) "Would you like us, then, to consider how we will produce men of this nature and lead them up to the light in the same way that, so the story goes, some people made the ascent from Hades to the gods?" "Of course, I would," he replied.

"This is an issue, it would appear, which would not be the spinning of a potsherd,[6] but would involve turning the soul round from a sort of day shrouded in darkness and bringing it to one with genuine daylight, that is, the journey upwards to reality, which we will define as a genuine love of wisdom." "No doubt about that."

(d) "Must we not, then, consider which branches of learning have the power to bring this about?" "Naturally."

"Well then, Glaucon, what form of learning could serve as the mechanism to haul the soul from the phase of creation to the final reality? . . . Did we not argue that these men at a very early age must be practised in warfare?" "We did indeed."

"Then this form of learning we are looking for must be a supplement to that." "What sort of thing do you mean?"

"That it must be something which is not without benefit to fighting men." "Of course, it must, if that is possible," he said.

"Earlier we were providing an education in gymnastics and music." "That was so," he said.

(e) "And gymnastics is well-adapted to development and decline; it controls the growth and decline of the body." "Clearly."

"That, then, would not be the form of learning we are searching for." (522a) "No."

"Well then, is it music, in terms of the description we gave of it earlier?"

"But, if you remember," he replied, "that served as the complement to gymnastics, in that it uses habits to educate our guardians; it transmits not knowledge but a well-tempered disposition in terms of harmony, and a well-measured grace in terms of rhythm; and it contains some other characteristics akin to these qualities in those tales which are mythical and those which come closer to the truth. But it entailed no form of learning which produces the sort of effect you are now searching for."

(b) "Your reminder is right on the mark," said I. "The reality is that it did not involve anything of that nature. But, Glaucon, good fellow that you are, what would have this capacity? We felt that all the crafts were mechanical."

6 Like flipping a coin for heads or tails.

"Of course we did. Moreover, what other form of knowledge is left which is unrelated to music, gymnastics and the crafts?"

"Come now," said I, "on the assumption that we cannot find anything else which is independent of these, let us find something which is a common denominator to them all." "What sort of thing?"

(c) "For example, that common denominator employed by all crafts, all faculties of thought and all forms of knowledge, one of the first things everyone must learn." "And that is?"

"This everyday matter of knowing the difference between one, two and three," I replied. "To put it in a nutshell, I am talking about number and computation. . . . (525a) "To take this a step further, the entire field of computation and arithmetic is focused on number." "Certainly."

"And these things provide guidance on the path to truth." "Absolutely."

(b) "Then it would appear that they are among the branches of learning for which we are searching. A grasp of them is indispensable, not only for a fighting man to deal with his formations for battle, but also for a philosopher as he emerges from the stage of being born on the upward journey he must make to reach the final reality. The alternative is to be without computational skills for ever." "You are right," said he.

"And it so happens that our guardian is both a fighting man and a philosopher." "Yes."

"Then, the appropriate course would be to draw up a law prescribing this branch of learning and to convince those who are going to participate in the most important affairs of our city to embark on the study of computation (c) and not to engage in it as amateurs, but to proceed to the point when their very intellect has reached the stage at which it can contemplate the nature of numbers. Their goal in engaging in this practice is not the purchase and sale of goods as if they were merchants or involved in retail trade, but for warfare and to enable the soul itself to make an easy transition from the developmental phase to truth and final reality." "You have put the case very well," he said.

"And, what is more," said I, "now that I have spoken about the branch of learning dealing with computation, (d) it occurs to me that it is a subtle practice which benefits us in a multitude of ways, provided that we engage in it in order to gain knowledge and not to peddle wares." [From this point until 532b Socrates explains the role that geometry, astronomy and music also have in the education of the "guardians" and in the learning of dialectic.]

5.10. The education of women in Plato's ideal state

Plato, *Republic* 451c–452b, 456d–457b

In the *Republic*, Plato prescribed an upbringing and an education for women who would take their place in the ideal state. An important question is the degree to which he was influenced by educational conditions for women in Sparta at this time (around 375), since we know that in other respects he was a keen observer of Spartan society. Socrates is the main speaker in this selection; his respondent is Glaucon. The views expressed here reflect Plato's beliefs, not those of the historical Socrates. Further reading: Pomeroy 1975: 115–19; Annas 1981: 181–85.

(451c) "In my opinion there is only one correct way for men who have been born and trained as we have described to possess and treat women and children. That is for them to proceed in keeping with the guiding principle we set at the beginning. In our discussion we tried, I believe, to make men similar to guardians of a flock." "We did."

(d) "Let us then follow this principle and provide women with a birth and training which parallels theirs. Then we can consider whether it is appropriate or not." "What do you mean?" he asked.

"Just this. Do we expect the female watch-dogs to have a duty to participate in guarding whatever the males guard? Do we expect them to join in the hunt and to share all their other activities? Or do we expect that they should stay at home on the grounds that they are incapable of other things because of their role in the birth and raising of pups, while the work and all the care involved in looking after the flocks fall to the males?"

"They will share everything," he replied, "except that our treatment takes into account the inferior strength of the females and the superior strength of the males."

(e) "Well then," I asked, "is it possible to use any creature for the same purpose as others without providing it with the same upbringing and training?" "No, it is impossible."

"So, if we intend to use men and women for the same ends, we must also provide women with an identical education." (452a) "Yes, we must."

"We gave men an education in the arts and gymnastics." "We did."

"Then women too will have to be provided with skills in these two areas. We must train them for war and treat them in exactly the same way as men." "That is the logical conclusion from your argument," he said.

"Many of our proposals are out of keeping with present practice," I said. "Perhaps they would appear ridiculous if they were carried out as suggested." "They would, indeed," he replied.

"What do you consider to be their most ludicrous feature?" I asked. "Is it not clear that you will see women exercising naked in the *palaistra* along with men? It will not be just the young ones you will see, (b) but those who are already rather old. They will be just like the old men in the gymnasia who are dedicated to exercise despite the fact that they are wrinkled and unpleasant to look at."

"Good Lord!" he replied, "that would appear ridiculous. At least it would by the standards of today." . . . .

(456d) "In the state we were founding, then, which men do you think will turn out better for us, the guardians who have received the type of education we described or the cobblers who have been trained in the art of shoemaking?" "What a silly question!" he replied.

"I quite understand," said I. "Of course, the guardians will be the best of all the citizens. Is that not so?" "Yes, by far."

(e) "And, of course, these women will be the best of the females. Do you not agree?" "That is also true. The best by far."

"Is there anything better for a state than the development of men and women of the best quality?" "No."

"This will be the result of the availability of an education in the arts and gymnastics, (457a) as we described?" "It will indeed."

"So we established an institution which is not only possible, but best for the state." "That is so."

"Since their excellent qualities will be what covers them, not clothes, our women guardians must strip down and play their part in war and all the responsibilities involved in the guardianship of the community. This must be the only thing they do. Because of the weakness of their sex we must assign the lighter duties to the women rather than the men. (b) But if any man laughs at the sight of naked women taking exercise for the best of reasons . . . he is, it seems, unaware what he is laughing at or what it is he's doing."

5.11. Education, the emotions, and the role of song and dance

Plato, *Laws* 653a5–c4, 654a6–b7

The *Laws* – Plato's final and longest work – is a dialogue between an unnamed Athenian (the main speaker below), a Cretan (Clinias, the Athenian's respondent in our extracts), and a Spartan (Megillus). Early in its second book, Plato offers a general definition of education in terms of a person's responses to pleasures, pains, and other irrational factors. He then

107

proposes that music and dance can condition these responses in such a way as to create a harmonious state in the soul (Anderson 1966: 64–110). This discussion of music's place in education continues as far as *Laws* 673d9 (Plato had presented his views on the topic earlier as well, in *Republic* 398b6–401e1). Further reading: Marrou 1956: 138–41; Morrow 1993: 297–318; Jaeger 1944: 213–62; Ferrari 1989: 104–8.

> (653a) It is my assertion that the first sensations that children experience are pleasure and pain, and that it is through these that goodness (*areté*) and vice (*kakia*) first develop in the soul. It is, however, a matter of good fortune if wisdom and true, unshakable opinions (*doxai*) develop in a person, even at an advanced age; at any rate, a man who possesses these qualities, as well as all the good things they entail, is perfect. (b) It is my assertion, then, that education (*paideia*) is that form of goodness (*areté*) which first develops in children. In fact, if feelings of pleasure, love, pain and hatred occur in their souls in the appropriate circumstances before they are capable of reasoning, and if, when they have acquired reason, these emotions are in harmony with reason as a result of correct training in appropriate habits, then this harmony, taken altogether, is goodness (*areté*). But correct upbringing in regard to pleasures and pains, (c) which produces hatred of what we ought to hate from start to finish, and love of what we ought to love – if you isolate this very thing in your account and call it "education," in my opinion you would be giving it the right name. . . .
>
> (654a) Are we then to begin by accepting this and to agree that our earliest education is the product of the Muses and Apollo? – Yes.
>
> Then, must we not postulate that the uneducated man will have no training in choral activities, (b) while the educated man will have adequate experience in them? – Absolutely.
>
> And choral activity as a whole includes both singing and dancing? – Inevitably.
>
> Then somebody who is well-educated would have the ability to sing and dance well? – So it would appear.

5.12. Children belong to the state

Plato, *Laws* 804c2–d6

It is Plato's view in the *Laws* that education should be compulsory because children belong to the state rather than to their parents (similarly Aristotle: **2.5**). The following passage immediately precedes the one in **5.14**, which presents Plato's opinion that education should be compulsory for girls as well as for boys. The Athenian (see **5.11**) is the speaker. Further reading: Lacey 1968: 189–90; Harris 1989: 100–101.

(c) Let us take up the next point. We have specified the buildings for public gymnasia and schools in three sites at the centre of the city. In three areas outside the city in its vicinity we have also described training grounds for horses and open spaces set up for archery and other forms of target-practice where the young can be trained and can practise. Assuming that we did not deal adequately with these issues earlier, I think we should discuss them now and provide detailed regulations. In all these places teachers for each subject who have been hired abroad must be in residence (d) and must provide their pupils with instruction in all the lessons related to war and the arts. It must not be at a father's discretion whether a child attends school or stays away from education, but every man and child ... must be compelled ... to receive an education, since they all belong to the state more than they do to their parents.

5.13. Legal enforcement

Plato, *Laws* 810a2–b4

This extract emphasizes the compulsory nature of education in Plato's state (cf. *Laws* 789d7–790b6). The Athenian is the speaker. Further reading: Morrow 1993: 337–43.

(810a) Neither a boy's father nor the boy himself, no matter whether he is fond of learning or hates it, shall have the right to increase or reduce the number of years [involved in the child's education], or to extend or shorten the period devoted to these studies. To do so will be against the law. Whoever fails to comply shall be excluded from the honours in education to be mentioned a little later. First of all, you must grasp exactly what the young should learn during this period and what their teachers should teach. (b) They must work hard at their letters until they are capable of reading and writing them. As far as speed and accuracy in the formation of letters are concerned, one must forget about attaining perfection in the case of those whose natural aptitude has not matured in the specified number of years.

5.14. Final thoughts from Plato on the education
of women

Plato, *Laws* 804d6–805b2

By the time that he wrote the *Laws* late in his life, Plato had changed his mind on many of his earlier beliefs about the best prescriptions for society, but his views about appropriate – and compulsory – education for women did not depart significantly from his earlier formulations in the *Republic* (see also *Laws* 794c–d, 813a–c). Further reading: Morrow 1993: 329–31; Saunders 1995.

(804d) My law would also lay down exactly the same provisions for females as for males, and they must do exactly the same training. (e) I would make this statement without any reservation whatsoever: if riding and physical training are appropriate for males, they are for females too. I am not only convinced by the old legends I have heard, but I practically know for certain that today there are countless thousands of women around the Black Sea, called Sarmatians, (805a) who participate with men not only in riding but in archery and the handling of other weapons as well; equal participation is mandatory, and they receive equal practice. Moreover, on this topic I have come to the following conclusion. It is my assertion that, if the establishment of such traditions is possible, current practices in our part of the world, where men and women do not follow the same pursuits with all their strength and with a single mind, are the most stupid of all. Under these circumstances, though it would cost no more money and effort to change, almost each state has been developing only half its potential, (b) and it would be an astonishing blunder for a lawgiver to permit that to continue.

5.15. The founding of Plato's school

(a) Diogenes Laertius, *Life of Plato* 3.7, (b) Diogenes Laertius, *Life of Speusippus* 4.1

Some time around 385, Plato founded a community of students and teachers about a kilometre beyond the Dipylon Gates which marked the limits of the city of Athens. The location of Plato's school – relatively isolated from the heavy traffic of the city – provides an interesting contrast with the activities of Socrates, who conducted many of his philosophical discussions in the agora, as well as in the *palaistrai* and gymnasia of his city. For the identity of Speusippus (**b**), see **5.16a**. Further reading: Jaeger 1934: 11–23; Marrou 1956: 67–68; Friedländer 1969: 85–107; Lynch 1972: 54–63; Guthrie 1975: 19–24; Riginos 1976: 119–23; Dillon 1983, 2003: 1–16; Baltes 1993.

a

When Plato returned to Athens [after his travels in Sicily], he carried on his discussions in the Academy. This is the gymnasium on the outskirts of the city, a wooded area, which takes its name from a hero, Hecademus.

110

b

Speusippus dedicated statues of the Graces (*Charites*) in the temple of the Muses (*Mouseion*) which Plato had established in the Academy.

5.16. Students in the Academy

(a) Diogenes Laertius, *Life of Plato* 3.46–47, (b) Themistius, *Oration* 33.295c–d

The list of students who attended the Academy during Plato's lifetime (**a**) is a who's-who of Athens' intellectual élite in the fourth century BC. Included are Plato's nephew Speusippus, who became head of the Academy upon Plato's death in 347 and introduced entrance fees (Diogenes Laertius, *Life of Speusippus* 4.2), and Xenocrates, who followed Speusippus. Aristotle was a student from 367 to 347. Of considerable interest is the mention of two women as Plato's pupils, Lastheneia and Axiothea (Pomeroy 1977: 58–60). Themistius explains Axiothea's decision to join Plato's school (**b**): she was inspired by reading Plato's *Republic* or *Laws*. If this explanation was formulated in order to account for a female presence in the Academy, the explanation must have been motivated by the remarkable prescriptions for equal education between the sexes which we find in those two works (**5.10, 14**). Further reading: Burnet 1928: 48–64; Riginos 1976: 128–38; Glucker 1978: 226–55; Dillon 1983, 2003: 1–16; Baltes 1993.

a

His pupils were Speusippus from Athens, Xenocrates from Chalcedon, Aristotle from Stageira, Philip from Opus, Hestiaeus from Perinthos, Dion from Syracuse, Amyclus from Heraclea, Erastus and Coriscus from Skepsos, Timolaus from Cyzicus, Euaeon from Lampsacus, Python and Heraclides from Ainos, Hippothales and Callippus from Athens, Demetrius from Amphipolis, Heraclides from Pontus, and many others. Among them were two women, Lastheneia from Mantinea and Axiothea from Phlius, who, according to Dicaiarchus, dressed like a man. Some claim that Theophrastus also was his pupil. Chamaeleon also includes the orators Hyperides and Lycurgus and is supported in this by Polemon. Sabinus, citing as his authority Mnesistratus of Thasos, states in the fourth book of his collection of *Meditations* that Demosthenes studied with him.

b

When Axiothea read one of the treatises on the principles of government, she left Arcadia and travelled to Athens. There she attended

Plato's lectures, disguising for some considerable time the fact that she was a woman, just like Achilles when he was with Lycomedes. When the Corinthian farmer [Nerinthus] became familiar with [Plato's dialogue] *Gorgias* ... he immediately abandoned his land and his vines and pledged his soul to Plato, as a sower and planter of Plato's ideas.

5.17. Plato as teacher on the comic stage

Epicrates fr. 10 Kassel-Austin

The following passage (from a lost comedy whose title is unknown) demonstrates not only the Academy's philosophical interest in classification and definition during Plato's own lifetime, but also the popular criticism that this interest came in for. Further reading: Jaeger 1934: 18–20; Friedländer 1969: 94–95; Riginos 1976: 148–50; Guthrie 1978: 463–64.

A: What about Plato, Speusippus and Menedemus? What are they spending their time on now? What idea and what argument are they investigating? ...

B: I do know and can tell you plainly. At the Panathenaia I saw a group of boys in the gymnasia of the Academy, and I heard strange talk that I can't describe. They were defining and classifying the natural world: the way that animals live, the nature of trees, and the species of vegetables. And in the middle of this they had a pumpkin and were investigating the species that it belonged to.

A: What definition did they give it, and what species did they say it belonged to? ...

B: Well, at first they all stood there in silence and bent over it for quite a while as they pondered the problem. Then suddenly, while the boys were still bent over and investigating, one of them said that it's a round vegetable, another that it's grass, another that it's a tree. A Sicilian doctor heard this and farted at them because of the nonsense they were talking.

A: I'm sure they got very angry and shouted that he was making fun of them. That wasn't a nice thing to do in that kind of discussion!

B: The boys didn't care. Plato was there and wasn't disturbed at all. He told them very calmly to define again, this time according to the species a fart belonged to. And so they kept on with their classifications.

5.18. Plato's lecture "On the Good"

(a) Aristoxenus, *Harmonics* 2.1–2, (b) Proclus, *On Plato's Parmenides* 127c (688.4–18 Cousin)

Although Plato taught for forty years in the school which he founded, the only surviving evidence for his teaching practice has to do with a single lecture which he gave during this time. The most famous witness for this story is Aristoxenus (**a**); his source is Aristotle, who presumably was present at the event which he related to Aristoxenus. Aristotle's reason for telling the story is to exemplify a general principle: a speaker should explain at once the subject of his lecture in order to lighten the mental burden on his audience. Proclus, a much later source (AD 410–85), adds details to the story which emphasize the lesson that a speaker must know his audience (**b**). It is safe to assume that Plato's lecture was delivered in the gymnasium in the Academy; that is also where the scene is set in **5.17**. Further reading: Cherniss 1945: 1–30; Düring 1957: 357–60; Riginos 1976: 124–26; Guthrie 1978: 424–26.

a

Aristotle would frequently explain that most of the people who heard Plato give his lecture "On the Good" had just this experience. Each of them arrived with the expectation that he would hear about one of those things that are considered human goods, such as wealth, health, power – in general, some extraordinary blessing. But when it became clear that his arguments were about mathematics, numbers, geometry, astronomy and, finally, that the Good is a single thing, it seemed, I think, absolutely outrageous to them. Some had a little contempt for the subject matter, while others criticized it openly.

b

After reaching this point in their study they ask whether philosophers should read their writings in the presence of certain people, as Zeno did; and they say that if they ever did this they should read the kinds of writings that are attuned to their listeners, in order not to have the same experience that Plato is said to have had when he announced his lecture "On the Good." A large and diverse crowd had gathered, but when the man himself was reading and they didn't understand what he was saying, one small group after another left until almost everyone was gone. But this happened to Plato even though he had known it would and had told his companions in advance not to prevent anyone from entering, since his reading would be directed only towards those who were close to him.

5.19. Philosophy is not an education for the real world

Plato, *Gorgias* 484c–485a, c–e

Callicles, one of Socrates' interlocutors in the *Gorgias* and his main antagonist in that dialogue, holds a deeply cynical view of morality and recognizes little practical value in philosophy. Although Isocrates expressed himself with far less sarcasm and acidity, he too saw the kind of study that Callicles has in mind as useless for life in the world of affairs (see **5.1, 6**). Both Callicles and Isocrates, however, share the opinion that philosophy does have a place in a person's education if it is studied at the right age. In fact, Callicles seems to view philosophy as an important element in a liberal education, that is, an education fitting for a free man (cf. **4.4**). This passage is often taken to reflect criticisms against Plato and his students. Further reading: Ostwald 1986: 244–50.

(484c) I'm sure philosophy is a charming thing, Socrates, provided a person deals with it in moderation at the right age. But if he spends more time with it than he should, it's the end of the human race. For even if he comes from excellent stock and practises philosophy well on into maturity, he's bound to prove inexperienced in all the things that a man who is going to be an outstanding and reputable member of society ought to be experienced in. (d) He is inexperienced in the customs of his city and in the ways of speaking which a person must use when dealing with others in private and public business, inexperienced in human pleasures and desires, and, in a word, inexperienced in the ways of people altogether. Whenever he enters upon some personal or political activity, he turns out to be ridiculous – (e) in the same way, I suppose, that politicians do whenever they enter upon your discussions and your kinds of arguments. There is truth in what Euripides says: "Each person is distinguished in this and strives towards it, allotting the better part of the day to that in which by chance he is at his best."[7] (485a) Whatever he is mediocre in, he avoids it and attacks it, but he praises the other thing because he thinks well of himself and believes that in this way he is praising himself. Yet in my opinion the most correct course of action is to engage in both of

---

7 From Euripides' lost play *Antiope*, fr. 184 Kannicht.

these. It's a fine thing to engage in philosophy so long as it's strictly for education (*paideia*), and while you're a boy it's not shameful to prac-tise philosophy, but whenever a man gets older and continues to do this, the whole thing is ridiculous, Socrates. . . .

(c) I'm delighted when I see philosophy in the possession of a young lad, and I think it's appropriate; in my opinion, this is a free-born person, whereas someone who doesn't practise philosophy is showing a lack of freedom and will never consider himself worthy of anything admirable or noble. (d) But whenever I see an older man still prac-tising philosophy and not giving it up, I think that this man now needs a flogging. For as I was saying a moment ago, even if this man is from a very good family, he will likely become unmanly as he avoids the centres of his city and the places of assembly – these are the places where, according to the poet, men become "preeminent"[8] – and instead lives the rest of his life skulking and whispering in a corner with three or four lads, (e) never uttering anything that is free, impor-tant, and effective.

5.20. Mathematical study in the Academy after Plato

Philip of Opus [?], *Epinomis* 990b8–c5, 991d5–992a6

An ancient tradition held that the entrance to Plato's school contained the inscription "Let no one enter who does not know geometry." Although the story is unlikely to be authentic (its earliest source is dated only to AD 362: Julian, *Against Heracleus the Cynic* 237c), it does reflect a well-known char-acteristic of the studies pursued within the Academy. The following extract is from the *Epinomis*, which was probably written not long after Plato's death as a supplement to the *Laws*, perhaps by Philip of Opus, a pupil of Plato; it is at any rate a product of the Academy. The main focus of the *Epinomis* is wisdom and the studies that lead to its acquisition. Of special significance is the central place that the author assigns to the mathematical sciences, clearly following the model set forth in the *Republic* (**5.9**). Further reading: Marrou 1956: 73–76; Tarán 1975: 69–79, 92–110; Riginos 1976: 138–47; Guthrie 1978: 447–52; Bulmer-Thomas 1984; Fowler 1987: 106–57, 197–202.

(990b) In order to avoid saying the same things on the same subjects again and again, (c) since it is difficult to understand all their other orbits which we discussed earlier, we must work constantly at teaching

---

8 Homer, *Iliad* 9.441.

a person many preliminary subjects and at making him accustomed to them when he is a child and a youth by preparing for this purpose those whose natures can understand them. That is why they require the mathematical sciences. [The speaker now sets out the subjects that a student should pursue: arithmetic, geometry, stereometry, and harmonics, in preparation for the study of astronomy.] ... (991d) In regard to all these subjects, we must understand that if someone grasps each of them correctly, according to the prescribed method, he receives a great benefit; otherwise it is better always to call on god. The prescribed method is as follows. ... (e) Every diagram and system of number, every combination of harmonious sounds and the unified system of the revolution of the stars, one thing that applies to all of them – these must all be revealed to the person who learns in the right way, and they will be revealed if, as we say, someone learns in the correct way by focusing on unity. (992a) For there is in nature a single bond embracing all of these, which will be revealed to those who study in this way. But if someone pursues these subjects by some other method, he must ... call on good luck. For without these subjects no one in cities will ever be happy. This is the method, this is the upbringing, these are the subjects of study; whether they are difficult or easy, it is along this path that we must proceed.

5.21. Education, character and law

Aristotle, *Nicomachean Ethics* 10.1179b20–1180a5

Aristotle here considers the roles that nature, habit and teaching play in the development of a person's character, in particular in the acquisition of goodness (*areté*). The relationship between these factors had been debated long before Aristotle turned his attention to the question; his main contribution to the debate is the argument in favour of legislation. Further reading: Guthrie 1981: 362–64; Lord 1982: 153–59; Curren 2000: 84–88.

(1179b) Some people think that we become good by nature, some that it is by habit, others that it is by teaching. Nature is obviously not in our control; those who are truly fortunate possess it through some divine cause. Reason and teaching, no doubt, are never effective in all cases, but as the earth which is going to nourish the seed must be prepared in advance, so also must the mind of the student be prepared in its habits in order for it to enjoy and hate the right things. For the man who lives in accordance with his emotions would not listen to an argument that tries to dissuade him, nor would he even understand it.

How can a person in this state be persuaded to change his thinking? It is apparently a general rule that emotion listens to force, not reason; we must therefore have from the start a character that is somehow related to goodness (*areté*), which is attracted to what is noble and shrinks from what is wicked. Yet it is difficult to obtain a correct training for goodness from our youth if we have not been raised under correct laws, since a sensible life that involves endurance is not a pleasant thing to most people, especially when they are young. That is why their upbringing and pursuits must be regulated by laws, for they will not be painful when they have become habitual. (1180a) But it is not enough, I suppose, to receive a correct upbringing and supervision when we are young; on the contrary, since we must continue to practise and habituate ourselves to these things when we are grown men as well, we will also need laws for them, and generally for our whole life, seeing that most people are obedient to compulsion rather than to reason, and to punishment rather than to consideration of what is noble.

5.22. Private or public education?

Aristotle, *Nicomachean Ethics* 10.1180a24–b16

Although Aristotle claims to favour public education, he acknowledges the superiority of private education, which focuses upon the needs of the individual. Elsewhere he takes a more rigid position in favour of the state's control over education (**5.21**). The issue would be discussed later by the Roman Quintilian (**8.13**). Further reading: Guthrie 1981: 399–400; Lord 1982: 48–51; Miller 1995: 229–34; Curren 2000: 75–79.

(1180a) It is only in Sparta, or a few other cities, that the lawmaker seems to have concerned himself with upbringing and daily pursuits; in most cities matters of this kind have been neglected, and each person lives as he wishes, "making laws over his children and wife,"[9] like the Cyclops. It is best that supervision be public and of the right kind, but if it is being completely neglected by the state, it would seem to be appropriate for each person to help his own children and friends along the path towards goodness (*areté*), or at least to choose this path; and . . . he would seem to be more capable of this if he becomes skilled at legislation. For it is clear that public supervision is carried out by means of laws, and supervision which is carried out through sound laws is good supervision. (b) It would seem to make no difference whether the laws are written or unwritten, or whether they will provide for the education of one person or many, just as in the case of music, physical education, and other pursuits. For as it is the laws and customs that prevail in states, so it is the father's words and habits that prevail in the home, all the more because of kinship and the benefits that it provides, since they are naturally predisposed towards affection and obedience.

Furthermore, individual education, like individual medical treatment, is superior to public education; for while it is generally true that a person who has a fever benefits from quiet and lack of food, another person might not; and the boxing master does not perhaps impose the same method of fighting on all his students. So the individual case, it would seem, is treated with greater precision when the supervision is of a personal kind, since each person is then more likely to obtain that which is suitable for him. But the best detailed supervision will be provided by a doctor or a trainer or anyone else who knows in general what is right for all people or for a given class; for the sciences are said to be, and really are, concerned with what is generally true.

5.23. Regulation by the state

Aristotle, *Politics* 7.1336b35–8.1337a21

The final part of book 7 and most of book 8 of Aristotle's *Politics* are given over to a discussion of education; in fact they contain Aristotle's most important reflections on the subject. Some passages from the *Politics* have already appeared (**2.5**); these were presented in order to illustrate Aristotle's views about Spartan education. In the first of those extracts he asserted that "the administration of this system [of education] must be public and not private, as it is now" (these words follow immediately after the extract printed below). He takes this view because the state has a profound interest in the kind of citizens it produces. Hence for Aristotle education serves politics since, by producing good citizens, it enables a good state to exist. Unlike Plato, however, he does not think that there can only be one kind of good state; it follows that the kinds of education necessary to produce the good democratic citizen and the good oligarchic citizen will differ. Further reading: Lord 1982: 36–67; Miller 1995: 229–34; Curren 2000: 63–156.

(1336b) When boys have reached the age of five, during the following two years until their seventh birthday they must now sit in as observers of the lessons they will be obliged to learn. There are two stages of their lives into which their education must be divided: the first from their seventh birthday until they reach puberty, the second from puberty until they are twenty-one. Those who divide the span of years into groups of seven are, for the most part, quite right, (1337a) and we must follow the divisions set by nature. It is the goal of all education and systematized training to fill the void left by nature. Consequently, we must consider first whether we should establish a fixed curriculum for children; second, whether it is advantageous to assume the responsibility for looking after them at the level of the state or to leave it to the private individual, as is the case in the majority of cities today; and third, the nature of that curriculum. No-one can doubt that the lawmaker must concern himself above all with the education of the young. States in which this is not done suffer harm to their constitutions, since they require educations that are consistent with each constitution. The spirit that is appropriate to each constitution usually safeguards that constitution, as it did its original establishment; thus the democratic spirit safeguards a democracy, and the oligarchic spirit safeguards an oligarchy. It is always the case that the better spirit is responsible for a better constitution. Furthermore, as in all arts and crafts we must undergo some preliminary education and habituation in order to perform each of them, so clearly also must we do so in the case of the activities of goodness (*areté*).

5.24. The core subjects

Aristotle, *Politics* 8.1337b22–33

In this extract Aristotle identifies the basic elements in the curriculum and assesses them according to the criterion of usefulness. He also applies, however, another criterion concerning the status of a subject, namely its value to us in our leisure hours. His comment on the purpose of music as a subject of study appeals exclusively to its aesthetic value and its role as a leisure activity. Later in the *Politics* (8.1339a11–1342b34) he has a great deal to say about the capacity of music to form the character of the student (Anderson 1966: 121–45). Further reading: Burnet 1903: 129–41; Marrou 1956: 138–41; Lord 1982: 68–150, 1996; Curren 2000: 88–91.

The basic areas studied today serve, as I stated earlier, a double purpose. There are more or less four subjects in which instruction is normally given: letters, physical training, music, and sometimes a fourth, drawing. Letters and drawing are useful, indeed extremely useful accomplishments in life; physical training contributes towards developing courage; as for music, there would seem to be considerable uncertainty today about its function. Although in contemporary

119

society the majority participate in the study of music for the pleasure it brings, originally men established it as part of the educational curriculum because it has often been remarked that nature herself seeks not only to make proper use of the time during which we are at work, but also to make seemly use of our leisure hours. And at the risk of repeating myself, this is at the root of everything.

6

THE HELLENISTIC PERIOD
(*c*. 335–30 BC)

Until the middle of the fourth century BC the Greek world was politically fragmented into many small states which asserted or attempted to assert their independence from one another. This situation changed in 338, when Philip II of Macedon imposed unity on the Greeks after his victory over the Athenians at the Battle of Chaironea (about 90 km northwest of Athens). The unity which the Macedonians imposed extended also to language. Previously the Greek tongue had been distinguished by its many dialects, with each city or region showing its own varieties of speech, in greater or lesser degree. For administrative and political purposes a new "common" dialect rapidly developed called the *koiné*, which was adopted first for official use and then by the general population for spoken and written communication. This common dialect was based heavily on the dialect spoken by Athenians in the fifth and fourth centuries BC.

As significant as these developments were for the way that Greeks lived their lives, far greater were the implications from the expansion of the Greek world under Philip's son, Alexander the Great. By the time of his death in 323 BC, Alexander had conquered and colonized lands as far east as modern Afghanistan and Pakistan. Until then, most of the people in many of these places had had limited or no contact with Greeks and Greek culture. For their part, the Greeks (including Alexander's veterans) who settled in towns and cities in Egypt, Asia Minor, the Near and Middle East, Persia and elsewhere had to overcome cultural isolation in order to preserve something like the life they had known in their homeland. These people constitited a ruling class, and in these towns and cities the Greek immigrants reproduced some of the institutions that were fundamental to Greek society and identity. Chief among them were the gymnasium, whose existence in these places is attested by both archaeological remains and written evidence, and a system of education which now took on a recognizable pattern throughout the hellenized world. The success of these immigrants was astonishing, not least because it derived from a new willingness to set aside the political differences that had bedevilled Greek city-states for centuries. A modern scholar has captured the cultural effects of this success (Lane Fox 1974: 483–84):

> Sophocles was read in Susa [Iran]; scenes from Euripides inspired Greek artists in Bactria [Afghanistan]; comic mimes were performed in Alexandria-in-the-Caucasus; Babylon had a Greek theatre and the tale of the Trojan horse was a favourite in Alexandria-in-Sogdia [Uzbekistan] where men must have read it in early Greek epic poets; Homer, deservedly, reached India and, together with Plato and Aristotle, ended by being enjoyed in Ceylon.

It would be impossible to overstate the importance of the gymnasium to the Hellenistic cities. It was the primary means by which Greek culture was transmitted to generations of young Greeks growing up in foreign lands. In the gymnasium the traditional athletic, musical and intellectual elements of Greek education were taught to the new ruling élite (**6.8–10, 18–20, 22, 24–25**). But the gymnasium was not merely for the young; older members of Greek society, many or most of them alumni of the local gymnasium, relied on it as a social centre for recreation and leisure, and these people also assumed many of the responsibilities for its operation (**6.18**). Sometimes the gymnasium was among a city's finest architectural treasures (e.g. Pergamon: **6.21**), and the person chosen to administer it (the *gymnasiarchos*) held a position which could bring great honour (**6.18–19**).

To Greeks of the Hellenistic period the gymnasium was therefore a symbol of civilized life, even an island, as they saw it, in a sea of barbarism. Little wonder, then, that promotion of the gymnasium and everything that went on in it became increasingly the concern of the state. It built the gymnasia and in many instances now provided for the education of its young people, including, in at least one instance, the education of girls and young women (**6.8**), whose educational opportunities expanded in this period (**6.15–17**). Little wonder, too, that this concern for the propagation of Greek culture very often took the form of endowments by private benefactors or by Hellenistic kings (**6.8–10, 13, 19, 25**).[1] Outside Sparta, public education was something new. Previously, proposals in favour of it came especially from theorists, most notably Plato and Aristotle (**2.5, 5.8–10, 12–14, 22**), and the only form of public education that had existed in Athens and some other cities was the mandatory military training called the *ephebeia* (**3.25–26**). Along with this public involvement in education came the construction of libraries for public use, where scholars sought to collect in one place the

---

1 **6.8–9** provide valuable evidence for rates of pay for teachers. The following denominations occur in these inscriptions and elsewhere in this chapter: 1 talent = 60 minas = 1,500 staters = 6,000 drachmas. For the sake of comparison, note that many skilled manual workers at this time received about one drachma per day.

literary production of the Greek past and undertook advanced scientific and literary research (**6.5–7**).

In the Hellenistic period there was also increased standardization of the educational curriculum. How far did this standardization go? Henri-Irénée Marrou, the author of the most widely read and cited book on ancient education, believed that a basic system emerged at this time which possessed a highly fixed curriculum; that this system was later taken over by the Romans in its essentials and in many of its details; and that, once fixed, it remained more or less intact for the rest of antiquity, as well as in both eastern and western medieval Europe. This is the system which came to be referred to by the name *enkuklios paideia*, a term which has been described as "one of the key-concepts in European culture and education" (de Rijk 1965: 24).

There is certainly a good deal of truth in Marrou's position, as some of the extracts in this chapter demonstrate, but it is impossible to confirm his highly influential assumptions with complete confidence. Although inscriptions and papyri, as well as literary and artistic evidence, enable us to know a great deal about education in the Hellenistic period, our knowledge is not as full or secure as is frequently believed. In particular, we possess a wealth of inscriptions from the period but lack extensive contemporary evidence from literary sources on which to base firm conclusions. Moreover, the origin and even the meaning of the term *enkuklios paideia* (and the alternatives *enkuklios paideusis* and *enkuklia mathemata*) are much debated. Although it gave rise to the English "encyclopaedia" and "encyclopaedic," *enkuklios paideia* does not denote a "complete" or "universal" education, as the English words might suggest. Instead it seems to mean literally "education in a circuit," signifying apparently a "broad" education, in contrast to a "technical" or "professional" education. The widespread use of this specific-sounding term by modern writers has had the effect of implying that it designates a precise Hellenistic curriculum. Yet the earliest reference by name to *enkuklios paideia*, by the Roman architectural writer Vitruvius (**9.3**: *encyclios disciplina*), can only be dated to the late first century BC. Ancient attributions of the phrase to fourth- and third-century Hellenistic writers, on the other hand, are not proof that the term was in use as early as that time (**6.2**).

There is little evidence, then, that for most of the Hellenistic period the system of basic education was designated by a unique name. Was there nevertheless a curriculum with a specific, fixed set of *subjects*? At a later time that was certainly the implication underlying the term *enkuklios paideia*, when it designated a curriculum that comprised especially the "seven liberal arts" (**9.2–5, 10.27–28**). But our evidence from the Hellenistic period points instead to a curriculum with a wider range of subjects and greater flexibility in the ones which an individual student might take. It is safe to say that the curriculum was not as clearly defined or homogeneous in the Hellenistic period as has often been supposed; rather it focused on a few basic and all-but-compulsory subjects, together with a larger number of "electives" (**6.3**, **7–9**, **20**, **25**). To the extent that the term *enkuklios paideia* was used in the Hellenistic period, it likely conjured in a person's mind the connotations of a broad, non-technical education.

General background: Green 1990: 155–70, 312–35; Koester 1995: 41–76; Pomeroy *et al.* 1999: 446–67. *Hellenistic education*: Marrou 1956: 95–226; Koller 1955; Mette 1960; de Rijk 1965; Koester 1995: 97–109; Cribiore 1996: 3–37, 2001; Morgan 1998; Russell 1989; Mitsis 2003. *Gymnasia*: Delorme 1960; Nilsson 1955: 78–80, 83–98; Jones 1940: 220–26; Wycherley 1978: 219–36; Kyle 1987: 64–92.

6.1. A teacher's notebook from Egypt

Guéraud and Jouguet, *Un livre d'écolier*

Many school exercises have survived from the Greek and Roman worlds (Cribiore 1996: 175–284). Some, like the ones presented below, were written on papyrus, others on wooden tablets. Wax tablets and ostraka also served as writing material for young students, since the first were reusable and the second were cheap, whereas papyrus could be expensive. All surviving examples on papyrus and wood were produced in Egypt. The following contains the reproduction of a substantial part of a remarkably well-preserved papyrus roll that dates to the second half of the third century BC. To judge from the high quality of the handwriting and the fact that the book begins with elementary exercises and proceeds by steps to fairly advanced literary study, this notebook apparently belonged not to a student but to a teacher. Sections **a** and **b** contain practice in forming simple letter combinations and sounds. Section **c** consists of monosyllabic nouns; a few of these words are rare (*stragx*, *knax*, *klagx*), and it seems probable that they were chosen for their use in teaching a young student how to enunciate letter combinations that were especially difficult for a Greek speaker (these were called *chalinoi*, "tongue-twisters": **8.4** [37]). Section **d** lists ten of the Olympian gods and goddesses; they are among the most common in Homer's *Iliad* and *Odyssey*, poems which were, of course, basic to the education of all Greeks (**1.9**, **3.9**, **5.8–9**). A list of rivers then follows in section **e**. Section **f** contains disyllabic words, usually separated according to their syllables by the use of a dicolon (:), though the author sometimes neglects this device; a similar pattern is followed in section **g**, which contains polysyllabic names. In both **f** and **g** the names are drawn mainly from Greek mythology and legend.

Even though this is the earliest school-book to survive from the Greek world, we know that the system described here for teaching children to form letters, syllables and individual words was not a Hellenistic innovation; it is essentially the system described by Plato in **3.15**, **3.19**, and *Republic* 402a–b. Moreover, it remained in use for many centuries to come (see **8.4**, **5**, **29**, **10.1**). In the section of this papyrus that follows the extracts printed below, lines from Euripides (*Phoenician Women* and *Ino*) and from Homer (*Odyssey*) appear, then some epigrams and elegiac couplets; these provide the student with an introduction to the reading and study of literature. Some mathematical exercises then follow. Further reading: Marrou 1956: 150–55; Bonner 1977: 165–72; Cribiore 1996: 269, 2001: 250–58.

a. Lines 2–8 ("kh", "ps" and "ph" represent transliterations for the Greek letters chi [χ], psi [ψ] and phi [φ]).

	kha	psa
	khe	pse
	khê	psê
	khi	psi
	kho	pso
	khu	psu
phô	khô	psô

b. Lines 9–15

an ban gan dan zan than kan man nan xan pan ran san tan phan khan psan
en ben gen den zen then ken men nen xen pen ren sen ten phen khen psen
ên bên gên dên zên thên kên mên nên xên pên rên sên tên phên khên psên
in bin gin din zin thin kin min nin xin pin rin sin tin phin khin psin
on bon gon don zon thon kon mon non xon pon ron son ton phon khon pson
un bun gun dun zun thun kun mun nun xun pun run sun tun phun khun psun
ôn bôn gôn dôn zôn thôn kôn môn nôn xôn pôn rôn sôn tôn phôn khôn psôn

c. Lines 27–37

thêr (beast)
pûr (fire)
pux (with the fist)
lax (with the foot)
khên (goose)   hûs (pig)
sarx (flesh)   kêr (heart)
aix (goat)   thin (meaning uncertain)
lugx (lynx *or* hiccup)   klagx (noise)
stragx (drop)   rhin (nose)
knax (milk)   pous (foot)
phlous (skin)   kheir (hand)

d. Lines 38–47

> Hera
> Hermes
> Poseidon
> Demeter
> Ares
> Athena
> Hephaistos
> Aphrodite
> Apollo
> Artemis

e. Lines 58–66

> Saggarios
> Pigrus
> Peneios
> Indos   Kal...
> Ebros   Arachotos
> Anakmôn   Melês
> Rhundakos   Skamandros
> Eridanos   Simois   Praktios
> Strumôn

f. Lines 67–70, 72–83

> Onomata disullaba (two-syllable nouns)
> Kastor Phoi : bos
> Thras : ôn Le : ôn
> Hek : tôr Dei : nôn
>
> Ar : ktos
> Nê : reus
> Nei : leus
> Nei : los
> Tho : as
> Gou : neus
> A : kmôn
> Zê : thos
> Ai : as
> Teu : kros
> Thê : rôn
> Or : pheus

g. Lines 86–92

> O : dus : seus

126

Phô : ku : los
Al ki nous
Pe li as
I : a : sôn
Tê : le : phos
A : khilleus

6.2. Early references to *enkuklios paideia*?

(a) Diogenes Laertius, *Life of Diogenes* 6.27–28, 73,
(b) D.L., *Life of Zeno* 7.32, 129, (c) Athenaeus,
Sophists at Dinner 13.588a

Several philosophers of the fourth and third centuries BC are presented here as attacking or defending conventional education. Diogenes of Sinope (*c.* 412–324) was founder of the Cynic school of philosophy; Zeno of Citium (*c.* 335–263) was the founder of the philosophical system called Stoicism; Chrysippus (*c.* 280–207) was one of Zeno's successors as head of the Stoic school; and Epicurus (*c.* 341–270) was founder of the Epicurean school of philosophy, which consistently criticized the standard curriculum. Although the term *enkuklios paideia* appears in **b** and **c**, as does a variant of it in **b** (*enkuklia mathemata*), their occurrence in these places is not evidence for the use of the terms by Zeno, Chrysippus and Epicurus themselves some 200–250 years before its first appearance in our sources. Instead, it probably reflects the terminology which the later writers Diogenes Laertius and Athenaeus were familiar with and therefore used to record the information they wanted to communicate (cf. **6.7**). If that is the case, the most that we can say is that the early Hellenistic philosophers Diogenes, Zeno and Epicurus had a low regard for the standard subjects that students were learning – a common position for ancient philosophers to take towards conventional education (**1.9, 4.19**) – but not that these subjects were in their time grouped under the title *enkuklios paideia* or *enkuklia mathemata*. If the information preserved in **a** faithfully represents the opinions of Diogenes, we can assume that the standard school subjects included reading and writing, rhetoric, music, geometry, astronomy, and mathematics – a list which is close to the one recorded by Teles (**6.3a**; cf. **4.5, 8, 5.9**) and represents most of the subjects that were later to constitute *enkuklios paideia* when its contents *were* formalized. Further reading: de Rijk 1965; Asmis 2001.

a

(27) Diogenes thought it remarkable that teachers of letters (*grammatikoi*) studied Odysseus' faults but were ignorant of their own; that

musicians, moreover, tuned the strings on the lyre but had souls whose characters were out of tune; (28) that mathematicians focused their attention upon the sun and the moon but disregarded the things right in front of them; that rhetors were eager to say what was right but not to do it. . . .

(73) [Diogenes believed that] music, geometry, astronomy and subjects such as these should be neglected on the grounds that they are useless and unnecessary.

b

(32) Some people, among them Cassius the Sceptic and his followers, condemn Zeno on many points, saying, first, that at the beginning of his *Republic* he declares the educational curriculum (*enkuklios paideia*) to be useless. . . .

(129) Chrysippus says that the subjects of the curriculum (*enkuklia mathemata*) are useful.

c

Since Epicurus was not initiated in the educational curriculum (*enkuklios paideia*), he considered as blessed those who had likewise managed to avoid it on their way to philosophy. Here is the kind of thing he said: "I consider you blessed, sir, because you've set out for philosophy, pure of all education (*paideia*)."

6.3. A Hellenistic curriculum

(a) Teles 5 (49–50 Hense), (b) [Plato], *Axiochus* 366d–e

Extract **a** can be dated to about 240 BC. The Cynic moralist Teles identifies two phases in a child's education before the child reaches the third stage called *ephebos* (eighteen years in Athens, though younger in some other cities): a primary level, which involves physical training, training in reading and writing, musical theory and drawing; and a second level, which consists of arithmetic, geometry and riding. In this scheme we find the basic core of a widespread curriculum, with its emphasis on letters on the one hand and mathematical subjects (including musical theory) on the other. Teles' reference to the student's "riding instructor" shows that he has in mind the education of a child who belongs to a wealthy family. Teles' description of the "ephebic stage" takes for granted most of the elements in the life of the *ephebos* which Aristotle mentions in **3.25** (see also **6.8, 20, 24**). The pseudo-Platonic *Axiochus* (**b**) was probably written in the second century BC; the evidence which it provides for Greek education therefore reflects conditions during the Hellenistic period. As Aristotle had done (**5.23**), this author assumes that the curriculum begins at the age of seven. Further reading: O'Neil 1977: ix–xxv; Hershbell 1981: 16–17, 59; Russell 1989: 218–19; Dudley 1998: 45–48, 84–88.

a

If it can only be the case that the happy life consists of a greater balance of pleasure, no man, says Crates,[2] would be happy. On the contrary, if one were to consider all the various stages throughout one's life, one would find a greater abundance of painful experiences. First, it is impossible to distinguish between pleasure and pain for one half of the entire span of our years, because we are asleep. Second, the first stage of life, when we are being raised as very young children, is full of discomfort. If the baby is hungry, its nurse puts it to bed; if it's thirsty, she gives it a bath; if it wants to be put down to sleep, she picks up its rattle and makes a horrible din. Suppose the child survives his nurse. He is then taken over by his *paidagogos*, his *paidotribés*, his *grammatodidaskalos*, his teacher of musical theory, and his art-teacher. He advances a bit in years and finds that he has also got a teacher of arithmetic, a geometer, and a riding-instructor. He wakes up at dawn and has no time to spend as he wishes. When he has reached the stage of *ephebos*, then he has the *kosmetés*, the *paidot-ribés*, the *hoplomachos* and the *gymnasiarchos* to be afraid of. He's got all these people to supervise him, to grab him by the scruff of the neck and to give him a flogging. Once his ephebic stage is over, he is now twenty years of age, but he still has the *gymnasiarchos* and *strategos* to fear and to look out for.

b

Once the child reaches the age of seven after enduring a host of sufferings, *paidagogoi*, *grammatistai* and *paidotribai* are set over him and exercise their tyrannical authority. When he is older, there are teachers of literary criticism, geometry and equestrian skills, a whole host of masters. Once he is enrolled among the *epheboi*, there are the *kosmetés* and the fear that his hands inspire, then the Lyceum, the Academy,[3] the *gymnasiarchos*, his rods and a countless number of misfortunes.

---

2 A Cynic philosopher from Thebes, *c*. 365–285 (**6.17**).
3 The author is referring to the gymnasia in these locations rather than to the Platonic and Aristotelian philosophical schools.

THE HELLENISTIC PERIOD (*c.* 335–30 BC)

6.4. The student's pain

Herodas, *Mimes* 3.58–73

The kind of punishment mentioned in **6.3a–b** is brought to life in this extract from a work whose probable date is about 265 BC. Kottalos is Merotime's son; Lampriskos is his teacher. Kottalos' fellow-students help in his beating. Further reading: Booth 1973.

> LAMPRISKOS: Merotime, enough of your imprecations! He'll get no less than he deserves. Euthies, Kokkalos, Phillos! Where are you? Hoist him onto your shoulders. Akeses' full moon is here and it's high time you exposed him to it. I just love the things you have been up to, Kottalos! Isn't it enough for you to have an honest game of knucklebones [dice], like these boys here? No, you've got to be hanging around the gambling dens, tossing coins with the hired hands. I am going to make sure that you're better behaved than a dainty miss and don't budge an inch, if that is all right with you. Where is my strap, the oxtail, the one which really stings and which I use to flog prisoners and those set aside for punishment? Somebody, put it in my hand before I choke on my bile.
>
> KOTTALOS: No! No! I beg you by the Muses, Lampriskos, by your beard, and by poor little Kottalos' life. Not a beating with the stinger! Use your other one!

6.5. The Library and Mouseion of Alexandria, and the Library of Pergamon

(a) pseudo-Aristeas, *Letter to Philocrates* 9–10, 29,
(b) Strabo, *Geography* 17.1.8, (c) Strabo 13.4.2

After Alexander the Great founded the Egyptian city of Alexandria in 331 BC, it became one of the intellectual centres of the Mediterranean world, home to the famous Mouseion ("temple of the Muses") and Library, and rivalled as a place of learning during the Hellenistic period only by Pergamon (in modern Turkey) and possibly Athens. The Alexandrian Library was the largest in the ancient world and was closely integrated with the scholarly activities pursued in the Mouseion. The Mouseion and the Library were probably founded some time during the reigns of Ptolemy I (305–282), who had been Alexander's close friend, and of his son, Ptolemy II (285–246, joint ruler of Egypt with his father for three years).

Since Demetrius of Phaleron, the key figure in **a**, fled to Alexandria in 294 (after being governor of Athens from 317 to 307), it seems safe to assume that the Library began its existence about the time of his arrival. His role is described by "Aristeas," a pseudonym for this unknown writer who is

130

generally believed to have been an Alexandrian Jew of the first half of the second century BC. Strabo's presentation of the Mouseion as a community of scholars (**b**) is likely to remind us of Plato's and Aristotle's schools (**5.15–20**), which also possessed libraries containing (at least) the works of their respective founders. The Mouseion, however, was open to the public, whereas use of the books in the Academy and Lyceum was restricted to their members. The library in Pergamon (**c**), founded by Eumenes II (reigned 197–158), was a distant second to Alexandria's in terms of size and influence. Its most famous head was Crates of Mallos, who played a central role in the spread of Greek learning in Rome (**7.7**). Further reading: Marrou 1956: 189–91; Pfeiffer 1968: 95–104, 234–51; Hansen 1971: 272–74; Fraser 1972: 1.305–35, 696–704, 2.970–72; Bowman 1986: 223–28; Canfora 1989; Reynolds and Wilson 1991: 5–20; Habicht 1997: 53–66; Radt 1998: 16–19; Nagy 1998.

a

(9) Demetrius of Phaleron was put in charge of the royal library and provided with large sums of money in order to collect, if possible, all the books in the known world. By making purchases and transcriptions he brought the king's project to completion as far as he could. (10) I was there when the king asked him, "How many thousands of rolls do we now have?" He replied, "Over two hundred thousand, Sire, but I shall see to the remainder in a short while so that the number reaches five hundred thousand." ... [Later in this work a letter from Demetrius to Ptolemy is quoted.] (29) "In pursuance of your order that the rolls which are still missing be added towards completion of the library, and that the rolls which are incomplete receive the appropriate repair, I have taken considerable care and now give an accounting to you. . . . "

b

The Mouseion is also a part of the royal palaces; it has a covered walkway, a sitting area, and a large house where the dining-hall is located for the scholars who share the Mouseion. This community has property that it holds in common and a priest in charge of the Mouseion, formerly appointed by the king but now by Caesar.

c

Eumenes built up the city [Pergamon] and cultivated the Nikephorion[4] with a grove; and he was the one who, from his love of beauty, added

---

4 A shrine dedicated to Athena Nikephoros, i.e. "Bringer of Victory."

sacred buildings and libraries and brought the settlement of Pergamon to its present state.

6.6. Homer's *Iliad* on papyrus

This papyrus fragment, copied some time between 145 and 140 BC and discovered in Tebtunis, Egypt, contains parts of Homer's *Iliad* bk. 2, lines 172–210. It owes its preservation to the fact that it was recycled as cartonnage (casing) for a crocodile mummy. As is usual for Greek texts at this time, it is written exclusively in upper-case letters, and there is no division between words. More papyrus fragments of Homer's *Iliad* and *Odyssey* have been unearthed than of all other ancient Greek authors combined, and those of the *Iliad* outnumber those of the *Odyssey* by about two to one

Figure 6.1 Homer's *Iliad*, Bk. 2, lines 172–210. Tebtunis Papyrus 4, Bancroft Library, University of California, Berkeley

(bks. 1 and 2 of the *Iliad* are especially common and were clearly the ones most often read in schools). These are sure signs of the cultural preeminence of Homer and of the educational dominance of the *Iliad*.

This papyrus is the earliest so far discovered to contain "critical" notations that scholars working in the Alexandrian library devised in the late third century and first half of the second; their purpose was to help in the analysis of Homer's poems. They are visible (circled) on the left-hand side of the fragmentary right-hand column and include: (1) the horizontal stroke or "obelos" – designating lines considered inauthentic – which appears adjacent to the first line of the right-hand column; (2) oblique strokes beside the second line and in the margin near the bottom of the column, possibly indicating the beginning of new sections of the poem; (3) between the two oblique strokes, an "antisigma" (ↄ), the significance of which is disputed. The most prominent of these Alexandrian scholars was Aristarchus (*c.* 216–144 BC), the date of whose death coincides roughly with the production of this papyrus. Further reading: Oldfather 1923: 62–78; West 1967: 11–28; Pfeiffer 1968: 210–33; Turner 1980: 100–112; Haslam 1997: 69–74, 84–87; Cribiore 2001: 194–97.

6.7. The persecutions by Ptolemy VIII

Athenaeus, *Sophists at Dinner* 4.184b–c

In this extract Athenaeus (writing *c.* AD 200) tells of the persecutions carried out by Ptolemy VIII, king of Egypt, not long after he ascended the throne in 145 BC (he reigned until 116). These persecutions marked the beginning of the decline of Alexandria's Library (the scholars who fled Alexandria included Aristarchus; see **6.6**). The claim in this passage that "the Alexandrians were the educators of all the Greeks and barbarians" should be contrasted with the more limited claims of earlier figures such as Pericles, who saw the Athenians as the educators of the Greeks alone (**3.1b**; cf. **2.1**). The remark reflects changed conditions in the Hellenistic world. Further reading: Rostovtzeff 1953: 1084–86; Marrou 1956: 213–215; Pfeiffer 1968: 252–54; Fraser 1972: 1.467–75; Reynolds and Wilson 1991: 17–18.

You are unfamiliar with the fact that Menecles, the historian from Barca, and Andron of Alexandria in his *Chronicles*, have recorded that the Alexandrians were the educators of all the Greeks and barbarians at the time when the system of general education (*enkuklios paideia*) was declining on account of the constant political disturbances which occurred during the period of Alexander's successors. There was a revival of all educational matters during the reign of Ptolemy VIII in Egypt, that is the Ptolemy whom the Alexandrians very properly called "the Malefactor." He put many Alexandrians to the sword and exiled no small number of those who had been *epheboi* at the same time as his brother, filling the islands and cities with *grammatikoi*, philosophers, geometers, musicians, painters, *paidotribai*, doctors and many others who were experts in their fields. Because of their poverty they were forced to teach what they knew and in so doing had a formative influence on many men of note.

6.8. Endowment of schooling at Teos by Polythrous

*SIG*³ 578

The following is the first half of a famous inscription from the late third century BC. It is an important source of information for many features of Hellenistic education: it demonstrates the increasing spread of education to ordinary citizens through state sponsorship; it provides an example of "euergetism," that is, the donation by a private benefactor (*euergetés*) to the operation of a state institution; it confirms that education, at least at its early levels, could be open to females; it furnishes evidence for the organization of the *ephebeia* outside Athens (clearly in Teos it was not exclusively military); and it provides information about teachers' rates of pay (cf. **6.9**; also n. 1 above). The gymnasium is referred to as a place where the teacher of letters (*grammatodidaskalos*) tests his students; literary education seems therefore to have been delivered in the gymnasium in Hellenistic Teos, as it was in other Hellenistic cities (**6.19** [Eretria], **6.25** [Delphi]). Further reading: Forbes 1942: 30–32; Marrou 1956: 112–13, 145–47; Pomeroy 1977: 52–53; Austin 1981: 211–13.

... and after the election of the *gymnasiarchos*, a *paidonomos* not younger than forty years [is to be appointed]. In order that all free-born children might be educated in keeping with the promises made to the people by Polythrous, son of Onesimus, in his concern for their future, he made a gift of 34,000 drachmas to fulfil his undertaking and thereby left a most honourable memorial of his dedication to establishing his own fame.

Each year, after the registrars have been chosen and when the magisterial elections are held, three *grammatodidaskaloi* are to be appointed to give instruction to both boys and girls. Six hundred drachmas a year are to be given to the teacher appointed to the first level of instruction, 550 to the teacher at the second level, and 500 to the teacher at the third level. Two *paidotribai* are also to be appointed and each is to receive 500 drachmas a year. A *kitharistés* or *psaltes*[5] is to be appointed and the appointee given a fee of 700 drachmas a year.

---

5 A player of the *psalsis*, a stringed instrument similar to the *kithara*.

The latter will instruct boys who are to enter the *ephebeia* and those a year younger in music. The instruction will take the form of teaching them to play on the lyre with the fingers or with a plectrum. He will also teach music to the *epheboi*. Any question regarding the age of these children is to be decided by the *paidonomos*. If we are observing an intercalary month, the teachers are to be paid an additional portion of their fee for that month. The *paidonomos* and the *gymnasiarchos* are to hire, after reference to the people, a *hoplomachos*, an instructor in archery and an instructor in throwing the javelin. These teachers are to give instruction to the *epheboi* and those children who have been designated to receive musical education. A fee of 250 drachmas is to be given to the man giving instruction in the use of the bow and javelin, 300 to the *hoplomachos*, whose period of instruction will be of not less than two months. It is to be the responsibility of the *paidonomos* and the *gymnasiarchos*, as is stipulated for each according to the law, to ensure that careful attention is paid to having the children and the *epheboi* properly exercised in their studies.[6] If a dispute arises among the *grammatodidaskaloi* over the number of children, the *paidonomos* is to have the final decision and they are to obey his ruling. The *grammatodidaskaloi* are to hold obligatory examinations in the gymnasium, and the instructor of music is to hold his in the council-chamber.

6.9. Endowment of the schools of Miletus by Eudemus

SIG[3] 577

This is another famous inscription, exceedingly informative about the organization of schooling in a Hellenistic city (Miletus, on the coast of Asia Minor). Like Polythrous (**6.8**), the Eudemus named here is an example of a private benefactor or *euergetés*; he too decided that the best way to memorialize himself was through an educational bequest. We notice again the highly regulated character of Hellenistic schools, but more important here are the suggestions, at least, of a system of universal public education. The date of this inscription is 200/199 BC. Further reading: Forbes 1942: 30–32; Marrou 1956: 112–13, 145–47; Austin 1981: 207–10.

Eudemus, the son of Thallion, deciding to benefit his people and to establish the finest permanent memorial to his desire for fame, promised to award on behalf of himself and his brothers, Menander and Dion, ten talents of silver for the education of freeborn

---

6 For an inscription which sets out the law for a *gymnasiarchos* in one Hellenistic city (Beroia, in Macedonia), see Austin 1981: 203–7.

children. Accordingly, the people of Miletus passed the following decree.

Eudemus is to receive the highest praise for the serious concern he has shown for this noble objective, and the responsibility for carrying out his purpose is to lie with the council and the people. In order to ensure that this endowment is properly managed, Eudemus must write out a draft for the sum of money specified above and give it to the treasurers in charge of regular revenues within the period defined in his undertaking, and the treasurers are to turn it over at once to those chosen to manage the state bank. The bankers will open a state account under the name of "the fund established by Eudemus for the education of freeborn children," enter the amount of the donation and look after it carefully. They shall then hand the sum over to the bankers chosen to succeed them until the people have come to a decision about the income from the endowment. Should they fail to hand it over as ordained, they are to be liable to pay back to the people double the amount. The assessors who manage the city's revenues are to set aside annually in their financial estimates 300 staters against the future income from the money, and in their expenditures they are to allocate on a monthly basis to each treasurer what is due to him. Should they fail to set that money aside as decreed, each of them will be liable to pay 500 staters, which will be consecrated to Hermes and the Muses.

Those who wish to give instruction as *paidotribai* or *grammatodidaskaloi* are to enter their names with the *paidonomoi* appointed for the following year, and this registration is to take place annually from the fifteenth to the twentieth of the month of Artemision [11–16 March], and the *paidonomoi* are to publish the names entered in the stoa of Antiochus. On the eighth day from the end of that same month, at a meeting of the assembly, a tripod and incense-burner are to be placed in the *orchestra*.[7] The priests, that is the priest of Hermes Enagonios in the boys' *palaistra* and the priest of the Muses, the sacred herald, the *paidonomoi* who have been elected and are about to enter office, Eudemus, during his lifetime, and, after his death, the eldest of his descendants, are to burn frankincense as an offering to Hermes, the Muses and Apollo Mousegetes ("leader of the Muses"). The sacred herald will offer a prayer on behalf of those participating in the assembly that good fortune may attend whosoever votes to elect as *paidotribai* and as *grammatodidaskaloi* those who he believes will give the best care to the children and does not allow his judgement to be

---

7 The semi-circular floor of a theatre on which the chorus danced.

affected by any matter of personal benefit contrary to the requirements of justice; and that his fortune be the opposite if he fails to do so. After this the *paidonomoi* must hand over to the secretary of the council the names submitted to him and bring each man forward one by one. As each steps forward, the priests and the sacred herald are to administer an oath to him. In the case of the *paidotribai* the text of the oath will be as follows: "I swear by Hermes not to approach any Milesian to influence him to vote for me, nor to instruct another man to do so on my behalf. I pray that good fortune attend me if I abide by my oath, ill fortune if I break it." The oath administered to the *grammatodidaskaloi* is to be exactly the same, except that they are to swear by Apollo and the Muses. From those who have come forward four *paidotribai* and four *grammatodidaskaloi* are to be elected and appointed.

The fee for each of the *paidotribai* is to be set at 30 drachmas a month, and for each of the *grammatodidaskaloi* at 40 drachmas a month. Contributions for their public declamations and other responsibilities are to be made according to the law regulating the *paidonomoi*. Those elected as *paidotribai* are to have the right to go abroad, if they wish to do so when they take contestants to any of the competitions at which crowns are awarded as prizes, but only after they have obtained permission from the *paidonomoi* and have left in their place somebody acceptable to the *paidonomoi* to look after the children. To ensure that each receives his due on a regular basis, the treasurers are to give the *paidotribai* and the *grammatodidaskaloi* their prescribed fee at the time of the new moon in each month. If any treasurer fails to do so, he is to be liable to pay 500 staters to be consecrated to Hermes and the Muses, and action will also be taken against him to recover the fees for the *paidotribai* and the *grammatodidaskaloi* under the terms of the law governing the responsibilities of the *agoranomos*.[8] The monies set aside for this purpose in accordance with the financial estimates may not in any way be transferred to any other activity. If anyone makes such a suggestion or proposal, or puts it to the vote, or does divert the funds, or allots less than the published amount, that man will be liable to pay 500 staters to be consecrated to Hermes and the Muses.

After the fees have been paid, the remainder of the sum set aside for this purpose is to be handed over to the *paidonomoi*, and they will send the finest ox available to Apollo of Didyma at the time of the Festival of Didyma[9] every fifth year and at the time of the Boigia in

8 An official who regulated the commercial activities of the marketplace (*agora*).
9 South of Miletus; the festival was held in honour of Apollo.

other years. They themselves, the boys selected by them, the elected supervisors of the boys, Eudemus, during his lifetime, and, after his death, the eldest of his descendants, are to take part in the procession. The *paidonomoi* are to sacrifice the offering sent and distribute a portion to all the boys and the others whose participation in the procession has been ordained.

Moreover, the children are to be released from their studies on the fifth day from the beginning of each month, and the *paidonomoi* are to include this day with the others in their registry of school-holidays, as is laid down in the law regulating the duties of the *paidonomoi.*

6.10. The owner of a *palaistra*

Theophrastus, *Characters* 5.7, 9–10

This extract, part of a description of the "typical" obsequious man, can be dated some time between about 320 and 310 BC. It illustrates both the importance of the gymnasium for the training of Athenian *epheboi* and the increasingly crucial role that private citizens played in the funding and operation of education and its institutions early in the Hellenistic period. Gymnasia were generally owned by the state, but *palaistrai* (wrestling grounds) were the property of individual people. Like gymnasia, *palaistrai* could be used not only for physical training (see **6.8**). Further reading: Marrou 1956: 114; Lynch 1972: 34–37; Diggle 2004: 235–36, 244–48.

He passes his time in the gymnasia where the *epheboi* are training. . . . He owns a small *palaistra* with its covering of sand, and an area for playing ball, which he goes around lending out to philosophers, soph-ists, drill-sergeants (*hoplomachoi*), and teachers of musical theory (*harmonikoi*) as a place in which they can demonstrate their talents. He himself turns up late at these events, when the members of the audience are already seated, so that they can say to each other, "That's the man the *palaistra* belongs to."

6.11. Public education on Rhodes

Polybius 31.31

It was not only private citizens who furnished financial support for a city's schools; Hellenistic kings also provided endowments. For Eumenes, mentioned below, see **6.5c**. The event which Polybius is describing took place in 161/0 BC. Further reading: Hansen 1971: 395.

The people of Rhodes accepted 280,000 *medimnoi*[10] of grain from Eumenes in order to lend out the proceeds and put the interest towards the fees for their sons' instructors and teachers. If someone were in tight personal circumstances for a short time, he might accept a gift like this from his friends in order not to let his children remain without an education because of his lack of money. But when times are good a person would put up with anything rather than go around asking his friends for money to pay teachers.

6.12. Epitaph for a teacher

IG 12.1.141

The following epitaph from Rhodes dates to the beginning of the second century BC. It is as a teacher that the deceased most wanted to be remembered.

This man taught letters for 52 years and is now resident in the region assigned to the pious. For Pluto and Persephone settled him there, and Hermes and Hecate the torch-bearer appointed him, as a man who showed kindness to all, to preside over the Mysteries due to his complete trustworthiness. Stranger, having visited, learn precisely the large number of pupils who crowned my grizzled brow.

6.13. An educational endowment for Delphi by Attalus II

SIG[3] 672

This inscription provides another example of royal support for education, in this instance at the express request of the city of Delphi. The inscription dates to 160/59; it is therefore almost exactly contemporary with **6.11**. Attalus was king of Pergamon from 158 to 138 but was called "king" even before the death of his brother Eumenes. Further reading: Hansen 1971: 126–27, 459–60; Austin 1981: 334–37.

This resolution was passed by the city of Delphi at a fully constituted assembly with the votes required by law. On the occasion of the embassies we sent to him regarding the education of boys ... King Attalus (II) ... listened sympathetically to our requests and forwarded to the city 18,000 Alexandrian silver drachmas for the education of boys and 3,000 drachmas for the honours and sacrifices, with the intention that the gift might stand for all time in perpetuity, that the fees

---

10 1 medimnos = approxinately 52 litres.

might be paid to teachers with regularity, and that the funds required for the honours and sacrifices might be produced from the interest accruing from lending the money out.

Accordingly, with the blessing of fortune, it has been decreed by the city that the funds shall be dedicated to the god and that no magistrate or private citizen shall be permitted to use the money for any other purpose, in any way whatsoever, either by decree of the people or resolution of the Council; that, if any magistrate or private citizen does so, he shall be charged with theft of sacred funds, the financial officials shall register a penalty against him eight times the sum decreed or otherwise transferred, and the decree or resolution shall be deemed null and void; that, if any surplus remains from the interest after the fees have been paid to the teachers as has been determined, it shall be turned over to the Council and the people, and that the resolution shall be binding; that, whomsoever the people elect, the three men chosen as trustees for the funds shall make the money available to be borrowed at an interest-rate of 6.67 per cent in the month of Amalios[11] during the archonship of Amphistratus [further conditions for treatment of the surplus follow]. . . .

In future years, the following arrangements shall be in place for the appointment of trustees and the management of the fund. The interest accruing from the 18,000 drachmas to be spent on teachers and the revenue from the 3,000 drachmas to cover the costs of the honours and sacrifices shall be subject to the following procedures: each year during the month of Poitropios, at the meeting of the assembly required by law, the archons who are in office at any given time shall draw up a formal list of three trustees from a list of proposed candidates chosen by the popular vote; those appointed trustees shall swear the oath taken by the other boards of magistrates, shall levy the interest yielded by the funds before the 15th of the month of Endyspoitrios, shall deposit in the temple the funds for the payment of the teachers in the month of Heraklios, shall pay the fees to the teachers monthly during the following year, and shall render an account of this to the city.

6.14. Charondas and Thurii

Diodorus of Sicily, *Library of History* 12.12.4–13.4

Charondas was a sixth-century lawgiver in Catane, on the eastern coast of Sicily. Greek writers frequently attribute important deeds to early lawgivers

---

11 22 December–25 January. Other months in this inscription: Poitropios = 22 November–21 December; Endyspoitrios = 27 March–25 April; Heraklios = 26 April–25 May.

even though these deeds really belong to a much later period (e.g. Solon: **1.2**, **3.3**; Lycurgus: **2.2**, **6**). We know that this is what Diodorus has done in the following passage, since he is here describing the constitution not of Catane but of the city of Thurii (eastern coast of southern Italy), whose foundation in 445 occurred long after the death of Charondas. The historical basis of the story can nevertheless be preserved if we believe (a) that a system of universal education existed in at least one part of the Greek world already in the middle of the fifth century, and (b) that in this place literacy was considered to be a necessary accomplishment. It is more likely, however, that the provision of universal education reflects the environment that existed in cities in the Hellenistic period (but see Muir 1982). Further reading: Dunbabin 1948: 68–75; Marrou 1956: 112, 388; Harris 1989: 98–99.

(12.4) Charondas enacted that all the sons of citizens should learn letters (*grammata*) and that the state should provide the fees for their teachers. He did so on the assumption that those who were poor would be unable to pay the fees from their private means and so would be deprived of the opportunity to participate in the noblest of pursuits. (13.1) The lawgiver gave precedence to the study of letters above the other branches of learning, and appropriately so, since it is by means of this skill that a man fulfils the majority and the most useful of the activities in life, such as voting, letters, contracts, laws, and the other things which are most conducive to keeping one's life on an orderly course.

(13.2) Who could compose a worthy eulogy on the importance of learning letters? By letters alone do the living preserve memory of the dead. By means of writing, those who are far away in a distant place maintain communication with those who are furthest away from them as if they were standing at their side. When nations and kings make treaties in times of war, letters provide security and a firm guarantee that the agreement will be kept. Indeed, in general, the art of letters alone preserves the most brilliant statements of the wise, the oracles of the gods, philosophy, and all the forms of learning, and it perpetuates them for all subsequent generations. (13.3) For that reason, while one must assume nature to be responsible for life, an education based on letters must be thought of as enabling one to live that life well.

Consequently, by this piece of legislation Charondas corrected the disadvantage of the illiterate in the belief that they were being excluded from considerable benefits. He believed that they merited the expenditure of care and money by the state. (13.4) Earlier legislators laid down that individuals who fell sick should be attended by doctors at public expense and so judged that their bodies warranted care. Charondas, however, gave healing attention to those whose inner souls were sickly for want of an education. That is the measure of his superiority over his predecessors. We pray that we may never have a need for these physicians, but we crave to spend all our time in the company of the teachers who give us an education.

6.15. Eurydice

Plutarch, *The Education of Children* 14b–c

Eurydice (born *c.* 410) was the mother of Philip II of Macedon and grandmother of Alexander the Great. She was the first in a long line of women in the Macedonian court who demonstrated educational and intellectual attainments and provided models for Hellenistic women in general.

> We must, therefore, try to adopt every appropriate mechanism to teach our children self-control and to follow the example of Eurydice, who, despite being an Illyrian and a barbarian thrice over, nonetheless embarked on her own education late in life in order to provide her children with an opportunity to be given instruction. The inscription which she dedicated to the Muses provides ample evidence of her affection for her children: "Eurydice, daughter of Sirras, dedicated this to the Muses of her city, since she had a longing for knowledge in her soul. For, as the mother of sons in the prime of their youth, she worked hard to learn her letters, the means by which words can be recorded for remembrance."

6.16. Why should a woman learn to read and write?

(a) Theophrastus fr. 662 Fortenbaugh, (b) Menander fr. 702 Körte

Theophrastus' view of a woman's education (**a**) is a practical one; it also reveals prejudices which were undoubtedly shared by many. From his position it is a short step to the view uttered in lines attributed to the comic playwright Menander (**b**). Yet these passages are intelligible only in a society in which it is not extraordinary for women to learn how to read and write. Further reading: Pomeroy 1975: 137–39, 1977: 60–62.

a

> In my view, it is essential that women receive training in letters, but just to the point where it will be useful to them for the running of the household. An education which is more detailed than that inclines them to laziness in other areas and makes them talkative and interfering.

b

The man who teaches a woman letters is making a mistake; he is giving extra poison to a frightening snake.

6.17. Hipparchia, wife of Crates the Cynic

Diogenes Laertius, *Life of Hipparchia* 6.97–98

Like her famous husband Crates, Hipparchia had a reputation for non-conformity. She was not, however, unique in her attraction to philosophy; cf. **5.16**, **10.23**, **25**. Hipparchia and Crates were married around 315 BC. Further reading: Pomeroy 1975: 136–37, 1977: 58–60; Dudley 1998: 49–52; Grams 2007.

(97) Hipparchia put on the same clothes as her husband and went about with him, maintaining their coexistence in public and going out to dinners with him. One day she attended the banquet given by Lysimachus and on that occasion defeated Theodorus the atheist in a debate. She used the following clever argument: if an action taken by Theodorus was not pronounced wrong, that same action could not be considered wrong if taken by Hipparchia; if Theodorus strikes himself, he does no wrong; therefore, if Hipparchia strikes Theodorus, she does no wrong. When Theodorus had no argument with which to meet hers, he tried to expose her by pulling up her cloak. Hipparchia, however, was quite unperturbed and showed none of the embarrassment to be expected in a woman. (98) When he said to her, "Is this the woman who has left her shuttle at the loom?" she retorted, "I am, indeed, Theodorus. But do you think I have made a bad decision if I spent on my education all the additional hours I was destined to waste on the loom?"

6.18. "Those from the gymnasium"

SEG 8.694

This inscription of the third or second century BC is from Luxor, Egypt, and records honours granted by "the members of the gymnasium" to the *gymnasiarchos* Boidas. The phrase is a formulaic expression – literally "those from the gymnasium" – which was very common in the Hellenistic period and after (cf. **10.18a–b**). Since the large majority of "those from the gymnasium" were undoubtedly its former students and *epheboi*, some have compared the expression to the English "old boys." Further reading: Rostovtzeff 1953: 1058–61; Nilsson 1955: 92; Marrou 1956: 104; Walbank 1981: 117–18.

The following resolution has been passed by the members of the gymnasium. Since Boidas, the Persian, son of Demetrius, the *gymnasiarchos* and *kosmetés,* among the many people contributing to the gymnasium, provided useful services and dedicated himself enthusiastically to everything which contributes to public benefit and, in the assistance he provided to the office of the *logistés*, made a major contribution to the securing of accounts from earlier periods which were not arranged under particular headings, it is decreed that, each year on the 28th of Hyperberetaeus [21 August] at the feast in honour of the king's birthday, he be commended publicly and be awarded a crown of fresh leaves, that a painted portrait of him be set up on public display, that a stone tablet inscribed with this resolution be set up in the most prominent location of the gymnasium, that he and his descendants receive anointing oil for life, and that the costs entailed in these honours be borne by the public treasury.

6.19. Honours to the *gymnasiarchos* Mantidorus in Eretria

IG 12.9.236

The following fragmentary inscription, dated to about 100 BC, was discovered in excavations of the gymnasium in Eretria (on the island of Euboea). As in **6.8** and **6.25**, the gymnasium is described as a place where literary instruction is offered; of special interest is Mantidorus' hiring of an Athenian literary scholar whose lessons are open to anybody who wants to attend. His provision of olive oil also rates mention here. Further reading: Richardson and Heermance 1896: 173–90; Kennell 2001.

Mantidorus, son of Callicrates, who was elected *gymnasiarchos* by the people, has, in the performance of all the duties associated with the office, conducted himself with distinction and in a manner worthy of himself, his ancestors and the faith placed in him by the people. When, on account of his competitive spirit, there was a gathering of a larger number of children (*paides*), *epheboi* and the others falling within the scope of his office, he provided leadership in ensuring orderly conduct in the place through the entire period of his office, residing in the gymnasium all year long. He made available an ample supply of olive oil and unguents as generously as he could. Utterly committed to help the young, he used his own resources to make available the Homeric scholar (*philologos*), Dionysius of Athens, son of Philotas, who gave lectures in the gymnasium to the *epheboi*, the children and all others properly disposed towards learning (*paideia*). Each month, on behalf of the children, the *epheboi* and all the others . . . , he performed sacrificial rites to Hermes and Heracles. . . .

6.20. Winners in competitions on Chios

SIG 959

This inscription from the island of Chios (early first century BC) records the names of winners in a wide range of competitions that reflect the traditional literary, musical and physical elements in Greek education. In at least one place (Miletus), *paidotribai* were allowed to take their students to participate in athletic competitions outside their city (**6.9**). To judge from the reference here to "junior," "intermediate" and "senior" *epheboi*, the *ephebeia* on Chios lasted three years, unlike the one in Athens and elsewhere. Further reading: Marrou 1956: 109, 158–59, 402–3.

> During the presidency of Athenodorus, when Hermesilaus son of Xouthos, Dinnuos son of Helixos and Nicias son of Metron served as *gymnasiarchoi*, the following boys (*paides*), *epheboi* and young men (*neoi*) were the victors in the competitions established by law and performed sacrifices to the Muses and Heracles from the funds assigned in accordance with the decree of . . . son of Lysias:

- reading – Agathocles son of Agathocles
- recitation of poetry – Miltiades son of Dionysius
- playing the lyre with the fingers – Xenon son of Timocles
- playing the lyre with a plectrum – Cleocydes son of Dionysius
- long-distance race for boys – Asclepiades son of Protogenes
- long-distance race for junior *epheboi* – Dionysius son of Callistratus
- long-distance race for intermediate *epheboi* – Protocles son of Timocles
- long-distance race for senior *epheboi* – Moschion son of Moschion
- long-distance race for men – Aeschrion son of Aeschrion

[Lists of five winners now follow for each of the sprint, return-race and wrestling, similar to the list for the long-distance race.]

6.21. The gymnasia in Pergamon

Pergamon boasted not only a famous library (**6.5c**) but also a spectacular set of three gymnasia, the most elaborate educational complex of its kind in the ancient world. These gymnasia were constructed in successive levels on the citadel on which the city was built. The illustration shows a reconstruction. The upper gymnasium was the largest of the three, surrounded on three sides by covered colonnaded walkways (porticoes). This gymnasium was used by the *neoi* or "young men," those who had already completed the *ephebeia*. The second, lower gymnasium, bounded to the rear by a long portico, was for the use of the *epheboi*. The lowest gymnasium was for

Figure 6.2 Reconstruction of the gymnasia in Pergamon

the youngest students (*paides*). These gymnasia underwent modifications between their initial construction and the second century AD. Further reading: Forbes 1933: 16–20; Hansen 1971: 253–59; Radt 1998: 13–14, 1999: 113–34.

6.22. Gymnasia and *ephebeia* in Jerusalem

2 Maccabees 4: 7–15

There were some in Jerusalem around 175 BC who sought to introduce Greek culture into the life of that city. The leading proponent of this movement was Jason, who became high-priest, then built a gymnasium and established an *ephebeia*. His ultimate goal seems to have been to transform Jerusalem into a Greek city. Further reading: Doran 1990; Koester 1995: 202–5; Hengel 2001: 16–22; Kennell 2005.

After the death of Seleucus and the succession to the throne by Antiochus (called Epiphanes), Jason, the brother of Onias, connived to gain the high priesthood by promising the king, through a petition, three hundred and sixty talents of silver and eighty talents from some other source of revenue. In addition to this he promised to pay one hundred and fifty talents if he was granted permission through the king's authority to establish a gymnasium and an *ephebeia*, and to inscribe those in Jerusalem as citizens of Antioch. The king gave his assent, and Jason acquired the office. At once he turned his fellow-citizens to the Greek way of life; he also rejected the royal favours for the Jews that were established through John, father of Eupolemos, who had conducted an embassy to the Romans to secure friendship and an alliance. Seeking to destroy the lawful institutions, he introduced new customs that were forbidden by the law. He gladly founded a gymnasium below the acropolis itself and, drawing up the strongest of the *epheboi*, he made them wear the *petasos*.[12] Through the overwhelming impurity of the unholy anti-high priest Jason, Hellenism reached such a peak, and adoption of foreign customs advanced so far that the priests were no longer eager for the services of the altar, but despising the temple, and disregarding the sacrifices, they hurried to share in the unlawful distribution in the *palaistra* when summoned by the discus.[13] They placed no value in their ancestral honours but considered Greek forms of renown to be the finest.

12 A wide-brimmed hat worn by *epheboi* and associated especially with them.
13 A gong which signalled the opening of the gymnasium.

6.23. Hellenistic wisdom literature

Ecclesiasticus 6: 32–37

Ecclesiasticus, an "apocryphal" book of the Bible, is contemporary with the events described in **6.22** if, as is widely believed, it dates from the 180s BC. The instructions set out here are highly reminiscent of the kinds of advice found in Hesiod and Theognis, and of the educational relationship favoured especially by the latter. Further reading: Doran 2001: 98–103.

> If you are willing, child, you will be taught, and if you apply your mind you will be clever. If you desire to listen you will receive knowledge, and if you pay attention you will be wise. Stand in the crowd of elders. Who is wise? Stick to him! Be willing to listen to every divine account, and do not let proverbs of wisdom escape you. If you see an intelligent man, go to him early, and let your foot wear down his doorstep. Reflect on the rules of the Lord and meditate constantly on his commandments. He is the one who will make firm your heart, and the desire for wisdom will be granted to you.

6.24. Evolution of the Athenian *ephebeia*

(a) *IG* II² 1006, lines 16–20, 58–65, (b) *IG* II² 1009, lines 6–9

Some time between 307 and 302 BC, the duration of the Athenian *ephebeia* was reduced to one year; late in the fourth century BC or early in the third it ceased to be compulsory, lost much of its exclusively military character, and increasingly emphasized its intellectual, athletic and social dimensions. It also became, predictably, a school for the city's élite. From 119 BC, students of sufficient means even came from places such as Rome, Alexandria, Antioch, Delos, and northern Greece to attend it (likewise some boys and young men from outside Sparta attended the *agogé*: Humble 2004).

By 122 BC (possibly three or four years earlier), *epheboi* were required to attend lectures by teachers from the city's main philosophical schools (**a**). A few years later (117), the further requirement was added that the *epheboi* provide a gift of 100 books to the public library (**b**). The final section of the inscription from which **a** is excerpted records that the *ephebeia* consisted of 58 *epheboi*; two hundred years earlier its enrolment had numbered several hundred. Further reading: Reinmuth 1929, 1971: 101–2; Nilsson 1955: 21–29; Marrou 1956: 107–8; Miller 1991: 140–45 (full translation of **a**); Habicht 1997: 110–11.

a

Since the *epheboi* ... continued supporting and obeying the *kosmetés* in the gymnasia throughout the year and, considering it most important and necessary to preserve the discipline of the lessons assigned by the people (*demos*), remained blameless and obedient to the orders given by the *kosmetés* and the teachers (*didaskaloi*); and since they were adherents of Zenodotus, attending his lectures in the Ptolemaion[14] and the Lyceum, and likewise all the other philosophers in the Lyceum and the Academy throughout the whole year. . . .

Since he [Dionysius, the *kosmetés*] provided for their education (*paideia*) in all things, and for their soundness of mind, setting them beside the philosophers and attending all their lectures throughout the year; and since he likewise took care over their improvement in reading and writing (*grammata*), devoting himself to Zenodotus . . . lessons and physical training. . . .

b

[The *epheboi*] dedicated a bowl to Demeter and Koré and to the Mother of the Gods, and, in accordance with the decree proposed by Theodorides of Piraeus, they were the first to deposit one hundred books in the library, falling short in neither effort nor desire for distinction. . . .

6.25. Delphi honours the *grammatikos* Menander

SIG[3] 739

Some teachers of grammar and literature (*grammatikoi*) achieved local recognition and honour. Menander seems to have earned Delphi's gratitude as much for his financial benefaction as for his contributions as a teacher. Once again we see that the gymnasium could be used for the teaching of letters and not simply for athletic endeavours (cf. **6.8, 19**). This inscription dates to 85 BC; seventy-five years earlier Delphi had been the recipient of an educational endowment from Attalus II (**6.13**). Further reading: Marrou 1956: 187.

The people of Delphi granted to the *grammatikos*, Menander . . . for himself and his descendants, the following: the status of public friend, the right of precedence in consulting the oracle, the right of priority in the courts, a guarantee of personal security, immunity from all public impositions, the privilege of a front seat at all games held by the community, and all the marks of honour reserved for other public

14 A gymnasium founded in the centre of Athens by Ptolemy VI (reigned in Egypt 180–145 BC).

friends and benefactors of the state. When he was present in Delphi, he dedicated as an offering to the god and the state the first revenues received for his lessons. When he took his seat off to one side in the gymnasium and gave the learned lectures for which he was highly esteemed, the state offered him a contribution towards his expenses, which he refused, saying that he had taken up residence at Delphi in order to honour the god and out of regard for the people of Delphi. In return for all this it was resolved to invite him to eat at the public table.

7

EARLY ROME TO
c. 100 BC

From the early centuries of Roman history two general features in Roman education stand out. The first is the duty – especially within the family – to inculcate in the young person such traditional Roman values as loyalty, truthfulness, piety, patriotism, courage and perseverance. This is clearly the essential aim of education in Rome's earliest days. The second feature is the increasing influence, from around the middle of the third century BC, of Greek culture and customs on the Roman model of education. The basis of this influence is apparent from the material in Chapter 3 and, in particular, Chapter 6.

The first two writers whose works are extracted below illustrate these main features and exemplify some of the problems involved in reconstructing early Roman education. The historian Livy (59 BC–AD 17) drew upon earlier historical writers and records in compiling his accounts of the first centuries of the Roman Republic. His motive for telling a story is frequently to convey a moral lesson which emphasizes what he considers to be a characteristic virtue of the Roman citizen. For this reason his accounts have to be interpreted cautiously. Sometimes they involve distortion and are clearly unhistorical, as some of the evidence which he provides for education in early Rome demonstrates (**7.1a–c**). The comedies of Plautus, which date to the late third and early second centuries BC, present a different kind of challenge. Plautus was heavily influenced by Greek "New Comedy," the most famous representative of which was the Athenian playwright Menander (**6.16b, 8.6**), and the degree to which it influenced him is a fundamental question in deciding whether evidence for educational practices in a given play simply reflects the content of the (now lost) Greek comedies on which he drew (**7.2**). His plays contain a strong Greek element in terms of their plots, characters, settings, and moral assumptions, but Plautus was writing at a time when Greek culture was beginning to have a heavy impact on Roman life, so it would hardly be surprising if his plays reveal this impact and reflect new realities in the Roman world.

In this period the Roman attitude to Greek culture and its influence was highly ambivalent. Perhaps the best example of this attitude is seen in

Marcus Porcius Cato (234–149 BC), whose education of his son (**7.3**) is widely accepted as an accurate expression of the traditional Roman ideal of upbringing (cf. **7.4–6**). Here and elsewhere Cato is characterized as highly critical and suspicious of things Greek. Yet we know that he had a fluent command of the Greek language and a thorough knowledge of Greek literature, and he was not averse to citing with approval the deeds of Greeks from the past. Cato is not alone in revealing this tension between scepticism towards the Greeks and admiration for them. Other Romans express hostility to aspects of Greek learning, such as music, rhetoric and philosophy, and even attempt to curtail their practice; but these same people frequently display an intimate acquaintance with and attraction to Greek culture (**7.7–12**).

Greek educational practices and ideals proved to be irresistible to the Romans. Despite the objections raised in several of the extracts below, Greek teachers, methods, and subject matter, as well as the Greek language and even travel to Greek cities for advanced education, would become increasingly widespread and dominant in the upbringing of young Romans from early in the first century BC onwards (Chapters 8–10).

The kinds of educational opportunities available to girls and young women during this period are difficult to determine with certainty. Direct, reliable evidence for their education is not plentiful, but the little that exists suggests that some girls attended school and learned to read and write (**7.1a, 2c–d, 4**).

General background: Jones and Sidwell 1997: 1–48, 273–76; Boatwright *et al.* 2004: 97–165; Marrou 1956: 229–64; Bonner 1977: 3–75; Gruen 1984: 203–72.

7.1. The earliest Roman school?

(a) Livy, *History of Rome* 3.44.4–6, (b) Livy 5.27.1–4,
(c) Livy 6.25.8–10, (d) Plutarch, *Roman Questions* 278e

Livy describes three events of the fifth and fourth centuries BC in which schools or formal schooling play a supporting role in his narrative. In **a** (set in 449 BC), the daughter of a centurion attends an elementary school in the Roman Forum. Extract **b** records the capture of the town of Falerii (about 50 km north of Rome) by the Romans in 394 BC. The moralizing story of the school-teacher's treachery is, however, probably a later addition to the story: Livy's description of the school-teacher as a *comes*, "escort," is a clear reference in Latin to the Greek position of *paidagogos*, but *paidagogoi* were not employed in non-Greek cities of Italy at the beginning of the fourth century BC. The elementary school is presented in **c** (set in 381 BC) as a familiar feature in the urban landscape (Tusculum) of early republican

Rome. Plutarch's statement in **d** flatly contradicts the three items of evidence in Livy, since his reference is to a much later event, around 230 BC. Further reading: Marrou 1956: 250, 267, 430; Pomeroy 1977: 52; Bonner 1977: 34–35; Ogilvie 1965: 685–87; B. Rawson 2003: 163–65.

a

(4) The daughter was a full-grown girl of exceptional beauty. Appius, beside himself with love for her, tried to seduce her with money and promises, only to find all his efforts blocked by her chastity – whereupon he set his mind on a cruel, presumptuous and violent resolution to the problem. (5) He instructed Marcus Claudius, one of his dependants, to claim that the girl was his slave and to make no concessions to any petitioning for her liberty. . . . (6) The girl was coming into the forum, which was where the elementary schools stood, in temporary buildings, when the henchman of the lecherous decemvir set his hand on her, declaring her a slave and the daughter of a slave belonging to himself.

b

(1) As a rule the people of Falerii would engage the same man as a school-teacher (*magister*) and escort (*comes*) for their children, with several boys simultaneously entrusted to this individual's responsibility, a practice which still prevails in Greece today. As usually happens, the children of the town's luminaries were tutored by the one considered the most learned. (2) In peacetime this person had established the practice of taking his boys out before the city to play and take exercise. Although the town was now at war, the teacher had not interrupted this practice, but he would draw them shorter or longer distances from the city gate, giving them different games and topics of conversation. One day he availed himself of the opportunity of a longer-than-usual stroll and brought the boys amongst the enemy outposts, then into the Roman camp and finally to Camillus in the commander's tent. (3) There he compounded his abominable behaviour with even more abominable talk, (4) telling the Romans that he had surrendered Falerii into their hands by delivering to them the boys whose fathers held power in the town.

c

(8) Camillus, who had established his camp before the city-gates, now wished to see whether all appeared as peaceful within the walls as in the countryside, and so he entered the city. (9) Here he found house-doors standing open, shops unbarred with all their merchandise on

display before them, tradesmen plying their various trades, elementary schools (*ludi litterarum*) humming with pupils' voices, streets packed with people, including women and children going this way and that as their respective commissions directed them (10) – nothing to suggest surprise, let alone fear.

d

The teaching of letters [in Rome] was considered to be an honourable thing, since people taught friends and relatives. It was not until later that they began to teach for pay. The first person to open an elementary school (*grammatodidaskaleion*) was Spurius Carvilius, a freedman of Carvilius, who was the first to divorce his wife.

7.2. Evidence from Roman comedy (Plautus)

(a) *The Bacchis Sisters* 419–48, (b) *The Merchant* 289–93, 303–4,
(c) *The Persian* 171–75

Some members of Plautus' audience would have understood in detail the references to the educational system that the pedagogue Lydus describes in **a**, but many would not, since in 189 BC (the probable date of the play's production) the Roman educational system had not yet adopted the most important and characteristic features of contemporary Greek education.[1] It is likely, however, that by the time of this play the position of *paedagogus* – occupied by Greek slaves – is one with which many Romans would have been familiar. Extract **b** takes it for granted that primary education begins at the age of seven, as it did in contemporary Greek society (**6.3b**), and that the child attends a school to learn how to read and write. As in **a**, it is hard to know how far this passage may be taken as reflecting contemporary educational practice in Roman society, or how far Plautus may have been reproducing elements from Greek comedies on which he relied.[2] The speaker in **c** is an *ancilla* (maid-servant), who is speaking to her mistress, a *meretrix* (courtesan). This passage assumes the existence of primary schooling, but it is uncertain evidence for the attendance of girls in schools in contemporary Roman society. *The Persian* probably dates to the 180s; its Greek source is unknown. Further reading: Marrou 1956: 242–54, 265–73, 397–98; Bonner 1977: 35, 37–46, esp. 39; Bradley 1991: 37–75.

---

1 In writing *The Bacchis Sisters*, Plautus seems to have drawn upon Menander's comedy *Double Deceivers*.
2 Plautus' main Greek source for *The Merchant* (produced *c*. 205 BC) was Philemon's *Emporos* (*The Merchant*).

a

LYDUS: Was this the same kind of education you had in your youth? I tell you that in your first twenty years you never had the opportunity of putting your foot an inch outside the house without your *paedagogus*. If you hadn't reached the *palaestra* before sunrise it was no trifling punishment you'd receive from the gymnasium director.[3] If that happened to you, you were even further penalized in that the disgrace was thought to be equally shared by the pupil and the teacher. At that time boys got their exercise in track-events, wrestling, the javelin, the discus, boxing, ball-games and jumping, not with tarts and necking! It was there that they spent their lives, not in shady dives. Then, when you'd got home from the track and the *palaestra*, you would sit on your chair in front of your teacher, your tunic all tightly belted up, and if you were one syllable wrong in reading your book your hide would be made more blotchy than a wet-nurse's apron! ...

PHILOXENUS: Things are different these days, Lydus.

LYDUS: That I fully realize. In the past a youngster would be voted into public office before he left his teacher's authority. Nowadays you take a boy who's not seven years old – just lay a finger on him and straightway he'll smash his *paedagogus'* head with his writing-tablet! You go to complain to the father and he says to his son: "You're a boy of mine as long as you can defend yourself against mistreatment!" The *paedagogus* is brought in. "Hey, you useless old good-for-nothing," says the father, "don't you put your hands on my son for showing some pluck." Off goes the teacher, crushed, like a lamp with a wet wick. And with this sentence given, the court adjourns. Can a teacher have authority in such a situation, if he's the first to take a beating?

b

DEMIPHON: How old do you think I am?

LYSIMACHUS: You're ready for Acheron, a decrepit old fogey.

DEMIPHON: There's something wrong with your eyes. I'm a boy, Lysimachus, just seven years old.

LYSIMACHUS: You're out of your mind, saying you're a boy.

DEMIPHON: But it's true! ... Today I started to attend primary school (*ludus litterarius*), Lysimachus. I now know three letters.

LYSIMACHUS: What do you mean, three letters?

DEMOPHON: A-M-O [I'm in love].

---

3 "Gymnasium director" translates *gymnasi praefectus*, which probably = Greek *gymnasiarchos*.

c

SOPHOCLIDISCA: I really thought you'd scrutinized me and my character enough by this time. You know, it's five years now that I've been attending you; I think if a sheep spent that much time in school it might have got a thorough grasp of the alphabet. But you, in all that time, girl or infant, still haven't learned my nature.

7.3. Marcus Porcius Cato

Plutarch, *Life of the Elder Cato* 20.4–7

Marcus Cato (234–149 BC) was a younger contemporary of Plautus. The approach that he took to the upbringing and education of his son has been thought to reflect the accepted Roman system before, during, and at least 50 years after Cato's lifetime. In embracing this system Cato implicitly rejected the more structured Greek approach, but it is interesting to note that the slave Chilo, whom he kept in his household and who is called "an accomplished *grammatistés*," was himself a Greek. Plutarch emphasizes the physical, moral and patriotic elements in the education that Cato's son received. For praise of the values espoused by Cato, see **9.15**. Further reading: Marrou 1956: 232–33; Bowen 1972: 170–72; Bonner 1977: 10–19; Astin 1977: 157–81; Gruen 1992: 52–83; B. Rawson 2003: 157–58.

(4) After the birth of his son, there was no task, the affairs of state excepted, which was so pressing that he failed to be present when his wife was giving the baby his bath and wrapping him in swaddling clothes. (5) Indeed, she fed the child with her own milk and frequently also allowed the babies of their slaves to suckle at her breast, thereby producing in them positive feelings towards their son as a result of their being fed together. As soon as he reached the age when the child's powers of comprehension begin to develop, Cato took charge of him personally and taught him letters, although he did own a slave by the name of Chilo, who was an accomplished *grammatistés* and was teaching a large number of children. (6) However, he did not consider that it was appropriate . . . that his son should be abused verbally by a slave or hauled up by his ears when he did not learn his lessons fast enough, and he had no wish to owe a slave a debt of gratitude for teaching such an important branch of education. Instead he personally taught his son letters (*grammata*), served as his instructor in the law, and gave him his training in physical education, teaching him not just how to throw the javelin, how to fight in armour and how to ride, but how to box, how to endure both heat and cold and how to use his strength to swim across the river where the water was swirling and

rough. (7) Cato himself tells how he used his own hand to compose his histories and wrote them out in large letters so that his son might have in his own home a means to benefit himself by becoming familiar with his country's past. He also relates that he took just as much care to avoid indecent language in the presence of his son as he would in that of the Vestals . . . and that he never took a bath in his company.

7.4. Cornelia and her sons, Tiberius and Gaius Gracchus

(a) Cicero, *Brutus* 104, (b) Plutarch, *Life of Tiberius Gracchus* 1.6–7, (c) Cicero, *Brutus* 211

By the time of Tiberius Gracchus' boyhood (born *c*. 163 BC), Greek culture, including especially Greek education, was being sought out by many upper-class Romans. In **a**, Cicero refers to the two main influences on Tiberius' education, his mother Cornelia[4] and the Greek Diophanes; elsewhere (*On Friendship* 37) he also mentions the Stoic philosopher Blossius (Tiberius' father died when his son was about ten years old). The second passage lays greater stress on the traditional familial influence in the education of the Gracchi brothers through its praise of the extraordinary Cornelia, often seen as the ideal Roman matron. The third passage (Cicero himself is the speaker) testifies to the powerful influence that a Roman mother could have on the education of her children, especially on the quality of their diction (cf. **8.11**; also Cicero, *On the Orator* 3.45, and Pliny, *Letters* 1.16.6). Further reading: Gruen 1984: 255–57; Hemelrijk 1999: 64–67, 192–203.

ⓐ

Thanks to the concern of his mother Cornelia, Gracchus received instruction from the time he was a child and was educated in Greek literature, for he always had teachers who were imported from Greece, including, in his youth, Diophanes of Mytilene, who was the finest orator in Greece at that time.

b

(6) Cornelia took charge of the children and the household. . . . (7) Her surviving children – one daughter, who was married to the younger Scipio, and two sons, Tiberius and Gaius, the subjects of this biography – were brought up by her with such dedication that, although there is general agreement that her sons displayed the best

---

4 Daughter of Scipio Africanus, who defeated Hannibal and the Carthaginians at the Battle of Zama in 202 and thus ended the Second Carthaginian (Punic) War.

natural aptitude in all Rome, it was believed that their preeminent qualities were more the product of their education than of their natural disposition.

c

"I have read the letters of Cornelia, the mother of the Gracchi, and it would appear that her sons were actually raised not so much in their mother's bosom as in her language! I have on numerous occasions heard Laelia daughter of Gaius in conversation, and could see that she had her father's refinement in diction, as did both her daughters the Muciae, with whose speech I am also familiar. Likewise, too, Laelia's grand-daughters, the Liciniae, both of whom I have heard speaking – and one of them, the wife of Scipio, you have also heard talking on occasion, I believe."

7.5. Study of law in republican Roman education

Cicero, *On the Laws* 2.59

One of the subjects which Cato taught his son was law. It seems, however, that by at least the middle of the first century BC it had ceased to be taught. In the following passage Cicero implies that in Roman education "the law" meant, first and foremost, the Twelve Tables, the set of wide-ranging prescriptions published in the middle of the fifth century BC which established rules concerning such basic matters as legal procedures, debt, the rights of the head of the family, and ownership of land. Further reading: Marrou 1956: 289–91; Ogilvie 1976: 111–24; E. Rawson 1985: 201–14; Fantham 2004: 102–30; Corbeill 2001: 275–76.

There are, moreover, other laws in the Twelve Tables for reducing the expense and mourning at funerals, and these were adapted largely from Solon. "Don't do more than this," the law says; "don't smooth the funeral pyre with an axe." You know what follows, since we learned the Twelve Tables as a required formula when we were boys. But no-one learns them now.

7.6. Roman and Greek education compared

Cicero, *On the Commonwealth* 4.3.3

Until about the middle of the second century BC, it was a characteristic of Roman society that responsibility for providing an education lay mainly in the hands of the child's family and that the state did not make much formal provision for it. The absence of the state from early Roman education, however, may not have been as complete as Cicero in this passage leads his reader to believe; cf. **7.11** (2): "Our ancestors stipulated the subjects they wished their children to learn, and the schools they wanted them to attend." Further reading: Bonner 1977: 47; B. Rawson 2003: 184.

> The Romans have never wanted a system of education for the free-born which is fixed or determined by laws, or made available at public expense, or of a single kind. The Greeks have worked hard at this in vain, and it is the one area in which our guest Polybius criticizes us for neglecting our institutions.

7.7. The early study of letters

Suetonius, *On Teachers of Grammar and Rhetoric* 1–2

By the second half of the third century BC, the cultural influence of the Greeks was being felt in Roman society. Here Suetonius tries to identify the beginnings of the systematic study of language and literature (*grammatica*) in Rome. His assessment is essentially correct: it was the visit to Rome in 168 by Crates of Mallos as a member of an embassy from Pergamon (see **6.5**) that was most decisive (but cf. **8.24**). Further reading: Gwynn 1926: 34–37; Marrou 1956: 242–54, 422; Pfeiffer 1968: 235–46; Bonner 1977: 20–23, 53; Wallace-Hadrill 1983: 30–38; Gruen 1984: 250–72; Clarke 1996: 11–15; Reynolds and Wilson 1991: 20–21; Kaster 1995: 42–68.

> (1.1) In Rome's early days *grammatica* was not even studied, much less held in respect. Of course our state was still uncivilized and belligerent and could not yet spare much time for liberal education. (1.2) The subject's early stages, too, were modest: its first teachers, who were both poets and half-Greeks – I mean Livius and Ennius,[5] who, it is recorded, taught in the two languages in Rome and elsewhere – merely translated the Greek authors and gave public readings of their own Latin compositions. (1.3) Some authors state that two books on letters and syllables and another on metres are by this same Ennius, but Lucius Cotta is right to maintain that these are not the work of the poet but of a later Ennius. . . .

---

5 Livius Andronicus, from Tarentum in southern Italy, was brought to Rome as a slave in 272 BC. He wrote tragedies and comedies and produced a Latin translation of Homer's *Odyssey*. Quintus Ennius (239–169 BC) was from southern Italy. In addition to his activities as a teacher he composed poetry in various genres.

(2.1) In my view it was Crates of Mallos who brought the study of grammar to Rome. A contemporary of Aristarchus,[6] he had been sent to the Senate by King Attalus,[7] right about the time of Ennius' death. . . . In the Palatine district he fell into a drain-opening and broke his leg, after which he spent the entire period of his embassy and convalescence delivering a large number of public lectures and giving instruction, thus providing an example for our fellow-citizens to follow. (2.2) But they followed only to the extent of applying detailed criticism to poetry that hitherto had limited circulation, poetry written by friends now deceased or by any other people whose work met with their approval, and their readings and commentaries also made these works well known to the public. This is what Gaius Octavius Lampado[8] did for Naevius' *Punic War*,[9] a work that was originally composed as a single undivided volume but which Lampado split into seven books. This, too, is what Quintus Vargunteius[10] later did for the *Annals* of Ennius, which he used to recite before great crowds on pre-arranged dates. It was what Laelius Archelaus and Vettius Philocomus did for the satires of their friend Lucilius[11] which Pompeius Lenaeus claims to have read at Archelaus' house and Valerius Cato at Philocomus'.

7.8. The Roman attitude to musical education

Macrobius, *Saturnalia* 3.14.6–7

Music was an essential ingredient of Greek education, but as the Romans gradually adopted and adapted the Greek educational curriculum, some took an ambivalent attitude towards the subject. Although it was recognized as a civilized pursuit, there was concern that it was soft and un-Roman. The words quoted in this extract were delivered in 129 in a speech which Scipio gave in opposition to a law for the reform of the law courts in Rome. Despite the impression conveyed by this passage, Scipio was far from hostile to Greek learning. Further reading: Marrou 1956: 247–48; Astin 1967: 15–17; Bonner 1977: 44; E. Rawson 1985: 167–69; Gruen 1992: 252–57; Corbeill 2001: 263–66; B. Rawson 2003: 170–73.

---

6 See **6.6–7**; he was appointed head of the Library in Alexandria around 153.
7 Attalus II became king of Pergamon in 158 BC (see **6.13**); it was therefore not Attalus who sent Crates to Rome, but his predecessor, Eumenes II.
8 A Roman scholar of the second century BC.
9 A writer of tragedies and comedies, as well as the narrative poem the *Punic War*; he was active in the second half of the third century BC.
10 Second half of the second century BC.
11 A writer of satire, *c*. 180–102 BC.

(6) Scipio Africanus Aemilianus attests that sons of the nobility and
... even unmarried daughters reckoned the practice of the dance
among their attainments. In his speech against Tiberius Gracchus' law
relating to the courts Scipio says: (7) "They are taught disgraceful
tricks. With a harp and a lute they go along with perverts to an actors'
school where they learn to sing songs which, in our ancestors' view,
should be considered shameful for decent people. Yes, they go along
with perverts to a dancing school – girls and boys of good family!
When someone told me this I could not imagine that noblemen taught
their children such things, but when I was taken to the dancing school
– my God! I saw in that school more than fifty boys and girls,
including ... one boy wearing the *bulla*,[12] no less than twelve years old
and the son of a man canvassing for public office, and he was
performing with castanets a dance of a kind that would have been
shameful even for a disgusting little slave."

7.9. The introduction of rhetoric in Rome

Suetonius, *On Teachers of Grammar and Rhetoric* 25.1–2

Rhetoric was a key element in Greek higher education. Since rhetorical skill
was especially important for aspiring politicians and lawyers, it is not
surprising that in the second century BC it was being adopted by the Romans
and incorporated into their system too. Here and in **7.11**, Suetonius provides
us with a valuable discussion of the way in which the study of rhetoric
became a central part of Roman education. The senatorial decree to which
he refers was passed in 161 BC; the censorial edict mentioned here appears
in **7.11**. Further reading: Gwynn 1926: 60–69; Bonner 1977: 65–66; Gruen
1990: 171–79; B. Rawson 2003: 147–48.

(1) The introduction of rhetoric to our society was much like that of
grammar (*grammatica*), except that it was slightly more difficult in
that ... its practice was periodically outlawed. (2) To eliminate any
doubt of this I shall include an old senatorial decree along with a
censorial edict: "In the consulship of Gaius Fannius Strabo and
Marcus Valerius Messala, Marcus Pomponius raised a matter in the
Senate. After discussing the question of philosophers and *rhetores*, the
Senators decreed that the praetor M. Pomponius should take steps
and measures ... to ensure that they not remain in Rome."

---

12 A pendant worn around a child's neck.

7.10. Lucius Licinius Crassus and Marcus Antonius

Cicero, *On the Orator* 2.1–4

Cicero wrote the dialogue *On the Orator* in 55 BC as a discussion of the characteristics of the perfect orator (the work's dramatic date is 91 BC). Thanks to information that he provides in this work, we know more about Lucius Licinius Crassus and Marcus Antonius[13] than we do about any other orators in the last decades of the second century and first decade of the first. These men were the most eminent orators of their day; hence the nature of the education they received is an especially important question for us. Cicero presents them as something of a contrasting pair, Antonius as largely unfamiliar with Greek literature and culture, Crassus as knowledgeable on a very wide range of subjects but scornful of Greek learning. In reality, both had a detailed knowledge of Greek practices. Further reading: Kennedy 1972: 80–90; Bonner 1977: 68–71; Fantham 2004: 26–48.

(1) Quintus, my brother, you may remember the common belief when we were boys that Lucius Crassus' learning went no further than what could be gained from the primary instruction boys received at that time, while Marcus Antonius was thought totally devoid of culture and intellectual attainment. There were many others who did not really believe this to be so but who were still willing to make such statements about those orators, the more easily to deter us from this branch of learning. . . . The theory was that, if men had attained a peerless acumen and incredible standard of oratory without any formal education, then we would judge all our own efforts to be futile and the attention devoted to our education by our good and enlightened father to be foolish.

(2) We used to rebut the claims of these people . . . by citing as witnesses members of our family: our father, our kinsman Caius Aculeo and our uncle Lucius Cicero. For father, Aculeo . . . and our uncle, who had gone to Cilicia with Antonius and accompanied him when he left – all three spoke long and often to us on Crassus' learning and his enthusiasm for his discipline. Furthermore, we were educated, along with our cousins, the sons of Aculeo, in those subjects which were dear to Crassus' heart, and we were also receiving our instruction from those teachers who were his associates. And so, since we were in his house, we often had occasion to remark . . . that he not only spoke Greek so well as to give the impression that it was his only language, but also that the subjects he proposed for investigation to our teachers,

13 Grandfather of Marcus Antonius (Mark Antony) the triumvir and opponent of Julius Caesar's assassins.

EARLY ROME TO *c.* 100 BC

and with which he himself dealt in all his discussions, revealed that nothing was unfamiliar to him or beyond his grasp. (3) In the case of Antonius, we had often been informed by our uncle . . . how he had engaged the finest scholars at Athens or Rhodes in discussion; even so I myself, in my early youth, often asked him many detailed questions. . . . I am sure that my words will come as no surprise to you. You have in the past often been told by me that after the many wide-ranging conversations I had with him I could see nothing that revealed inexperience or ignorance on his part, at least nothing in the realm of those studies about which I could hold an opinion.

(4) There was, however, a difference between the two men. Crassus was not so much eager to be thought lacking in education as he was to give the impression of disdaining it, and of esteeming the practical wisdom of our people above that of the Greeks in every area. Antonius, on the other hand, thought his oratory would win greater acceptance with our people if he were thought never to have received any formal education at all. And this was how they each thought that they would carry greater weight, one by giving the impression of despising the Greeks, and the other of not even knowing them.

7.11. The early practice of declamation

Suetonius, *On Teachers of Grammar and Rhetoric* 25.2–4

Suetonius continues his discussion (begun in **7.9**) of the way in which the study of rhetoric became a central part of the Roman system. Two of the figures whom he mentions here, Lucius Licinius Crassus and Marcus Antonius, have appeared in **7.10**. The censorial edict against "Latin *rhetores*" which is quoted here was issued in 92 BC; its purpose was probably to prevent the acquisition of rhetorical skill outside the aristocracy, where it was traditionally learned within the family and through an apprenticeship rather than in schools (cf. **7.12** [93–94]). Later (**9.10–15**) we shall hear more about the practice of rhetorical "declamation" which Suetonius discusses briefly here. Further reading: Gwynn 1926: 60–69; Marrou 1956: 252–53; Kennedy 1972: 53–55, 80–96, 1994: 115–17; Bonner 1977: 65–75; Wallace-Hadrill 1983: 31–32; E. Rawson 1985: 143–55; Gruen 1990: 179–91; Kaster 1995: 273–75; Clarke 1996: 10–22, 45–49; Corbeill 2001: 268–75; B. Rawson 2003: 148–51.

(2) Some time later[14] the censors Gnaeus Domitius Ahenobarbus and Lucius Licinius Crassus issued the following edict: "It has been

---

14 I.e. after the expulsion of *rhetores* and philosophers from Rome in 161 BC. (**7.9**).

brought to our notice that there are men who have introduced a new kind of teaching, and that our young people are attending their schools. They have given themselves the title Latin *rhetores*, and our young men idle away whole days in their company. Our ancestors stipulated the subjects they wished their children to learn, and the schools they wanted them to attend, and these departures from the traditional practice of our forefathers both displease us and appear to us to be wrong. Wherefore, we feel obliged to express our sentiments to both the proprietors of such schools and their devotees: we do not like them."

(3) Gradually rhetoric came to be regarded as both beneficial and reputable, and many took it up to win renown as well as to defend themselves. Cicero declaimed in Greek, too, right up to the time of his praetorship, and he continued declaiming in Latin late in his life, in fact along with Hirtius and Pansa, later to be consuls, whom he would call his "students" and his "overgrown boys." According to certain historians, Gnaeus Pompeius returned to the practice of declamation just before the civil war in order to be more fluent in arguing with Gaius Curio, . . . while Marcus Antonius, and Augustus, too, did not discontinue the exercise even during the war at Mutina.[15] Nero Caesar gave a public declamation in the first year of his rule, having already done so twice before that. Several of the orators even published declamations. As a result there was increased interest among the general public, which brought professors and teachers flooding to Rome, where they did so well that some of them rose from the lowest condition to senatorial rank and the highest offices of the state. (4) But they did not as a body have a uniform teaching method, and even individuals did not always follow the same procedure in their own teaching – they diversified their instruction. For their practice was to vary their analysis of cultivated oratory, examining all its figures of speech, its cases and the stories used, and they would develop the exposition of a case at one time tersely and concisely, at another in a more detailed and prolix manner. Sometimes they would translate works of the Greeks, and praise or criticize famous personages.

7.12. The language question in Roman rhetoric

Cicero, *On the Orator* 3.93–95

As Cicero recognizes in this extract, rhetoric was a Greek invention and its teaching adhered to Greek principles; hence it would be artificial to try to

---

15 April 43 BC; Mutina (Modena) is in northern Italy.

divorce it from its Greek basis. Licinius Crassus, who is one of the characters in *On the Orator*, here explains the reasons behind the decree which
Suetonius quoted in the previous selection. Further reading: Marrou 1956:
255–64; Kennedy 1972: 90–96, 205–30; Bonner 1977: 70–74; Clarke 1996:
50–61; Fantham 2004: 36–37, 90–93.

(93) As for choice of vocabulary, its positioning in the sentence and
the formation of periods, the theory is easy, as is the actual practice,
considered apart from the theory. Of subjects there is a large range
and, since the Greeks no longer monopolized them and our young
men therefore virtually forgot them as they were learning them, there
grew up during the past two years Latin teachers of rhetoric, if you can
believe it! When I was censor I had used my decree to banish them.
Not that I was unwilling to see the sharpening of our young people's
intellects, as some purportedly claimed; quite the reverse, I didn't
want their intellects blunted and their arrogance reinforced. (94) I
could see that, whatever their other qualities, the Greeks at least had,
beyond this verbal proficiency, some kind of learning and knowledge
befitting a civilized man, whereas I realized that these new teachers
could teach nothing but recklessness, something to be studiously
avoided in itself even when it accompanies decent qualities. In fact,
this was the one thing being taught, and their school was a school of
arrogance; and I accordingly considered it a censor's job to see the rot
spread no further. (95) These conclusions of mine do not mean that I
despair of seeing the subjects we have discussed presented in a
polished form in Latin, for both our language and the normal development of things are conducive to the adaptation to our common practice of the venerable and preeminent sagacity of the Greeks. But we
need men of learning, and in this field, at least, we have so far had
none. If they ever do emerge they will have to be rated even above the
Greeks.

8

READING, WRITING, AND LITERARY STUDY

Late Roman Republic and Empire

The story of Roman education up to the early part of the first century BC can be characterized as one culture's uneasy responses to the increasing influence of another. In that period the ideal education for a Roman child was seen to be mostly or solely in the hands of the child's family and friends. How often that ideal was realized is a matter for debate, but it is at any rate strikingly different from the ways in which Greeks during the same time – from the fifth century through the Hellenistic period – thought that a child's education should be delivered. But as Roman dominance over the Greeks increased and the political importance of the Greeks declined in the third and second centuries (the decisive blow was the Roman destruction of Corinth in 146 BC and Rome's subsequent domination of Greece), Greek culture exerted a growing impact upon the Romans in all areas. The poet Horace expressed this paradox in often-quoted words: "Captured Greece captured her savage conqueror" (*Epistles* 2.1.156). The Romans were captured through their exposure to the monuments of the Greek world, but even more by their contact with individual Greeks, both abroad and, increasingly, in Rome itself.

By the time Horace wrote his famous line late in the first century BC, the effect of Greek education on Roman was pervasive. It is not simply that some Romans – Cicero, Horace, Julius Caesar, Augustus, to name a few – travelled to Greece to continue their education (**8.25, 9.16**). It is rather that the practices which Greeks used successfully throughout the Hellenistic world were adopted by the Romans, from the earliest stages of a child's education to the study of rhetoric and philosophy. Romans in this period often acknowledge their pedagogical indebtedness to the Greeks (e.g. **8.4** [37], **23**), but frequently it is material discovered in the Mediterranean world outside Italy that confirms this reliance on Greek methods. The Hellenistic towns and cities of Egypt are an especially plentiful source of evidence for Greek practices (**8.5, 7b, 29, 31a, 33**), and documents from these places demonstrate both the high level of homogeneity in the delivery of education in the Greco-Roman world and a striking continuity of practice over a long period.

Several observations about Greek and Roman education in the late Republic and the Empire need to be made. First, the extent and variety of the available source-material for this period far exceeds what we have been able to draw upon so far. Apart from an enormous quantity of literary evidence, there is also the evidence of a vast number of inscriptions, papyri, tablets of wax and wood, ostraka, sculptures and paintings (**8.2, 5, 6, 7b**, **10**, **15b**, **16**, **17b**, **20**, **22**, **28–29**, **31a**, **32d**, **33**). Only a representative sample of this evidence can be presented here and in the next two chapters. Secondly, our study of elementary and literary education in this period is dominated by one figure: Marcus Fabius Quintilianus (Quintilian), born *c.* AD 40 in Spain, died *c.* 100 in Rome. Quintilian recorded his beliefs and expressed his principles about the ingredients that characterize a good education in a long work on the training of orators. The work is unique in ancient literature for the detailed information it provides about education as it was actually practised; although Quintilian's focus is on the orator's training, the first book of *Training in Oratory* deals with a child's earlier education (**8.4**, **8a**, **9a**, **11–13**, **27**, **30**, **34**). Thirdly, much or most of our evidence relates especially to educational conditions as they existed for the aristocratic and well-connected classes of Rome; indeed, it was through this segment of society that Greek culture made its inroads into Roman culture in the first place.

The picture which emerges from this mass of evidence is in some respects predictable. Students as young as six or seven arrive at school in the morning (**8.1**) and learn how to form letters, syllables, and whole words, how to pronounce what they see (**8.3–5**), and how to do simple arithmetic (**8.7**). Later, they write, read and memorize well-known sayings and sentiments, especially those by the comic poet Menander (**8.6**), which required knowledge of the Greek language (**8.12**). All this elementary work leads in a few years to the study of grammar and literature (**8.26–30**), lasting as long as to the age of fifteen. What passes for literary criticism is, however, little more than the memorization and regurgitation of trivia, sometimes organized and classified (**8.31–33**). Whether students attend a school or receive their instruction at home depends mainly on their families' means (**8.13–17**). Educational opportunities were open to girls and women, too (**8.18–20**).

This picture, however, is too schematic. The image of a student who attends elementary school to learn how to read and write from an elementary teacher (*grammatistés* or *litterator*), then proceeds to the secondary level for more advanced literary and grammatical study with the *grammaticus* (or *litteratus*), then progresses to higher education, is so familiar from our own experience that it has long been assumed to be the standard path that Roman children followed. There are indeed some clear instances of students who adhered to this sequence of instruction (e.g. **8.26**, **10.8**), but it is far from obvious that they represent the norm. On the contrary, many children learned how to read and write at home, and from there went directly to the lessons of the *grammaticus* when they attended their first school (**8.13, 25**), bypassing the *grammatistés* altogether. Nor is it the case that the subjects taught by the *grammatistés* on the one hand and the *grammaticus* on the other were as clearly defined and segregated as is often supposed (**8.23**). Factors which could influence the pattern of educational experience that a student might follow included the talents and aspirations of a given teacher, the availability of a range of teachers who could provide different kinds of instruction (determined especially by the size of town or city in which a student lived), and the ability of parents to impart basic skills in literacy to their children.

General background: Jones and Sidwell 1997: 18–82; Boatwright *et al.* 2004: 225–352; Marrou 1956: 265–313; Bonner 1977: 97–111.

8.1. Opening-time

Martial, *Epigrams* 9.68

Martial's complaint about the noise caused by the early opening of schools reflects the fact that teaching was often conducted out of doors under less than formal circumstances. Unlike Rome in the late first century AD, Athens in the fifth and fourth centuries BC had laws which prevented the opening of schools before dawn (**3.3**). Martial was born in Spain around AD 40 and died there around 100. Further reading: Bonner 1977: 126–27.

> What have you to do with us, damned schoolteacher, a creature hated by boys and girls alike? The crested roosters have not broken their silence and already your bloodthirsty growling and beatings sound like thunder. . . . We your neighbours do not ask to sleep the entire night – to be awake is of little importance, but to be awake all night is serious! Dismiss your students. Are you ready to take as much cash for your silence as you do for your shouting, big-mouth?

8.2. Late arrival

This relief sculpture from the second or third century AD apparently depicts a student's late arrival to class. The teacher faces the viewer; to our right is a student holding a scroll. Another student, nearly the mirror-image of this one, sits on the other side of the teacher (not shown here).

Figure 8.1 Teacher with two pupils; detail of relief on a *stele*. Rheinisches Landesmuseum, Trier, Germany

8.3. A day at school

Hermeneumata (Vindobonensis suppl. gr. 43, lines 18–22, 27–35)

The *Hermeneumata* are school-readers which contain narratives that describe a day in the life of a student. These narratives are bilingual – Greek and Latin – and were probably composed to help Greek-speaking students learn Latin. Although none of the eight surviving *Hermeneumata* is itself older than the Middle Ages, their content stems probably from the third century AD or earlier. They are valuable not only because they inform us about the daily activities of students in their schools but also because they provide examples of the kind of elementary material with which students learned to read. Further reading: Marrou 1956: 263–64; Dionisotti 1982: 90–92, 120–25; Cribiore 2001: 15–18; Gwara 2002: 110–17.

I go out to the school of the accountant, of the stenographer, of the Greek grammarian, of the Latin grammarian, of the orator.[1] I entered the school and said: "Hello teacher, hello instructor." He greeted me

1 The repetition here and elsewhere was intended to introduce the student to a wider range of vocabulary.

in return. He gives me a lectern and tells me to read five pages to him, and I read accurately and clearly. Then I gave the book to another student. Later I go off to the assistant-teacher. I greet him and my fellow-students, and they greeted me in return. Then I sat in my place, on the bench or seat or step or stool or chair. As I sit there my slave who is carrying my writing-case hands me my tablets and my writing-case, my straight-edge, my tablet, and my lupines. . . . I erase and I write beside the line, and I write and show it to my teacher. And he praised me because of my good writing. I reread what I wrote syllable by syllable. I recite. I have recited before you. Lies. I do not lie. "If you speak truly," my *paedagogus* said to me, "let us go home, so that we may be able to go to the Greek and the Latin grammarian." Then we are dismissed to go to the *palaestra*, for Latin and Greek studies. I entered the school of the Greek teacher and the lecture-room of the Latin teacher. I learn my texts. If I am ready, I give them back immediately; otherwise, I read them again. . . . I took a reading, verses, notes. An unknown book is explained to me, or an unknown reading. An explanation is provided to me. I take a passage, and others along with me read it *ex tempore*, and the rest repeat it accurately. With an assistant-teacher the younger children practise translations and syllables, declension of sayings,[2] grammar of all kinds, speech; the declension of nouns, genders of nouns, numbers, grammatical forms, words letter-by-letter, letters (vowels and semi-vowels and voiceless consonants) – they divide, shorten, and pronounce them with raised pitch.

8.4. First lessons

Quintilian, *Training in Oratory* 1.1.24–37

Quintilian sets out the best way for a child to learn how to read, write, and pronounce the words he or she sees. The method which he recommends had been in established use for several centuries (**3.15**, **6.1**; also Plato, *Republic* 402a–b). His advice in regard to the memorization of moral maxims and to practice in handwriting can be illustrated from many school-book papyri (Cribiore 1996: 43–47). Further reading: Marrou 1956: 269–71; Bowen 1972: 185–87; Bonner 1977: 165–72; Muir 1984; B. Rawson 2003: 157–58.

(24) I do not like the generally accepted practice of having young boys learn the names and order of the letters before their shapes. (25) This

---

2 As in **8.27a**.

impedes the recognition of the alphabet, for the children will not concentrate on the outlines of the letters but rather resort to their memories, which move faster than their eyes. This is why teachers, after sufficiently drilling the alphabet into boys in the conventional order, reverse that order and use various randomly selected sequences, until their students recognize the letters by their form rather than from the order in which they come. Accordingly, the best system is for pupils to learn the appearance of the letters along with their names. . . . (26) However, the problem that we have with the alphabet will not occur with syllables. I do not, nevertheless, rule out the well-known practice of stimulating young children to learn by giving them letters made of ivory to play with, or anything else that can be devised to enhance the enjoyment of children of that age, anything that it is pleasurable to touch, examine and find the name for.

(27) Now, when the boy has developed the ability to trace the outlines of letters, it will be expedient to have those outlines carved as accurately as possible on a wooden panel, so that the child's pen can be guided along them, keeping to the grooves. The pen will not slip, as it does on wax, since it will be restrained by the borders on each side, and will not be able to leave the track marked out for it, while tracing these prearranged outlines with increasing speed and frequency will steady the boy's fingers and make it unnecessary for him to have the help of someone guiding his hand by putting his own hand on it.[3] (28) Attention paid to writing well and rapidly is not inapposite, despite the general neglect of it by people of distinction. In fact, the ability to write is of fundamental importance in intellectual activities, and the only means by which genuine progress, based on sound foundations, can be achieved in these areas. A slow pen is an obstacle to contemplation; a clumsy and obscure one is undecipherable, calling for the further effort of dictating material to be copied to a secretary. (29) Accordingly, it will, in general, prove gratifying not to have neglected even this aspect of education, but it is especially gratifying when one comes to writing personal letters to one's friends.

(30) With syllables there is no shortcut. They all have to be learned, nor should one follow the generally accepted practice of postponing the most difficult ones so that they are acquired when the pupil reaches the stage of writing nouns. (31) And one must avoid placing too much confidence in a child's memory. Better to repeat the syllables and drill them into him over a period of time and, when he is reading, not hurry him on to connected or more rapid reading, except

---

3 For the technique described here, see Muir 1984; compare the advice in **3.15**.

when the way the letters are joined together is so smooth and obvious that the child does not have to stop and think. The pupil should then begin to join these syllables to form words, and with the words construct continuous prose. (32) It is hard to believe how far reading can be retarded by excessive haste; for when what children are trying to do is beyond their capabilities, the result is hesitation, breaks in continuity and repetitions, and, after making mistakes, children become diffident even about the things which they know. (33) So, at the start, reading should be confident; then it should develop continuity and remain quite slow for a long period until, through practice, speed can be achieved without mistakes. (34) For looking ahead to the right, as is universally taught, is not only methodologically sound, but also a matter of practice: the pupil must simultaneously utter the words that he has passed and look at what is to come, performing the extremely difficult task of dividing his attention between vocal and visual activity.

When, following the traditional practice, the boy begins to write out nouns, it will prove advantageous to ensure that he does not waste his time on pedestrian, everyday words. (35) He can from the start memorize the meanings of more recondite vocabulary . . . as he goes along, and he can acquire during his elementary schooling something which later on would require time of its own. And, while we are on peripheral matters, see that the verses given to the pupil as a model for his handwriting do not contain worthless maxims, but ones which offer sound moral guidance. (36) These remain in the memory into one's advanced years, and, when they are instilled in a mind not yet mature, they will aid moral development. The pupil can also amuse himself memorizing the sayings of famous men and choice passages, chiefly drawn from the poets (poetry having greater attraction for children). For a good memory is, as I shall explain at the appropriate point, absolutely indispensable, and it is by practice that this is strengthened and nourished. Furthermore, at the stage of development of which we are now talking, which is intellectually unproductive, the memory is about the only faculty that can be developed by education.

(37) To improve elocution and clarity of pronunciation, it would be a good idea to have pupils of this age reel off as quickly as they can some names and lines of verse, chosen for their difficulty, which are strung together from a number of syllables fitting together very badly, and which are therefore harsh on the ear (these are called *chalinoi* in Greek[4]). An apparently small matter this, but overlooking it leads to many defects in pronunciation which persist thereafter, incurable and perverse, unless they are eliminated in the earliest years.

---

4 Literally "bridles," i.e. "tongue-twisters"; see **6.1c**.

8.5. Some elementary exercises

(a) Milne 1908: 121–22, (b) *P.Rain.Unterricht* 7
(Harrauer and Sijpesteijn 1985)

The material in these extracts illustrates some practical applications of the advice Quintilian gives in **8.4**. **8.5a** was written on an ostrakon (pottery fragment) and discovered in upper Egypt, probably in the ancient town of Thebes; its date is believed to be some time around AD 150. **8.5b** shows a more elaborate set of alphabetic exercises, this time on papyrus, and dated to the first century AD. They illustrate Quintilian's advice (25) that children should be presented with letters out of their normal sequence. Hence in **a** the letters of the alphabet are matched up in two pairs of vertical columns, the first letter (A) with the last (Ω), the second (B) with the second-last (Ψ), and so on. In **b**, line 2 shows the alphabet in reverse order (a very common exercise); lines 3 and 4 consist of nonsense words which test the student's ability to pronounce some difficult syllables (so-called *chalinoi*, mentioned by Quintilian in **8.4** [37]); and line 5 has the letters of the alphabet in the sequence first letter/last letter, second letter/second-last letter etc. The evidence for the child's learning of all possible syllables (lines 12–18) and their combination into words predates Quintilian by several hundred years (see **8.4**, introduction). Further reading: Cribiore 1996: 184, 191–92.

a

A	Ω		I	Π
B	Ψ		K	O
Γ	X		Λ	Ξ
Δ	Φ		M	N
E	Y			
Z	T			
H	C			
Θ	P			

b

αβγδεζηθι]κλμνξοπρστυφχψω	1
ωψχφυτσ]ρποξνμλκιθηζεδγβα	2
]θυπτησφλεγμοδρωψ	3
]ψχθωινπληκτρονσφι[ξ	4
αωβψγχ]δφευζτησθριπκολξμν	5

da	za	tha	12
de	ze	the	13
dê	zê	thê	14
di	zi	thi	15
do	zo	tho	16
du	zu	thu	17
dô	zô	thô	18

8.6. Practising on Menander

This wax tablet from the second century AD contains two lines of iambic verse written out neatly at the top by a teacher: (1) "Accept advice from a wise man." (2) "Do not put trust carelessly in all your friends." Underneath, in a much less fluent hand, a student has copied these verses twice, with the letters confined between sets of parallel lines. The first verse is by Menander; the second may be as well. Further reading: Marrou 1956: 156–57; Bonner 1977: 172–77; Morgan 1998: 120–51; Rowlandson 1998: 308–9.

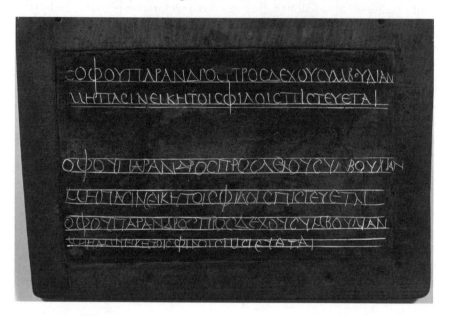

Figure 8.2 Verses from Menander on wax writing tablet. British Library, Add. 34186

8.7. Simple arithmetic

(a) Horace, *The Art of Poetry* 323–32, (b) *PSI* 763, ll. 26–35

Horace contrasts the practical focus of Roman education with the literary orientation of the Greeks (**a**). While the stereotype that Horace draws here may have had some foundation in truth, we know that around the same time Greek children too were learning basic kinds of calculation, as the fragment of a first-century AD papyrus from Egypt indicates (**b**). Further reading: Marrou 1956: 157–58; Bonner 1977: 180–88; Cribiore 2001: 180–83.

a

To the Greeks, . . . the Muse granted talent and the ability to speak in a smooth style. Roman boys, with lengthy sums, learn to divide a penny into a hundred parts. "Let Abinus' son tell us this: if one twelfth is taken away from five twelfths, what is left? . . . You could have answered by now!" "One third." "Splendid! You'll be able to look after your affairs! If a twelfth is added, what does it become then?" "A half." But once this blight and love of money has tainted the soul, can we hope for poems to be fashioned that are worth smearing with oil of cedar and keeping in a bookcase of smooth cypress?

b

First, consider how much ¼ drachma is. – 1½ obols.

And how much is ¹⁄₁₂ drachma? – It's ½ obol.

Add 1½ obols and ½ obol, which equal 2 obols, and consider what part of the drachma it is. – ⅓.

So ¼ and ¹⁄₁₂ added together is ⅓.

8.8. The carrot . . .

(a) Quintilian, *Training in Oratory* 1.1.20, (b) Horace, *Satires* 1.1.25–26

It was helpful to give young children some encouragement to learn lessons such as those described in **8.4** and presented in **8.3, 5, 6**.

a

I am not so insensitive to age-differences as to think that pressure should be cruelly put on young minds from the start, and that work should be clearly demanded of them. For one should above all else see to it that a boy not yet able to love his studies will not begin to hate them, and that he will not, even after the passage of the formative years, shrink away from the bitter taste he once received from them. Let him have fun learning. He should be asked questions and given praise, and he should never feel happy about not achieving a goal. Sometimes, if he is recalcitrant, let another receive his lesson so that he may envy him; and let him occasionally be in competition, and feel more often than not that he is the winner. He should even be enticed by the prizes that boys of that age strive for.

b

Cajoling teachers sometimes give their boys little pastries to make them want to learn the rudiments.

8.9. . . . and the stick

(a) Quintilian, *Training in Oratory* 1.3.14–15,
(b) Horace, *Epistles* 2.1.69–71

Quintilian's disapproval of corporal punishment (**a**) doubtless reflected a minority viewpoint. More typical was the behaviour of Orbilius (**b**), one of whose students was Horace. It is from Horace in particular that we hear of Orbilius' irascibility and occasionally violent behaviour (see also Suetonius, *On Teachers of Grammar and Rhetoric* 9). Further reading: Marrou 1956: 272–73; Booth 1973; Bonner 1977: 143–45; Kaster 1995: 125–37; B. Rawson 2003: 175–77.

a

(14) I have very little time for corporal punishment of students, even though it is accepted practice and Chrysippus[5] is not opposed to it. In the first place it is offensive, and appropriate only for slaves, and it is assuredly an indignity, as one will see if its use is imagined at another age. Moreover, if a student is so uncouth that he fails to respond to criticism, he will, like the worst slaves, also become insensitive to beatings. Finally, such punishment will even be superfluous if the boy has someone strictly supervising his studies. (15) These days it seems that it is generally a matter of correcting the results of the *paedogogus'* slovenliness: rather than being *obliged* to do the right thing, boys are punished for *not* doing it. Finally, coerce a small child with beatings and what will you do when he is a young man? Such intimidation cannot work on him, and he has more important things to learn.

b

But I am not attacking, nor do I recommend destroying, the poetry of Livius,[6] poetry which I remember "slogger" Orbilius dictating to me when I was a boy.

8.10. Furius Philocalus, *magister*

This relief sculpture and accompanying inscription date to the late first century BC or early first century AD. Furius Philocalus was an elementary teacher; since he was responsible for young children, this inscription's praise

---

5 For Chrysippus, see **6.2**.
6 Livius Andronicus; see **7.7**, with n. 5.

Figure 8.3 Funerary epigram and relief sculpture for Furius Philocalus. *CIL* 10.3969
(Capua, Italy)

of his upright behaviour (a quality not to be taken for granted in teachers,
e.g. Quintilian, *Training in Oratory* 1.2.4–5, 2.2.1–8) comes as no surprise.
Furius sits in the middle of the relief, holding a writing tablet, as does the
boy on his right. A girl stands on his left. Further reading: B. Rawson 1999:
85–86, 2003: 160–61.

All the time that he had his soul locked in its stronghold, and he was
amongst the living, he lived his entire life to his final day with thrift
and modesty. He was an Auruncan, called Furius Philocalus, a teacher
of elementary school (*magister ludi literari*), a man of consummate
morality with regard to his pupils, and also a scrupulous writer of wills.
He never refused anyone, and he hurt nobody. And so, a trusted man,
he spent his life without fear. His bones now lie here, placed there by
the centuries.

8.11. The difference that parents can make

Quintilian, *Training in Oratory* 1.1.6–7

Quintilian acknowledges the influence of supportive parents on the education of their children (cf. **7.4c**). Further reading: Bonner 1977: 98–104.

(6) In parents I would like to see the maximum possible education, and I am not just talking about fathers. For we have been told that their mother Cornelia contributed greatly to the eloquence of the Gracchi, and her truly erudite oratorical style has also been transmitted to posterity in her letters. Laelia, too, the daughter of Gaius Laelius, is said to have reproduced the elegance of her father in her way of speaking, and the speech before the triumvirs delivered by Quintus Hortensius' daughter Hortensia is read today, and not only as a mark of honour to her sex. (7) Those men, too, who have not had the advantage of an education themselves should not be less interested in educating their sons. In fact, they should for this very reason be all the more diligent about helping them in every way they can.

8.12. The Greek language in the Roman curriculum

Quintilian, *Training in Oratory* 1.1.12–14

The censorial edict of 92 BC against "Latin *rhetores*" (**7.11**) demonstrates that at that time Romans were wrestling with the role of Greek in their own educational curriculum. By Quintilian's day the issue was no longer a matter of controversy: Greek was now on an equal footing with Latin, and might even be given priority over it. Further reading: Marrou 1956: 255–64; Adams 2003: 9–18.

(12) I prefer the boy to begin with Greek. Latin, which is in more frequent use, he will absorb come what may, and, at the same time, since it is from the Greek academic disciplines that ours are derived, he should be instructed in these first. (13) On the other hand, I would not have this practice followed so scrupulously that the boy for a long time speaks and learns nothing but Greek, as is the fashion these days. This produces numerous imperfections in pronunciation, which then has a foreign intonation, and in phraseology, with Greek modes of expression embedded in it through habit, and obstinately lingering on even when it is another language that is being spoken. (14) Thus Latin should come hard on the heels of Greek, and soon accompany it; and

in this way, when we have put both languages on an equal footing, the one is not likely to impede the other.

8.13. Home or school?

Quintilian, *Training in Oratory* 1.2.1–3

The question that Quintilian tackles – whether a child's education should be conducted at home or in a school – had already been considered by Aristotle (**5.22**). In the paragraphs that follow this passage (not included here), Quintilian explains his preference that children be educated in school. Since the child he is now discussing has already learned to read and write (**8.4**), it is apparent that, in the case he envisages, the student's first school is that of the *grammaticus*, not the *grammatistés*. Private education was more expensive and was therefore restricted to relatively wealthy families. Further reading: Kennedy 1969: 43–44; Bonner 1977: 104–8; Booth 1979a: 2–4; B. Rawson 2003: 160–64.

(1) Little by little our boy must grow up, leave his mother's arms and pay serious attention to his studies. This, then, is the most appropriate point at which to deal with the question of whether it is preferable that his education be conducted at home, within his own house, or be entrusted to a crowded school and to "public" teachers. (2) I realize that it is the latter which has commended itself to those responsible for the moral codes of the most renowned communities, as well as those who are the most distinguished experts in this area. But we cannot pretend that there are not some people who have convictions of their own, and disagree with this generally accepted system of education. These seem to have two things in particular in mind. First, they claim that they are taking the pupil's morals into account by having him avoid contact with a large number of people who are at an age which is particularly susceptible to vice, and which has often been the cause of scandalous behaviour. . . . Secondly, whoever the teacher, it seems likely that he will give more freely of his time to a single pupil than if he is sharing that time amongst a number of them. (3) The first point is certainly an important one. For if it were established that schools advanced intellectual development at the expense of moral development, it would be my opinion that learning to live decently is more important even than learning to be an excellent orator. But, in my view, at least, the two are inextricably connected: I do not think anyone can be an orator unless he is a good man, and I would not want him to be, even if he could.

8.14. Private instruction

(a) Cicero, *Letters to his brother Quintus* 2.4.2 (March 56 BC),
(b) Cicero, *Letters to Atticus* 4.15.10 (27 July 54 BC)

Cicero was wealthy enough to have a private tutor in his own home for his ten-year-old nephew Quintus (**a**). Theophrastus of Amisos (southern coast of the Black Sea), nicknamed Tyrannio, came to Rome in the early 60s and gained a reputation as a teacher and literary scholar. In addition to his teaching he also organized Cicero's private library (*Letters to Atticus* 4.4a.1). Marcus Pomponius Dionysius (**b**) was a learned freedman (ex-slave) who received his freedom from Cicero's close friend Titus Pomponius Atticus. He continued to serve Atticus as his secretary; to judge from this letter, he provided instruction as well. Further reading: Pfeiffer 1968: 272–73; Marshall 1975: 259–61; Bonner 1977: 28–32; B. Rawson 2003: 153–57.

a

Your son Quintus, a fine boy, is receiving an excellent education – I notice it all the more these days because Tyrannio is teaching him at my house.

b

Give my good wishes to Dionysius, and ask him to press you [i.e. Atticus] to come as soon as possible so that he can teach my son Cicero, and me, too.

8.15. Students away from home

(a) Cicero, *Letters to his Friends* 16.21.3–6, (b) *POxy* 1296

Cicero's son Marcus was 21 or 22 when, in early August 44, he wrote from Athens to Tiro, his father's freedman and secretary (**a**). Earlier that year his father had complained to Marcus about his laziness and dissolute behaviour. In **b**, Aurelius Dius, who is studying away from his home in the Egyptian town of Oxyrhynchus, likewise attempts to ease his father's anxieties. The date of this papyrus letter is the third century AD. Further reading: Cribiore 2001: 108–14.

(3) My relationship with Cratippus,[7] you can be sure, is more that of a son than a pupil. I happily attend his lectures, and I am also very much taken with his delightful personality. I spend entire days with him, and often a part of the evening, too, as I beg him to have dinner with me as often as he can. Since this close relationship has been established between us, he often drifts in on us unexpectedly, and when we are at dinner and casting aside the seriousness of philosophy, he will share a joke with us like a friend. So do your best to get to see this man who possesses such qualities – a man so pleasant, and so outstanding – as soon as you can.

(4) What am I to say about Bruttius? At no time do I let him leave my company – his life-style is frugal and ascetic, but living with him is also a great delight. For humour is certainly not isolated from our scholarship and the shared inquiries we hold each day. I have rented quarters for him close by, and as far as I can I give him assistance in his straitened circumstances from my slender means.

(5) In addition, I have begun declamation in Greek with Cassius, but in Latin I want training with Bruttius. As my close friends and daily companions I have the men whom Cratippus brought with him from Mytilene, learned fellows who are very well thought of by him. Epicrates . . . is with me a lot of the time, and so too are Leonides and all the other people like these.

But enough about me. (6) With regard to the comments you make on Gorgias, he was of use to me in my daily practice of declamation, but I made everything else secondary to obeying my father's orders, for he had sent me written instructions to dismiss him immediately. I did not want to hesitate in case any excessive support for the man raised my father's suspicions. And then it also occurred to me that judging my father's judgement in the matter was a serious thing.

b

Warmest greetings from Aurelius Dius to Aurelius Horion, my father whom I love so dearly. Each day I fall down before the gods here and appeal to them on your behalf. Do not worry yourself, father, about my studies. I am working hard and obtaining some relaxation. I will be just fine. . . . I pray that you remain in good health, father. Deliver this to Aurelius Horion from his son Dius.

---

7 A Peripatetic (Aristotelian) philosopher. Of the other figures named in this letter, nothing is known of either Bruttius or Cassius; Epicrates has not been securely identified; Leonides was a correspondent of Cicero senior; Gorgias is mentioned elsewhere as a noted teacher of rhetoric.

8.16. Finding and keeping a good teacher

(a) *SB* 3.6262 (b) *POxy* 930, (c) *PGiss* 80

Parents and students often experienced difficulty in securing the services of a competent teacher. The following papyri describe different sets of circumstances. In **a** (early third century AD), the homesick and neglected Thonis is in danger of losing his teacher, apparently because his father has failed to come to a financial arrangement with him. In **b** (second or third century AD), the teacher Diogenes seems to have departed from Oxyrhynchus in search of better prospects in Alexandria. This letter is from a parent to his or her son (named Ptolemaeus in the portion of the letter not presented here). Heraidous in **c** (*c*. AD 120) is a girl, probably in her teens, though the sender of this letter is unknown. The letter belongs to an archive of over two hundred which all have to do with members of a single family in Hermopolis, Egypt (Rowlandson 1998: 118–24; Bagnall and Cribiore 2006: 139–63). The term *kathegetés* in **b** and **c** was applied to private teachers, whether at the elementary, secondary or rhetorical level; cf. **9.17**. Further reading: Pomeroy 1988: 715–21; Cribiore 2001: 94–101, 111–14, 216–18.

a

Greetings from Thonis to Arion my father and lord. . . . .Please note that this is the fifth letter I have written to you, but that, with just one exception, you have not written to me, not even about your health; nor have you come to visit me. Although you gave me your guarantee that you were on your way, you have not come even to find out whether my teacher was giving me his attention or not. He himself asks me on an almost daily basis whether I have heard any news about your now being on your way, to which I just reply "Yes."

Please, then, make it a priority to come to me quickly so that he undertakes my instruction as he is eager to do. If you had come with me on my journey up here, I would have received that instruction long ago. As you travel, bear in mind those matters about which I have written to you on several occasions. Come and see me quickly before he makes his departure for regions further up-river. Please give my best wishes to all members of our household by name, together with those who hold us in affection, and give my greetings also to my teachers. I pray, my father and lord, that it will be my good fortune that you remain in good health for many years along with my brothers – may they be protected against the evil eye. And please remember our young pigeons. To my father Arion from. . . .

b

Please do not hesitate to write to me about anything you may need from here. I was sorry to discover from the daughter of our tutor (*kathegetés*) Diogenes that he had moved down the river, since my anxieties had been allayed by the knowledge that he intended to concentrate on you to the best of his ability. In my concern I sent to find out about your state of health and to learn what you were reading. He informed me that you were reading the sixth book [of Homer's *Iliad*] and provided me with a detailed report on your *paidagogos*. Thus, my son, in these circumstances you and your *paidagogos* must see to it that you are placed under the care of a suitable teacher. Your sisters, the children of Theonis (may they be protected against the evil eye) and the various members of the household by name send you their best wishes. Give my best to Eros your *paidagogos* whom I hold in the highest regard.

c

Greetings from Heraidous . . . Helena, Tinoutis, her papa, the entire household, and the mother of our dearest Heraidous. Please send the young pigeons and small birds which I do not normally eat . . . to the tutor (*kathegetés*) of Heraidous. Apollonius' mother, Helena, appeals to you to maintain control over her son Hermaeus. Please send whatever I did not eat when I . . . from you to my daughter's tutor (*kathegetés*) in order that he may devote special attention to her. I pray that you are in good health. Choiak 17.[8]

8.17. Pliny's gifts

(a) Pliny, *Letters* 4.13.3–9, (b) *CIL* 5.5262

Selection **a** is from a letter which Pliny wrote in AD 104 to his friend, the orator and historian Cornelius Tacitus (**9.6, 14a, 15a**). Most families could not afford private tuition for their children. In Greek cities in the Hellenistic period the cost of schooling was sometimes met by a private benefactor (*euergetés*), who provided the necessary funds to enable a city to hire teachers for its young people (**6.8–9, 11, 13**). The arrangement which Pliny sets up in **a** should be distinguished from the Hellenistic examples of "euergetism," since it is clear that in this case education will be provided for those

---

8 The Egyptian month Choiak = 27 November–26 December (cf. **9.17**).

children whose fathers contribute to the overall cost of hiring the teachers, not for all students regardless of their ability to pay. The discussion in this letter is about the hiring of a teacher of rhetoric (*rhetor*); that is the reason for Pliny's writing to Tacitus, as the final part of this letter shows (not included here). Selection **b** is the longest of three related inscriptions produced after Pliny's death (*c.* 112). It records his benefactions to his hometown of Comum, which included money for the support of boys and girls during his own lifetime, as well as a library and the funding for its upkeep. Further reading: Marrou 1956: 304–5; Bonner 1977: 107–9, 156–57; B. Rawson 2003: 184–87.

a

(3) I was recently in my hometown, and the young son of a fellow-townsman of mine came to pay his respects to me. "Are you a student?" I asked him. "Yes," he replied. "Where?" "In Milan." "Why not here?" to which his father (who was in fact present, having himself brought the boy) answered: "Because we have no teachers here."

"Why not?" I asked. (4) "It is very much in the interests of those who are fathers" – and as luck would have it there were a number of fathers listening – "to have your children go to school here rather than elsewhere. For where could they spend their time more enjoyably than in their own town? Where have a more pure upbringing than under their parents' eyes, and where one less expensive than at home? (5) How little it would cost to hire teachers if you pooled your money, adding to the teachers' fees the amount that you now spend on lodging, travel and what is bought out of town – and everything is bought out of town! I do not yet have children, and I am personally ready to make a grant of a third of whatever sum you decide to raise, and will do this for our community as though it were for a daughter or a parent. (6) I would actually undertake to supply it all were I not fearful that at some stage my gift might become the object of sharp practice, as I see to be happening in many places where teachers are hired at public expense. (7) For such malfeasance there is but one remedy, namely to leave exclusively to the parents the right to hire the teachers, and by obliging them to contribute funds to see to it that they are scrupulous about making the right choice. (8) For those who may perhaps be negligent with other people's money will certainly be careful with their own, and will make every effort to see that only a reputable person takes money from me if he will also be taking money from them.

(9) "So you should reach an agreement together and take encouragement from my good will – I want the contribution that I have to make to be as great as possible. There is nothing finer that you can

offer your children, nothing for which your hometown will be more grateful. Let the children who are born here be brought up here, and right from infancy let them love, and live on, their native soil. And my hope is that you bring in such eminent teachers that an education will be sought here by those in neighbouring towns, and that other people's children will soon come in droves to this place as your children now go elsewhere."

b

Gaius Plinius Caecilius Secundus . . . ; in his will he bequeathed baths at a cost of . . . sesterces, as well as 300,000 sesterces[9] to furnish them, . . . with the interest on 200,000 sesterces for their maintenance; likewise for the support of his one hundred freedmen he bequeathed to the city 1,866,666 sesterces, the interest of which he wanted subsequently to be used for a dinner for the city's people; likewise in his lifetime he gave 500,000 sesterces for support of the city's boys and girls, and he left a library and 100,000 sesterces for its maintenance.

8.18. Should daughters receive the same education as sons?

Musonius Rufus 4

Musonius (c. AD 30–c. 100) was a Roman knight and a Stoic philosopher. In this extract he bases his arguments on the belief that females and males have an equal capacity for virtue (areté). It is clear that his thoughts on the education of women were influenced by Plato (**5.10, 14**). Further reading: Hemelrijk 1999: 60–64; Nussbaum 2002: 286–93, 300–313; B. Rawson 2003: 201–3.

Since men and women [share the same virtues], it is absolutely inescapable that the same education and upbringing are appropriate for both, since, in the case of every animal and plant, the care it is given, if properly applied, must produce the virtue peculiar to it. If a man and a woman needed to have a similar ability to play the flute, and if this were an essential dimension of life for each of them, we would teach the art of flute-playing to both without discrimination, as would be the case if each needed to play the lyre. And if both of them, the one just as much as the other, need to achieve competence in the virtue appropriate to a human being, to have the ability to use their minds in the same way, to exercise self-control, and to share together qualities of

---

9 The sesterce was a gold coin. Its value fluctuated over time; in the middle of the first century BC a labourer earned about 1,000 sesterces a year.

courage and justice, shall we not then provide each with the same education and shall we not teach both without discrimination that skill in particular which has the capacity to produce a virtuous human being? But, of course, this, and no other, is the policy we must follow. . . .

Consequently, I believe that we are justified in providing the same education to both male and female in matters relating to virtue. Starting right from infancy, they must be taught that one particular act is good, another bad (and that this applies to both sexes), that one act is beneficial, another harmful, and that they should do one thing, but not another. This is the process which results in prudence being developed in students, girls and boys alike, and without any distinction between them. Then we must inculcate a sense of shame when confronted with anything that brings disgrace. If these two characteristics are present, it is inevitable that men and women will show self-control. Moreover, those properly educated, whoever they may be, male or female, must become accustomed to endure suffering, to have no fear of death and not to allow themselves to collapse in face of adversity, since these are the habits which produce manly courage, and I established the fact a little earlier that women, too, must have their share of manly courage. Furthermore, the finest lesson one can teach, and one which produces justice in those who learn it, is to avoid greed, to show respect for principles of fairness, and to have an innate impulse, as a human being, to confer benefits on others and to avoid doing them harm. Is there any reason why a man should have a better right to be given this instruction?

If, for Heaven's sake, it is appropriate that women should have a sense of justice, both sexes must be given the same instruction in the most important and critical principles. If it turns out that a man has some piece of knowledge of minor importance, which falls within the scope of a particular skill, and a woman does not, or conversely that she does and he does not, that does not prove that each has received a different education. Just ensure each sex does not learn different lessons on the most important principles in life, and that here their instruction is identical. If someone were to ask me which branch of knowledge is to take precedence in this form of education, my answer will be that, just as is the case with a man, without philosophy no woman would be properly educated. By this I do not mean to say that women must be capable of remarkable clarity or cleverness in argumentation, if they are to apply their education in philosophy as women (in fact, I do not particularly approve of this in the case of men). What I do mean is that women ought to have a disposition marked by its goodness and a character marked by its nobility, and philosophy is nothing but the cultivation of the habit of nobility.

8.19. Educated women

(a) Pliny, *Letters* 4.19.4, (b) Pliny, *Letters* 5.16.1–3,
(c) Sallust, *The Catilinarian Conspiracy* 25.2–5

Pliny's bequest (**8.17b**) was for both boys and girls, and his references in **a** and **b** below make it clear that women of his class had the opportunity to receive an education in reading, writing and music. In his famous character-ization of the aristocratic Sempronia (**c**), Sallust finds fault on several grounds (not least Sempronia's alignment with the conspirator Catiline in 63 BC), but Sempronia's educational and intellectual attainments seem to have been the least of his concerns. Further reading: Pomeroy 1975: 170–76; E. Rawson 1985: 46–48; Hemelrijk 1999: 60–64; B. Rawson 2003: 197–209; D'Ambra 2007: 62–65.

a

She [i.e. Pliny's young wife Calpurnia] even sings my verses and adapts them to the lyre, with no expert giving her instruction – only love, which is the finest teacher.

b

I am very sad writing you this letter, for the younger daughter of our friend Fundanus is dead. . . . .How she loved all her nurses, her peda-gogues and her teachers for their various services! How attentive and intelligent was her reading, how sparing and restricted her amuse-ments! The most recent illness she bore with such self-control and patience, and even with resolve!

c

(2) Sempronia was a woman who, in pedigree and looks, as well as in her husband and children, was very well blessed. She was versed in Greek and Roman literature, and could dance and sing with a refine-ment greater than a respectable woman needs; and she was possessed of numerous other qualities that suit the life of luxury. (3) But to her anything was more precious than decency and modesty, and one would have found it hard to say whether it was to her finances or her reputation that she did more damage. (4) She had such a frenzied libido that she was more often chasing men than being chased by them. She had often before this broken her word, denied on oath her debts, been an accessory to murder, and gone headlong into perdition through a combination of high living and poverty. (5) But there was

nothing wrong with her intellect. She could write poetry, keep people entertained, employ a mode of conversation that was modest or alluring or outrageous. In short, she was full of wit, and full of charm.

8.20. Hermione

Girton College, Cambridge

This is a portrait of a young woman named Hermione. Painted on linen, the portrait covers a mummy discovered in 1911 in Hawara, Egypt. It is dated to the first half of the first century AD. The name of the young woman (no older than about 25 at the time of her death) is written in Greek capitals

Figure 8.4 Mummy portrait of Hermione *grammatiké*. Girton College, Cambridge

(below her chin), and beneath her name appears the term *grammatiké*. This term must mean one of two things: either it is the feminine form of *grammatikos* and indicates that Hermione was a teacher of letters, or it means "literate," "skilled in letters." Further reading: Rowlandson 1998: 300–301; Cribiore 2001: 78–83; D'Ambra 2007: 135–36.

8.21. Giton and Hermeros

Petronius, *Satyrica* 58

Hermeros, the speaker in this extract from Petronius' novel *Satyrica* (middle of the first century AD) is a freedman (ex-slave). He is indignant that the boy Giton, whom he considers to be a slave, has received a liberal education, which by definition was an education fit for a free (*liber*) person (cf. **9.4**); hence his scornful reference to "geometries," "illogics," and "wraths" (an allusion to the study of Homer's *Iliad*). He believes instead that practical training in the rudiments of reading and writing and in simple arithmetic is good enough for a slave (cf. Martial, *Epigrams* 10.62). Further reading: Forbes 1955: 323–28; Booth 1979b.

> Either I don't know who I am or you're going to stop that laughing, even if you've a golden beard. I'm going to see that Athena vents her anger on you and that man who first made you into a "come and get it" boy. I didn't learn your "geometries," your "criticals," your "illogics," or your "wraths," but I know my capital letters and can do my percentages in asses, pounds and sesterces. O.K., let's you and I put on a little bet, if you like; come on, I'm putting down my cash. Now you'll find out your father wasted the school-fees, even if you do know rhetoric.

8.22. A trade for the slave Chaeramon

POxy 724

The following papyrus letter from Oxyrhynchus was written in AD 155. It is the contract for a slave to learn shorthand from a shorthand-writer (*semiographos*). Further reading: Forbes 1955: 328–34; Marrou 1956: 312.

> Panechotes, also known as Panares, the former *kosmetés*[10] from the city of Oxyrhynchus, brings his greetings to the shorthand-writer, Apollonius, through the person of his friend Gemellus. I have placed

---

10 For this position, see **6.3b**.

my slave Chaeramon with you to learn the symbols of which your son Dionysius has knowledge. This apprenticeship is to be for a period of two years, excluding feast-days, commencing from the present month of Phamenoth[11] in the eighteenth year of the reign of our lord Antoninus Caesar and at the fee of 120 silver drachmas which we agreed to. Of this sum you have received the first instalment of 40 drachmas; the second payment of 40 drachmas you will receive once the boy has absorbed the contents of the entire manual; the third payment of the remaining 40 drachmas you will receive at the completion of the period when the boy is writing and reading flawlessly from every kind of prose. If you complete his training within this period, I will not wait until the end of the apprenticeship stipulated. However, I will have no right to remove the boy from you before the end of the period, and he will remain with you after it for however many days or months as he may have done no work.

8.23. Teachers' titles

Suetonius, *On Teachers of Grammar and Rhetoric* 4.1–3

Quintilian consistently uses the names *grammatista* (Latin version of Greek *grammatistés*) for the elementary teacher and *grammaticus* for the secondary teacher; he does this despite the fact that the corresponding Latin names *litterator* and *litteratus* were also available to him. Yet the subjects which the *grammatistés/litterator* and the *grammaticus/litteratus* taught were not as tightly defined or restricted as is often thought, and the one class of teacher frequently taught material more commonly associated with the other. In this extract Suetonius provides us with some idea of the confusion that existed over the meanings of these titles and the areas of expertise that the different levels of teacher claimed. Further reading: Booth 1979a, 1981; Kaster 1988: 443–46, 1995: 60–86.

> (1) It was Greek usage that made the term *grammaticus* gain in popularity [among the Romans], though originally such men were called *litterati*. Furthermore, in a short treatise in which he draws a distinction between *litteratus* and *eruditus*, Cornelius Nepos states that the expression *litterati* is commonly used of people who have the ability to discuss or write upon a topic with precision, insight and expertise, but that it is correctly applied to those who interpret the poets, the men called *grammatici* by the Greeks. (2) That the latter were also called

---

11 The Egyptian month Phamenoth = 25 February–25 March.

litteratores is proved by Messala Corvinus in one of his letters where he says he has no truck with Furius Bibaculus, nor even with Ticidas or the *litterator* Cato, his reference clearly being to Valerius Cato, well known both as a poet and grammarian (*grammaticus*). (3) There are some who distinguish between a *litteratus* and a *litterator*, as the Greeks do between a *grammaticus* and a *grammatista*, considering the former a thorough expert in the area and the latter reasonably well-versed in it. Orbilius[12] lends weight to their judgment with examples. In the time of our forefathers, he observes, when someone's house-hold slaves were put up for sale, it was not usual for the term *litteratus* to be indiscriminately written on the notice of sale; *litterator* was written instead, on the grounds that the slave had some literary back-ground, but was no expert.

8.24. Early *grammatiké* in Rome

Suetonius, *On Teachers of Grammar and Rhetoric* 3

The following passage from Suetonius appears after some remarks about the early days of literary education (*grammatiké*) in Rome (**7.7**). By repre-senting those first efforts as limited and unfocused, Suetonius gives the impression that the study of language and literature in the city of his day owed nearly everything to Romans and little to Greeks. Further reading: Kaster 1995: 68–86.

(1) The teaching of *grammatiké* was undertaken and promoted in all respects by Lucius Aelius from Lanuvium and his son-in-law, Servius Clodius.[13] Both were Roman knights with extensive and varied experi-ence in politics as well as scholarship. (2) Aelius bore two cognomina: *Praeconinus* because his father had been a town-crier, and *Stilo* because he used to write speeches for all the nobility. . . . (3) Servius pirated a book of his father-in-law's before its publication, and for this was disowned by him. He left Rome tired and ashamed, and fell prey to the gout. . . .

(4) Subsequently the subject became ever more popular and more studied. Even the most distinguished people were not reluctant to write on it themselves, and at times there are reported to have been more than twenty famous schools in the city. (5) Moreover, the fees charged by the grammarians (*grammatici*) and the incomes they received were so large that, as is well known, Lutatius Daphnis . . . was

---

12 See **8.9b**.
13 *C.* 150–85 BC and *c.* 120–60 BC respectively; see Kaster 1995: 68–72.

bought by Quintus Catulus for 700,000 sesterces and then manumitted a short while afterwards, and Lucius Appuleius was hired at an annual fee of 400 sesterces by the wealthy Roman knight Aeficius Calvinus to teach at Osca. (6) For *grammatiké* had now penetrated into the provinces as well, and some of its best-known teachers taught abroad, especially in Cisalpine Gaul. These included Octavius Teucer, Sescenius Iacchus and Oppius Chares, the last of whom kept teaching to the end of his days when he was not just lame but blind as well.

8.25. Horace at school

(a) Horace, *Satires* 1.6.71–82, (b) *Epistles* 2.2.41–48

In **a**, Horace speaks of elementary education and secondary (literary) education not as distinct stages but as alternatives: he *could* have gone to Flavius' school along with the sons of centurions, where, it appears, he would have learned basic reading and writing; instead his father aspired to have his son receive the kind of education that the son of a knight or senator would receive. The first sentence in **b** makes it clear that this loftier curriculum included Homer's *Iliad*, whose subject is "the wrath of Achilles." Since Horace gives us no hint that his education in the more prestigious school was preceded by basic instruction in reading and writing, it seems safe to assume that the instruction which he received from the *grammaticus* represented his first formal education and that he learned to read and write either at home or from the *grammaticus* himself. The second sentence in this extract reveals that Horace's education in Athens included philosophy. Horace was born in 65 BC; his education therefore took place in the 50s and 40s. Further reading: Booth 1979a: 2–3; E. Rawson 1985: 74–75.

a

Though a poor man on a meagre farm, my father refused to send me to the school of Flavius to which would go the eminent sons of eminent centurions, with writing case and tablet dangling from the left arm and their eight asses in their hand on the Ides of the month.[14] No, my father ventured rather to take his boy to Rome to be taught the subjects which any knight or senator would teach his children. Anyone seeing my clothes and the slaves attending me . . . was sure to believe that my means derived from inherited wealth. My father himself served as my guardian, an absolutely incorruptible one, doing the rounds of all my teachers with me.

---

14 The fifteenth of March, May, July and October, the thirteenth of all other months.

b

It was my lot to be brought up at Rome and to be taught the damage the wrath of Achilles inflicted on the Greeks. Good old Athens made a further contribution to my training, making me keen, of course, to distinguish between right and wrong, and search for truth in the groves of the Academy.

8.26. An education in three stages

Apuleius, *Florida* 20

Apuleius was born around AD 125 in Madaura (in modern Algeria) and educated in Carthage, Rome and Athens. Writing in the AD 160s, he indicates that his education traced the sequential path of *litterator* (*grammatistés*), *grammaticus*, and *rhetor* (followed also by the study of philosophy). Contrast the experience of Horace (**8.25**).

A wise man made this famous comment on dining: "The first cup," he said, "is to quench the thirst, the second is to promote jollity, the third to promote pleasure, and the fourth to promote madness." With the Muses it's the opposite: the more numerous and stronger the cups, the better they are for the health of the soul. The first cup trims the spirit with the *litterator*'s elementary lessons; the second equips it with the learning of the *grammaticus*; the third arms it with the eloquence of the *rhetor*. Most people drink to this extent. As for myself, I have drunk other cups, too, at Athens.

8.27. A plan of study

Quintilian, *Training in Oratory* 1.4.1–5

Once a child had completed his early education he could read and write, and by now he had also been introduced to literature through passages carefully chosen for their moral value (cf. **3.15**, **5.8**, **8.4** [35–36], **6**, **30** [4]). The next stage concentrated upon the study of grammar and literature – *grammatiké* – and was usually considered to be the responsibility of the *grammaticus*. For those who would continue their education, it preceded intensive training in rhetoric. Quintilian raises a question here which resonates with modern debates over the literary "canon": which poets and which of their works should students read at the secondary stage. Further reading: Marrou 1956: 251–52; Bowen 1972: 187–88; Bonner 1977: 212–49; O'Sullivan 1997.

(1) After the boy has acquired the ability to read and write, the *grammaticus* has the most important position. What I have to say is equally applicable to a Greek or a Latin teacher (though I should prefer a Greek teacher first); the approach will be the same for the two. (2) The profession is concisely described as encompassing two areas, namely the art of correct oral expression and the interpretation of the poets, but it involves more than is readily apparent. (3) For writing is connected with oral expression, and reading without error is a prerequisite for literary interpretation, while criticism is involved in all of these activities. The *grammatici* of old were so rigorous in their criticism that they not only granted themselves the right to mark lines of verse with an obelos,[15] and to reject from an author's *œuvre*, as one might illegitimate children from a family, books which they considered of spurious authorship, but they also drew up a prescribed list of authors, to which some were admitted while others were entirely expelled.

(4) Reading the poets is not enough for the *grammaticus*, either; every literary genre should be attentively examined, not simply for its content but also for its vocabulary, which is often sanctioned through its use by the authors. Furthermore, the *grammaticus'* training cannot be complete without a study of music, for he has to discuss metre and rhythm, and without a knowledge of astronomy he could not understand the poets who, other things aside, often use the rising and setting of the heavenly bodies as indicators of time. Philosophy cannot be overlooked, either, because there are a large number of passages, in almost all the poems which we have, that are derived from highly esoteric topics of natural philosophy, and especially because of Empedocles in Greek, and Varro and Lucretius in Latin, who committed their philosophical teachings to verse. (5) Eloquence is required, too, and in no short measure, for the *grammaticus* to be able to discuss in an appropriate and eloquent fashion each of the topics mentioned above. So one should not tolerate the criticism that this discipline [i.e. *grammatiké*] is trivial and sterile, for unless one has by means of it laid down a solid basis for the prospective orator's education, whatever you build on top will collapse. It is a discipline that is essential for boys, a joy to the aged, the pleasant companion of our private lives and, of all intellectual activities, the one in which appearance most falls short of the content.

15 See **6.5–6**.

8.28. In memory of a *grammatikos*

IG 9.1.880

On the island of Corcyra (modern Corfu), some time probably in the first century AD, a Greek inscription on stone was dedicated to the memory of the *grammatikos* Mnaseas, who taught astronomy, geometry and literature (especially Homer's poems). It is for his expertise as a teacher that he most wanted to be remembered and hoped to achieve some small measure of immortality.

> Traveller, stand for a moment beside the tomb and learn the exact truth. Know that the man buried here was called the son of Athenion. You must address him as Mnaseas, a name which will never die. Become familiar with the stories which were the source of his wise delight, how he told of the hallowed secrets of the universe and the fiery pathway through the stars which speed their way across the sky, how he explained the art of land-surveying, which uses lines to trace its plans. Well he knew the immortal books of Homer, in the folds of which are to be found the lengthy travels of the son of Laertes and the oppressive wrath. Having gained an accurate knowledge of all matters, he won a distinguished reputation. He left behind a wife and young son in his prime to whom he transmitted his craft. After gazing upon the light beneath the sun for forty years, he passed below this earth, a man sorely missed by the people of this city.

8.29. Exercises from Egypt

(a) British Museum Add. MS 37516, (b) Brit. Mus. Add. MS 37533, (c) Brit. Mus. Add. MS 37533

It is especially from papyri and other documentary sources that we are able to catch glimpses of the *grammatikos/grammaticus* in action. The following are translations of representative exercises from wooden tablets discovered in Egypt, all of which date to the third century AD. In order to understand and appreciate the teacher's methods it is necessary to know that, like many ancient and modern languages (e.g. Latin, German and the Slavic languages), ancient Greek is an "inflected" language. That is, the relationship between words in an ancient Greek sentence is determined mainly by the endings of those words, not by word-order, and the endings of words change according to the role which they play from one sentence to another (compare English "they" and "them"). In **a**, a sentence which appears first in a straightforward structure is then modified in its successive appearances by conversion of the grammatical subject ("the philosopher Pythagoras") into its other possible functions, each requiring a different "case" ending (only the first four of fifteen sentences have been translated here). Precisely this kind of exercise is prescribed in **9.8b** (5). The sentence itself is an example of a *chreia* (**9.8b** [3], **9.9** [26]). The other side of this tablet (not reproduced below) presents in a systematic way over one hundred of the forms in which the verb "to defeat" (*nikân*) can be expressed. Selection **b** is drawn from a book which consists of eight wooden tablets stitched together by a cord; it seems to have belonged to a student named Epaphroditus. Five sides contain a single exercise (sides 1a–4b; three sides are blank) in which 217 verbs are listed in groups of synonyms, arranged in columns (only the first ten phrases are translated here). Selection **c** contains material that appears on the fourth and fifth tablets; it consists of questions and answers intended to convey basic truths. Further reading: Kenyon 1909: 29–36; Marrou 1956: 275–77; Cribiore 1996: 46–47, 264–65; Hock and O'Neil 2002: 56–59, 62–66.

a

- Pythagoras the philosopher [grammatical subject: nominative case], after he had landed and was teaching letters, advised his students to abstain from red meat.
- A story is recounted of Pythagoras the philosopher [genitive case], after he had landed and was teaching letters, advising his students to abstain from red meat.
- It seemed good to Pythagoras the philosopher [dative case], after he had landed and was teaching letters, to advise his students to abstain from red meat.
- They say that Pythagoras the philosopher [accusative case], after he had landed and was teaching letters, advised his students to abstain from red meat.

b

Page 1b: I honour him / I extol him / I put him first / I reward him / I revere him / I dishonour him / I consider him worthless / I insult him / I revile him / I criticize him. . . .

c

What is it that teaches things? Experience.
What is it that is enjoyable in life? Being in good spirits.

What is it that persuades mankind? Speech (*logos*).
What is it that is strong in life? Wealth and virtue. . . .
What is it that pleases the gods? Justice.
What is the good thing that is done in bad circumstances? Daring or force.
What teaches mankind? Necessity or time.
What is the ugly face of life? Toil.

8.30. What should a student read?

Quintilian, *Training in Oratory* 1.8.4–12

Starting from the assumption that students will be fluent in both Latin and Greek, Quintilian goes into detail here on the question of what a student should read (cf. **8.27** [4]). Homer tops the list, and Virgil has by now also achieved the status of a "classic." Quintilian's recommendation of tragedy reflects the fact that Euripides was a favourite in the schools. We know as well that the comic playwrights Menander (**8.6**) and (among Roman students) Terence were standard authors. Despite the fact that Quintilian views the learning of *grammatikē* as a preliminary to the study of rhetoric, his reading-list contains no prose-writers, only poets. Further reading: Marrou 1956: 277–78; E. Rawson 1985: 267–81.

(4) Above all, since boys' minds are young and likely to absorb more deeply anything implanted in them when they are immature and totally ignorant, the goal of our pupils' education should be not only eloquence but also, and more importantly, integrity. (5) Accordingly, the accepted practice that reading commence with Homer and Virgil is excellent, though a boy does need more mature judgement to appreciate these poets' finer points (but there is time for this since they will be read more than once). For the time being just let his soul be uplifted by the sublime character of epic poetry; let him draw inspiration from the magnificence of its subject matter; let him be permeated with the most noble ideals. (6) Tragedy will prove useful; the lyric poets will add sustenance, too. But in the case of the latter, you must not only select the authors but also excerpt from their works, for the Greek lyricists contain much that is salacious, and there are parts of Horace which I would prefer not to elucidate. If possible, elegy, and especially love-elegy, should be removed from the reading-list, as should hendecasyllables, which are merely truncated Sotadic verses; failing that, at least they should be held in reserve for the more mature students. (7) Comedy can make a significant contribution to rhetoric because every kind of character and emotion falls within its purview, and how this can be used for the education of boys I shall presently explain at the

appropriate point, for, once the child's moral welfare is assured, it should figure amongst his most important reading matter. (8) I am referring to Menander, but without intending to exclude others, for Latin authors will also prove useful. But boys should be reading in class things that best develop the intellect and expand the mind; the long years that follow will provide the time for other material that belongs exclusively in the sphere of academic scholarship.

Even the archaic Latin dramatists will help greatly (although the majority of them were stronger in natural talent than artistic sophistication), particularly when it comes to their rich vocabulary, which can be seen to possess nobility in their tragedy, and elegance and a kind of Atticism in their comedy. (9) The arrangement of their material is also more carefully executed than that of most modern authors, who think that terse aphorisms are the highlight of any literary creation. At all events, one should be looking for nobility in their work, and a virility, so to speak, since even the way we deliver speeches these days has degenerated into all manner of decadent frills.

(10) Finally, let us take our cue from the greatest orators who use the poetry of the older authors to enhance the credibility of their cases or to embellish their rhetoric. (11) In Cicero especially, but often, too, in Asinius and the other orators of the recent past, we see lines quoted from Ennius, Accius, Pacuvius, Lucilius, Terence, Caecilius and others; and these are not only an attractive display of the speaker's erudition but also a pleasure for the audience, since their enjoyment of the poetry grants their ears some respite from the fierceness of forensic rhetoric. (12) There is a further, and not inconsiderable, advantage: the orators use the aphorisms of the poets almost as evidence for the arguments which they have put forward. Now what I said earlier will be of more relevance to younger boys, but the later advice will apply to the more mature students, for a love of *grammatiké* and the activity of reading are not limited to one's time at school, but continue throughout one's life.

8.31. The grammarian's catechism

(a) *PSI* 19, (b) Suetonius, *Life of Tiberius* 70.3

The kind of "literary criticism" that students engaged in during their reading of Homer, Virgil and other authors seems to have involved especially the memorization of mythological detail and historical facts. One of the main methods used to drill students and test their knowledge was a system of simple question-and-answer quizzes. Although the first example is from a papyrus that dates to the fifth century AD, it accurately reflects a practice that had been in existence for hundreds of years. The emperor Tiberius, for one, was attracted to the arcane learning encouraged by the kind of test illustrated here and in **8.32**. Further reading: Marrou 1956: 167–69; Bonner 1977: 238–39; Cribiore 2001: 207–9.

a

Who were on the side of the barbarians? Ares, Aphrodite, Apollo, Artemis, Leto and Scamander. Who was the king of the Trojans? Priam. Who was their commander-in-chief? Hector. Who served as their advisers? Polydamas and Agenor. Who were their prophets? Helenus and Cassandra, Priam's children. Who were their heralds? Idaeus and Eumedes, the father of Dolon, and perhaps Dolon himself.

b

But Tiberius was most interested in mythology, an interest he took to ridiculous and laughable extremes. He would challenge the *grammatici* – a class of men that he especially cultivated, as I noted above – with such questions as: "Who was Hecuba's mother?," "What was Achilles' name amongst the young ladies?," "What was the song the Sirens used to sing?"

8.32. Problems, criticisms and caricature

(a) Epictetus, *Discourses* 2.19.6–7, (b) Juvenal, *Satires* 7.229–36,
(c) *The Laughter-Lover* 197, (d) *SEC* 192

Epictetus criticizes the "grammarian's catechism" implicitly as rote-learning which requires no independent judgement from the student (**a**). Juvenal for his part (**b**) objects to the exercise because it encourages the belief that the teacher knows, and is always ready to offer, the answer to every trivial question. It also became the object of ridicule and the butt of jokes. *The Laughter-Lover* (*Philogelos*) is a collection of amusing stories and jokes that may have been compiled as early as the third century AD or as late as the sixth, but its spirit reaches far back into Greek and Roman culture (**c**). The final selection is a graffito found in Cyrene (northern Libya) and is probably a student's attempt at parody. Further reading: Baldwin 1983: iv–viii; Kaster 1984.

a

I was not born for this purpose, to test my own impression, to compare the statements people make, and to form an opinion of my own on the subject. For this reason I am just like the teacher (*grammatikos*):

"Who was Hector's father?" "Priam." "Who were his brothers?" "Alexander and Deiphobus." "Who was their mother?" "Hecuba. This story was handed down to me." "By whom?" "By Homer. Hellanicus also writes on the same topics, I believe, and perhaps others."

b

Still, go ahead, you parents, and impose your merciless terms! Demand that the teacher have faultless grammar, that he read all the historical examples and know all the authors as well as he knows his fingers and fingernails. Demand that, if he happens to be asked a question on the way to the public baths or those of Phoebus, he can give the nurse of Anchises, the name and homeland of Anchemolus' stepmother, how many years Acestes lived, and how many jars of Sicilian wine he gave the Phrygians.

c

A stupid teacher (*grammatikos*) was asked, "What was Priam's mother called." He was stumped and said, "Out of respect we call her 'Lady'."

d

Question: Who was the father of Priam's children?

8.33. Famous firsts

POxy 1241

This papyrus from Oxyrhynchus (Egypt) was written in the first half of the second century AD, but the information contained in it was compiled in the late first century BC or early first century AD. Its unifying theme is its concern with important "firsts." It thus reflects the kind of erudition that contemporary schools promoted through exercises such as those presented in **8.31–32**. The translation below begins a few lines into the papyrus, and there are gaps in the segment of it which is translated here. Further reading: Marrou 1956: 161–62; Bonner 1977: 239–40.

Tradition has it that the first to form a military camp was Asias, from whom they say that Asia gets its name. Apis, son of Phoroneus, led forth an army after arming his followers with clubs and hides. It is recorded that the first man to embark on a civil war was Agenor, who gathered shepherds together and, having attacked Pelasgus, drove him out of the land, and that the first man to sack a Greek city was Amphitryon, with the assistance of Cephalus of Athens, their enemies being the Taphians in Cephallenia. Aristotle, however, records that this first happened in the case of Pallene, and others claim that Pallene was not only enslaved by Cleisthenes when he attacked it with his Sicyonian army, but that the wives and daughters of its inhabitants who were taken prisoner were forced into prostitution. They say that Heracles was the first to hand back the dead under a truce. . . . that the first to recover the bodies of those who lost their lives in war was Theseus in the conflict with the Thebans, when he retrieved and buried the bodies of those who had participated in the expedition of the Seven against Thebes and remained unburied.

Aitolus is said to have been the first to have shed the blood of a kinsman, having killed Apis, the son of Ion, when he competed against him in the games established by Cepheus in honour of Azon, although some claim that the first case of shedding a relative's blood was Ixion's killing of his father-in-law Eioneus. Phoroneus, son of Inachus, established a single court for those who shed the blood of their kin and put them on trial. Tradition has it that the first occurrence of fratricide occurred at Thebes when Ismenus and Caantus, the sons of Oceanus, fought over their sister Melias. Some people claim that weapons of war were fabricated by Ares, although others state that this was done by the Cyclopes in a cave in Euboea called Teuchion. Whereas men of earlier generations used hides to protect their bodies, the first to equip himself with armour was Briareus, although others record that Ares was first. Others again claim that weapons of war were first made in Thrace by Zeus' son Enyalios, who was imprisoned by Aloeus and his children, who were slain by Apollo when he rescued him. Others say that the Curetes in Euboea were the first to manufacture and dress themselves in bronze armour, when they armed their followers and [attacked] Cymindis, queen of. . . .

8.34. A *grammaticus* should not know everything

Quintilian, *Training in Oratory* 1.8.18–21

Quintilian demonstrates here a disdain for pedantry and a preference for practical educational goals. His target is those scholars, working mainly in Alexandria between the third and first centuries BC, who wrote detailed commentaries (*hypomnemata*) on works of literature, above all on Homer's *Iliad* and *Odyssey* (see **6.5–6**). Further reading: Turner 1980: 112–24; Pfeiffer 1968: 274–79; Reynolds and Wilson 1991: 9–15.

(18) There will also be the interpretation of historical allusions in the texts, and this should be executed carefully, without, however, going into non-essential detail. It suffices to relate the generally accepted versions, or those given by reputable authorities. To go into what every third-rate writer has said is a tedious waste of time or useless pedantry, diverting and encumbering minds which would be better occupied with other matters. (19) Anyone closely scrutinizing every single page of writing that is not even worth reading is capable of giving serious attention to old wives' tales as well; and yet the treatises of *grammatici* are replete with stumbling-blocks of this kind, treatises which are barely familiar even to their authors. (20) Thus it is on record that Didymus, whose literary output has no equal, once challenged the authenticity of a certain story, and then one of his own books was brought forward which actually contained that particular story.[16] (21) This arises especially with unhistorical subjects where matters can reach ridiculous and even disgraceful heights, inasmuch as anyone with no principles is at such liberty to invent things that he can safely fabricate whatever he likes about entire books and authors; for in the case of non-existent people detection is impossible, whereas, when material is more familiar, inquisitive people will often catch them out. Accordingly, in my eyes, being ignorant of some things will count amongst a *grammaticus'* merits.

---

16 Didymus (first century BC) was reputed to have written between 3,500 and 4,000 books. For a discussion of his carelessness, see West 1970: 288–96.

9

TEACHING AND LEARNING THE LIBERAL ARTS AND RHETORIC

Cicero to Quintilian

The changes which rhetorical education underwent in Rome and throughout the Empire during the period covered by this chapter were little less than astonishing. In 92 BC a censorial edict was passed against the so-called "Latin *rhetores*" (**7.11**); a senatorial decree against *rhetores* and philosophers had preceded it in 161 (**7.9**). But by the late first century AD the landscape had altered completely. So successfully had Greek learning penetrated Roman culture, especially élite culture, that the emperor Vespasian not only established an official position in Rome for teachers of Latin and Greek rhetoric but exempted *rhetores* and *grammatici* from taxes as well (**9.20c**). By now rhetoric had proved itself to the Romans to be a supremely useful skill. It was also the focus of minute study and discussion, above all by Cicero and Quintilian, whose writings on the subject form the basis of what we know about the theory and practice of rhetoric from the first century BC to the first century AD (and well beyond).

Cicero and Quintilian agree that a good orator must have a broad but thorough education, focused especially on language and literature (**9.1**). Technical ability is not enough; the goal instead is to produce "a good man, skilled in speaking" (**8.13**). Greeks and Romans paid considerable attention to the content and organization of this earlier "liberal" education, to its relationship with subsequent studies, and to its intrinsic value (**9.2–5**), even as an agent of cultural assimilation (**9.6**). The preparatory work which preceded the study of rhetoric often – perhaps usually – contained some rudiments of rhetorical training (**9.8**); indeed, the territory to be covered by the teacher of literature (*grammaticus*) and the teacher of rhetoric (*rhetor*) respectively was a matter of considerable dispute (**9.7**). The system which Romans and Greeks in the late Republic and the Empire adopted and developed for the training of an orator took advantage of the education which the child had undergone prior to this stage. Rhetorical exercises called *progymnasmata* drew upon the knowledge of the mythological, legendary and historical past which the student had acquired (**9.8–9, 12**).

This feature is especially evident in the rhetorical practice-speeches or "declamations" through which students were taught the art of persuasion (**9.10**). These practice-speeches were a form of exercise whose origin can be traced back to the Greek sophists of the fifth century BC (**9.11**). Although students were attracted to this kind of training (**9.13**), it was roundly criticized, even seen as ludicrous, by many observers (**9.14**). Most of these critics faulted declamation for its irrelevance to the real world; some also lamented the fact (as they saw it) that rhetorical education and the practice of oratory had fallen so far from the loftier heights of a few generations earlier (**9.15**). The ideal at the beginning of the second century AD which writers such as Tacitus and Pliny envisaged was instead something very like the education that Cicero received, which was essentially an apprenticeship (**9.15–16**). Of course, the rhetorical education which Cicero acquired was not so readily available to everyone, as an important letter on papyrus shows (**9.17**). Not surprisingly, disapproval of a different kind was voiced as well, this time directed at women who showed too much interest and learning in literature, rhetoric and philosophy (**9.18**). The rhetorical ideal was a practical training which – as both Cicero and Quintilian agreed – relied less on handbooks and mock-speeches than on wide learning, good judgement, and innate talent (**9.19**).

General background: Boatwright *et al.* 2004: 353–92; E. Rawson 1985: 3–114; *Rhetoric*: Marrou 1956: 284–91; Clarke 1967; Wooten 1988; Kennedy 1994: 128–200; Pernot 2005: 128–201.

9.1. Laying the groundwork

(a) Cicero, *On the Orator* 1.19–20, (b) Quintilian, *Training in Oratory* 1.1.10

Writing about 150 years apart, Cicero and Quintilian both see the first and second stages of a child's education as leading to the study of rhetoric and the production of a skilful orator. They also agree that the would-be orator needs a broad education; without it, the result (as Cicero says) is "a meaningless outpouring of words." Further reading: Kennedy 1972: 210–15; Bonner 1977: 76–89; B. Rawson 2003: 147–53.

a

(19) So let us stop wondering why there is a dearth of eloquent men, for oratory comprises a complex of areas, making headway in each of which is an arduous task. Let us rather encourage our children, and all others whose fame and standing we hold dear, to come to terms with the magnitude of the discipline. Let us encourage them not to feel

confident that they can reach their goal through rules or teachers or exercises that everyone uses, but that there are other means of doing so. (20) In my opinion, no one will be able to become an accomplished orator, praiseworthy in all respects, unless he has gained a mastery of all the great fields of enquiry and knowledge. It is from proficiency in these fields that oratory should derive its vigour and its flourish, and unless such a substructure of knowledge is acquired and understood by the orator, his oratory will be only a meaningless and almost childish outpouring of words.

b

If anyone thinks that I am asking a lot [in setting out the orator's educational program], he should bear in mind that the training of an orator is difficult even when his education contains no gaps, and that there remain ahead problems more numerous and difficult. For what is needed is constant study, outstanding instructors and a broad spectrum of subjects.

9.2. The liberal arts and rhetoric

(a) Cicero, *On the Orator* 1.187–88, (b) Cicero, *In Defence of Archias* 1.2

Cicero and Quintilian believed in the importance of a broad education for the aspiring orator (**9.1**); this breadth derived from the study of the liberal arts (*artes liberales*). The relationship between these disciplines was the focus of considerable discussion and debate, especially among philosophers (**5.20, 10.3, 7**). The subjects which Cicero identifies here embrace most of the seven traditional *artes liberales*: grammar, rhetoric and dialectic (the literary arts), and geometry, arithmetic, astronomy and musical theory (the mathematical arts). These two sets would later have a profound influence on medieval education as, respectively, the *trivium* and *quadrivium* (**10.27–28**). Further reading: Kidd 1978: 7–15, 1999: 6–8; Chadwick 1981: 108–11; E. Rawson 1985: 132–42; B. Rawson 2003: 168–73.

a

(187) Practically all the subjects now encompassed by the arts were formerly separate and lacking classification. In music, for example, there were rhythms, notes and tunes; in geometry, lines, figures, dimensions and proportions; in astronomy, the rotation of the sky, the rising, setting and the movements of the stars; in literature, the detailed examination of the poets, the study of history, the interpretation of words and their pronunciation; finally, in oratorical theory,

with which we are now involved, invention, rhetorical embellishment, arrangement, mnemonics, and delivery – these were unknown[1] to all men, and appeared to them unconnected. (188) Accordingly, a particular rationale was applied from another, unrelated area, one to which the philosophers lay exclusive claim [i.e. dialectic], so that it can give cohesiveness and some kind of schematic arrangement to an otherwise disjointed and orderless subject.

b

All the arts which are oriented towards culture are interconnected and related to each other.

9.3. The liberal arts and architecture

Vitruvius, *On Architecture* 1.1.11–12

Like Cicero (**9.2a–b**), the architectural writer Vitruvius (late first century BC) views the liberal arts as both preliminary – not to rhetoric, however, but to architecture – and interconnected. The following extract contains the earliest reference to or use of the term *enkuklios paideia*, in the hybrid Latin phrase *encyclios disciplina*. Just before the point at which this extract begins, Vitruvius has been explaining the relevance of letters, drawing, mathematics, historical studies, philosophy, music, medicine, law, and astronomy to the study and practice of architecture. Further reading: E. Rawson 1985: 185–200; B. Rawson 2003: 191–92.

(11) Since a subject of study as great as this one is embellished with and abounds in learning of many different kinds, I do not think that those people can rightly claim suddenly to be architects unless, by ascending the steps of these subjects from boyhood, they have been nourished on the knowledge of many arts and sciences and have reached the summit of the temple of architecture. (12) And perhaps it will seem remarkable to inexperienced people that human nature can master and remember such a large number of subjects. But when they have realized that all subjects are connected with and relate to one another, they will easily believe that it can happen; for a broad education (*encyclios disciplina*) is made up of these parts as though it were a single body. Therefore those who are trained from tender years in the various subjects identify in all the arts the same characteristics and the relationship between all the disciplines, and by this fact they more easily come to know everything.

---

1 There is a problem with the Latin at this point in the text.

9.4. The liberal arts and philosophy

Seneca, *Moral Letters* 88.1–2, 20, 23

Writing in the AD 60s, Seneca sees the liberal arts – here equated with *enkuklios paideia* – as preparatory to philosophy, not as an end in themselves. At the end of this extract the phrase "the only liberal arts" is a reference to philosophy, and was probably a formulation by the philosopher Posidonius (*c.* 135–*c.* 50 BC). For another view of the relationship between the liberal arts and philosophy, see Cicero, *On the Orator* 1.9–10. Further reading: Kidd 1988: 359–65.

(1) You want to know what I think about liberal studies. I admire none; nothing which sets out to acquire money do I count in the rank of good things. They are skills for hire, useful only so far as they prepare the intellect and do not hold it back. We have to linger over these studies as long as our mind can do nothing greater; they are our first lessons, not our professions. (2) You see why they are called liberal studies: it is because they are worthy of a free (*liber*) man. But there is one truly free pursuit which makes a person free, namely the pursuit of wisdom [i.e. philosophy], something lofty, powerful, noble; everything else is puny and childish. [Seneca proceeds to dismiss the case for grammar, music, arithmetic, geometry and astronomy.]

(20) "Well, then, do liberal studies contribute nothing to our well-being?" They contribute much to other things; to goodness they contribute nothing. For these admittedly lowly skills which depend on manual labour [mentioned earlier in the letter] contribute a great deal to life's accessories, yet they have nothing to do with goodness. "So why do we educate our sons in the liberal studies?" Not because they can impart goodness, but because they prepare the mind to receive goodness. Just as that first training in letters (as people in the past used to call it) by which children gain the rudiments does not teach the liberal arts but prepares the ground for children to acquire these soon after, so do the liberal arts not lead the soul to goodness but clear a path for it. [Seneca goes on to record Posidonius' views on the liberal arts.] . . .. (23) Those arts which the Greeks call *encyclic*, and we [Romans] call liberal, relate to children and are something like the liberal arts. But the only liberal arts – or rather, to put it more accurately, the only arts characteristic of a free man – are those concerned with goodness.

9.5. A Jewish Platonist discusses the liberal arts, philosophy and wisdom

Philo, *Intercourse with the Preliminary Subjects* 73–76, 79–80

Philo was a prominent member of the Jewish community in Alexandria until his death around the middle of the first century AD. His voluminous writings focus on the Greek translation of the Old Testament (the Septuagint), applying both a wide knowledge of Greek philosophy and the literary technique of allegory. Like Seneca, he is interested in the relationship between the liberal arts and philosophy, but he looks past philosophy to wisdom itself. Further reading: Russell 1989: 222–23; Snyder 2000: 122–37.

(73) When Abraham is about to marry the handmaid of wisdom – that is, the general curriculum (*enkuklios paideia*) – he didn't forget the agreements he made with his mistress, but he knew that the one was his wife by law and choice, while the other was by necessity and the force of opportunity. This is how it is for every lover of learning: the person who has experience will prove the most infallible witness. (74) For example, when I was first aroused by the goads of philosophy to desire her, I associated when I was quite young with one of her handmaids, grammar (*grammatiké*), and I dedicated to her mistress all the things which I begat from her, writing, reading, and the study of the poets' words. (75) Then I came together with another, geometry, and although I was delighted by her beauty – for she had a symmetry and proportion in all her parts – I didn't take any of her offspring as my own but instead brought them as a gift to my lawful wife. (76) I was eager to come together with a third as well – her rhythm, harmony and melody were fine, and she was called music – and from her I begat diatonics, chromatics, and enharmonics, conjunct and disjunct melodies which correspond to the consonance of the fourth, fifth and octave intervals. Again I didn't hide any of them away, to ensure that my lawful wife would be wealthy and cared for by a vast array of servants. . . .

(79) Furthermore, just as the general subjects (*enkuklia*) contribute to the acquisition of philosophy, so also does philosophy contribute to the possession of wisdom. For philosophy is the cultivation of wisdom, and wisdom is the knowledge of divine and human matters and their causes. So just as the general culture (*enkuklios mousiké*) is the servant of philosophy, so also must philosophy be the servant of wisdom. (80) Philosophy teaches control of the belly and control of the parts below it, and control also of the tongue. These powers of self-control are said to be worth choosing in their own rights, but they

would appear holier if they were to be practised to honour and serve God.

9.6. Education for Romanization

Tacitus, *Life of Agricola* 21.2

As governor of the Roman province of Britain from AD 78 to 85, Gnaeus Julius Agricola employed the traditional educational curriculum as a way to assimilate (and pacify) aristocratic Britons. For the education of the Gauls, with whom the Britons are here compared, see **10.9–10**. Further reading: Salway 1981: 141–43, 505–16.

Agricola provided an education in the liberal arts for the children of the leading Britons and ranked the natural talents of the Britons above those of the Gauls, despite their training. The result was that those who were recently rejecting the Latin language were now eager for its eloquence. Roman dress also became popular with them, and the toga was a common sight. Little by little they strayed towards the enticements of degeneracy: assembly-rooms, baths and dinner parties. All this the inexperienced called civilization, though it was really a part of their servitude.

9.7. Educational turf-wars

(a) Quintilian, *Training in Oratory* 2.1.1–3, (b) Suetonius,
On Teachers of Grammar and Rhetoric 4.4–6

By around AD 100 there was considerable disagreement over the responsibilities that should belong to the *grammaticus* on the one hand and to the *rhetor* on the other (cf. **8.23**). Quintilian believed that *grammatici* had stepped into a pedagogical area that the *rhetores* vacated out of their desire to avoid teaching less advanced students (**a**). Suetonius' view of the contemporary grammarian's activities, and his reconstruction of the past relationship between *grammaticus* and *rhetor* (**b**), differ from Quintilian's in important ways. Whereas Quintilian maintains that *grammatici* are increasingly assuming responsibilities that *rhetores* once held, Suetonius believes that *grammatici* are withdrawing from those previous practices; and whereas Quintilian believes that the *grammaticus'* welcome encroachment on territory formerly held by the *rhetor* is a recent development, Suetonius traces the teaching of rhetorical rudiments back to "the *grammatici* of old" (cf. *On Teachers of Grammar and Rhetoric* 7.1–2, on Marcus Antonius Gnipho). For declamation, mentioned in these two passages, see **9.10–14**. Further reading: Kaster 1995: 99–105, 269–71.

a

(1) It has become a common practice . . . for boys to be sent to teachers of rhetoric later than reason dictates, invariably in the case of Latin teachers, but occasionally in the case of Greek ones, too. There are two reasons for this: *rhetores*, especially our [i.e. Latin] ones, have given up some of their customary branches of instruction; and, secondly, *grammatici* have appropriated those belonging to others. (2) *Rhetores* now believe their sole function is to declaim and to teach the theory and practice of declamation, confining themselves, moreover, to deliberative and judicial themes (for they consider all else to be beneath their profession); and the *grammatici*, in turn, think that what has been left to them is insufficient (for which, incidentally, they deserve our thanks), and so are even getting into character-speeches and hortatory speeches, where the orator's task is greatest of all. (3) That is why material which used to constitute the primary stages of the one sphere now constitutes the last stages of the other, and students, at an age when they should be devoting themselves to higher studies, are stuck in a lower school being trained in rhetoric under the *grammatici*. So we have the absolutely ridiculous situation of a boy apparently not being ready to be sent to a teacher of declamation until he is able to declaim!

b

(4) The *grammatici* of old would also teach rhetoric, and text-books by many of them on both subjects [i.e. grammar and rhetoric] are still in circulation. (5) It was because of this practice, I think, that later on, too, even though the two vocations had separated, *grammatici* still retained or established certain types of exercises designed for oratorical training – topics for debate, for example, paraphrasing, hortatory addresses, aetiologies and the like – the aim obviously being to prevent boys being passed on to the *rhetores* totally inarticulate and untrained. (6) This practice, I see, has now been discontinued because some of the students are too lazy or too young, and not, I think, because the subjects have fallen into disfavour. When I was young, I remember, one teacher called "Princeps" used to offer declamations and instructional debates on alternate days, or sometimes he would limit the instruction to the morning and remove his desk and declaim in the afternoon. I used to be told, too, that in the days of our forefathers some people went directly to the forum [i.e. the site of the law courts] from the school of the *grammaticus*, and that they were regarded as being amongst the foremost advocates of the day.

9.8. *Progymnasmata* (I)

(a) Aelius Theon, *Exercises* 59, (b) Quintilian, *Training in Oratory* 1.9, (c) O.Bodl. (uncatalogued)

Grammatici sometimes presented their students (both Greek and Roman) with written rhetorical exercises before these students progressed to the *rhetor* himself. These were called *progymnasmata*, "preliminary exercises," and we possess extensive evidence about their nature especially from the surviving textbooks of four Greek authors: Aelius Theon (believed to be first century AD, though possibly as late as the fifth), Hermogenes (second half of the second century AD), Aphthonius the sophist (second half of the fourth century AD), and Nicolaus the sophist (late fifth century AD). In **a** below, Aelius Theon explains his belief that students need adequate preparatory work before they begin the intensive study of rhetoric (cf. **9.1**). In **b**, Quintilian provides a succinct discussion of the *progymnasmata* taught by *grammatici*. An example of these is provided by **c**, the fragment of a student's exercise written on an ostrakon which was discovered in Egypt and is dated to the third century AD. The student's mistakes are reflected in this translation (e.g. "abandoned" in the second sentence has no clear subject). Further reading: Milne 1908: 128, 130; Hock and O'Neil 1986: 115–49; Kennedy 1994: 202–8, 2003; Cribiore 1996: 46–47, 261; Webb 2001; Heath 2002/3.

a

The rhetoricians of long ago ... did not think that a person should come to rhetoric at all before having some grasp of philosophy and being filled with the elevated thinking that comes from it. Today, however, most people are so far from paying attention to such studies that they dash off to speak in public without even the slightest involvement in the so-called general subjects (*enkuklia mathemata*). What is most ignorant of all is that without even practising on the appropriate topics they proceed to judicial and popular themes (*hypotheseis*). . . . Let others write about the other things that a person has to learn who is going to study rhetoric. I am now going to try to explain what a person must know and appropriately practise before he deals with themes, not because others have not written about these things, but because I hope that I too will provide a good deal of help to those who choose to speak in public.

b

(1) That completes my account of the two areas which are claimed to lie within the purview of *grammatici*, namely the principles of rhetoric

211

and literary interpretation (the former known as *methodiké* and the latter as *historiké*). We should, however, add to their responsibilities some elementary exercises in speaking, designed for those pupils not yet sufficiently advanced for instruction by the *rhetor*. (2) Boys should learn to recount orally the fables of Aesop (the next step up from the tales told by children's nurses) in a straightforward style, with no hyperbole, and then learn how to put into writing this same neat and simple method of expression, starting with the breaking down of verses, then advancing to explaining them in different words, and finally moving on to freer paraphrasing that permits abbreviation and embellishment, but without altering the poet's meaning. (3) This is an exercise difficult even for the most accomplished professors, and a person coping with it properly will be able to learn anything.

The student should also, in the schools of the *grammatici*, write out maxims (*sententiae*), anecdotes (*chriae*) and character-sketches (*ethologiae*) (with explanations supplied for the aphorisms), for these arise in his reading. The principle of all of these forms of expression is the same, though their form is different: a maxim is a statement of a universal nature, while the character-sketch is confined to persons. (4) We are presented with numerous types of anecdotes. One is like the maxim, framed as a simple statement and beginning "He said" or "He was in the habit of saying"; another is in the form of a reply, beginning "When asked, he said..." or "When this was said to him, he answered..."; a third is not unlike this one, beginning "When someone had said something, or done something..." (5) It is even thought that an anecdote can be represented in the actions of people, as, for example, in "On seeing an ignorant boy, Crates struck the boy's *paedagogus*," or, almost identical to this (but one to which people do not venture to apply the same name, "anecdote," calling it rather "anecdote-like"), "Milo carried around the bull, having grown accustomed to carrying it as a calf." In all of these the declension goes through the same cases, and account is taken of actions as well as deeds.[2]

(6) As for short stories which the poets have made famous, I think they should be handled by students simply for their general knowledge, rather than for enhancing their eloquence. By abandoning other exercises requiring greater effort and fervour, the Latin *rhetores* have made these the obligatory domain of the *grammatici*. The Greeks know better the importance and the extent of their duties.

---

2 For an example of this kind of exercise, cf. **8.29a**, **10.1**; also described by Aelius Theon, *Exercises* 101, and by Nicolaus, *Preliminary Exercises* 18 (Kennedy 2003: 19–20, 139–40); see also Morgan 1998: 185–89.

c

After the end and death of Achilles, Calchas the seer tells the Achaeans to fetch from Lemnos Philoctetes, who had Heracles' bow and arrows. For he abandoned him after he was stung by the water-snake and was not cared for. Odysseus and Diomedes bring him back and Machaon the son of Asclepius cares for him. And Philoctetes. . . .

9.9. *Progymnasmata* (II)

Quintilian, *Training in Oratory* 2.4.1–3, 18–26, 33

The *progymnasmata* were not the exclusive responsibility of the *grammaticus*; the *rhetor* taught more advanced forms of these written exercises. Here Quintilian explains these *progymnasmata*. The works of the four Greek authors cited in **9.8** provide more detail still, and contain specific examples of the exercises. For *suasoriae* and *controversiae* (26, 33 below), see **9.10**. Further reading: Marrou 1956: 172–75.

(1) I shall now commence the discussion of the elements which I feel should come first when *rhetores* give instruction, putting off for the moment consideration of that which is exclusively called, in popular parlance, "the art of rhetoric" (*ars rhetorica*). And in my opinion the most appropriate start can be made with something that resembles what the boy has already learned under the *grammatici*. (2) We accept that there are three types of narrative, apart from the type which we use in court-cases: mythological narrative, which occurs in tragedy and epic poetry, and which is far removed not only from reality but from any semblance of it; the argument, which is found in comedy and which, though unreal, has verisimilitude; and the historical narrative, which involves a presentation of hard facts. We leave poetic narratives to the *grammatici*, and the *rhetor* should start with the historical, the strength of which will depend on its closeness to the truth. (3) But what I consider to be the best way to organize such a narrative I shall reveal when we discuss forensic training. In the meantime suffice it to say by way of recommendation that it should be neither dry nor insipid – for what is the point of devoting such effort to our studies if it be considered adequate to present facts baldly and without embellishment? – nor yet should it be convoluted, and wallowing in irrelevant descriptions, into which many speakers are drawn, imitating the license of poetry. . . .

(18) A useful exercise subjoined to narrative is that of refuting or corroborating the narratives themselves, which is called [in Greek] *anaskeué* and *kataskeué*. This can be used not only with subjects drawn

from mythology or poetry, but also with actual historical records. Take, for example, the question of the plausibility of the story of the raven perching on Valerius' head, while he was fighting, to strike the face and eyes of his Gallic opponent with its beak and wings – on both sides there will be many topics for discussion. (19) Then there is the snake from which Scipio was purportedly born, the wolf of Romulus, and Numa's Egeria. . . .

(20) From here the student will proceed gradually to more important things, the praise of famous men and the censure of the wicked, which serve more than one purpose. First, the intellect receives training from the widely varied material, and then the personality is developed through the study of good and bad behaviour. Extensive general knowledge also accrues from this, equipping the student with examples (of great weight in all manner of cases) which he will use as the occasion requires. (21) Next after this comes the "comparison exercise," examining the relative merits and faults of two people. This entails similar work to the aforementioned exercises, but it means a doubling of the material and also includes assessment of the degree of virtues and vices discussed, as well as the nature of them. . . .

(22) Now on to "commonplaces," by which I mean those which we normally use to oppugn vices themselves, without attacking specific individuals (like adultery, gambling or debauchery). These are the substance of court-cases, and are actual prosecutions, if one adds a defendant's name. Here too, however, one generally shifts away from general treatment to specific instances by, for example, representing the adulterer as being blind, the gambler as poor, or the debauchee as an old man. On occasion, commonplaces are also used in defence. (23) We may speak in defence of extravagance or love, and sometimes a case is made for a pimp or a parasite, worded in such a way as to meet the charge against him rather than defend the man himself.

(24) "Theses" are based on comparison – for example, "is life better in the town or in the country?" or "is the lawyer or the soldier more praiseworthy?" – and, offering as they do a remarkably attractive training in public speaking, are extremely useful, whether it be for the practice of hortative or forensic oratory. Indeed, the second of the two topics cited above is given very full treatment by Cicero in his case for Murena. (25) Then there are those topics which belong almost exclusively to deliberative oratory – "should a man marry?" or "should one seek public office?" Just add specific individuals and these will become hortative speeches.

(26) My instructors used to prepare us for conjectural cases by a form of exercise which was useful and at the same time enjoyable for us, telling us to examine and enlarge upon the themes "Why is Venus armed in Sparta?" and "Why was Cupid conceived of as being a boy

and winged, armed with arrows and a torch?" and so forth. In doing these exercises we were investigating the matter of intention – the frequent issue of *controversiae* – and this can be seen as a sort of "aphorism" (*chria*). . . .

(33) The praise and criticism of laws calls for greater strengths, strengths which are able to meet virtually the greatest tests of oratory. As to whether such an exercise is more relevant to *suasoriae* or to *controversiae*, that depends on the practice and legal convention of the various states. In Greece, the proposer of legislation was called before a judge, whereas in Rome it was the practice to urge acceptance or rejection of laws before an assembly of the people. In both cases, however, arguments used are few and of an almost uniform pattern.

9.10. Declamation

Quintilian, *Training in Oratory* 2.10.1–4

Progymnasmata were designed to be preparatory to the main exercises that the *rhetores* prescribed. These were speeches on fictional themes which they required their students to produce. The "declamations" were of two kinds: (1) the *suasoria*, which required the student to offer advice on a historical or mythical situation presented to him; and (2) the *controversia*, which required the student to take the part of an advocate on one side of a legal case. *Suasoriae* were considered the simpler of the two; they were therefore thought to be better suited for younger students and were taught earlier than the *controversiae* (see **9.14a**). Further reading: Kennedy 1972: 316–18; Bonner 1977: 84–85, 277–87; Fairweather 1981: 151–239; Kaster 2001: 317–37.

(1) When the student has received thorough instruction and training in these preliminary stages (of no small importance in their own right, but constituting nonetheless individual parts of a more important whole), it will be almost time for him to put his hand to deliberative and forensic topics; but before embarking upon these I should speak briefly about the general principles of declamation, the most recently invented, but also by far the most beneficial, of all the rhetorical exercises. (2) For it encompasses everything we have discussed so far and is not far removed from the real world, for which reason it has become so popular that many think it can on its own suffice to provide an education in oratory. Indeed, there is no laudable quality in public speaking, at least in continuous speaking, which is not also found in this particular rhetorical exercise. (3) Now, in fact, because of the shortcomings of the teachers, the activity has so deteriorated that the permissiveness and ignorance of the declaimers are amongst the prime

215

reasons for the debasement of oratory. (4) Even so, one may put to good use something which is by its nature good. Accordingly, the subjects for composition should be as realistic as can be, and the declamation should, as far as possible, follow the lines of those court-cases for which it was invented as training.

9.11. The origins of declamation

(a) Quintilian, *Training in Oratory* 2.4.41–42, (b) Philostratus, *Lives of the Sophists* 481

Quintilian tentatively associates declamation's introduction into the curriculum with Demetrius of Phaleron (**a**), who governed Athens from 317 to 307 BC and died in 283 (cf. **6.5a**). Philostratus' description of speeches that present "sketches of the poor, the wealthy, princes, tyrants and the specific themes to which a study of history leads" (**b**) shows that he is thinking in terms of declamations, and his association of this innovation with Aeschines, son of Atrometus, places its introduction some time between 330 and 315 BC, when Aeschines established his school of rhetoric in Rhodes. Although its seeds were planted by the sophists in the second half of the fifth century BC (**4.9**), we can reasonably accept that declamation as it came to be known did originate late in the fourth century. Quintilian's last sentence implies that declamation was introduced into Rome shortly before 92 BC, the year in which Lucius Crassus had the teaching of Latin rhetoric banned (see **7.9–10**, **9.14a**). Further reading: Bonner 1949: 1–50; Sussman 1978: 2–17; Fairweather 1981: 104–31; Russell 1983: 1–20.

a

(41) It is generally agreed that the procedure of speaking on imaginary topics, by way of imitating the practice of the law courts and political assemblies, goes back to about the time of Demetrius of Phaleron in Greece.
(42) Whether this type of training was invented by Demetrius himself I have been unable to establish with certainty . . .; but even those who make this claim most emphatically have no reliable source on which to base it. Latin professors of rhetoric, so Cicero informs us, began towards the end of Lucius Crassus' day, and the best-known of them was Plotius.

b

Even when the old style of sophistic proposed to discuss philosophical subjects, its exposition was lengthy and diffuse. For it would discuss courage, justice, gods and heroes, and how the universe was given its shape. The sophistic which followed (and one should call it the second rather than the new sophistic, since it has existed for some time) provided sketches of the poor, the wealthy, princes, tyrants and the specific themes to which a study of history leads. The earlier sophistic started in Thessaly on the initiative of Gorgias of Leontini; the second was founded by Aeschines, son of Atrometus, who was deprived of his civic rights in Athens and took up residence in Caria and Rhodes. Masters of his school dealt with their themes according to the rules of their craft, while those who followed Gorgias did so as they deemed appropriate.

9.12. Some declamatory themes

(a) Elder Seneca, *Suasoriae*, Themes 3, 6, 7, (b) Elder Seneca, *Controversiae* 1.1, 1.2, 1.6, 4.5, 5.5, 10.3

Many Roman declamations survive, mainly those which the Elder Seneca had heard as a young man and transcribed from memory late in life (full translations in Winterbottom 1974), and those which are attributed (some, at least, falsely) to Quintilian. Each of Seneca's *suasoriae* and *controversiae* is prefaced with a summary of the problem that the speaker is addressing. A sample of themes is presented below. Further reading: Bonner 1949; Marrou 1956: 201–4, 286–87; Sussman 1978; Fairweather 1981, 1986; Beard 1993; Kennedy 1994: 166–72.

a

3. Agamemnon considers the sacrifice of Iphigeneia since Calchas claims that sailing is otherwise against the will of heaven.
6. Cicero considers whether he should beg Antony for mercy.
7. Cicero considers burning his writings since Antony promises to spare him if he does so.

b

1.1 THE UNCLE WHO DISINHERITS HIS NEPHEW.

Law: Children are to maintain their parents or be imprisoned.

Two brothers, one having a son, were in dispute. The son's uncle fell on hard times, and the young man maintained him over the father's objections. He was disinherited for this, but did not protest. He was adopted by the uncle. The uncle received a legacy and became wealthy. The father began to fall on hard times and the young man is maintaining him over the uncle's objections. He is in the process of being disinherited.

1.2 THE PRIESTESS WHO IS A PROSTITUTE.

Law: A priestess should be virtuous and the daughter of virtuous parents, pure and the daughter of pure parents.

A girl who was a virgin was captured by pirates and put on sale. She was bought by a pimp and made a prostitute. When clients came to her she begged them to be charitable to her.[3] She was unable to persuade a soldier who had come to her, and when he struggled with her and tried to rape her she killed him. She was accused, acquitted and returned to her family. She is a candidate for a priesthood.

1.6 THE CHIEF PIRATE'S DAUGHTER.

Captured by pirates, a man sent his father a written request for ransom, but was not ransomed by him. The pirate chief's daughter made him swear an oath to marry her if he were to be set free by her, and he took the oath. The girl abandoned her father and went with the young man. He returned to his father and married her. An orphaned girl now appears and the father orders the son to divorce the chief pirate's daughter and marry the orphan. When he refuses the father disinherits him.

4.5 THE STEPSON WHO IS A DOCTOR.

A man disinherited his son, who then studied medicine. When the father became ill and the doctors claimed a cure was impossible, the son cured him, and was made his heir again. Later his stepmother fell ill and the doctors lost all hope for her. The father asks the son to cure the stepmother, and disinherits him when he refuses. The son objects.

5.5 THE HOUSE THAT IS BURNED WITH THE TREE.

Law: Anyone knowingly doing damage should pay four times the amount of the damage caused; anyone doing so unknowingly should simply cover the damage.

A rich man asked a poor neighbour to sell him a tree that, he claimed, was obstructing his view. The poor man refused, and the rich man set

---

3 I.e. to give her money without receiving sex.

fire to the plane tree, but the neighbour's house also burned down with it. The rich man makes a commitment to pay four times the cost of the tree, but just the value of the house.

10.3 A MAN THOUGHT INSANE BECAUSE HE FORCED HIS DAUGHTER TO DIE.

Law: Insanity should be prosecuted.

In a civil war a woman accompanied her husband although she had her father and a brother on the other side. Her side was defeated and her husband killed, so she came home to her father. Not being welcomed into the home, she said: "How do you want me to give you satisfaction?" The father replied "You must die." She hanged herself before his door, and the father is accused of insanity by his son.

9.13. A student's attraction to declamation

Cicero, *Letters to his brother Quintus* 3.3.4 (21 October 54 BC)

Having practised declamation himself, Cicero saw value in it, but he did not, apparently, consider it the best way to become an accomplished speaker. Cicero is writing here about his nephew Quintus, aged 12 at this time. The teacher Paeonius is otherwise unknown.

Your boy Cicero – our boy, rather – is very taken with his teacher of rhetoric, Paeonius. Paeonius is, I think, a skilful and good man, but you are aware that my kind of teaching is a little more profound and intellectual. I personally do not want to see Quintus' development in this discipline obstructed and, moreover, the boy himself evidently finds the declamatory style more attractive and appealing. Since I myself took that path, let us permit him to follow in my footsteps, for I am sure that he will arrive at the same goal. Even so, if I take him with me into the country somewhere, I shall then acquaint him with my own methodology and practice. What I am offered by you as a fee is certainly considerable, and if I fail to earn it it will be through no fault of my own.

9.14. Critics of declamation

(a) Tacitus, *Dialogue on Orators* 35, (b) Juvenal, *Satires* 7.150–67, (c) Petronius, *Satyrica* 1–2

Despite its central place in rhetorical education, declamation was severely criticized by numerous writers. The criticism focused principally on its apparent irrelevance to real-world contexts and concerns. Quintilian blamed teachers for the deterioration in the practice of declamation but considered the exercise itself to be exceedingly useful (**9.10** [3]). The three witnesses presented below were far less sympathetic. Further reading: Bonner 1949: 71–83; Marrou 1956: 287–89; Kennedy 1972: 460–62, 515–21, 548–51, 1978: 171–78; Crook 1995: 163–67.

a

The *rhetores* made their appearance just before the time of Cicero and met with our forefathers' disapproval, as is clear from the injunction for the closure of their "school of arrogance" (to use Cicero's expression[4]) issued by the censors Crassus and Domitius.[5] But, to continue, the young men are taken to such schools in which it is difficult to say whether they sustain more intellectual harm from the actual surroundings, from their fellow-students or from the kind of subjects they study. There is nothing impressive about the surroundings: no-one enters who is not as ignorant as the others. The fellow-students are of no benefit: boys among boys and young men among young men, they speak with as much indifference as they are heard. And then the exercises themselves are to a great extent intellectually damaging. There are, of course, two types of declamatory themes which are dealt with by the *rhetores*: *suasoriae* and *controversiae*. The former are assigned to young boys in the belief that they are evidently less taxing and require less intelligence, whereas the stronger students are given the *controversiae* – but exercises of what quality, I ask you, and how implausibly contrived! On top of this, a highly rhetorical style is used to present this subject-matter which is divorced from reality. So, in an inflated style, we get the rewards of tyrant-slayers, the options of deflowered virgins, remedies for the plague, mothers' incestuous acts and the other everyday subjects of the rhetorical school that rarely or never arise in the courts.

b

You teach declamation? Ah, you must have the steely heart of a Vettius to listen when a crowded class is killing off the cruel tyrants! For, whatever it is that the student has just read in his seat, this he will repeat verbatim standing up, and drone on with it in exactly the same lines, the rehashed cabbage killing his wretched teachers. The appropriate line of defence, the nature of the case, the main question at the

4 See **7.12**.
5 In 92 BC; see **7.11**.

heart of it, and the shots that will possibly come from the other side –
this is what everyone wants to know, but no-one wants to pay the fee.
"You are asking for a fee? But what have I learned?"

"It's the teacher's fault, of course, that the young clodhopper has
no beating in the left of his breast. His frightful Hannibal is dinned
into my head every sixth day, whatever the debate – be it whether he
should head for Rome from Cannae, or whether he should be cautious
after that cloud-burst and lightning, and lead his storm-drenched
cohorts to shelter. Name any price you like and take it right now –
what I'd give to get his father to hear him as often as I do!" This is
what six or more other sophists cry out in unison. . . .

<h3 style="text-align:center">c</h3>

(1) [Encolpius, main character and narrator of the *Satyrica*, is the
speaker.] Surely our declaimers are in the grip of some other kind of
furies, bawling out as they do: "These wounds I suffered for the
freedom of the people! This eye I lost for your sakes! Give me a guide
to take me to my children; for my knees cannot hold up my body – the
tendons are severed!"

Even this could be tolerated if it helped those who would study
rhetoric along their way. As things are, these people with their gran-
diose subjects and noisy and trite platitudes only serve to make
students coming to the Forum think they have been brought to
another planet! And the reason for my thinking that our youngsters
are actually being made into total dunderheads in the schools is this:
they neither hear nor see anything that we have in the real world.
Instead, we have pirates standing on the shore in chains! We have
tyrants writing proclamations ordering sons to cut off their fathers'
heads! We have oracular responses for the removal of a plague which
call for the sacrifice of three or more virgins! We have honeyed knobs
of verbiage and everything that is said and done more or less coated
with poppy-seed and sesame!

(2) Those brought up in this environment have as much chance of
becoming discerning as those living in a kitchen do of smelling nice.
Pardon me for saying so, but you *rhetores* were the first to destroy
eloquence. By producing a sort of entertainment with your trivial and
inane utterances you have brought about the weakening and death of
the substance of oratory. Young men were not yet at the point of being
hidebound by declamation when Sophocles and Euripides found the
words to express themselves appropriately. Not yet had the seques-
tered professor destroyed the pure intellect when Pindar and the nine
lyric poets shrank from composing in Homeric verse. And – not to cite
just poets as evidence – I see for sure that neither Plato nor

Demosthenes ever touched this kind of exercise. [Agamemnon, a teacher of rhetoric, proceeds to defend himself against Encolpius.]

9.15. Rhetorical teaching as it used to be

(a) Tacitus, *Dialogue on Orators* 34, (b) Pliny, *Letters* 8.14.4–8

Tacitus' account (**a**) of how rhetorical education had been practised in Rome two hundred years before his time displays considerable nostalgia for simpler times and less formal standards, when teaching was in the hands of a student's relatives and education was more clearly relevant to its purpose. Pliny (**b**) was a contemporary of Tacitus and student of Quintilian, and like Tacitus he looked fondly upon the days when young men gained their training for public life through the imitation and emulation of prominent older Romans, especially members of their own families. Further reading: Bonner 1977: 10–19; Kennedy 1994: 186–96; Pernot 2005: 84–87, 128–34.

a

Now, in the days of our forefathers the young man who was being trained for a career in forensic oratory would have the groundwork laid for him by instruction at home, and after a thorough education in the liberal arts he would be taken by his father or his relatives to the person who ranked highest in the community as an orator. He would make it his practice to follow this man about, act as his escort and attend all his speaking engagements, whether in court or in public assemblies, to the point of even taking in his courtroom repartee, being present at his verbal skirmishes and learning, so to speak, to fight in the ranks. Young men right from the start derived from this considerable experience, a large measure of self-confidence and great critical acumen, for they were conducting their studies in broad daylight and in the thick of the fray where no-one can get away with stupid or illogical remarks without incurring the judge's displeasure, criticism from the opposition and, on top of that, censure from one's own supporters. Thus their training was from the start in an oratory that was real and uncorrupted, and though they attended only a single teacher they nevertheless came to know all the advocates of the day from attending a large number of legal proceedings. They also had the occasion to observe the very different partialities of the public, easily recognizing what won approval or incurred displeasure in each speaker's case.

So it was that they were provided with a teacher – and a fine, hand-picked one at that, the kind of person who could show them the true features of oratory and not just a pale imitation. But they were also provided with an opposition and adversaries who fought not with fake swords but the real thing, and with an audience which was invariably packed and differently composed, made up of antagonists as well as partisans, so that no remark went unnoticed, felicitous or not. You know that a great and durable reputation in oratory is acquired as much in the opposition benches as one's own – indeed, that is where it sprouts more robustly, where it gains a firmer strength. I swear that if the young man under discussion had teachers like that; if he was the student of practising orators, an auditor in the forum, an assiduous attender at the law courts; if he gained practical instruction from the experiences of others and knowledge of the laws from listening to them each day; if he recognized the faces of the jurymen, had made it his common practice to observe public assemblies and had had considerable experience of the proclivities of the general public – that young man was, all on his own, immediately qualified for any case whatsoever, whether he represented the prosecution or the defence.

b

(4) In days of old, learning from our elders was the established practice, using eyes as well as ears to find out what one's duties were and what, in turn, should be passed on to the next generation. (5) Boys therefore received a military training right from the early years, the object being to learn to command through obedience and to lead through following others. Thus when they became candidates for public office, they would stand at the doors of the Senate-house and observe state politics before taking part in them. (6) Every boy's father served as his instructor; if there was no father, some distinguished older person served in his place. So boys were taught by example, the most effective means of instruction, and thus learned the powers of those proposing legislation and the rights of members in expressing an opinion, the authority of the magistrates and the prerogative of the other senators. They learned when to give way; when to put up a fight; when to remain silent and how long to speak; how to distinguish between conflicting points of view and how to make amendments to legislation already proposed – in short, the entire operation of the Senate. In our day it was different. (7) True, we were in the army, but at a time when courage raised suspicion and cowardice won reward, when officers possessed no authority and common soldiers showed them no respect, when a command and obedience likewise meant nothing, when the whole system was slack, undisciplined and in complete confusion – better forgotten than remembered. (8) We, too, observed the Senate, but a Senate frightened and mute,

when speaking one's mind was dangerous and saying what you didn't mean distressing.

9.16. Cicero's intellectual journey

Cicero, *Brutus* 305–10, 314–16

In important respects, Cicero's rhetorical education was that of an upper-class Roman of his time, involving as it did a personal and persistent contact with an eminent public figure whom he could observe and from whom he could learn how distinguished men conducted themselves in public. It was, in other words, essentially an apprenticeship, of the kind described admiringly by both Tacitus and Pliny (**9.15**). The person to whom Cicero attached himself was Quintus Mucius Scaevola, who was eighty years old at the time (89 BC; see Cicero, *On Friendship* 1–3). Then, in 79 BC, at the age of 26, Cicero left Rome to further his rhetorical and philosophical education. He travelled to many Greek cities, including Athens, Sparta, Corinth, Rhodes and Smyrna (modern Izmir, Turkey). At that time, this kind of educational "grand tour" was unusual, but it would not remain so. The dates of events which Cicero refers to are given in square brackets. Further reading: Marrou 1956: 233–34, 289–91; Stockton 1971: 4–6; Shackleton Bailey 1971: 7–12; Bonner 1977: 84–96; E. Rawson 1983: 1–28, 1985: 6–12; Fantham 2004: 105–6; Pernot 2005: 84–87, 105–7.

(305) My daily round of writing, reading and practice-speeches left me discontented with being confined to rhetorical exercises alone. The next year [89 BC], Quintus Varius left the country, condemned under his own law. (306) I then became mostly a devotee of Quintus Scaevola son of Quintus for the study of civil law. Scaevola did not put himself at anyone's disposal for the purpose of instruction, but he nevertheless gave instruction to those eager to hear him by his replies to clients who consulted him. The year after this one was that of the consulship of Sulla and Pompeius [88 BC]. At that time Publius Sulpicius, in his capacity as tribune, gave public addresses every day, and from that I came to know his entire oratorical style inside out. And in this same period Philo, the head of the Academy, had come to Rome, having fled from home with some prominent Athenians during the war with Mithridates; and I, stirred with an amazingly strong passion for philosophy, dedicated myself entirely to him. In the process, although the wide range of the issues of philosophy and their supreme importance kept me enthralled, I remained even more steadfastly at his side because it seemed as if the system of the courts had been removed in perpetuity. (307) Sulpicius had died during that year, and in the year that followed [87 BC], three orators of three different generations –

Quintus Catulus, Marcus Antonius and Gaius Julius – were brutally killed. In the same year I also devoted myself, at Rome, to Molon of Rhodes, who was a great practising lawyer as well as a teacher. . . .

(308) For about three years the city was free of armed conflict. . . . During this entire period I was night and day occupied with the study of all the branches of learning. (309) I spent time with the Stoic Diodotus, who lodged at my home and spent his days with me, and some time ago died at my house. Under Diodotus I trained most diligently in all the disciplines, and especially in dialectic, which should be regarded as a condensed and concise eloquence. Even you, Brutus, have opined that, without dialectic, it is impossible to attain that true eloquence which is considered an amplified form of it. I applied myself to Diodotus' instruction and his many various studies, but making sure that no day passed free of rhetorical exercises. (310) I would do my declamatory practice – that is the expression they use now – often with Marcus Piso or with Quintus Pompeius or anyone else, on a daily basis, and I would do it in Latin much of the time, but more often in Greek. This was for two reasons: the Greek language, providing greater stylistic elaboration, would habituate me to speak Latin in a like manner; and also it was only by speaking Greek that I could receive correction and instruction from the greatest Greek teachers. . . . . .

(314) So it was that after having spent two years pleading cases, and when my name was by now well known in the forum, I left Rome [79 BC]. (315) After reaching Athens, I spent six months in the company of Antiochus, the well-known and sagacious philosopher of the old Academy. Under this great authority and teacher I resumed the study of philosophy, which I had never really forsaken and which I had followed from early youth. But at the same time in Athens I regularly immersed myself in my exercises under the direction of Demetrius the Syrian, a veteran teacher of rhetoric who was not without distinction in the field. After that I travelled all over Asia in the company of its greatest orators, who were themselves quite happy to have me practise declamation with them. The most important of these was Menippus of Stratonicea who, in my view, was the most eloquent man in all of Asia at that date; and if the mark of "Attic" speakers is a style free of frippery and bombast, he is an orator who can truly be numbered amongst them.

(316) But the one most in my company was Dionysius of Magnesia, and along with him also Aeschylus of Cnidus, and Xenokles of Adramyttion. These were reckoned the leading *rhetores* of the day in Asia. Not satisfied with them, however, I came to Rhodes, where I joined the school of Molon, whose teachings I had earlier followed at Rome. For he was a leading advocate in real cases and in

speech-writing, as well as being a real expert in identifying and criticising defects and in giving training and instruction. He made every effort to check, as far as he could, the effusive and superfluous elements of my style, which arose from some youthfully hasty and unrestrained manner of expressing myself, and to keep its excesses from, as it were, overflowing the banks. And so I returned two years later [77 BC], not just more proficient but almost a changed man! The strain on my voice had subsided, my speech had simmered down, so to speak, my lungs had acquired strength and my physique had taken on some growth.

9.17. A letter from Neilos to his father Theon

POxy 2190

The following letter on papyrus was written late in the first century or in the second century AD. It was discovered in Oxyrhynchus though probably composed in Alexandria. Neilos, the letter's author, was a student of rhetoric. The difficulties which he experienced in finding a suitable teacher and school are of special interest (cf. **8.16**, **10.19, 23**), as are the measures that he took to overcome these obstacles. These measures included his search for a tutor (*kathegetés*; cf. **8.16b–c**) and a scholar (*philologos*; cf. **6.19**), and his attendance at rhetorical displays (probably declamations). Further reading: Glucker 1978: 127–33; Cribiore 1996: 167, 2001: 56–59, 118–23; Winter 2002: 19–39, 256–60.

> The warmest of greetings from Neilos to Theon, his father and his lord. You freed me from my present depression when you revealed that the episode involving the theatre was of little concern to you. I, for my part, did not hesitate to sail down the river to obtain distinguished. . . . and I have achieved something to match my eagerness. While I was seeking out a scholar (*philologos*), the tutor (*kathegetés*) Chaeremon, and Aristocles' son Didymus, men with whom I hoped that I, too, might achieve some success, I found them no longer in the city. Instead I found rubbish, men with whom most students take the road which leads straight to their own destruction.
>
> I wrote to Philoxenus and his companions, giving instructions that they, too, should turn the business over to. . . . who is held in high regard. . . . so that I may find a tutor (*kathegetés*) immediately, now that I have obtained my release from Theon, since I, too, personally found fault with him. . . . for the lack of care he showed about his behaviour. When I shared your thoughts with Philoxenus, he agreed that you were right and suggested that just this very shortage of sophists was a reflection of the state of the city. However, he did say that

Didymus, who it turns out is a friend of his and has a school, would travel down the river and would devote greater care to our education than the others. He also persuaded the sons of Apollonius son of Herodas to go to Didymus for instruction, since they too, along with Philoxenus, have been searching until now for a tutor (*kathegetés*) with superior skills, now that the scholar (*philologos*) whose school they used to attend is dead.

Personally, if only I had come across reputable tutors (*kathegetai*), I would have prayed never to set eyes on Didymus even from a distance. I find the reality of this situation utterly discouraging, that this individual who used to teach out in the country has decided to compete with the rest of the field. Accordingly, well aware of the fact that, quite apart from paying larger fees to no purpose, there is no benefit to be derived from a tutor (*kathegetés*), I am depending on my own initiative instead. If you have any good advice to give, write to me quickly. As Philoxenus also observes, I do have Didymus, who is always ready to devote his time to me and is always providing me with everything within his power. In addition, by listening to those who offer displays of rhetoric, including Posidonius, I shall soon achieve some success, the gods being willing.

I am quite depressed about these circumstances, something which is forcing me to ignore my physical needs, because those who have not yet attained success should not have to be concerned about these issues, especially when there are none who are contributing any income. At one time the useful Heraclas used to provide some obols on a daily basis. But, damn him! Having been imprisoned by Isidorus as he deserved, he has now made his escape and returned to join you, I believe. You may rest assured that he would never hesitate to scheme against you. He showed no embarrassment at gossiping quite happily in the city, in front of the whole world, about the episode in the theatre and spreading the sort of lies that not even an accuser would allege in court. He did this despite the fact that he did not suffer the punishment which was his due, but obtained his release and is conducting every aspect of his life as a free man.

Nonetheless, if you are not sending him back here, you might turn him over to a carpenter, since I hear that a young fellow makes two drachmas a day. Or else attach him to some other form of work which will produce a greater income, so that his earnings can be collected and sent to us in due course. For you are aware that Diogas too is learning letters. While you send me the small one, we will look about to find greater space in a private home, since the space we have at present, in order to be next door to Dionysius, is far too small. We did receive the basket, which contained exactly what you described in your letter, and the vessels, including the half-*cadus* jar, in which we found a total of 22 *choes*,[6] not 18. To each of those you mentioned in your letter I have sent a half-*cadus* of unprocessed lentils together with a note. I received the six measures, a full *coion* of vinegar, 126 lbs of pickled meat, the contents of the *cadus* and the 30 loaves of bread. I trust that you are in good health. Choiak 4.

9.18. The problem with learned women

Juvenal, *Satires* 6.434–56

Juvenal's attack on educated women is part of a larger assault in his sixth *Satire* on women in general. Compare Sallust's more balanced assessment of Sempronia (**8.19c**). Further reading: Pomeroy 1975: 170–76, 1977: 60–62.

But that woman is harder to bear who, as soon as she has reclined for dinner, starts praising Virgil and pardoning the doomed Elissa; and who pits the poets against each other and compares them, placing Maro [i.e. Virgil] on one side of the scale and Homer on the other. The *grammatici* give in, the *rhetores* are defeated, and the whole attendance falls silent. A lawyer will not get a word in, and neither will the auctioneer – or another woman! Such a mass of words comes crashing down. One would say that umpteen pans and bells were being all crashed together. No one now should wear out trumpets or brass – one woman alone will suffice to help the eclipsing moon! The philosopher sets a limit even on virtues. The woman who has an overwhelming desire to appear learned and eloquent should tuck her clothes up to the knee, sacrifice a pig to Silvanus and go to the baths for a penny. The matron who reclines for dinner beside you should not have an oratorical style and should not be hurling a curved syllogism with combative tongue. She should not know all the tales from history, and some of what she finds in books she should not understand. For my part, I truly hate the woman who, always preserving the rules and laws of language, checks up and leafs through Palaemon's grammar, and who, with her love of archaism, remembers poetry I don't know. These are men's concerns? Let her find fault with her stupid girl-friend's language, and give her husband leeway to commit his solecism.

9.19. Book-learning is not enough

(a) Cicero, *Against Caecilius* 47, (b) Quintilian, Preface 24, 26

Both Cicero and Quintilian express scepticism about the value of textbooks and their rules.

6 Approximately 65 litres.

a

For if you are able to answer me on any of the points I am making, if you depart by a single word from that book of yours, that book compiled from others' speeches which some schoolmaster gave to you, then I shall consider you to have ability. I shall think you not lacking the competence for that trial, too, and that you are talented enough for that case and for discharging your responsibilities to it. But if you prove to be of no account in this preliminary engagement, what are we to think your performance will be in the real fight with the keenest of opponents?

b

(24) Generally speaking, those stark textbook rules, straining as they do after excessive subtlety, only enervate and destroy whatever nobility there is in one's oratorical style. They drain it of all its natural vitality and uncover its bones – which, indeed, should be there and should be bound together by the sinews, but they should also be covered with flesh. . . . (26) However, I must emphasize one point in particular: rules and techniques are of no avail if natural talent is not there to help. So such writings would be of no more use to the student who lacks natural ability than writings on agriculture would be to barren lands.

9.20. Vespasian's support for Greek and Latin *rhetores*

(a) Suetonius, *Life of Vespasian* 17–18, (b) Cassius Dio,
History of Rome 66.12.1a, (c) *FIRA* 1.77

Vespasian, emperor from AD 69 to 79, provided support for education through the establishment of official positions ("chairs") for teachers of Greek and Latin rhetoric (**a**), probably one for each language. The historian Dio Cassius adds the information (**b**) that this occurred in 71 and that Vespasian's initiative did not extend beyond Rome (the first holder of the Latin chair was Quintilian). But Vespasian promoted teachers in another, equally significant way: he exempted them (and physicians) from taxation (**c**). The Greek inscription which records this measure is from Pergamon and is dated to 27 December AD 75. Further reading: Marrou 1956: 301–2; Bowersock 1969: 30–42; Bowen 1972: 197–99; Wallace-Hadrill 1983: 36; Coleman 1985: 3108–11.

a

(17) Vespasian was exceedingly generous to all ranks of people. . . .
(18) He gave special encouragement to learning and the liberal arts.
He was the first to establish from the public treasury an annual salary
of 100,000 sesterces each for the Latin and Greek teachers of rhetoric
(*rhetores*).

b

After Jerusalem was sacked, Titus returned to Italy [AD 71], where he
and his father [Vespasian] celebrated their triumph. . . . Afterwards
Vespasian established teachers of Latin and Greek education in
Rome, who received their pay from the public treasury.

c

The emperor Caesar Vespasian Augustus . . . declares: since the professions that are suitable for free men are considered publicly and
privately useful to cities and sacred to the gods, namely the profession
of the *grammatikoi* and the *rhetores*, who, by the guidance of Hermes
and the Muses, train the minds of the young towards gentleness and
civic goodness, and, by the guidance of Apollo and Asclepius, the
profession of the physicians and healers, since the care of bodies has
been assigned to the followers of Asclepius alone – because these men
are called holy and god-like, I order that no billeting be done with
them and that no taxes be exacted in any manner. If any of those under
my rule dare to commit a crime against, or require security from, or
bring a charge against, any physician or teacher or healer, let those
who have committed the crime pay a fine of 10,000 drachmas to
Jupiter Capitolinus. Whoever cannot pay, let him sell his property,
and let the fine assigned by the official appointed for these matters be
consecrated to the god immediately. Likewise, if they find him trying
to escape detection, let them indict him in whatever court they choose,
and let no-one prevent them from this. Let them be permitted to
convene meetings as well, wherever they choose, in sanctuaries, sacred
places, and temples, since these places provide safety. Whoever forces
them out, let him be subject to trial by the Roman people for impiety
against the imperial household. I, emperor Caesar Vespasian, signed
this and ordered it to be displayed in public.

10

PAGANS AND CHRISTIANS

From the second century AD to the end of Antiquity

By the beginning of the second century AD the system of formal education in the Mediterranean world was fixed within fairly well-defined limits for both native Greek and native Latin speakers. Students at the elementary stage learned the rudiments of reading and writing, as well as some basic arithmetic, using methods that had been followed for centuries. This instruction often took place inside the home rather than in a classroom. Many children did not advance beyond this level, but those who did were introduced to literature and a kind of literary criticism, most often, though not invariably, by the *grammaticus* alone. By now the authors (and works) that were to be studied had hardened into a standardized list: above all, Homer, Hesiod, Euripides, Menander (though Aristophanes would replace him), and Demosthenes in Greek, and Virgil, the comic playwright Terence, Cicero, and the historian Sallust for Latin speakers. Students who continued their education usually came under the direction of the *rhetor*, though their rhetorical training often commenced with the *grammaticus*. For some, philosophical study then followed.

The emergence of Christianity as the dominant religion in the Roman Empire had the potential to end this pedagogical continuity. Many of the beliefs, values and practices of the early Christians were, after all, fundamentally at odds with those of the pagan Greeks and Romans. Hence it might be assumed that Christians would have established their own distinct system of education, focusing on the Bible and other Christian texts. This, however, did not happen. The traditional methods for teaching children to read and write could not be improved upon, so it made no sense to discard them (**10.1**). The subjects that students learned continued to include the literary, mathematical and artistic pursuits familiar since at least the Hellenistic period (**10.2–3**). Moreover, Christians studied the same authors and works that their pagan counterparts had read at school in the past and continued to read.

Yet Christians had to confront the question: how could traditional education and the study of the standard school authors be reconciled with the spiritual life they had chosen? One response was to view the curriculum as preliminary to the acquisition of a knowledge of the one true God – in other words, as the means to a higher end (**10.3**). Another was to argue against a Christian's teaching of pagan literature but not a child's learning of it (**10.4**). It was not only Christians, however, who recognized the potential hypocrisy involved in a Christian's teaching of pagan literature. The emperor Julian, who strove to re-establish paganism throughout the Empire, objected as well, and even legislated against the practice (**10.5**). Although this measure is said to have provoked a remarkable attempt to produce a set of Christian works of literature to take the place of the traditional classics (**10.6**), the more practical response was that of St. Basil, St. Augustine and Pope Gregory, who treated pagan literature, again, as a preliminary stage, but one which was beneficial in itself (**10.7**) – though it is apparent that Augustine was conflicted over his attraction to Latin literature, in particular to Virgil (**10.8**). It is not surprising, then, that in the fourth century the famous teacher Ausonius and his grandson Paulinus, both raised and educated in Gaul, and both Christian, received traditional educations (**10.9–10**). St. Basil's sister Macrina, however, avoided pagan literature altogether, focusing instead on the Bible (**10.11**), and St. John Chrysostom favoured chastening stories from the Bible (and threats) as alternatives to corporal punishment (**10.12**).

A distinctive feature of this period is the degree to which the state sought to regulate and promote various aspects of education. This activity is apparent not only in the philosophical appointments initiated by the emperor Marcus Aurelius in 176 and in the creation of the "municipal" chair of rhetoric which preceded them (**10.13–14**), but also in a variety of other measures (**10.15–17, 26**). At a local level this activity can be seen (as before) in the operations of gymnasia and the *ephebeia* (**10.18**).

The official attention given to teaching and learning during the later Roman Empire reflects both the desire to encourage education at all levels and the need to safeguard the position of Christianity in a world in which pagan culture still played a prominent role. Of special interest is the tremendous prestige which skill in rhetoric continued to enjoy among pagans and Christians up to the end of antiquity (**10.19–21**), a status which can be seen in the substantial salaries commanded by the teacher of rhetoric (the *rhetor* or sophist). The competition for students was intense, and loyalty to one professor or another could be fierce (**10.20–21**). Declamation continued to be an important part of rhetorical training, even among Christians as late as the sixth century AD (**10.22**); critics found the same shortcomings in it that had been identified since at least the first century AD (**9.14–15**).

In certain respects the teaching and study of philosophy thrived from the second century AD. Plato's writings in particular attracted dedicated followers, especially in Athens and Alexandria, which were the main centres of philosophical study. The most notable of these followers was Plotinus, about whose methods of teaching we possess much useful information, as we do also about the approaches taken by some of his successors (**10.23–24**). Although there was a great deal about Platonic philosophy that Christians could relate to, it also – like all pagan philosophy – posed problems that a Christian could not overcome. This conflict is most famously reflected in the decree of 529 by the emperor Justinian concerning the teaching of philosophy (**10.26**), but it can also be seen in the fate of Hypatia, a prominent Platonist in Alexandria in the early fifth century (**10.25**). In spite of this difficult environment, Platonic philosophy exercised an enduring influence on the shape of medieval education through the aggregate of subjects called the *quadrivium* (arithmetic, geometry, astronomy, musical theory), a term first attested in western Europe by Boethius (**10.27**). This set of four subjects went by the name *tetraktys* in the Greek east, where the old terms *enkuklios paideia* and *enkuklios paideusis* were also still used to describe the curriculum of which these subjects formed a part, even in the eleventh century and beyond (**10.28**).

General background: Bowersock 1990: 1–13; Brown 1992: 118–58; Maas 2000: 46–58 (translated sources); Clark 2004: 78–92; Mitchell 2007: 225–55. *Christianity and pagan education*: Marrou 1956: 314–50; Jaeger 1961; Bowen 1972: 217–345; Young, Ayres and Louth 2004: 91–104, 222–38, 464–84.

10.1. A student's notebook

PBour 1 (= *PSorb* inv. 826)

The Greek papyrus-notebook from which the following extracts are taken leaves little doubt that by the fourth century AD (the date of the papyrus), the way children learned the rudiments of reading and writing had not changed appreciably since the fifth century BC. The notebook, eleven pages long, begins with a column of monosyllabic words in alphabetic sequence, followed by columns of two-, three-, and four-syllable words, again in alphabetic sequence; these words include gods, characters of legend, historical figures, authors, and a few "tongue-twisters" (*chalinoi*: **6.1c**, **8.4** [37]). Five anecdotes (*chreiai*) then follow; twenty-four sayings in iambic-trimeter verse come after these; the papyrus then ends with a longer passage, the introduction to the *Fables* of Babrius (a very popular author in schools). The word-lists concentrate on items that would serve students in their later reading of Homer, tragedy, comedy, and historical writing, while the anecdotes and sayings are of the kind used in the composition of *progymnasmata* (see **9.8b** [3–5]). From a modern perspective, however, the anecdotes and sayings do not always follow the advice of Protagoras (**3.15**), Plato (*Republic* 386a–387b) and Quintilian (**8.4** [35–36]) that students should be required to learn passages of high moral value.

The only features that alert us to the fact that this is the work of a

Christian student are the appearance of the word *theos*, "God," at the top of the first page, and the "christogram" (interlocked Greek letters *chi* [χ] and *rho* [ρ], the first two characters in the name "Christ") at the start of each page. The five anecdotes and some of the sayings are translated below. In each of the anecdotes, the Cynic philosopher Diogenes is the subject of "seeing." Further reading: Marrou 1956: 324–26; Cribiore 1996: 276; Morgan 1998: 185–89; Hock and O'Neil 2002: 5–12.

- Seeing a fly on his table, he said: "Even Diogenes keeps parasites."
- Seeing a woman being taught letters, he said: "That's quite a sword that's being sharpened!"
- Seeing one woman giving advice to another, he said: "An asp is being given poison by a viper."
- Seeing an Ethiopian eating white bread, he said: "Look, night is swallowing day."
- Seeing an Ethiopian shitting, he said: "That's quite a kettle that's been pierced!" ...
- Letters are the most important starting-point for thinking.
- Honour an old man, the image of god.
- Eros is the oldest of all the gods.
- You will live the best life if you overcome emotion.
- Avoid bad character and wicked profit.
- The sea, fire, and a woman – the third evil.
- The mind is the most prophetic god in us.
- Arrogance is the greatest evil for people.

10.2. The seven liberal arts, and more

Galen, *Exhortation to Learn the Arts* 14

Galen was a Greek physician, born in Pergamon in AD 129; he spent part of his career there before moving to Rome, where he died in 216. Of the eleven intellectual pursuits named in this extract, two – sculpture and painting – are presented as an afterthought. The unusual prominence of medicine in this list can be explained by the fact that Galen was himself a physician, while law was included because it had long held a place in Roman education (see **7.5**). The other *technai* comprise the standard list of the seven liberal arts. Further reading: Russell 1989.

If someone thinks that you should prepare yourself for an occupation that is secure and well regarded, practise a skill that will stay with you throughout your life. Now, the primary difference among the crafts (*technai*) is twofold: some of them are rational and held in respect, while others provoke our contempt and are carried out through bodily labour – these of course are the ones which are called the jobs of tradesmen and manual workers. It would therefore be preferable to pursue one of the first class of skills, since the second kind normally fails practitioners when they become old. In the first class are medicine, rhetoric, music, geometry, arithmetic, logic, astronomy, letters and law. To these add sculpting and painting if you like, for although sculptors and painters work with their hands, what they make does not require youthful strength. Therefore, if the young man's spirit is not altogether like an animal's, he should take up and practise one of these skills, preferably the best of them, which, as we claim, is medicine.

10.3. The liberal arts in a Christian education

(a) Clement of Alexandria, *Miscellanies* 1.5.30.1–2,
(b) Lactantius, *The Divine Instructions* 3.25–26

The Christian "Church Fathers" Clement (roughly contemporary with Galen) and Lactantius (*c.* AD 240–320) both see the usual subjects of study – the liberal arts – as representing a preliminary stage. In Clement's view (dependent on Philo's, **9.5**), they are preliminary to philosophy, which is itself preliminary to wisdom or "knowing God." For Lactantius too these subjects are preliminary to philosophy, but he is unwilling to grant that philosophy contributes to the acquisition of true wisdom (which, again, consists of knowing God), since he views this wisdom as the common property of all people, whereas philosophy is only for the few. Further reading: Ellspermann 1949: 79–88; Brown 1992: 121–26; Osborn 2005: 81–105, 197–212.

a

(1) But as the subjects in a general education (*enkuklia mathemata*) contribute to their mistress philosophy, so also does philosophy herself assist in the acquisition of wisdom (*sophia*), since philosophy is the cultivation of wisdom and wisdom is the knowledge of divine and human things and of their causes. Now, wisdom is superior to philosophy, as philosophy is superior to preliminary education (*propaideia*); (2) for if philosophy promises control over one's speech and stomach and the parts below the stomach, and if it is to be chosen for its own sake, then it will appear holier and more authoritative, provided it is practised for the purpose of honouring and knowing God.

b

(25) But if human nature has the capacity for wisdom, then workmen, peasants, women, and all who have human form should be taught so that they may be wise, and a population of wise people should be formed from every tongue, condition, sex and age. So the strongest proof that philosophy neither leads towards wisdom nor is itself wisdom is the fact that its mystery is observed only by the beard and the pallium.[1]

The Stoics realized this, for they said that both slaves and women should practise philosophy; and so did Epicurus, who invites those without any literary education to study philosophy; and likewise Plato, who wished to construct a city of wise men.[2] Those men tried to do what the truth demanded of them, but it was not possible to advance beyond words because, in the first place, it requires many arts to be able to approach philosophy. Those letters that we all use must be learned for the practice of reading, since, when there are so many different things, everything can neither be learned by hearing nor retained in the memory. You must devote sufficient attention to grammar so that you may know the correct way of speaking; by necessity this takes many years. Not even rhetoric should be ignored, so that you can present and express what you have learned. Geometry, too, and music and astronomy are required, because these arts have some connection with philosophy. Women are unable to learn all these subjects to completion since, when they are old enough, they have to be taught the duties that will soon be beneficial to managing a home; nor can slaves learn them, since it is especially in the years in which they can learn them that they must serve; nor can the poor, or workmen, or peasants, since they must seek out their sustenance with their labour every day. This is the reason why Cicero said that "philosophy avoids the crowd."[3]. . .

(26) Therefore, what those men [i.e. the philosophers mentioned above] realized must be done according to the demands of nature – though they themselves could not do it and saw that it could not be done by philosophers – this heavenly doctrine alone accomplishes, because it alone is wisdom.

---

1 The beard and *pallium* (a Roman cloak) were external features of the philosopher.
2 For the views of the Stoics, see **8.18**; of the Epicureans, see **6.2c**; of Plato, see **5.10**, **14**.
3 Cicero, *Tusculan Disputations* 2.1.4.

10.4. The perils of pagan education

Tertullian, *On Idolatry* 10.5–7

Tertullian's general view of the relationship between pagan thought and Christian life is expressed most famously through his rhetorical questions: "What does Athens have to do with Jerusalem? What does the Academy have to do with the Church?" (*Prescriptions against All Heresies* 7). Yet Tertullian himself was well schooled in classical authors and literature (Helleman 1994). In *On Idolatry*, written around 200, he wrestled with the problem of how a Christian life can be lived in the presence of widespread pagan practices. A particularly difficult manifestation of this problem confronted many Christians before him and after: can a Christian child be taught the pagan curriculum, and can a Christian teacher teach it? Further reading: Ellspermann 1949: 23–42; Barnes 1971: 186–210; Osborn 1997: 24–47.

(5) Let us look, then, at the necessity of an education in literature, and let us take into account that it cannot be partly accepted and partly avoided. Believers may learn literature rather than teach it, since learning and teaching involve different ways of thinking. If a believer teaches literature, there can be no doubt that, by teaching about the idols which he proclaims as part of his teaching, he is recommending them, by passing on their stories he is confirming them, by mentioning them he is bearing witness to them. (6) He gives the gods themselves his seal of approval with this name [i.e. "gods"], although, as I said, the law forbids that they be called gods and that this name be assigned in vain. It is as a result of this that the first belief in the devil is built from the beginnings of education. Consider whether the person who catechizes about idols is committing idolatry!

But when a believer learns these things, if he already knows who he is, he neither accepts them nor receives them. If he does not yet know who he is, or when he has begun to know, all the more should he know first what he has learned first, namely, about God and faith. Therefore he will abhor those things and not accept them, and he will be as safe as one who recognizes poison and, though accepting it from a person who does not recognize it, does not drink it. (7) This person has necessity as his excuse, since he cannot learn in any other way. However, it is easier not to teach letters than it is not to learn them.

10.5. A ban on Christian teachers

Julian, *Letters* 61c

By the time Julian became emperor in AD 361 at the age of 30, Christianity had held a secure position in the Roman Empire for about 50 years. Julian, however, was a dedicated pagan, steeped in Platonic philosophy, and was troubled by the prospect of a Christian teaching children what he (the teacher) did not believe. On 17 June 362 he acted on his convictions by passing a famous law which forbade Christians from practising as teachers (*Theodosian Code* 13.3.5). The letter which follows was probably addressed to Christian teachers. Julian died only a year after the law was enacted, and it was repealed almost at once (*Theodosian Code* 13.3.6). Further reading: Marrou 1956: 323–24; Bowen 1972: 292–94; Browning 1975a: 167–74; Bowersock 1978: 82–85; Wilson 1983: 8–18.

A good education (*paideia*) is not, in my opinion, lavish fluency in words and speech, but a healthy disposition of thought and good judgement, as well as correct opinions about what is good and evil, attractive and disgraceful. A person who holds one set of beliefs but teaches his students another seems to me to have failed in this education as much as he has failed in being a good man. If the difference between what he thinks and what he says concerns minor matters, that is bad but in some ways tolerable. But if on the most important matters a person has certain thoughts but teaches the opposite of what he thinks, that is surely the behaviour of dishonourable peddlers. Their life is that of the most corrupt people, who praise to the skies what they consider least valuable, tricking and entrapping with their words of praise those with whom they want to exchange, I believe, their own inferior merchandise.

All who profess to teach any subject should therefore be of good character and carry opinions in their soul which do not conflict with their public practices. All the more should this be the case, I think, for those who teach literature to the young, who are interpreters of ancient writings, whether *rhetores* or *grammatikoi* or, above all, sophists, since they want to be teachers not only of how to speak but also of how to live, and they claim that political philosophy is their special area of expertise.

Let us leave aside whether this claim is true or not. While I praise them for striving after such fine professions, I would praise them even more if they did not lie and prove that they think one thing and teach their students another. Well? What of Homer, Hesiod, Demosthenes, Herodotus, Thucydides, Isocrates and Lysias – weren't the gods their guides in their entire education? Didn't some consider themselves sacred to Hermes, and others to the Muses? In my opinion, it is absurd for those who interpret the words of these authors to dishonour the gods whom the authors honour. But even though I think this is absurd, I am not saying that those who teach the young must change their opinions. I am giving them a choice: not to teach what they do not consider to be a matter of serious study, or, if they wish to teach, to teach first by their actions and persuade their students that neither Homer nor Hesiod nor any of those whom they interpret [was as stupid as they wanted their students to believe] when they accused them of impiety, foolishness and error in regard to the gods. But since they earn their living from these authors' writings, they are acknowledging that they are the most greedy of men and that they put up with anything for the sake of a few drachmas.

Until now, there were many reasons for not going to the temples, and the fear that everyone felt at all times justified concealing one's real beliefs about the gods. But since the gods have given us freedom, it seems absurd to me that people should teach what they do not believe is right. But if they consider as wise the people whom they interpret and in regard to whom they sit as prophets, as it were, then let them emulate first their piety towards the gods. If, on the other hand, they suppose that the poets are in error against the most honourable gods, let them go to the churches of the Galilaeans to interpret Matthew and Luke . . . .[4] You set down laws against participation in animal sacrifice; I want your ears and your tongue to be born again, as you would say, while you abstain from those things in which I would like to be involved always, along with anyone who thinks and does what is pleasing to me.

For professors and teachers, this is how the general law is laid down. Any young person who wishes to go to school, however, is not prevented, since it would be neither reasonable nor rational to prevent children who are still ignorant in which direction they should turn from taking the best path, out of fear that they will be led against their will to our ancestral customs. Yet it would be right to heal these people against their will as it would be to heal the insane, except that we excuse them all for a disease such as this. For we must teach the foolish, I believe, and not punish them.

---

4 Some words have been lost in the transmission of Julian's text, probably the result of an excision by a Christian scribe.

10.6. A response to Julian's law

Socrates, *Church History* 3.16

Julian's law is said to have inspired a father and son (both bearing the name Apollinarius) to recast the books of the Bible into the forms and styles characteristic of Greek literature (epic, tragedy, dialogue etc.). Since their attempt to produce a body of Christian literature to rival that which was already so well established was unsuccessful, the venture demonstrates that Christians were generally satisfied with the use of pagan literature in their children's education. As one modern scholar has put it: "what the Christians wanted their children to learn was not the bogus classics of the Apollinarii but the real thing" (Jones 1966: 351). In the following extract Socrates, a lawyer and church historian in Constantinople in the fifth century, explains the reasons for this failed attempt. Yet the project was not unique: some 75 years after the Apollinarii, Eudocia, wife of the emperor Theodosius II, turned Biblical stories into Homeric-style hexameter verse (Cameron 1982: 282–85; Urbainczyk 1997: 32–35). Further reading: Marrou 1956: 324.

The imperial law which prohibited Christians from participating in Greek education (*paideia*) cast in a more distinguished light the Apollinarii, whom I mentioned earlier. They were both expert in letters – the father in grammar, the son in rhetoric – and for this reason they proved themselves useful to the Christians in their current crisis. Since the father was a *grammatikos*, he compiled a manual on grammar suited to Christians; he also turned the books of Moses into what is called heroic verse, and all the historical books of the Old Testament he either compiled in dactylic verse or worked up into the form of dramatic tragedy. He used every poetic meter to ensure that there was no manner of expression in Greek that Christians did not hear. The younger Apollinarius, who was well trained in oral expression, presented the Gospels and the teachings of the apostles in dialogue form, following the style of Plato among the pagan Greeks. By showing themselves in this way to be useful to Christianity, they overcame the emperor's scheme through their personal labours. But God's providence proved greater than their industry and the emperor's impulse, since it was not long before his law was revoked, as I shall proceed to show, and their labours are now counted for no more than if they had not been written.

Someone will quickly raise an objection with us: "How can you say that this came about because of God's providence? The emperor's swift death was clearly to the advantage of Christianity, but there was no such advantage from abandoning the Christian compositions written by the Apollinarii or from having children undertake Greek education, since Greek education does harm by teaching polytheism."

In reply to these objections I will make such points as I can. Neither by Christ nor by his disciples was Greek education accepted as divinely inspired or rejected as harmful. They did what they did, in my opinion, with full awareness. For many Greek philosophers have not been far from knowing God. . . . Therefore, since they do not prevent us from learning the works of Greek literature, they left it to the judgement of those who want to study it. Consider this my first argument against the objection that has been presented. The second argument is as follows. The divinely inspired Scriptures teach admirable and truly holy doctrines, and they produce in their listeners much piety and an upright life, providing their students with a faith that is beloved to God. Yet they do not teach skill in speaking, which enables a person to confront those who want to do battle with the truth. The enemy is utterly defeated whenever we use his own weapons against him; but Christians would not have had this opportunity through the writings of the Apollinarii.

10.7. How Christians can accommodate pagan literature

(a) St. Basil, *Advice to the Young on Reading Pagan Literature* 1–2,
(b) St. Augustine, *On Christian Teaching* 2.139, 144–46,
(c) Gregory the Great, *Commentary on the First Book of Kings* 5.30

At some time probably in the 360s, St. Basil of Caesarea (in Cappadocia) wrote a short work which describes an appropriate method for Christian children to read the great works of pagan Greek literature that were an established part of the educational curriculum (**a**). St. Augustine wrote *On Christian Teaching* (**b**) over a period of about 30 years, beginning in the late 390s. Basil and Augustine both apply the practical criterion of "usefulness" in explaining the accommodation of pagan literature to the needs of the Christian student; and as Clement and Lactantius had done (**10.3**), they see the pagan curriculum as a preliminary stage. Writing around 600 – about 200 years after Augustine and nearly 250 years after Basil – Gregory the Great expresses some very similar views about the relationship between secular education and Christian faith (**c**). Further reading: Ellspermann 1949: 174–247; Howie 1969: 209–39; Richards 1980: 26–29; Kaster 1988: 77–78, 84–89; Rousseau 1994: 48–57; Brown 2000: 256–66; Smith 2004: 122–25.

a

(1) If you receive my words eagerly, you will belong to the second class among those who are praised in Hesiod's poem; but should you fail to do so, I would not like to say anything unpleasant, but remember on your own the verses in which he says: "Best is the man who compre-

hends for himself what must be done, and outstanding is that man too who follows what is demonstrated by others; but he who is suited for neither is useless for everything."[5] Do not be surprised if I say to you, who attend classes each day with teachers and associate with famous ancient men through the words which they have left behind, that I myself have discovered something of special advantage to you.

This is the very thing that I have come to advise you on, that you should not surrender to these men once and for all the rudders of your mind, as if it were a ship, and follow them wherever they lead. Rather, you should accept from them only what is useful, and you should know what ought to be disregarded. What these things are and how we shall distinguish between them is the lesson which I shall teach you from this point on. [Basil explains that only those pursuits have value that contribute to the "other life."] . . .

(2) It is to this life that the Holy Scriptures lead, completing our education through mysteries. But so long as your age prevents you from understanding the depth of their meaning, in the meantime, through analogies that are not entirely different, as if through shadows and mirrors, we give a preliminary training to the eye of the soul, imitating those who practise military tactics; for after they have gained experience through exercises for the arms and through dance-steps, they have in their competitions the benefit they derive from their training.

We must recognize that before us, too, a contest is set, the greatest of all contests, for which we must do everything and perform every task, as far as we can, to prepare for it, and we must associate with poets, prose-writers, orators, and all men from whom we are likely to derive some benefit for the care of the soul. Just as dyers first prepare by certain treatments that which is going to receive the dye, and then apply the colour, whether purple or some other shade, in the same way will we (if the glory of the good is destined to abide with us indelibly) then understand the sacred and mystical teachings after we have received preliminary initiation by those external [i.e. pagan] means. And like those who have become accustomed to seeing the [reflected] sun in water, so will we direct our eyes to the light itself.

b

(139) It therefore seems to me that the following instructions are to the benefit of young people who are studious and intelligent, and who fear God and seek a happy life. Do not venture to follow carelessly any teachings that are conducted outside the church of Christ, as if to

---

5 Basil is paraphrasing Hesiod, *Works and Days* 293–97; see **1.3**.

obtain a happy life, but distinguish them sensibly and carefully. Whichever ones you find of human origin – they are of different kinds because of the differing intentions of those who established them, and they are obscure because of the uncertain thoughts of fallible people – reject these completely and abhor them, especially if they have a connection with demons that was produced, as it were, through contracts and agreements to use certain hidden meanings. Do not let your study have anything to do with the unnecessary and extravagant institutions of mankind, but do not neglect those human institutions which, in view of the needs of this life, are important for an orderly society. . . .

(144) If by chance those who are called philosophers, especially the Platonists,[6] have said things that are true and consistent with our faith, not only should these not inspire fear but they should be claimed for our own use as well, as if from owners who have no claim to them. . . . (145) . . . all the teachings of the pagans possess false and superstitious fantasies and heavy loads of pointless labour, and we should all abhor and avoid this as we depart, through Christ's guidance, from the company of pagans. In addition to that they contain subjects of liberal study appropriate to the experience of truth, and some very useful moral lessons. A number of truths are also found in their writings concerning the worship of the one God himself. Those nuggets, like gold and silver, they themselves did not invent but dug out from the mines, as it were, of divine providence, which penetrates everywhere, and they use them misguidedly and harmfully, to serve demons. When a Christian is separating himself in spirit from their wretched company, he should remove these treasures from them and apply them to their correct purpose of preaching the Gospel. Their clothing – that is, human institutions suited to human society, which we cannot do without in this life – we may accept and keep by converting it to Christian use. (146) Many good Christian believers have done just this.

c

Although the learning to be obtained from secular books is not directly beneficial to the saints in their spiritual conflict, yet, when it is united to the study of Holy Scripture, men attain to a profounder knowledge of Scripture itself. The liberal arts ought, therefore, to be cultivated, in order that we may gain through them a more accurate knowledge of God's Word. But the evil spirits expel the desire for

---

6 Augustine is thinking in particular of Plotinus and his "Neoplatonic" successors (**10.23–24**).

learning from the hearts of some, to the intent that, being destitute of secular knowledge, they may be unable to reach the loftier heights of spiritual knowledge. For the devils know well that by acquaintance with secular literature we are helped in sacred knowledge. . . . If we are ignorant of profane science, we are unable to penetrate the depth of the Sacred Word.

10.8. Augustine's education in Greek and Latin literature

St. Augustine, *Confessions* 1.13–14

In the following extract (written shortly before 400), Augustine describes his personal experiences as a student of Greek and Latin literature. In doing so he also provides indications that his education followed the sequential path set out by the *litterator* (*grammatistés*) first, then the *grammaticus*. He was subsequently trained in rhetoric. Further reading: Howie 1969: 241–76; Brown 2000: 23–28.

(13) Not even now am I sure why it was that I hated Greek literature, in which I received instruction as a young boy; for I loved Latin literature – not that taught by the elementary teachers (*primi magistri*), but that taught by the so-called *grammatici*. In fact, I found my elementary Latin instruction – learning to read, write and count – as tiresome and painful as the Greek. And why so, unless this arises from sin and vanity of a life which made me "flesh and a wind that passeth away, and cometh not again"?[7] For the elementary studies were assuredly better because they were more certain, and by them there was, and is, imparted to me the ability which I have to read anything I find written, and to write anything I wish – better studies, indeed, than those which made me learn by heart the wanderings of some Aeneas or other, forgetting my own wandering from the true path, and weep for the dead Dido because she killed herself for love – when all the while, my God, my life, I could with dry eyes, miserable man that I was, bear my own self dying far from you! For what is more miserable than a miserable man who has no pity for himself, a man who weeps for the death of Dido, which came from loving Aeneas, but does not weep for his own death, which came from not loving you, O God. . . . [Further reference to Augustine's literary training and to Virgil's *Aeneid* follows.]

(14) So why is it that I hated *Greek* literature which tells of such things? For Homer, too, is a skilful weaver of tales like that and is

7 Psalm 77.39.

pleasantly inconsequential; yet as a boy I found him unappetising. I expect Greek boys find the same thing with Virgil, when they are forced to learn him by heart, as I did with Homer. Naturally, there is the difficulty, the real difficulty, of learning a foreign language, which virtually sprinkled gall on all those pleasant Greek fables and stories. For I knew none of the vocabulary, but intense pressure, in the form of cruel threats and punishments, was put on me to learn it. At some point in my childhood I knew no Latin vocabulary, either; yet this I learned simply by paying attention, and with no intimidation or torture – learned it as my nurses cajoled me, as people laughed and joked with me, and as my friends happily played with me. I learned, indeed, with no painful burden imposed on me by teachers urging me to learn; my own intellect was urging me to produce its own thoughts, something that would not have happened had I not learned some vocabulary, not from formal teaching, but from people talking to me and listening to whatever thoughts I had. Thus it is quite clear that an untrammelled curiosity is more efficacious for this type of learning than compulsion based on fear.

10.9. Ausonius

(a) Ausonius, *The Professors* 10.1–13, (b) Ausonius,
Various Prefaces 1.15–27

Decimus Magnus Ausonius, a Christian, was born around AD 310 in Bordeaux, where he lived the greater part of his life. He received most of his education there and in Toulouse. From 364 to 379, he lived in Trier while serving as tutor to the young emperor Gratian. From Ausonius' writings it is apparent that in Bordeaux there was no strict adherence to a rigid sequence of primary and secondary education. In **a** we learn that his earliest education was in *grammatiké* (literary and grammatical instruction); Macrinus, his first teacher, was therefore a *grammaticus* (cf. **8.25**). Selection **b** shows that Ausonius' own career as a teacher moved easily between *grammatiké* and *rhetoriké*. Such wholesale movement within the teaching profession seems, however, to have been unusual. Further reading: Haarhoff 1958: 46–48; Booth 1979a: 5–8, 1982; Kaster 1983: 331–32, 1988: 455–62; Green 1991: xxiv–xxxii; Stirling 2005: 138–64.

a

Now, as the sacred obligation of my melancholy duty brings each to my mind, I shall give an account of those who, though of lowly birth, station and merit, nevertheless introduced to the raw intellects of the men of Bordeaux the study of *grammatiké*. Let Macrinus be amongst these, to whom were initially entrusted my years of boyhood. . . .

b

I myself turned to *grammatiké*, and subsequently I also became quite well versed in *rhetoriké*. The courts of law I attended, too, but I was more dedicated to the practice of teaching. I won some fame as a *grammaticus*, not indeed so great that my reputation came close to that of Aemilius, Scaurus or Probus of Beirut, but such that I could look upon many of our own people, the famous Aquitaine names, as one comparable to them, not set beneath them. Then, after three decades passed on the calendar, my teaching in a provincial town ended; ordered to approach the golden palace of the emperor, I taught the emperor's progeny first as a *grammaticus*, and then also as a *rhetor*.

10.10. Paulinus

Paulinus of Pella, *Eucharisticon* 61–84, 113–40

Paulinus, grandson of Ausonius, was born around 375 in Pella (Macedonia) and raised in Bordeaux as a Christian. He began his education at the age of six; it consisted of Greek literature first, then Latin literature. Since Paulinus states that his parents forced him to learn "the first characters of the alphabet," we can surmise that he learned how to read and write at home rather than in the class of a *grammatistés*. Further reading: Kaster 1983: 333–34.

My parents were ever adept at combining my instruction with varied inducements to learning, and their well-controlled endeavours were able to instil in me the essence of good character, bringing rapid development to my coarse intellect and making me learn, almost along with the first characters of the alphabet, how to sidestep the ten special marks of ignorance and also avoid those faults of common sense. For a long time now none of these disciplines has been seriously practised, thanks to the corrupt times in which we live, but I admit I am more in favour of the old Roman practice, and an old man is better disposed to a time-period that is in keeping with his age.

Early on, when the time of my first lustrum was about over, I was compelled to read and learn the tenets of Socrates, Homer's martial fictions and the wanderings of Ulysses. Then I was immediately told to wade through Maro's [i.e. Virgil's] books as well, though I barely had a grip on the Latin language, since I had been accustomed to conversation with Greek slaves, to whom I had become close after a long period of playing games together. Thus, I admit, it was too great an effort for me as a boy to grasp those eloquent works written in a language I did not know. This twofold education is appropriate for more robust intellects, and confers a double glory on those who succeed in it; but in my case the linguistic division, as I now realize, easily exhausted the meagre capacity of my all too barren mind.

But I return to my life-story and the times which I passed through in that period when, intent on the study of grammar, I gladly thought that I could feel myself making some of the progress that I longed for in that enormously difficult enterprise, pushed along as I was by a Greek as well as a Latin teacher. I might even have derived some appropriate benefit from this had not a severe quartan fever suddenly descended on me, to bring to nothing my willing attempts at my studies, at the time when I had barely completed the fifth triennium of my life. . . .

10.11. The education of a Christian girl

Gregory of Nyssa, *Life of St. Macrina* 3–4

The author of this extract was the brother of Macrina and St. Basil (cf. **10.7a**). Gregory's purpose in composing this biography was not only to commemorate his remarkable sister but also to make known the important influence she had on her brother Basil. Despite the impression he leaves in this passage that secular education was something to be avoided, Gregory regularly reveals in his other writings a very close acquaintance with, and attachment to, pagan literature. Macrina's devotion to the Psalter (Book of Psalms) reflects the important place it came to have in Christian education. For her attraction to the reading of wisdom literature (i.e. the Wisdom of Solomon), cf. **1.3**, **5**, **4.9b**, **6.23**, **10.7a**. Further reading: Momigliano 1987.

When Macrina had passed the stage of infancy, she quickly learned the subjects that are taught to children, and the young girl's nature shone through in any subject her parents decided she should study. Her mother was eager to educate her daughter, but not in that secular, broad education (*enkuklios paideusis*) that children in their early years of study are taught. She thought that it was shameful and completely inappropriate that the tragic passions of women, which provided poets with their inspiration and their themes, or the obscenities of comedy, or the causes of the disasters in Troy should be taught to a gentle, docile nature, and defile it in some way through stories about women that are too indecent. But all teachings in the Scripture inspired by God, which children in their early years find easier to grasp – this was the child's programme of study, in particular the Wisdom of

Solomon and, furthermore, all the lessons that lead to a morally good life. There was, moreover, not a Psalm that she did not know, since she recited each part of the Psalter at particular times of the day, when she rose from bed, engaged in her duties and rested from them, took food and left the table, went to bed and arose to say her prayers. . . . Growing up with these and similar activities, and after becoming unusually skilful at working wool, she reached her twelfth year. . . .

10.12. A Christian view of corporal punishment

St. John Chrysostom, *On Vainglory* 30, 39

Augustine tells of the "cruel threats and punishments" that he endured as a young student (**10.8**). St. John Chrysostom (*c.* 350–407) urges that corporal punishment should be replaced by threats and fear alone, including the fear evoked by certain biblical stories. John was bishop of Constantinople from 398 to 403; Libanius (**10.19**) was one of his teachers. Further reading: Kelly 1995: 51–54, 85–87.

(30) Do not constantly use the rod or allow your son to grow accustomed to receiving that sort of discipline. For once he realizes that he is being forever subjected to chastisement, he will learn to despise it; and once he has learned to despise it, he has frustrated everything you are trying to achieve. On the contrary, see that he is always afraid of a beating, but that he never receives one. Shake your tawse at him and threaten him with it, but do not deliver the blow. While you must ensure that your threats are not carried through to the point of fulfilment, you must also, however, not allow it to be obvious that what you say will not go beyond a threat, since a threat is only useful if it is believed that it will become reality. Once the offender has learned the principles under which you are operating, he will feel contempt for them. So, though your son must not be disciplined, you must see that he expects it, so that there be no extinguishing of his fear. . . .

(39) "God immediately received Abel up into Heaven. But his brother, his murderer, lived on for many years amid terrible suffering and with fear and trembling as his constant companions. He suffered countless torments and was chastised daily." Speak to the child about the punishment with some emphasis, and do not simply say: "He heard from God that he would live groaning and trembling upon the earth." A young child does not understand what that implies. Say to him instead: "You tremble with fear when you stand before your schoolmaster and are tortured with anxiety about whether you are going to be given a beating. Every moment of Cain's life was like that after he had offended God."

THE SECOND CENTURY AD TO THE END OF ANTIQUITY

10.13. Public support for philosophical teaching

Lucian, *Eunuch* 3

In AD 176 the emperor Marcus Aurelius established professorships
("chairs") of philosophy in Athens for each of the four main philosophical
schools: Stoic, Platonic, Epicurean, and Aristotelian (or "Peripatetic"); cf.
10.14. This step reinvigorated the study of philosophy in the city. The
Eunuch is Lucian's satirical account of an apparently fictional competition
for one of these chairs. Lucian was born around AD 120 in Syria and wrote in
Greek. Further reading: Marrou 1956: 303, 441; Oliver 1981: 213–25; Millar
1992: 213–25.

LYCINUS: As you are aware, Pamphilus, the emperor has set up a
considerable fund to support the various branches of philosophy,
specifically the Stoics, the Platonists, the Epicureans, and also the
Peripatetics; the amount set aside is the same in each case. He
made it a requirement that, when one of the holders of the chairs
died, he should be replaced by someone else whom the leading
citizens had reviewed and approved. The reward is no shield of ox-
hide or animal for sacrifice, as you find in Homer,[8] but a fee of ten
thousand drachmas for providing instruction to the young.

PAMPHILUS: I am aware of that. Rumour has it that one of them
has just died, one of the Peripatetics, I believe.

LYCINUS: That's the Helen over whom they were locked in single
combat with each other. So far there was nothing ludicrous in the
situation, except perhaps for the fact that men who claimed to be
philosophers and to despise money were fighting over it as they
would if their country, their ancestral shrines, and the graves of
their forebears had been at risk.

10.14. Herodes Atticus

Philostratus, *Lives of the Sophists* 566–67

Herodes Atticus (*c*. AD 101–77) was given the responsibility of choosing the
four philosophers who would fill the professorial positions discussed in
10.13. Herodes was an extraordinarily wealthy Athenian who not only was a
man of letters and a skilful orator but had very good relations with the
Romans, as well, having been one of Marcus Aurelius' tutors, and also
consul in Rome in 143. At the same time that philosophers were being

---

8 *Iliad* 22.159–61.

chosen for the four chairs in 176, a decision was also made about candidates for a chair of rhetoric, likewise funded by the emperor. As we see here, a publicly funded chair of rhetoric (a "municipal chair") already existed when the imperial chair was established (see *Lives of the Sophists* 526–27). The first holder of the imperial chair was an Athenian, Julius Theodotus. Further reading: Marrou 1956: 305, 442; Bowersock 1969: 94–100; Kennedy 1972: 565–66; Kennell 1997: 346–56.

> My narrative now brings me to the sophist Theodotus, who held some authority over the people of Athens at the time when they were at odds with Herodes. Theodotus did not reach the point of showing animosity towards him in public. A man of low character and adroit at using circumstances to his advantage, he conducted secret intrigues against him behind the scenes. At any rate, he became closely attached to Demostratus' faction, so much so that he had a hand in writing the speeches against Herodes which they worked on from time to time. Theodotus was also the first to be given a chair to teach the young in Athens at a salary of ten thousand drachmas granted by the emperor. This detail is perhaps not worth mentioning, since not all of those who occupy this chair are men of note. I mention it because, while Marcus Aurelius charged Herodes with the responsibility of making the selection of Platonic, Stoic, Epicurean and Peripatetic philosophers, he personally picked out Theodotus as teacher of the young on the basis of his reputation, calling him an expert in political rhetoric and a boon to the art of rhetoric in general. Theodotus had attended the lectures of Lollianus and, indeed, had also been found at those of Herodes. He occupied the chair for two years and lived beyond his fiftieth birthday.

10.15. The role of the state in the lives of students and teachers

Theodosian Code 14.9.1

One of the prominent features of education in the Roman Empire was the increasing role that the state assumed (e.g. **9.20**, **10.13**, **16–17**). Some of the clearest evidence for this development is contained in the *Theodosian Code*, a collection of the decrees issued by Roman emperors between 313 and 438, the year in which the *Code* was promulgated. The collection is named after the emperor Theodosius II, who commissioned its production. The decree below was published on 12 March 370. Other relevant decrees include 13.3.1, 3, 5–7, 10–11, 16–18, 14.9.2–3 (Pharr 1952: 387–90, 414–15). Further reading: Pharr 1952: xvii–xxii; Marrou 1956: 306–8; Downey 1957.

> Emperors Valentinian, Valens, and Gratian Augustuses to Olybrius, Prefect of the City: All persons who come to the City because of their

desire for learning shall first of all upon arrival present to the master of tax assessment the requisite written documents from their several provincial judges, by whom the right to come to the City must be given. These documents shall contain the name of the municipality from which each student comes, together with his birth certificate and letters of recommendation certifying to his high attainments. In the second place, immediately upon matriculation the students shall indicate the profession for which they intend to study. In the third place, the office of tax assessment shall carefully investigate the life of the students at their lodging places, to see that they actually do bestow their time on the studies which they assert they are pursuing. These same officials of tax assessment shall warn the students that they shall severally conduct themselves in their assemblies as persons should who consider it their duty to avoid a disgraceful and scandalous reputation and bad associations, all of which We consider as the next worst thing to actual criminality. Nor shall the students attend shows too frequently nor commonly take part in unseasonable carousals. We furthermore grant to you as prefect the authority that, if any student in the City should fail to conduct himself as the dignity of a liberal education demands, he shall be publicly flogged, immediately put on board a boat, expelled from the City and returned home. Of course, permission shall be granted for all students to remain in Rome till their twentieth year, if they industriously apply themselves to the work of their profession, but if after the expiration of this time any student should neglect to return home of his own accord, by the administrative action of the prefect he shall be returned even more disgracefully to his municipality.

In order that these provisions may not perhaps be perfunctorily enforced, Your Exalted Sincerity shall admonish the office of tax assessment that for each month he shall enroll on his register the students who come, whence they come, and those who must be sent back to Africa or to the other provinces according to the periods of time. Only those students shall be excepted who are attached to the burdens of the guilds. Similar registers, moreover, shall be dispatched each year to the bureaus of Our Clemency, in order that We may learn of the merits and education of the various students and may judge whether they may ever be necessary to Us.

10.16. Teachers' salaries

Diocletian, *Edict on Maximum Prices* 7.65–71

In 301 the emperor Diocletian attempted (unsuccessfully) to curb rampant inflation by decreeing maximum prices for a wide range of goods and services, including teachers' monthly wages. Comparisons of teachers' wages with those for other workers are difficult to make, since variables differ from occupation to occupation. For instance, the daily wage for a farm labourer was fixed at 25 denarii, for a carpenter at 50, and for a wall painter at 75, while the wage for a first-rate scribe was set at 25 denarii per 100 lines (the denarius was worth 4 sesterces: Chapter 8 n. 9). The punishment for violating the decree was death or exile. Further reading: Frank 1940: 310–421 (full translation of Diocletian's *Edict*); Cameron 1965.

> For a *paedagogus*, per month for each boy: fifty denarii
> For a *magister institutor* (elementary teacher), per month for each boy: fifty denarii
> For a *calculator* (teacher of arithmetic), per month for each boy: seventy-five denarii
> For a *notarius* (teacher of shorthand), per month for each boy: seventy-five denarii
> For a *librarius* (teacher of manuscript writing) or *antiquarius* (teacher of palaeography), per month for each boy: fifty denarii
> For a Greek or Latin *grammaticus* and *geometres* (teacher of geometry), per month for each boy: two hundred denarii
> For an orator or sophist, per month for each boy: two hundred and fifty denarii

10.17. The "University of Constantinople"

Theodosian Code 14.9.3

The following decree from the *Theodosian Code* is an important document for the history of education in the eastern half of the Roman Empire and for the Byzantine world which followed it. It dates to 27 February 425 and records provisions made by the emperor Theodosius II for the foundation of the so-called University of Constantinople. Despite high and low points in its history, this institution survived until Constantinople's fall to the Turks in 1453. Further reading: Buckler 1948: 201–2, 216–20; Marrou 1956: 307–8; Cameron 1982: 285–87.

> We order to be removed from the practice of vulgar ostentation all persons who usurp for themselves the name of teachers and who in their public professorships and in their private rooms are accustomed to conduct with them their students whom they have collected from all quarters. Thus if any of these teachers, after the issuance of the words of this divine imperial sanction, should perhaps again attempt to do that which We prohibit and condemn, he shall not only undergo the brand of infamy that he deserves, but he shall know that he will also be

expelled from the very city where he conducts himself thus illicitly. But by no threat of this kind do We prohibit those teachers who are accustomed to give such instruction privately within very many homes, if they prefer to keep themselves free for such students only whom they teach within the walls of private homes. If, moreover, there should be any teacher from the number of those who appear to be established within the auditorium of the Capitol, he shall know that in every way he is interdicted from teaching such studies in private homes. He shall also know that if he should be apprehended doing anything contrary to the imperial celestial statutes, he shall obtain no benefit from those privileges which are deservedly conferred upon those persons who have been commanded to teach only in the Capitol.

Therefore, Our auditorium shall have three orators and ten grammarians, first of all among those teachers who are commended by their learning in Roman oratory. Among those professors also who are recognized as being proficient in facility of expression in Greek, there shall be five sophists in number, and likewise ten grammarians. Since it is Our desire that Our glorious youth should be instructed not only in such arts, We associate authorities of more profound knowledge and learning with the aforesaid professors. Therefore, it is Our will that to the other professors, one teacher shall be associated who shall investigate the hidden secrets of philosophy, two teachers also who shall expound the formulas of the law and statutes. Thus Your Sublimity shall provide that to each of these teachers a designated place shall be specifically assigned, in order that the students and teachers may not drown out each other, and the mingled confusion of tongues and words may not divert the ears or the minds of any from the study of letters.

10.18. Gymnasium and *ephebeia* in the third century AD

(a) *POxy* 1202, (b) *POxy* 2186, (c) *IG* 12.5.292

The first of these documents, a papyrus letter which dates probably to 217, is a petition by a father to have his son enrolled among the *epheboi* of Oxyrhynchus, Egypt, since his son has now reached the age of 14 and has already become a member of the gymnasium. The second document dates to 260; it is an application on behalf of the author's son for his admission into the gymnasium of Oxyrhynchus. The application is supported by the boy's ancestry: his father can trace membership in the gymnasium six generations back on his own side and four on his wife's. The third document, a third-century inscription from the island of Paros, is of special interest, since it provides evidence for a woman's service in the role of *gymnasiarchos*. The *ephebeia* does not seem to have survived as an institution beyond the fourth century either in Egypt or elsewhere (Kennell 2006: xiv–xv).

a

To the almighty Aurelius Severus, deputy-*epistrategos*, from Aurelius Ptolemaeus ... from the city of Oxyrhynchus. Ever since it was our good fortune to receive the competition of the *epheboi* as a gift from our masters, Severus and the mighty Antoninus, the tradition has been established that those serving as district-secretaries of the city at any given time should, as the date for the competition draws close each year, send forward and publish the list of those who are about to become *epheboi* in order that each should attain the status of *ephebos* at the appropriate time. Accordingly, since our son Aurelius Polydeuces, who is close to the point at which he would become an *ephebos* and who has been designated for membership in our gymnasium, having reached the age of fourteen in the 25th year [i.e. of the emperor Caracalla's reign] and passed the selection process for membership of the gymnasium[9] during the same 25th year in conformity with the requirements of age and birth, has been omitted, perhaps in error, by the current district-secretary of the city, Aurelius Serapion, from his recently published list of those who are about to become *epheboi* in auspicious circumstances, I must, in order to secure assistance, resort to a petition to you that my son be entered on the list of the *epheboi* in the same way as his age-group. May you continue to be blessed with good fortune. Dictated by Aurelius Ptolemaeus.

b

To the Aurelii, Cronius and ... , former *gymnasiarchoi*, senators of the city of Oxyrhynchus, and chairmen of the selection process, from Aurelius, son of Sarapion and whose mother was ... lia from the city of Oxyrhynchus. In keeping with the regulations governing the process for judging the applications of those who seek membership in the gymnasium to determine whether they meet the requirements of birth, my son, whose mother ... , was registered in the ward of. ... In this the 7th year, he is 14 years of age, he bears a scar on his left cheek, his brow is small and he is easily recognized by his height.

Therefore, I have appeared for the judgement on the application for membership and make the following disclosures: that, at the judgement of the applications for membership in the gymnasium which took

---

9 Literally: selection among "those from the gymnasium," a formulaic expression which occurs twice in **b** as well; see **6.18**.

place during the 5th year of the deified Vespasian [AD 74], the great-grandfather of my grandfather, Dionysius son of Philon, was approved for admission in the ward of Metrous on the basis of the proofs which he presented to the effect that his grandfather Dionysius, son of Philon, also was registered in the 34th year of the deified Caesar [AD 7] [five further generations of membership are recounted]. . . . that, at that same judgement which took place in the 5th year of the deified Vespasian, Apollonius, son of Apollonius, the great-grandfather of the grandfather of my son's mother, was registered from the ward of . . . [five further generations of membership are recounted]. . . .

I solemnly swear by the fortune of the Caesars, Valerianus, Gallienus, and Cornelius Salonius Valerianus, our lords the Augusti, that the details I have entered above are true, that . . . is the natural son of myself and . . . , that he is neither adopted nor suppositious, that I have not used either credentials which belong to others or false identities based on the same name. If I have, may I be liable to the consequences of perjury under oath. . . . Witnesses testifying to identity are the Marci Aurelii, Macrinus son of Maron, and whose mother is Aune, also known as Apia, and Leon, also known as Cercion . . . all of them residents of the same city.

c

The most illustrious city of the people of Paros, in return for many great services, and receiving honour rather than giving it: in accordance with its frequent decrees, it erected in the gymnasium, which she constructed and restored when it had been in a state of disrepair for many years, a marble statue of the *gymnasiarchos*, Aurelia Laeta, daughter of Theodotus; wife of Marcus Aurelius Faustus, the leading citizen in the city, who inherited from his forebears the chief-priesthood of the Augusti and Caesars for life and also served as priest of Demeter and *gymnasiarchos*; a lady most distinguished and virtuous in every respect, dedicated to the pursuit of knowledge, to her husband, to her children and to her country. . . . Faustus, a man of distinction, could not have held in greater honour his wife Laeta, a mother of a noble family of children, a woman who was characteristically wise.

10.19. Libanius' education in Athens

Libanius, *Autobiography* 16–17, 24–25

Libanius was one of the most prominent orators and teachers of rhetoric in the Mediterranean world during a lifetime which spanned most of the fourth century AD (314–*c.* 404). Born in Antioch (Syria), he studied in Athens, taught in Constantinople and Nicomedia, and then returned to his home-town; here he took up a chair of rhetoric, became one of Antioch's leading citizens, and remained there for the rest of his life. In the following extracts, Libanius tells about his days as a student of rhetoric in Athens. Some of the teachers he meets are charlatans; his experience is in this regard similar to that of Neilos in Alexandria in the late first century AD (**9.17**). The competition for students was intense, and the methods of recruitment used by sophists not always scrupulous (cf. **10.20**). Students swore an oath to support their teacher and attend his lectures, underwent an initiation, but were also permitted to listen to the lectures of other prominent sophists. The series of events which Libanius describes in the second paragraph occurred in 339. Further reading: Walden 1909: 296–333; Norman 1965: vii–xxxi, 1992: 7–28; Kennedy 1983: 150–63; Russell 1996: 1–15; Cribiore 2007: 47–52.

(16) I sailed into Geraistos and then into one of the harbours of Athens, where I spent the night. By evening of the following day I was in the city and in the hands of those I would have preferred to avoid. The next day I was in the hands of still other people, though again I had no great wish to be with them. I was unable even to see the man with whom I had come to study, since I was confined in a space of limited dimensions, almost like a wine-jar, this being the way they treat students when they arrive. My professor of rhetoric had been robbed of me and I of him, and far apart as we were we called out for each other. Those who had taken possession of me took no notice of my cries and, although I was a Syrian, I was kept under guard until I had taken the oath, just like an Aristodemus.[10] When I had sworn my oath to tolerate the present circumstances, someone opened the door and immediately I began to attend the lectures of my captor[11] as his regular student, and those of the other two professors[12] as well, in keeping with the regulations governing public declamation.

(17) The thunderous applause the performances aroused might deceive those who were hearing them then for the first time, but I gradually realized that the performances at which I was present were not so very wonderful and that the direction of the studies of the young had been usurped by men who were not much superior to the students themselves. I left the impression that I was committing a sin

---

10 A peace envoy to Philip of Macedon in 346 BC, together with Demosthenes and Aeschines.
11 Diophantus; see **10.21**.
12 Epiphanius and Prohaeresius; see **10.20, 21**.

against Athens and deserved to be punished for my failure to respect the teachers in charge of me. I appeased their wrath only with some difficulty, by claiming that my respect was expressed in silence, because I couldn't raise my voice due to ill-health. In the end I showed them some compositions of my own in my notebooks and they believed that my behaviour was in other respects quite reasonable, even if I did not openly display my admiration. . . .

(24) This, then, was the splendid scheme devised by Fortune. There was also the fact that I followed the guidance of the right people and, therefore, had no need of any doctors to attend to my body. As a result, I was involved in my labours every single day, except for the days on which they celebrated festivals, and I don't think there were many of these. Since there was a general feeling that the greatest achievement was to be judged worthy of one of the chairs at Athens, Fortune also applied her mind to bringing this about and presented the gift to me in the following manner.

(25) The governor was a presumptuous man from Italy who believed that the young people in the city should never put a foot wrong. After some student riots, he dismissed their teachers, on the grounds that as shepherds they were incapable of properly tending their flock, and he sought out three others to replace them as directors of the students' studies. Consequently, an Egyptian and a compatriot of mine, both of whom were present in Athens, were recommended to him. Although I was only twenty-five years of age, while the Egyptian was ten years older and the other appointee even older, my labours had brought me success which quite matched their own and I was obliged to show up when I received the invitation. The passage of time stilled the governor's wrath and the professors of rhetoric kept their chairs. I had, however, enjoyed the distinction of being selected for the post. Because of this, suspicion ruled, and sleep was impossible for both my colleagues and myself; in their case their plots caused them to stay awake at night, in mine it was the expectation that I had something rather unpleasant to look forward to. Still, even here Fortune had not abandoned me to the reckless conduct of the young; though they were absolutely furious and enraged, she kept them under control.

10.20. Prohaeresius

Eunapius, *Lives of the Philosophers* 485

Prohaeresius was born in Cappadocia in AD 276 and died in Athens in 366. Even though none of his speeches survives he deserves our attention, since he was one of the most celebrated rhetoricians of his time. He was invited to the court of the emperor Constans in Gaul when he was in his seventies, subsequently distinguished himself in Rome, where a statue with an inscription was erected in his honour, and held the chair of rhetoric in Athens, where his students, pagan and Christian, included (among other notables) the future emperor Julian, St. Basil of Caesarea, and Basil's friend St. Gregory of Nazianzus. Eunapius (a pagan) is here describing the circumstances of his arrival in Athens to study with Prohaeresius, probably in 362 or very shortly after. It is September or October, when classes are set to begin. The passage presents a vivid picture of the competition for students that professional teachers engaged in, perhaps even keener than it had been in Libanius' time a generation earlier (a similar scene is described by Gregory of Nazianzus in his *Funeral Oration for Basil the Great* 15–16). Eunapius was born around AD 346 in the city of Sardis (in Lydia, a region of modern Turkey) and died there around 414. Further reading: Marrou 1956: 303, 323; Kennedy 1983: 9–10, 138–41; Booth 1985: 14–15; Rousseau 1994: 30–33; Cribiore 2007: 52–54.

> The author of this book crossed over to Europe and Athens from Asia during his sixteenth year, when Prohaeresius, on his own admission, had reached his eighty-seventh. . . . His rhetorical abilities were still so strong and his weary body was so revived by the youthfulness of his mind that this author believed him to be ageless and immortal, and focused his mind on what he had to say. . . . I arrived at Piraeus about the time of the first watch, suffering from a violent fever which had come upon me during the journey, and was accompanied on the voyage by a large number of my relatives. Though the hour was late, the captain rushed straight off to Athens before any of the traditional practices had occurred; the ship, you see, was from Athens and, when boats came into the harbour, they would regularly find lying in wait for them crowds of people with a fanatical devotion to their own particular school (*didaskaleion*). The others went on foot, and, because I was unable to walk, several people took their turn in supporting me, and in this way I was transported to the city.
>
> It was now the very dead of night, at the season of the year when the sun moves further to the south . . . and night-hunting was imminent. The captain, who was, I suppose, an old friend of Prohaeresius, knocked at his door and brought into his house this large crowd of students. There were so many, in fact, that, at a time when battles were being fought over one or two lads, those who had just arrived appeared sufficient to fill up a sophist's entire school. Some were endowed with perfect physical strength, in the case of others there was greater strength in their wallets, while others fell between the two. But the only accomplishment of this writer, then in a pitiable state, was his capacity to recite most of the books of the authors of the past.

10.21. A battle for sophistic preeminence

Eunapius, *Lives of the Philosophers* 487

The event which Eunapius describes here occurred about 330. It demonstrates both the astonishing international status held by the more skilful rhetoricians and the position which Athens still enjoyed as a centre for the teaching of rhetoric (cf. **10.19**). The Julian who is mentioned at the beginning of this extract was the preeminent rhetorician of his time in Athens. Further reading: Kennedy 1983: 136–42; Penella 1990: 79–94; Cribiore 2007: 51–52.

When Julian died, many men in Athens passionately desired to succeed him in the advantages he had enjoyed as teacher of rhetoric. Although so many others entered their names to secure control of the sophistic school that it would be a bother even to enumerate them, the following were approved and elected by unanimous decision: Prohaeresius, Hephaistion, Epiphanius, Diophantus, Sopolis (who was a poor man and belonged to a class which was normally disregarded and pushed aside), and Parnasius (whose status was even more humble). According to Roman law, there was a requirement that there should be at Athens a large number to give lectures and a large number to attend them. After they had been elected, those of less distinguished status enjoyed only the title which went with their position. However, their influence was confined to the benches in their lecture-rooms and the platform on which they came forward to deliver their lectures. In contrast, the city was immediately divided in its support of the more influential. Nor was this division limited to the city alone, but it affected all nations under Roman control. The strife these sophists engaged in was not merely over rhetorical matters, but to win over entire nations because of their rhetorical skills. The eastern provinces were clearly reserved for Epiphanius as his prize, Diophantus obtained Arabia, Hephaistion, who was intimidated by Prohaeresius, abandoned Athens and the society of men, while the whole of Pontus and the neighbouring regions sent students to Prohaeresius because of their admiration for the man as a treasure from their own country.

10.22. Late declamation and its faults

Synesius, *On Dreams* 20

Synesius was bishop of Ptolemais (Libya) from 410 until his death in 413. His ridicule of declamation has the same basis as the criticisms that were levelled against it 300 years before and earlier (**9.14**). Declamation continued to be practised by Christians into the sixth century, when it featured some of the same themes that had been employed since at least the time of the Elder Seneca (Kennell 2000: 72–80, 151–63, on the declamations of Ennodius, Bishop of Pavia). Further reading: Marrou 1956: 286–89; Kennedy 1983: 35–44, 1994: 252–54.

In my opinion it is inappropriate to practise one's skill on Miltiades, Cimon, and unnamed characters, too, and on the political enemies "rich man" and "poor man." I saw two old men in the theatre locked in battle over these themes. They were both very serious about philosophy, and each of them dragged around, I would guess, a talent's weight of beard, but their serious manner didn't stop them from abusing one another and getting very heated, or from waving their arms around aimlessly while they delivered their lengthy speeches. At the time, I thought it was all in support of men they knew, but, as people were quick to correct me, far from being their friends, those men neither existed nor ever had lived; indeed, they weren't even in the real world at all. For where can there be a form of government which allows a hero to kill his political rival as a reward? When a person makes a contest out of a fiction at the age of ninety, for what occasion is he putting off the study of the truth?[13]

10.23. Plotinus, his students and his school

Porphyry, *Life of Plotinus* 3, 7, 9

The *Life of Plotinus*, written by Plotinus' student Porphyry (*c.* 234–*c.* 305), is an account of the founder (204–70) of the Neoplatonic system of philosophy. It contains biographical information – most notably how Plotinus discovered the teacher who was to have the greatest influence on him – but it also provides a uniquely informative picture of educational conditions and practices in one ancient philosophical school. Here we gain the impression of a learning environment in which questions are encouraged and discussion is carried on in an unstructured, even chaotic way, and where two kinds of student are involved, those committed to a life of serious philosophical inquiry and those more casually associated with the school, such as the public figures who are named below. It also appears that Plotinus' students included women. Further reading: Lamberton 2001: 433–48; Gerson 1994: xiii–xvi.

---

13 Synesius is referring to Libanius (**10.19**). Since Libanius was born in AD 314, the events described in this passage must have occurred around 404.

(3) Until Plotinus was eight years old, he used to go to his nurse, bare her breasts, and want to suck, even though he was attending school, but when he heard one day that he was a nuisance, he felt ashamed and stopped. When he was twenty-eight years old he had an urge to study philosophy and was recommended to the teachers who had the highest reputation at that time in Alexandria, but he returned from their lectures so discouraged and full of distress that he told one of his friends what had happened. Understanding what Plotinus wanted, his friend took him to Ammonius, whom Plotinus had not yet tried. After he entered and listened, he said to his friend, "This is the man I was looking for." From that day he stayed with Ammonius continuously and gained such skill in philosophy that he was eager to try the philosophy that is practised among the Persians and the one that prevails among the Indians. . . .

[At the age of forty, Plotinus came to Rome.] For a long time Plotinus continued to write nothing but composed his lectures on the basis of his study with Ammonius. He continued like this for ten complete years, teaching some but writing nothing. He would encourage his students to ask questions, so that his teaching was very disorderly and there was a lot of useless talk, as Amelius explained to us. . . . (7) He had many listeners, including some who associated with him enthusiastically for the sake of philosophy. Amelius was among them, whose family name was Gentilianus. . . . Another of his listeners was a doctor, Paulinus of Scythopolis. . . . There was another doctor too, Eustochius of Alexandria, who became familiar with him in the last part of Plotinus' life and tended to him continuously until his death. . . . Zoticus, a critic and poet, also associated with him. . . . Zethus, an Arab by race, was another of his companions, and he married the daughter of Theodosius, who was the companion of Ammonius; he too was a doctor. . . .

[Castricius, called Firmus], who had chosen a political career, also revered Plotinus. A considerable number of senators listened to Plotinus' lectures; of these, Marcellus Orrontius and Sabinillus worked hardest at philosophy. From the Senate there was also Rogatianus, who renounced this way of life to such a degree that he gave up all his property, dismissed all his servants, and renounced his rank as well. . . . Serapion of Alexandria also associated with him; he was a rhetorician early in his career and was later devoted to the study of philosophy as well. . . . (9) There were women, too, who were greatly devoted to him: Gemina, in whose house he also lived, her daughter Gemina, who had the same name as her mother, and Amphiclea, who became the wife of Ariston, son of Iamblichus. These women were greatly devoted to philosophy.

10.24. What should students of Plato read?

(a) Albinus, *Introduction to Plato's Dialogues* 4,
(b) Anonymous, *Introduction to Plato's
Philosophy* 26.13–44

It was probably not long after Plato's death that attempts to classify and
organize his writings were first made. This activity was motivated in large
part by the effort to find the best way to introduce students to Plato's
thought: what should be the first dialogue that they read, and what should
be the sequence of works that they then follow? A process of compression
occurred, especially from the first century AD onwards: the writings that
were believed to contain the essence of Plato's thought were identified and
became the core of a Platonist education. Although it is possible to identify
an educational "canon" of essential Platonic works that emerged over time,
the following extracts show that different authorities had somewhat different opinions about the contents of their reading-lists and about the
sequence in which the works should be read. Albinus (**a**) lived in the second
century AD, while the anonymous *Introduction* (**b**) is a sixth-century work.
Further reading: Dunn 1976; Lamberton 2001: 444–45.

a

Let us say next what kind of dialogues readers should begin with when
encountering Plato's thought. There have been different opinions.
Some people begin with the *Letters*, others with the *Theages*. Some
have divided the dialogues into tetralogies and arrange the first
tetralogy in the following group: *Euthyphro* (because Socrates
receives his indictment in it), *Apology* (because Socrates has to make
his defence speech), *Crito* (since Socrates then spent time in prison),
and *Phaedo* (because Socrates' life comes to an end in it). This is the
opinion [about arrangement] of Dercyllides and Thrasyllus;[14] their
intention is, I believe, to impose order on characters and on circumstances of their lives. This goal is perhaps useful for some purpose
other than what we want now; for we want to discover a principle and
an arrangement for instruction in wisdom. Now, we say that there is
no single, fixed principle behind Plato's thought, since it seems perfect,
with a circle's perfect form; as a circle's principle is not single and
fixed, so Plato's thought is not either.

---

14 Thrasyllus (died AD 36) was court astrologer for the emperor Tiberius. Little is known of
Dercyllides, including his dates.

THE SECOND CENTURY AD TO THE END OF ANTIQUITY

b

The divine Iamblichus[15] separated all the dialogues into twelve main ones, and of these he called one group "physical," the other "theological." Likewise he subsumed these twelve works under two, the *Timaeus* and the *Parmenides*, with these at the head of all the physical and theological dialogues respectively. It is worth inquiring into the order of these dialogues, since these are the ones that everyone has thought deserving of study. The *Alcibiades* should be studied first, since in this dialogue we come to "know ourselves,"[16] and it is right that we know ourselves before we know what is outside us. For how can we know that if we do not know ourselves? The *Philebus* should be studied last, since the subject of discussion in it is "the good," which is beyond all things; therefore it should be beyond all the other dialogues, and last.

10.25. The story of Hypatia

Socrates, *Church History* 7.15

Hypatia, a Neoplatonic philosopher and teacher in Alexandria, was probably around 60 years old when she was murdered in 415. The motive for her murder seems not to have been her pagan teaching *per se* but rather the influence that she held over some of the city's officials, who were engaged in a struggle for authority with the city's bishop, Cyril. Hypatia's students included both pagans and Christians; the most famous of the latter was the bishop Synesius (**10.22**). Her willingness to expound philosophical principles to whoever wanted to listen suggests that her teaching had a highly public character. Further reading: Rist 1965; Brown 1992: 115–17; Cameron and Long 1993: 40–62; Dzielska 1995; Haas 1997: 308–16.

Hypatia, the daughter of Theon the philosopher, achieved such a high level of learning that she surpassed all the philosophers of her time, succeeded to the Platonic school that derived from Plotinus, and set forth all the philosophical principles to those who wanted to hear them. It is for this reason that people everywhere who wished to practise philosophy travelled to be at her side. Because of the dignified frankness that she had acquired from her education, she would enter into open and sensible discussion with those in power; nor was it a

---

15 Neoplatonic philosopher, *c.* AD 245–325.
16 A maxim carved on the front of the temple of Apollo in Delphi, and one of the central themes of the *Alcibiades*.

cause of shame for her to be among men, for they all respected and admired her the more for her extraordinary intelligence.

At this time, hostility took up arms against her. The fact that she frequently met with Orestes aroused the false accusation among the Christian population that she had prevented him from reconciling with the bishop.[17] Some of them, led by a reader[18] named Peter, were incensed and formed a conspiracy. They watched for the woman as she returned home from somewhere; they threw her out of her carriage and dragged her to the church called Caesareum. They stripped off her clothes and then murdered her with broken pieces of pottery. After tearing her to pieces, they carried off her limbs to the place called the Cinaron and burnt them completely. This act brought considerable criticism upon Cyril and the Alexandrian Church, since murders, battles and the like are utterly foreign to the Christian spirit.

10.26. Justinian's decree of 529

(a) John Malalas, *Chronicle* 18.47, (b) *Code of Justinian* 1.11.10

Scholars frequently assert that in 529 the emperor Justinian "closed" the Neoplatonic school in Athens, also often referred to as Plato's Academy. Our direct evidence for the event is a terse and enigmatic account (**a**) by the historian John Malalas (*c.* 480–570). While a decree which forbids the teaching of philosophy could be expected to prevent a philosophical school from being viable, there is evidence that the Academy continued to function for several decades more, until the middle of the sixth century. Its success during this time was owed largely to the leadership of its head, Damascius. Indeed, Justinian's attack on philosophical teaching was probably inspired by the school's success prior to 529, since Damascius had been leading the school from around 515. The connection between philosophy, astronomy and dice (mentioned here) lies probably in the interest that their practitioners might be thought to have had in divining the future – a blasphemous act, especially if it involved pagan gods. The other piece of evidence usually presented for the closure of the Academy is a law in the *Code of Justinian* which, among other anti-pagan measures, prohibited pagans from teaching and from receiving state support (only the most relevant section is presented in **b**). It is uncertain, however, whether this law is the one that Malalas refers to. Further reading: Cameron 1967, 1971, 1985: 21–23; Bowen 1972: 297–302; Blumenthal 1978; Watts 2004; Wildberg 2005: 329–33.

---

17 Cyril (later St. Cyril), Bishop of Alexandria from 412 to 444; he vigorously suppressed paganism and Judaism in Egypt. Orestes was the prefect of Egypt.
18 A position in the early Church.

a

In the consulship of Decius, the emperor issued a decree and sent it to Athens, forbidding anyone from teaching philosophy or expounding astronomy,[19] and forbidding the use of dice in any of the cities, since some dice-throwers had been discovered in Byzantium who engaged in terrible blasphemies. They had their hands cut off and were paraded around on camels.

b

We forbid any subject to be taught by those who suffer from the madness of the unholy pagans, so that, accordingly, they do not pretend to teach those who come to them miserably as their students, when they are in reality corrupting the souls of those they teach. Moreover, we forbid them to receive benefit from public maintenance, since they do not have freedom or licence on the basis of sacred scriptures or pragmatic sanction[20] to lay claim to anything of this kind for themselves.

10.27. In Plato's footsteps

Boethius, *Training in Arithmetic* 1–2

Even as early as the fifth-century sophist Hippias, the so-called "mathematical arts" – arithmetic, geometry, astronomy and musical theory – were seen by some to form a related and coherent set of subjects (**4.5**). In parts of western Europe in the Middle Ages these four subjects were called the *quadrivium* and constituted the second stage of a formal education; the first stage was the *trivium*, consisting of the "literary arts" – grammar, rhetoric and dialectic. The first author to use the term *quadrivium* in referring to this set of subjects was Boethius (*c.* 480–*c.* 524),[21] who saw its purpose as enabling the student to transcend the intellectual limits of the physical world in order to comprehend perfect, unchanging reality. In his beliefs Boethius was heavily dependent upon the educational curriculum which Plato's "guardians" are required to undergo in his ideal state (**5.9**; cf. **5.20**). Two authors roughly contemporary with Boethius wrote handbooks on the *trivium* and *quadrivium*: Martianus Capella, a pagan (*The Marriage of Mercury and Philology*: Stahl 1971–77), and Cassiodorus, a Christian

---

19 Most editors of the Greek text read "the law" instead of "astronomy."
20 A decree formally issued by the emperor.
21 Boethius uses the alternative spelling *quadruvium*.

(*Introduction to Divine and Human Readings*: Jones 1946). Both books were widely used in the Middle Ages. Further reading: Clarke 1971: 139–51; Chadwick 1981: 69–107; Kibre 1981; White 1981; Wagner 1983; Smith 2004: 126–29.

(1) Amongst those authorities of old . . . there is general agreement on this, that in the various fields of philosophy one can reach the peak of perfection only if the investigation of this noble wisdom is conducted by the kind of study known as the *quadruvium*. This fact will not elude the intelligence of a clear-thinking mind. For wisdom lies in the comprehension of the truth of things that exist and that are endowed with an immutable substantiality of their own.

We say that the things that exist are those which do not grow through extension, or decrease through diminution, or change through variation, but which continually maintain their own character, protecting their nature by relying on their own resources. (2) These things are the following: qualities, quantities, geometrical figures, largeness, smallness, equalities, relations, acts, dispositions, places, times, and everything that is found attached to the physical, as it were. These are by their very nature incorporeal, and their essence lies in their inherent immutability, but when they are joined with the physical they are subject to change, and through their contact with what is variable they become instead inconstant and mutable. Accordingly, since they have been allotted by nature a changeless substance and constitution, these are the entities which are rightly and properly said "to exist." It is thus the knowledge of these things, that is, of those which properly exist and which are given the appropriate name "essences," that philosophy professes to encompass.

10.28. *Enkuklios paideia* in the Middle Ages

Anna Comnena, *Alexiad* Preface 1.2, 15.7.9

Throughout the Middle Ages, Greeks adhered to the practices of ancient education more closely than their counterparts did in western Europe. Not only were the same subjects taught and learned – reading and writing, followed by the liberal arts, then (for some students) rhetoric and philosophy – but the same classical authors continued to be studied (with greatest emphasis upon the memorization of Homer, especially the *Iliad*: Browning 1975b: 15–21). Moreover, the terms *enkuklios paideia* and *enkuklios paideusis* were still applied to the education which students received in preparation for a higher education, though these terms were not applied with complete consistency (Buckler 1948: 205–7). Medieval Greeks also considered the four mathematical arts to constitute a distinct component in a formal education, applying the Greek name *tetraktys* to it rather than the Latin *quadrivium* (cf. **10.27**).

The following extracts are from the *Alexiad*, the story told by Anna Comnena (1083–1153) of her father, the Byzantine emperor Alexius. Since Anna was a member of the royal household, it cannot be assumed that many girls and young women reached the level of education that she did. Further reading: Buckler 1928: 165–221; Runciman 1933: 223–39; Marrou 1956: 340–42; Clarke 1971: 130–39; Bowen 1972: 305–12; Mango 1980: 125–48; Wilson 1983: 18–27; Browning and Kazhdan 1991: 677–78; Browning 1997: 95–116; other relevant Byzantine texts in Geanakoplos 1984: 393–410.

(Preface 1.2) I, Anna, am not ignorant of letters, but supremely studious in the Greek language, and not without training in rhetoric. I have read thoroughly the treatises of Aristotle and the dialogues of Plato, and have strengthened my mind with the quartet (*tetraktys*) of subjects. . . .

(15.7.9) But now the study of these lofty subjects, and of the poets and prose-writers and the knowledge gained from them, is not even an afterthought; the rage now is gambling and other illegal practices. I mention this because of my distress over the utter neglect of broad education (*enkuklios paideusis*). It burns my soul because I have spent so much time over the same subjects and, when I was freed from my occupation with them as a child, I proceeded to study rhetoric, touched on philosophy, and amidst these sciences took to the poets and prose-writers, thereby polishing up my tongue's rough spots. Then, with the help of rhetoric, I condemned the overwrought complexity of grammatical parsing.

BIBLIOGRAPHY

Adams, J.N. (2003) *Bilingualism and the Latin Language*, Cambridge: Cambridge University Press.

Adkins, A.W.H. (1960) *Merit and Responsibility: A Study in Greek Values*, Oxford: Oxford University Press.

Anderson, G. (1986) *Philostratus: Biography and Belles Lettres in the Third Century AD*, London: Croom Helm.

Anderson, W.D. (1966) *Ethos and Education in Greek Music: The Evidence of Poetry and Philosophy*, Cambridge, MA: Harvard University Press.

Annas, J. (1981) *An Introduction to Plato's Republic*, Oxford: Oxford University Press.

Asmis, E. (2001) "Basic education in Epicureanism," in Y.L. Too (ed.) *Education in Greek and Roman Antiquity*, Leiden: Brill, 209–39.

Astin, A.E. (1967) *Scipio Aemilianus*, Oxford: Oxford University Press.

—— (1978) *Cato the Censor*, Oxford: Oxford University Press.

Bagnall, R.S., and R. Cribiore (2006) *Women's Letters from Ancient Egypt, 300 BC–AD 800*, Ann Arbor: University of Michigan Press.

Baldwin, B. (1983) *The Philologos or Laughter-Lover*, London Studies in Classical Philology 10, Amsterdam: J.C. Gieben.

Baltes, M. (1993) "Plato's school, the Academy," *Hermathena*, 155: 5–26.

Barnes, T.D. (1971) *Tertullian: A Historical and Literary Study*, Oxford: Oxford University Press.

Barrow, R. (1976) *Greek and Roman Education*, London: Macmillan.

Bassett, S. (2004) *The Urban Image of Late Antique Constantinople*, Cambridge: Cambridge University Press.

Beard, M. (1993) "Looking (harder) for Roman myth: Dumezil, declamation and the problems of definition," in F. Graf (ed.) *Mythos in Mythenloser Gesellschaft: Das Paradigma Roms*, Colloquium Rauricum 3, Stuttgart: Teubner, 44–64.

Beck, F.A.G. (1964) *Greek Education, 450–350 BC*, London: Methuen.

—— (1975) *Album of Greek Education*, Sydney: Cheiron Press.

Benson, H.H. (1997) "Socrates and the beginnings of moral philosophy," in C.C.W. Taylor (ed.) *Routledge History of Philosophy*, vol. 1: *From the Beginning to Plato*, London: Routledge, 323–55.

Bett, R. (1989) "The sophists and relativism," *Phronesis*, 34: 139–69.

Blank, D.L. (1985) "Socrates versus sophists on payment for teaching," *Classical Antiquity*, 4: 1–49.

Blumenthal, H.J. (1978) "529 and its sequel: What happened to the Academy," *Byzantion*, 48: 369–85.

Bonner, S.F. (1949) *Roman Declamation in the Late Republic and Early Empire*, Liverpool: Liverpool University Press.

—— (1977) *Education in Ancient Rome: From the Elder Cato to the Younger Pliny*, Berkeley: University of California Press.

Booth, A.D. (1973) "Punishment, discipline and riot in the schools of antiquity," *Échos du monde classique/Classical Views* 17: 107–14.

—— (1979a) "Elementary and secondary education in the Roman Empire," *Florilegium*, 1: 1–14.

—— (1979b) "The schooling of slaves in first-century Rome," *Transactions of the American Philological Association*, 109: 11–19.

—— (1981) "Litterator," *Hermes*, 109: 371–78.

—— (1982) "The academic career of Ausonius," *Phoenix*, 36: 329–43.

—— (1985) "Douris' Cup and the stages of schooling in Classical Athens," *Echos du monde classique/Classical Views* 4: 274–80.

—— (1987) "On the date of Eunapius' coming to Athens," *Ancient History Bulletin* 1: 14–15.

Boring, T.A. (1979) *Literacy in Ancient Sparta*, *Mnemosyne* Supplement 54, Leiden: Brill.

Bowen, J. (1972) *A History of Western Education*, vol. 1: *The Ancient World*, New York: Methuen.

Bowersock, G.W. (1969) *Greek Sophists in the Roman Empire*, Oxford: Oxford University Press.

—— (1978) *Julian the Apostate*, Cambridge, MA: Harvard University Press.

—— (1990) *Hellenism in Late Antiquity*, Ann Arbor: University of Michigan Press.

Bowman, A.K. (1986) *Egypt after the Pharaohs: 332 BC–AD 642, from Alexander to the Arab Conquest*, Berkeley: University of California Press.

Bradley, K.R. (1991) *Discovering the Roman Family: Studies in Roman Social History*, New York: Oxford University Press.

Bremmer, J. (1980) "An enigmatic Indo-European rite: Pederasty," *Arethusa*, 13: 279–98.

Brickhouse, T.C., N.D. Smith (2000) *The Philosophy of Socrates*, Boulder, CO: Westview Press.

—— (2004) *Plato and the Trial of Socrates*, New York: Routledge.

Brown, P. (1992) *Power and Persuasion in Late Antiquity: Towards a Christian Empire*, Madison: University of Wisconsin Press.

—— (2000, 2nd edn) *Augustine of Hippo: A Biography*, Berkeley: University of California Press.

Browning, R. (1975a) *The Emperor Julian*, London: Weidenfeld and Nicolson.

—— (1975b) "Homer in Byzantium," *Viator*, 6: 15–33.

—— (1997) "Teachers," in G. Cavallo (ed.) *The Byzantines*, trans. T. Dunlap, T.L. Fagan, C. Lambert, Chicago: University of Chicago Press, 95–116.

Browning, R., and A.P. Kazhdan (1991) "Education," in A.P. Kazhdan (ed.) *The Oxford Dictionary of Byzantium*, vol. 1, New York: Oxford University Press, 677–78.

Buckler, G. (1929) *Anna Comnena: A Study*, Oxford: Oxford University Press.

—— (1948) "Byzantine education," in N.H. Baynes and H. St. L.B. Moss (eds)

Byzantium: An Introduction to East Roman Civilization, Oxford: Oxford University Press, 200–20.

Bulmer-Thomas, I. (1984) "Plato's astronomy," *Classical Quarterly*, 34: 107–12.

Bundrick, S.D. (2005) *Music and Image in Classical Athens*, Cambridge: Cambridge University Press.

Burkert, W. (1985) *Greek Religion*, trans. J. Raffan, Cambridge, MA: Harvard University Press.

—— (1992) *The Orientalizing Revolution: Near Eastern Influence on Greek Culture in the Early Archaic Age*, trans. M.E. Pinder and W. Burkert, Cambridge, MA: Harvard University Press.

Burnet, J. (1903) *Aristotle on Education*, Cambridge: Cambridge University Press.

—— (1928) *Platonism*, Berkeley: University of California Press.

Burnyeat, M. (1977) "Socratic midwifery, Platonic inspiration," *Bulletin of the Institute of Classical Studies*, 24: 7–16.

Calame, C. (1999) "Indigenous and modern perspectives on tribal initiation rites: Education according to Plato," in M. Padilla (ed.) *Rites of Passage in Ancient Greece: Literature, Religion, Society*, Cranbury, NJ: Associated University Presses, 278–312.

Cameron, A. (1965) "Roman school fees," *Classical Review*, 15: 237–38.

—— (1967) "The end of the ancient universities," *Cahiers d'Histoire mondiale*, 10: 653–73.

—— (1971) "The last days of the Academy at Athens," *Proceedings of the Cambridge Philological Society*, 17: 7–29.

—— (1982) "The empress and the poet: Paganism and politics at the court of Theodosius II," *Yale Classical Studies*, 27: 217–89.

—— (1985) *Procopius and the Sixth Century*, Berkeley: University of California Press.

Cameron, A., and J. Long (1993) *Barbarians and Politics at the Court of Arcadius*, Berkeley: University of California Press.

Canfora, L. (1989) *The Vanished Library: A Wonder of the Ancient World*, trans. M. Ryle, Berkeley: University of California Press.

Cartledge, P. (1978) "Literacy in the Spartan oligarchy," *Journal of Hellenic Studies*, 98: 25–37.

—— (1981) "The politics of Spartan pederasty," *Proceedings of the Cambridge Philological Society*, 207: 17–36.

—— (2001) *Spartan Reflections*, Berkeley: University of California Press.

—— (2004) *The Spartans: The World of the Warrior-Heroes of Ancient Greece*, New York: Vintage Books.

Cartledge, P., and A. Spawforth (2002, 2nd edn) *Hellenistic and Roman Sparta: A Tale of Two Cities*, London: Routledge.

Castleden, R. (2005) *Mycenaeans*, London: Routledge.

Chadwick, H. (1981) *Boethius: The Consolations of Music, Logic, Theology, and Philosophy*, Oxford: Oxford University Press.

Chadwick, J. (1967, 2nd edn) *The Decipherment of Linear B*, Cambridge: Cambridge University Press.

—— (1968) "The organization of the Mycenaean archives," in A. Bartonek (ed.) *Studia Mycenaea: Proceedings of the Mycenaean Symposium, Brno, April 1966*, Brno: Universita J.E. Purkyne.

—— (1976) *The Mycenaean World*, Cambridge: Cambridge University Press.

Cherniss, H. (1945) *The Riddle of the Early Academy*, Berkeley: University of California Press.

Clark, G. (2004) *Christianity and Society*, Cambridge: Cambridge University Press.

Clarke, M.L. (1967) "Quintilian: A biographical sketch," *Greece & Rome*, n.s. 14: 24–37.

—— (1971) *Higher Education in the Ancient World*, Albuquerque: University of New Mexico Press.

—— (1996, 2nd edn) *Rhetoric at Rome: A Historical Survey*, revised by D.H. Berry, London: Routledge.

Cohen, D. (1987) "Law, society and homosexuality in Classical Athens," *Past and Present*, 117: 3–21.

Coldstream, J.N. (1977) *Geometric Greece*, London: Methuen.

Coleman, K.M. (1985) "The Emperor Domitian and literature," *Aufstieg und Niedergang der Römischen Welt*, II.32.5, Berlin, 3087–115.

Cribiore, R. (1996) *Writing, Teachers, and Students in Graeco-Roman Egypt*, American Studies in Papyrology 36, Atlanta: Scholars Press.

—— (2001) *Gymnastics of the Mind: Greek Education in Hellenistic and Roman Egypt*, Princeton: Princeton University Press.

—— (2007) *The School of Libanius in Late Antique Antioch*, Princeton: Princeton University Press.

Crombie, I.M. (1964) *Plato: The Midwife's Apprentice*, London: Routledge and Kegan Paul.

Crook, J.A. (1995) *Legal Advocacy in the Roman World*, London: Duckworth.

Curren, R.R. (2000) *Aristotle on the Necessity of Public Education*, Lanham, MD: Rowman & Littlefield.

D'Ambra, E. (2007) *Roman Women*, Cambridge: Cambridge University Press.

Delorme, J. (1960) *Gymnasion: Étude sur les monuments consacrés a l'éducation en Gréce (des origins à l'Empire romain)*, Paris: Éditions E. de Boccard.

Diggle, J. (2004) *Theophrastus:* Characters, Cambridge Classical Texts and Commentaries 43, Cambridge: Cambridge University Press.

Dillon, J. (1983) "What happened to Plato's Garden?," *Hermathena*, 133: 51–59.

—— (2003) *The Heirs of Plato: A Study of the Old Academy*, Oxford: Oxford University Press.

Dillon, J., and T. Gergel (2003) *The Greek Sophists*, London: Penguin.

Dionisotti, A.C. (1982) "From Ausonius' schooldays? A schoolbook and its relatives," *Journal of Roman Studies*, 72: 83–125.

Doran, R. (1990) "Jason's gymnasium," in H.W. Attridge *et al.* (eds) *Of Scribes and Scrolls*, Lanham, MD: University Press of America, 99–109.

—— (2001) "The high cost of a good education," in J.J. Collins and G.E. Sterling (eds) *Hellenism in the Land of Israel*, Notre Dame, IN: University of Notre Dame Press, 94–115.

Dover, K.J. (1968) *Aristophanes: Clouds*, Oxford: Oxford University Press.

—— (1972) *Aristophanic Comedy*, Berkeley: University of California Press.

—— (1974) *Greek Popular Morality in the Time of Plato and Aristotle*, Oxford: Oxford University Press.

—— (1988) "Greek homosexuality and initiation," in *The Greeks and their Legacy: Collected Papers*, vol. 2, Oxford: Oxford University Press, 115–34.

—— (1989, 2nd edn) *Greek Homosexuality*, Cambridge, MA: Harvard University Press.

Downey, G. (1957) "Education in the Christian Roman Empire: Christian and pagan theories under Constantine and his successors," *Speculum*, 32: 48–61.

Ducat, J. (2006) *Spartan Education: Youth and Society in the Classical Period*, trans. E. Stafford, P.J. Shaw, A. Powell, Swansea: The Classical Press of Wales.

Dudley, D.R. (1998, 2nd edn) *A History of Cynicism*, London: Bristol Classical Press.

Dunbabin, T.J. (1948) *The Western Greeks: The History of Sicily and South Italy from the Foundation of the Greek Colonists to 480 BC*, Oxford: Oxford University Press.

Dunn, M. (1976) "Iamblichus, Thrasyllus, and the reading order of the Platonic dialogues," in R. Baine Harris (ed.) *The Significance of Neoplatonism*, Norfolk, VA: International Society for Neoplatonic Studies, 59–80.

Düring, I. (1957) *Aristotle in the Ancient Biographical Tradition*, Göteborg: Elanders Boktryckeri Aktiebolag.

Dzielska, M. (1995) *Hypatia of Alexandria*, trans. F. Lyra, Cambridge, MA: Harvard University Press.

Ehrenberg, V. (1973, 2nd edn) *From Solon to Socrates: Greek History and Civilization during the 6th and 5th Centuries BC*, London: Methuen.

Ellspermann, G.L. (1949) *The Attitude of the Early Christian Latin Writers toward Pagan Literature and Learning*, Washington, DC: Catholic University of America Press.

Fairweather, J. (1981) *Seneca the Elder*, Cambridge: Cambridge University Press.

—— (1984) "The Elder Seneca and declamation," *Aufstieg und Niedergang der Römischen Welt*, II.32.1, Berlin, 514–56.

Fantham, E. (2004) *The Roman World of Cicero's* De Oratore, Oxford: Oxford University Press.

Ferrari, G.R.F. (1989) "Plato and poetry," in G.A. Kennedy (ed.) *The Cambridge History of Literary Criticism*, vol. 1, Cambridge: Cambridge University Press, 92–148.

Field, G.C. (1967, 3rd edn) *Plato and his Contemporaries: A Study in Fourth-Century Life and Thought*, London: Methuen.

Finley, M.I. (1978, 2nd edn) *The World of Odysseus*, Harmondsworth: Penguin.

Forbes, C.A. (1929) *Greek Physical Education*, New York: Century.

—— (1933) *Neoi: A Contribution to the Study of Greek Associations*, American Philological Association Monographs 2, Middletown, CT: American Philological Association.

—— (1942) *Teachers' Pay in Ancient Greece*, University of Nebraska Studies in the Humanities 2, Lincoln: University of Nebraska Press.

—— (1955) "The education and training of slaves in antiquity," *Transactions and Proceeding of the American Philological Association*, 86: 321–60.

Ford, A. (1999) "Reading Homer from the rostrum: Poems and laws in Aeschines' *Against Timarchus*," in S. Goldhill and R. Osborne (eds) *Performance Culture and Athenian Democracy*, Cambridge: Cambridge University Press, 231–56.

Fowler, D.H. (1987) *The Mathematics of Plato's Academy: A New Reconstruction*, Oxford: Oxford University Press.

Frank, T. (1940) *Economic Survey of Ancient Rome*, vol. 5, Baltimore: Johns Hopkins University Press.

Fraser, P.M. (1972) *Ptolemaic Alexandria*, 2 vols, Oxford: Oxford University Press.

Friedländer, P. (1969) *Plato: An Introduction*, Princeton: Princeton University Press.

Geanakoplos, D.J. (1984) *Byzantium: Church, Society, and Civilization seen through Contemporary Eyes*, Chicago: University of Chicago Press.

Gerson, L.P. (1994) *Plotinus*, London: Routledge.

Glucker, J. (1978) *Antiochus and the Late Academy*, Hypomnemata 56, Göttingen: Vandenhoeck and Ruprecht.

Golden, M. (1990) *Children and Childhood in Classical Athens*, Baltimore: Johns Hopkins University Press.

—— (2004) *Sport in the Ancient World from A to Z*, London: Routledge.

Graf, F. (2003) "Initiation: A concept with a troubled history," in D.B. Dodd and C.A. Faraone (eds) *Initiation in Ancient Greek Rituals and Narratives: New Critical Perspectives*, London: Routledge, 3–24.

Grams, L. (2007) "Hipparchia of Meroneia, Cynic cynosure," *Ancient Philosophy*, 27: 335–50.

Gray, V.J. (1985) "Xenophon's *Cynegeticus*," *Hermes*, 113: 156–72.

Green, P. (1990) *Alexander to Actium: The Historical Evolution of the Hellenistic Age*, Berkeley: University of California Press.

Green, R.P.H. (1991) *The Works of Ausonius*, Oxford: Oxford University Press.

Griffith, M. (2001) "Public and private in early Greek institutions of education," in Y.L. Too (ed.) *Education in Greek and Roman Antiquity*, Leiden: Brill, 23–84.

Gruen, E. (1984) *The Hellenistic World and the Coming of Rome*, vol. 1, Berkeley: University of California Press.

—— (1990) *Studies in Greek Culture and Roman Policy*, Leiden: Brill.

—— (1992) *Culture and National Identity in Republican Rome*, Ithaca, NY: Cornell University Press.

Guthrie, W.K.C. (1969, 1981) *A History of Greek Philosophy*, vols 3, 6, Cambridge: Cambridge University Press.

Gwara, S. (2002) "The *Hermeneumata pseudodositheana*, Latin oral fluency, and the social function of the Cambro-Latin dialogues called *De raris fabulis*," in C.D. Lanham (ed.) *Latin Grammar and Rhetoric: From Classical Theory to Medieval Practice*, London: Continuum, 109–38.

Gwynn, A. (1926) *Roman Education from Cicero to Quintilian*, Oxford: Oxford University Press.

Haarhoff, T. (1958, 2nd edn) *Schools of Gaul, a Study of Pagan and Christian Education in the Last Century of the Western Empire*, Johannesburg: Witwatersrand University Press.

Haas, C. (1997) *Alexandria in Late Antiquity: Topography and Social Conflict*, Baltimore: Johns Hopkins University Press.

Habicht, C. (1997) *Athens from Alexander to Antony*, trans. D.L. Schneider, Cambridge, MA: Harvard University Press.

Hadot, I. (1984) *Arts libéraux et philosophie dans la pensée antique*, Paris: Etudes augustiniennes.

Hansen, E.V. (1971, 2nd edn) *The Attalids of Pergamum*, Ithaca, NY: Cornell University Press.

Harrauer, H. and P.J. Sijpesteijn (eds) (1985) *Neue Texte aus dem antiken Unterricht*, Mittheilungen aus der Papyrussammlung der österreichischen Nationalbibliothek in Wien, NS XV, Vienna: Österreichische Nationalbibliothek.

Harris, W.V. (1989) *Ancient Literacy*, Cambridge, MA: Harvard University Press.

Harrison, E.L. (1964) "Was Gorgias a sophist?," *Phoenix*, 18: 183–92.

Haslam, M. (1997) "Homeric papyri and transmission of the text," in I. Morris and B. Powell (eds) *A New Companion to Homer*, Leiden: Brill, 55–100.

Heath, M. (1985) "Hesiod's didactic poetry," *Classical Quarterly*, 35: 245–63.

—— (2002/3) "Theon and the history of the *progymnasmata*," *Greek, Roman and Byzantine Studies*, 43: 129–60.

Held, G.F. (1987) "Phoinix, Agamemnon and Achilles: Parables and *paradeigmata*," *Classical Quarterly*, 37: 245–61.

Helleman, W. (1994) "Tertullian on Athens and Jerusalem," in Helleman (ed.) *Hellenization Revisited: Shaping a Christian Response within the Greco-Roman World*, Lanham, MD: University Press of America, 361–81.

Hemelrijk, E.A. (1999) *Matrona Docta: Educated Women in the Roman Élite from Cornelia to Julia Domna*, London: Routledge.

Hengel, M. (2001) "Judaism and Hellenism revisited," in J.J. Collins and G.E. Sterling (eds) *Hellenism in the Land of Israel*, Notre Dame, IN: University of Notre Dame Press, 6–37.

Hershbell, J. (1981) *Pseudo-Plato, Axiochus*, Chico, CA: Scholars Press.

Hindley, C. (2004) "*Sophron eros*: Xenophon's ethical erotics," in C. Tuplin (ed.) *Xenophon and his World: Papers from a Conference held in Liverpool in July 1999*, Stuttgart: Franz Steiner, 125–46.

Hock, R.F., and E.N. O'Neil (1986) *The Chreia in Ancient Rhetoric*, vol. 1: *The Progymnasmata*, Atlanta, GA: Scholars Press.

—— (2002) *The Chreia and Ancient Rhetoric: Classroom Exercises*, Atlanta, GA: Society of Biblical Literature.

Hodkinson, S. (1997) "The development of Spartan society and institutions in the Archaic Period," in L.G. Mitchell and P.J. Rhodes (eds) *The Development of the Polis in Archaic Greece*, London: Routledge, 83–102.

Howie, G. (1969) *Educational Theory and Practice in St. Augustine*, London: Routledge and Kegan Paul.

Humble, N. (2004) "Xenophon's sons in Sparta? Perspectives/perceptions on *xenoi* in the Spartan upbringing," in T.J. Figueira (ed.) *Spartan Society*, Swansea: The Classical Press of Wales, 241–59.

Ingalls, W.B. (2000) "Ritual performance as training for daughters in Archaic Greece," *Phoenix* 54: 1–20.

Jaeger, W. (1934) *Aristotle: Fundamentals of the History of His Development*, trans. Richard Robinson, Oxford: Oxford University Press.

—— (1947, 1943, 1944) *Paideia: The Ideals of Greek Culture*, vols 1–3, trans. G. Highet, Oxford: Oxford University Press.

—— (1961) *Early Christianity and Greek Paideia*, Cambridge, MA: Harvard University Press.

Jameson, M.H. (1960) "A decree of Themistokles from Troizen," *Hesperia*, 29: 198–223.

Jeffery, L.H. (1961) *The Local Scripts of Archaic Greece: A Study of the Origin of the*

Greek Alphabet and its Development from the Eighth to the Fifth Centuries BC, Oxford: Oxford University Press.

—— (1982) "Greek alphabetic writing," in J. Boardman *et al.* (eds) *The Cambridge Ancient History*, 3.1, Cambridge: Cambridge University Press, 819–33.

Johnson, R. (1957) "A note on the number of Isocrates' pupils," *American Journal of Philology*, 78: 297–300.

—— (1959) "Isocrates' methods of teaching," *American Journal of Philology*, 80: 25–36.

Joint Association of Classical Teachers (JACT) (1984) *The World of Athens: An Introduction to Classical Athenian Culture*, Cambridge: Cambridge University Press.

Jones, A.H.M. (1940) *The Greek City from Alexander to Justinian*, Oxford: Oxford University Press.

—— (1966) *The Decline of the Ancient World*, London: Longman.

Jones, L.W. (1946) *An Introduction to Divine and Human Readings by Cassiodorus Senator*, New York: Columbia University Press.

Jones, P., and K. Sidwell (1997) *The World of Rome: An Introduction to Roman Culture*, Cambridge: Cambridge University Press.

Kaster, R.A. (1983) "Notes on 'primary' and 'secondary' schools in late antiquity," *Transactions of the American Philological Association*, 113: 323–46.

—— (1984) "A schoolboy's burlesque from Cyrene?," *Mnemosyne*, 37: 457–58.

—— (1988) *Guardians of Language: The Grammarian and Society in Late Antiquity*, Berkeley: University of California Press.

—— (1995) *C. Suetonius Tranquillus: De Grammaticis et Rhetoribus*, Oxford: Oxford University Press.

Kelly, J.N.D. (1995) *Golden Mouth: The Story of John Chrysostom – Ascetic, Preacher, Bishop*, Ithaca, NY: Cornell University Press.

Kennedy, G. (1963) *The Art of Persuasion in Greece*, Princeton: Princeton University Press.

—— (1969) *Quintilian*, New York: Twayne.

—— (1972) *The Art of Rhetoric in the Roman World, 300 BC–AD 300*, Princeton: Princeton University Press.

—— (1983) *Greek Rhetoric under Christian Emperors*, Princeton: Princeton University Press.

—— (1994) *A New History of Classical Rhetoric*, Princeton: Princeton University Press.

Kennell, N.M. (1995) *The Gymnasium of Virtue: Education and Culture in Ancient Sparta*, Chapel Hill, NC: University of North Carolina Press.

—— (1997) "Herodes Atticus and the rhetoric of tyranny," *Classical Philology*, 92: 346–62.

—— (2001) "*Most necessary for the bodies of men*: Olive-oil and its by-products in the later Greek gymnasium," in M. Joyal (ed.) *In Altum: Seventy-Five Years of Classical Studies in Newfoundland*, St. John's: Memorial University of Newfoundland, 119–33.

—— (2005) "New light on 2 Maccabees 4:7–15," *Journal of Jewish Studies*, 56: 10–24.

—— (2006) *Ephebeia: A Register of Greek Cities with Citizen Training Systems in the Hellenistic and Roman Periods*, *Nikephoros* Beihefte 12, Hildesheim: Weidmann.

Kennell, S.A.H. (2000) *Magnus Felix Ennodius: A Gentleman of the Church*, Ann Arbor: University of Michigan Press.

Kenyon, F.G. (1909) "Two Greek school-tablets," *Journal of Hellenic Studies*, 29: 29–40.

Kerferd, G.B. (1950) "The first Greek sophists," *Classical Review*, 64: 8–10.

—— (1981) *The Sophistic Movement*, Cambridge: Cambridge University Press.

—— (1997) "The sophists," in C.C.W. Taylor (ed.) *Routledge History of Philosophy*, vol. 1: *From the Beginning to Plato*, London: Routledge, 244–70.

Kibre, P. (1981) "The Boethian *De Institutione Arithmetica* and the quadrivium in the thirteenth century university milieu at Paris," in M. Masi (ed.) *Boethius and the Liberal Arts*, Utah Studies in Literature and Linguistics 18, Berne: P. Lang, 67–80.

Kidd, I.G. (1978) "Philosophy and science in Posidonius," *Antike und Abendland*, 24: 7–15.

—— (1988) *Posidonius*, vol. 2: *The Commentary* (i), Cambridge: Cambridge University Press.

—— (1999) *Posidonius*, vol. 3: *The Translation of the Fragments*, Cambridge: Cambridge University Press.

Kirk, G.S. (1970) *Myth: Its Meaning and Function in Ancient and Other Cultures*, Berkeley: University of California Press.

Koehl, R.B. (1986) "The Chieftain Cup and a Minoan rite of passage," *Journal of Hellenic Studies*, 106: 99–110.

—— (1997) "Ephoros and ritualized homosexuality in Bronze Age Crete," in M. Duberman (ed.) *Queer Representations: Reading Lives, Reading Cultures*, New York: New York University Press, 7–13.

Koester, H. (1995, 2nd edn) *History, Culture, and Religion of the Hellenistic Age*, New York: Walter de Gruyter.

Koller, H. (1955) "Ἐγκύκλιος παιδεία," *Glotta*, 34: 174–89.

Konstan, D. (1997) *Friendship in the Classical World*, Cambridge: Cambridge University Press.

Kyle, D.G. (1987) *Athletics in Ancient Athens*, Mnemosyne Supplement 95, Leiden: Brill.

Lacey, W.K. (1968) *The Family in Classical Greece*, Ithaca, NY: Cornell University Press.

Lane Fox, R. (1973) *Alexander the Great*, London: A. Lane.

Lardinois, A. (1994) "Subject and circumstance in Sappho's poetry," *Transactions of the American Philological Association*, 124: 57–84.

Lloyd-Jones, H. (1971, 2nd edn) *The Justice of Zeus*, Sather Classical Lectures 41, Berkeley: University of California Press.

Lodge, R.C. (1947) *Plato's Theory of Education*, London: Russell & Russell.

Long, A.A. (2005) "Law and nature in Greek thought," in M. Gagarin and D. Cohen (eds) *The Cambridge Companion to Ancient Greek Law*, Cambridge: Cambridge University Press, 412–30.

Loomis, W.T (1998) *Wages, Welfare Costs and Inflation in Classical Athens*, Ann Arbor: University of Michigan Press.

Lord, C. (1982) *Education and Culture in the Political Thought of Aristotle*, Ithaca, NY: Cornell University Press.

—— (1996) "Aristotle and the idea of liberal education," in J. Ober and C. Hedrick (eds) *Demokratia: A Conversation on Democracies, Ancient and Modern*, Princeton: Princeton University Press, 271–88.

Loraux, N. (1986) *The Invention of Athens: The Funeral Oration in the Classical City*, Cambridge, MA: Harvard University Press.

Lynch, J.P. (1972) *Aristotle's School: A Study of a Greek Educational Institution*, Berkeley: University of California Press.

Maas, M. (2000) *Readings in Late Antiquity: A Sourcebook*, London: Routledge.

MacDowell, D.M. (1978) *The Law in Classical Athens*, London: Thames and Hudson.

Mango, C. (1980) *Byzantium: The Empire of New Rome*, London: Weidenfeld and Nicolson.

Marrou, H.I. (1956) *A History of Education in Antiquity*, trans. G. Lamb, Madison: University of Wisconsin Press.

Marshall, A.J. (1975) "Library resources and creative writing at Rome," *Phoenix*, 30: 252–64.

Mette, H.J. (1960) "Ἐγκύκλιος παιδεία," *Gymnasium*, 67: 300–07.

Millar, F. (1992, 2nd edn) *The Emperor in the Roman World*, Ithaca, NY: Cornell University Press.

Miller, F.D., jr. (1995) *Nature, Justice, and Rights in Aristotle's* Politics, Oxford: Oxford University Press.

Miller, S.G. (1991, 2nd edn) *Arete: Greek Sports from Ancient Sources*, Berkeley: University of California Press.

Milne, J.G. (1908) "Relics of Graeco-Egyptian schools," *Journal of Hellenic Studies*, 28: 121–32.

Milne, M.J. (1924) *A Study in Alcidamas and his Relation to Contemporary Sophists*, Diss: Bryn Mawr.

Mitchell, L.G. (1997) "New wine in old wineskins: Solon, *arete* and the *agathos*," in L.G. Mitchell and P.J. Rhodes (eds) *The Development of the Polis in Archaic Greece*, London: Routledge, 137–47.

Mitchell, S. (2007) *A History of the Later Roman Empire, AD 284–641: The Transformation of the Ancient World*, Malden, MA: Blackwell.

Mitsis, P. (2003) "The institutions of Hellenistic philosophy," in A. Erskine (ed.) *A Companion to the Hellenistic World*, Oxford: Blackwell, 464–76.

Momigliano, A. (1987) "The life of St. Macrina by Gregory of Nyssa," in *On Pagans, Jews, and Christians*, Middletown, CT: Wesleyan University Press, 206–21.

Morgan, T. (1998) *Literate Education in the Hellenistic and Roman Worlds*, Cambridge: Cambridge University Press.

—— (1999) "Literate education in classical Athens," *Classical Quarterly*, 49: 46–61.

Morris, I., and B.P. Powell (2006) *The Greeks: History, Culture, and Society*, Upper Saddle River, NJ: Pearson Prentice Hall.

Morrison, J.S. (1949) "An introductory chapter in the history of Greek education," *Durham University Journal*, 41: 55–63.

Morrow, G.R. (1993, 2nd edn) *Plato's Cretan City: A Historical Interpretation of the Laws*, Princeton: Princeton University Press.

Mueller, I. (1997) "Greek arithmetic, geometry and harmonics: Thales to Plato," in C.C.W. Taylor (ed.) *Routledge History of Philosophy*, vol. 1: *From the Beginning to Plato*, London: Routledge, 271–322.

Muir, J.R. (2005) "Is our history of educational philosophy mostly wrong? The case of Isocrates," *Theory and Research in Education*, 3: 165–95.

Muir, J.V. (1982) "Protagoras and education at Thourioi," *Greece & Rome*, n.s. 29: 17–24.

—— (1984) "A note on ancient methods of learning to write," *Classical Quarterly*, 34: 236–37.

Murray, O. (1980) *Early Greece*, Glasgow: Fontana.

Nagy, G. (1998) "The library of Pergamon as a classical model," in H. Koester (ed.) *Pergamon, Citadel of the Gods: Archaeological Record, Literary Description, and Religious Development*, Harvard Theological Studies 46, Harrisburg, PA: Trinity Press International, 185–232.

Nightingale, A.W. (2000) "Sages, sophists, and philosophers: Greek wisdom literature," in O. Taplin (ed.) *Literature in the Greek and Roman Worlds: A New Perspective*, Oxford: Oxford University Press, 156–91.

—— (2001) "Liberal education in Plato's *Republic* and Aristotle's *Politics*," in Y.L. Too (ed.) *Education in Greek and Roman Antiquity*, Leiden: Brill, 133–73.

Nilsson, M.P. (1955) *Die hellenistische Schule*, Munich: C.H. Beck.

Norman, A.F. (1965) *Libanius' Autobiography (Oration 1)*, London: Oxford University Press.

—— (1992) *Libanius: Autobiography and Selected Letters*, vol. 1, Cambridge, MA: Harvard University Press.

Nussbaum, M.C. (2002) "The incomplete feminism of Musonius Rufus, Platonist, Stoic, and Roman," in M.C. Nussbaum and J. Sihvola (eds) *The Sleep of Reason: Erotic Experience and Sexual Ethics in Ancient Greece and Rome*, Chicago: University of Chicago Press, 283–326.

Ober, J. (2001) "The debate over civic education in classical Athens," in Y.L. Too (ed.) *Education in Greek and Roman Antiquity*, Leiden: Brill, 175–207.

Ogilvie, R.M. (1965) *A Commentary on Livy, Books 1–5*, Oxford: Oxford University Press.

—— (1976) *Early Rome and the Etruscans*, Glasgow: Fontana.

—— (1978) *The Library of Lactantius*, Oxford: Oxford University Press.

Oldfather, C.H. (1923) *The Greek Literary Texts from Greco-Roman Egypt: A Study in the History of Civilization*, University of Wisconsin Studies in the Social Sciences and History, 9, Madison: University of Wisconsin.

Oliver, J.H. (1981) "Marcus Aurelius and the philosophical schools at Athens," *American Journal of Philology*, 102: 213–25.

Osborn, E. (1997) *Tertullian, First Theologian of the West*, Cambridge: Cambridge University Press.

—— (2005) *Clement of Alexandria*, Cambridge: Cambridge University Press.

Osborne, R. (1996) *Greece in the Making, 1200–479 BC*, London: Routledge.

Ostwald, M. (1986) *From Popular Sovereignty to the Sovereignty of Law: Law, Society, and Politics in Fifth-Century Athens*, Berkeley: University of California Press.

O'Sullivan, N. (1997) "Caecilius, the 'canon' of writers, and the origins of Atticism," in W.J. Dominik (ed.) *Roman Eloquence: Rhetoric in Society and Literature*, London: Routledge, 32–49.

Palaima, T. (2003) "'Archives' and 'scribes' and information hierarchy in Mycenaean Greek Linear B records," in M. Brosius (ed.) *Ancient Archives and*

Archival Traditions: Concepts of Record-Keeping in the Ancient World, Oxford: Oxford University Press, 153–94.

Parker, H.N. (1993) "Sappho schoolmistress," *Transactions of the American Philological Association*, 123: 309–51.

Pélékidis, C. (1962) *Histoire de l'éphébie attique des origines à 31 avant J.-C.*, École française d'Athènes, Travaux et Mémoires 13, Paris: de Boccard.

Pendrick, G.J. (2002) *Antiphon the Sophist: The Fragments*, Cambridge Classical Texts and Commentaries 39, Cambridge: Cambridge University Press.

Penella, R.J. (1990) *Greek Philosophers and Sophists in the Fourth Century AD: Studies in Eunapius of Sardis*, Leeds: F. Cairns.

Percy, W.A. (1996) *Pederasty and Pedagogy in Archaic Greece*, Urbana: University of Illinois Press.

Pernot, L. (2005) *Rhetoric in Antiquity*, trans. W.E. Higgins, Washington, DC: Catholic University Press.

Pfeiffer, R. (1968) *History of Classical Scholarship: From the Beginnings to the End of the Classical Age*, Oxford: Oxford University Press.

Pharr, C. (1952) *The Theodosian Code and Novels and the Sirmondian Constitutions*, Princeton: Princeton University Press.

Pleket, H.W. (1969) "*Collegium juventum nemesiorum*. A note on ancient youth organization," *Mnemosyne*, 22: 281–98.

Polinskaya, I. (2003) "Liminality as metaphor: Initiation and the frontiers of ancient Athens," in D.B. Dodd and C.A. Faraone (eds) *Initiation in Ancient Greek Rituals and Narratives: New Critical Perspectives*, London: Routledge, 85–106.

Pomeroy, S.B. (1975) *Goddesses, Wives, Whores, and Slaves: Women in Classical Antiquity*, New York: Shocken Books.

—— (1977) "*Technikai kai mousikai*: The education of women in the fourth century and in the Hellenistic period," *American Journal of Ancient History*, 2: 51–68.

—— (1988) "Women in Roman Egypt: A preliminary study based on papyri," *Aufstieg und Niedergang der Römischen Welt*, II.10.1, Berlin: Walter de Gruyter, 708–23.

—— (2002) *Spartan Women*, Oxford: Oxford University Press.

—— (2004) "Xenophon's Spartan women," in C. Tuplin (ed.) *Xenophon and his World: Papers from a Conference held in Liverpool in July 1999*, Stuttgart: Franz Steiner, 201–13.

Pomeroy, S.B., S.M. Burstein, W. Donlan and J.T. Roberts (1999) *Ancient Greece: A Political, Social, and Cultural History*, Oxford: Oxford University Press.

Poulakos, T. (1997) *Speaking for the Polis: Isocrates' Rhetorical Education*, Columbia, SC: University of South Carolina Press.

Powell, A. (2001, 2nd edn) *Athens and Sparta: Constructing Greek Political and Social History from 478 BC*, London: Routledge.

Powell, B.P. (1991) *Homer and the Origin of the Greek Alphabet*, Cambridge: Cambridge University Press.

Pritchard, D. (2003) "Athletics, education and participation in Classical Athens," in D.J. Phillips and D. Pritchard (eds) *Sport and Festival in the Ancient Greek World*, Swansea: The Classical Press of Wales, 293–349.

Proietti, G. (1987) *Xenophon's Sparta: An Introduction*, *Mnemosyne* Supplement 98, Leiden: Brill.

Raaflaub, K.A. (2000) "Poets, lawgivers and the beginnings of political reflection in

Archaic Greece," in C. Rowe and M. Schofield (eds) *The Cambridge History of Greek and Roman Political Thought*, Cambridge: Cambridge University Press, 23–59.

Radt, W. (1998) "Recent research in and about Pergamon: A survey (*c.* 1987–97)," in H. Koester (ed.) *Pergamon, Citadel of the Gods: Archaeological Record, Literary Description, and Religious Development*, Harvard Theological Studies 46, Harrisburg, PA: Trinity Press International, 1–40.

—— (1999) *Pergamon: Geschichte und Bauten einer antiken Metropole*, Darmstadt: Primus.

Rankin, H.D. (1983) *Sophists, Socratics and Cynics*, Beckenham, UK: Croom Helm.

Rawson, B. (1999) "Education: The Romans and us," *Antichthon*, 33: 81–98.

—— (2003) *Children and Childhood in Roman Italy*, Oxford: Oxford University Press.

Rawson, E. (1969) *The Spartan Tradition in European Thought*, Oxford: Oxford University Press.

—— (1983, 2nd edn) *Cicero: A Portrait*, London: Duckworth.

—— (1985) *Intellectual Life in the Late Roman Republic*, Baltimore: Johns Hopkins University Press.

Redfield, J. (1990) "Drama and community: Aristophanes and some of his rivals," in J.J. Winkler and F.I. Zeitlin (eds) *Nothing to do with Dionysus: Athenian Drama in its Social Context*, Princeton: Princeton University Press, 314–35.

Reinmuth, O.W. (1929) *The Foreigners in the Athenian Ephebia*, University of Nebraska Studies in Language, Literature, and Criticism 9, Lincoln: University of Nebraska Press.

—— (1971) *The Ephebic Inscriptions of the Fourth Century BC,* Mnemosyne Supplement 14, Leiden: Brill.

Reynolds, L.D., and N.G. Wilson (1991, 3rd edn) *Scribes and Scholars: A Guide to the Transmission of Greek and Latin Literature*, Oxford: Oxford University Press.

Rhodes, P.J. (1993, 2nd edn) *A Commentary on the Aristotelian* Athenaion Politeia, Oxford: Oxford University Press.

Richards, J. (1980) *Consul of God: The Life and Times of Gregory the Great*, London: Routledge and Kegan Paul.

Rihll, T.E. (2003) "Teaching and learning in classical Athens," *Greece & Rome*, n.s. 50: 168–90.

de Rijk, L.M. (1965) "Ἐγκύκλιος παιδεία: A study of its original meaning," *Vivarium*, 3: 24–93.

Rist, J.M. (1965) "Hypatia," *Phoenix*, 19: 214–25.

Robb, K. (1994) *Literacy and Paideia in Ancient Greece*, New York: Oxford University Press.

Robbins, E. (1993) "The education of Achilles," *Quaderni Urbinati di Cultura Classica*, n.s. 45: 7–20.

de Romilly, J. (1992) *The Great Sophists in Periclean Athens*, Oxford: Oxford University Press.

Rostovtzeff, M. (1953, 2nd edn) *The Social and Economic History of the Hellenistic World*, 3 vols, Oxford: Oxford University Press.

Rousseau, P. (1994) *Basil of Caesarea*, Berkeley: University of California Press.

Rowe, C. (2000) "*Cleitophon* and *Minos*," in C. Rowe and M. Schofield (eds)

The Cambridge History of Greek and Roman Political Thought, Cambridge: Cambridge University Press, 303–09.

Rowlandson, J. (1998) *Women and Society in Greek and Roman Egypt: A Sourcebook*, Cambridge: Cambridge University Press.

Runciman, S. (1933) *Byzantine Civilization*, London: Edward Arnold.

Russell, D.A. (1983) *Greek Declamation*, Cambridge: Cambridge University Press.

—— (1989) "Arts and sciences in ancient education," *Greece & Rome*, n.s. 36: 210–25.

—— (1996) *Libanius: Imaginary Speeches*, London: Duckworth.

Rutherford, R.B. (1995) *The Art of Plato: Ten Essays in Platonic Interpretation*, Cambridge, MA: Harvard University Press.

Salway, R. (1981) *Roman Britain*, Oxford: Oxford University Press.

Sansone, D. (2004) *Ancient Greek Civilization*, Malden, MA: Blackwell.

Saunders, T.J. (1995) "Plato on women in the *Laws*," in A. Powell (ed.) *The Greek World*, London: Routledge, 591–609.

Scanlon, T.F. (1988) "*Virgineum gymnasium*: Spartan females and early Greek athletics," in W.J. Raschke (ed.) *The Archaeology of the Olympics: The Olympics and Other Festivals in Antiquity*, Madison: University of Wisconsin Press, 185–216.

Schofield, M. (2000) "Approaching the *Republic*," in C. Rowe and M. Schofield (eds) *The Cambridge History of Greek and Roman Political Thought*, Cambridge: Cambridge University Press, 190–232.

Scholz, P. (2003) "Philosophizing before Plato: On the social and political conditions of the composition of the *Dissoi Logoi*," in W. Dietel, A. Becker and P. Scholz (eds) *Ideal and Culture of Knowledge in Plato*, Philosophie der Antike 15, Stuttgart: Franz Steiner, 201–30.

Scolnicov, S. (1988) *Plato's Metaphysics of Education*, London: Routledge.

Sedley, D. (2004) *The Midwife of Platonism: Text and Subtext in Plato's* Theaetetus, Oxford: Oxford University Press.

Sergent, B. (1986) *Homosexuality in Greek Myth*, trans. A. Goldhammer, Boston: Beacon Press.

Sharples, R.W. (1985) *Plato:* Meno, Warminster: Aris and Phillips.

Siewert, P. (1977) "Ephebic oath in fifth-century Athens," *Journal of Hellenic Studies*, 97: 102–11.

Skinner, M.B. (2005) *Sexuality in Greek and Roman Culture*, Malden, MA: Blackwell.

Slings, S.R. (1999) *Plato:* Clitophon, Cambridge Classical Texts and Commentaries 37, Cambridge: Cambridge University Press.

Smith, A. (2004) *Philosophy in Late Antiquity*, London: Routledge.

Snodgrass, A. (1980) *Archaic Greece: The Age of Experiment*, Berkeley: University of California Press.

Snyder, H.G. (2000) *Teachers and Texts in the Ancient World: Philosophers, Jews and Christians*, London: Routledge.

Stahl, W.H., R.W. Johnson, with E.L. Burger (1971, 1977) *Martianus Capella and the Seven Liberal Arts*, 2 vols, New York: Columbia University Press.

Stirling, L. (2005) *The Learned Collector: Mythological Statuettes and Classical Taste in Late Antique Gaul*, Ann Arbor: University of Michigan Press.

Stockton, D. (1971) *Cicero: A Political Biography*, Oxford: Oxford University Press.

de Strycker, E., and S.R. Slings (1994) *Plato's* Apology of Socrates*: A Literary and Philosophical Study with a Running Commentary*, *Mnemosyne* Supplement 137, Leiden: Brill.

Sussman, L.A. (1978) *The Elder Seneca*, *Mnemosyne* Supplement 51, Leiden: Brill.

Tarán, L. (1975) *Academica: Plato, Philip of Opus, and the Pseudo-Platonic Epinomis*, Philadelphia: American Philosophical Society.

Tarrant, H. (1988) "Midwifery and the *Clouds*," *Classical Quarterly*, 38: 116–22.

Thomas, R. (1992) *Literacy and Orality in Ancient Greece*, Cambridge: Cambridge University Press.

—— (1995) "The place of the poet in archaic society," in A. Powell (ed.) *The Greek World*, London: Routledge, 104–29.

Thornton, B.S. (1997) *Eros: The Myth of Ancient Greek Sexuality*, Boulder, CO: Westview Press.

Tomin, J. (1987) "Socratic midwifery," *Classical Quarterly*, 37: 97–102.

Too, Y.L. (1995) *The Rhetoric of Identity in Isocrates: Text, Power, Pedagogy*, Cambridge: Cambridge University Press.

—— (2000) *The Pedagogical Contract: The Economies of Teaching and Learning in the Ancient World*, Ann Arbor: University of Michigan Press.

—— (2001) "Legal instruction in Classical Athens," in Y.L. Too (ed.) *Education in Greek and Roman Antiquity*, Leiden: Brill, 111–32.

Turner, E.G. (1968, 2nd edn 1980) *Greek Papyri: An Introduction*, Oxford: Oxford University Press.

Urbainczyk, T. (1997) *Socrates of Constantinople: Historian of Church and State*, Ann Arbor: University of Michigan Press.

Van Nijf, O. (2004) "Athletics and *paideia*: Festivals and physical education in the world of the Second Sophistic," in B.E. Borg (ed.) *Paideia: The World of the Second Sophistic*, Berlin: Walter de Gruyter, 203–27.

van Wees, H. (1997) "Growing up in early Greece: Heroic and aristocratic education," in A.H. Sommerstein and C. Atherton (eds) *Education in Greek Fiction*, Nottingham Classical Literature Studies 4, Bari: Levante Editori, 1–20.

Ventris, M., and J. Chadwick (1973, 2nd edn) *Documents in Mycenaean Greek*, Cambridge: Cambridge University Press.

Vidal-Naquet, P. (1986) *The Black Hunter: Forms of Thought and Forms of Society in the Greek World*, trans. A. Szegedy-Maszak, Baltimore: Johns Hopkins University Press.

Vlastos, G. (1975) "Plato's testimony concerning Zeno of Elea," *Journal of Hellenic Studies*, 95: 136–62.

Wagner, D.L. (1983) "The Seven Liberal Arts and classical scholarship," in Wagner (ed.) *The Seven Liberal Arts in the Middle Ages*, Bloomington: Indiana University Press, 1–31.

Walcot, P. (1966) *Hesiod and the Near East*, Cardiff: University of Wales Press.

Walden, J.W.H. (1909) *The Universities of Ancient Greece*, New York: C. Scribner's Sons.

Wallace-Hadrill, A. (1983) *Suetonius: The Scholar and his Caesars*, London: Duckworth.

Waterfield, R. (2004) "Xenophon's Socratic mission," in C. Tuplin (ed.) *Xenophon and his World: Papers from a Conference held in Liverpool in July 1999*, Stuttgart: Franz Steiner, 79–113.

Watts, E. (2004) "Justinian, Malalas, and the end of Athenian philosophical teaching in AD 529," *Journal of Roman Studies*, 94: 168–82.

Webb, R. (2001) "The *progymnasmata* as practice," in Y.L. Too (ed.) *Education in Greek and Roman Antiquity*, Leiden: Brill, 289–316.

West, M.L. (1978) *Hesiod:* Works and Days, Oxford: Oxford University Press.

—— (1999) *The East Face of Helicon: West Asiatic Elements in Greek Poetry and Myth*, Oxford: Oxford University Press.

West, S. (1967) *The Ptolemaic Papyri of Homer*, Papyrologica Coloniensia 7, Köln: Westdeutscher Verlag.

—— (1970) "Chalcenteric negligence," *Classical Quarterly*, 20: 288–96.

White, A. (1981) "Boethius in the medieval quadrivium," in M. Gibson (ed.) *Boethius: His Life, Thought and Influence*, Oxford: Blackwell, 162–205.

Wildberg, C. (2005) "Philosophy in the age of Justinian," in M. Maas (ed.) *The Cambridge Companion to the Age of Justinian*, Cambridge: Cambridge University Press, 316–40.

Wilson, N.G. (1983) *Scholars of Byzantium*, London: Duckworth.

Winter, B.W. (2002, 2nd edn) *Philo and Paul among the Sophists: Alexandrian and Corinthian Responses to a Julio-Claudian Movement*, Grand Rapids, MI: Eerdmans.

Winterbottom, M. (1974) *The Elder Seneca*, 2 vols, Cambridge, MA: Harvard University Press.

Wooten, C.W. (1988) "Roman education and rhetoric," in M. Grant and R. Kitzinger (eds) *Civilization of the Ancient Mediterranean*, vol. 2, New York: C. Scribner's Sons, 1109–20.

Wycherly, R.E. (1961) "Peripatos: Athenian philosophical scene—I," *Greece & Rome*, n.s. 8: 152–63.

—— (1962) "Peripatos: Athenian philosophical scene—II," *Greece & Rome*, n.s. 9: 2–21.

Young, F., L. Ayres and A. Louth (eds) (2004) *The Cambridge History of Early Christian Literature*, Cambridge: Cambridge University Press.

Young, N.H. (1987) "*Paidagogos*: The social setting of a Pauline metaphor," *Novum Testamentum*, 29: 150–76.

GENERAL INDEX

INDEX OF PASSAGES